RESILIENCE AND COURAGE

Resilience

AND

Courage

Women, Men, and the Holocaust

Nechama Tec

YALE UNIVERSITY PRESS   NEW HAVEN & LONDON

Designed by Rebecca Gibb and set in Bulmer type by Integrated Publishing Solutions. Printed in the United States of America by R.R. Donnelley & Sons.

Library of Congress Cataloging-in-Publication Data
Tec, Nechama.
Resilience and courage : women, men, and the Holocaust / Nechama Tec.
p. cm.
ISBN 0-300-09355-1 (alk. paper)
1. Jewish women in the Holocaust. 2. Holocaust, Jewish (1939–1945)—Personal narratives.
3. Holocaust, Jewish (1939–1945)—Psychological aspects. 4. World War, 1939–1945—Jewish resistance. 5. Holocaust survivors—Interviews. I. Title.
D804.47 .T43 2003
940.53′18′082—dc21
2002012150

A catalogue record for this book is available from the British Library.

The paper in this book meets the guidelines for permanence and durability of the Committee on Production Guidelines for Book Longevity of the Council on Library Resources.

10 9 8 7 6 5 4 3 2 1

To my husband, Leon, and my grandchildren, Liam and Rome

Contents

1

Voices from the Past

Over the phone, the man's voice asked, "Are you the daughter of Ester Bawnik? You must be. For a long, long time I have been thinking about your mother. What a difference her selflessness, her caring attention made in my life, in the lives of so many others!"

What I heard took me to a different world, a ruined world, a world buried under many seemingly forgotten memories. The man identified himself as Samuel Gruber. In 1939, as a soldier in the Polish army, he had been captured by the rapidly advancing German forces. In 1941 he came with other former Polish Jewish soldiers to the work camp Lipowa 7 in Lublin, my birthplace. In the late summer of 1942, Gruber escaped into the surrounding forests where, as a partisan leader, he survived the war.

In the Lipowa 7 camp many of the Jewish prisoners of war became ill with typhus. The Germans isolated the sick POWs from the rest of the inmates and put them into a makeshift hospital. Dirty mattresses, scattered on equally dirty floors, served as beds. The patients stayed there, receiving hardly any help and little food and water.

I don't know how my mother managed to sneak into this hospital, a place that was off-limits to civilians. I don't know how she dared defy the authorities. Nor do I know how she managed to disregard the danger of contracting the disease.

Now, forty years later, I listened as Gruber recalled that the only bright moments in his otherwise gloomy confinement had been my mother's daily visits. He remembered so much more than I, telling me how Mother would come, loaded with baskets of food and drink. How smiling gently she would divide what she had brought among the feverish men. With these lifesaving provisions came spoken assurances that their ordeal was about to end, that they must not despair. She fed the men who were too weak to feed themselves. She wiped their hot faces with a cold wet rag. Gruber was convinced that my mother's promises of a better future had been just as important as her offers of food. She restored both spiritual and physical health to him and his comrades.

When Gruber mentioned a quiet little blue-eyed blond girl who carried some of the baskets, the images took on clearer outlines. Even the feelings of pity and sadness came back. I was that little girl.[1]

It is ironic that a man whom I did not remember had to remind me of my mother's behavior. It is more ironic that this telephone conversation lay dormant in my subconscious for about ten years. It resurfaced only when my research made me realize that in the grip of Nazi terror women were confronted with challenges and opportunities unlike those faced at any other time in our living memory. When telling me about Mother's selfless help, Gruber was reconstructing a part of our shared past. In my case this resurfaced memory had been short-lived; it had receded quickly. Why? Probably because neither the experiences nor my mother's actions had been unique. The extreme wartime circumstances had led to many strange and unprecedented actions and reactions.

Faced with the German assaults upon their lives and values, Jewish women and men searched for ways to cope with their respective circumstances. First and most basic, their reactions were dictated by the Nazi policies of Jewish annihilation, which contained measures that aimed at the biological elimination of European Jewry. But though all Jews were slated for death, the actual application of these policies and measures of destruction varied over time, by place, and in degree of ruthlessness. These variations were reflected in four recurring stages of Jewish annihilation. The first was the legal definition and identification of Jews by the Nazis. Next came the confiscation of Jewish property and removal of Jews from gainful employment. These were followed by procedures that isolated Jews from the rest of the population. The fourth and final phase was the actual murder. Integral to each of these stages were special degradations and sporadic killings.

Some of these anti-Jewish measures were punctuated by assaults aimed specifically at either women or men. These gender-specific measures inevitably had different consequences for men and women. Raul Hilberg has argued that "'the Final Solution' was intended by its creators to ensure the annihilation of all Jews. Most often, men and women were rounded up simultaneously for transport to a death camp or to be shot in front of a ditch. Their bodies were burned in the same crematory or buried in the same mass grave . . . Yet the road to annihilation was marked by events that specifically affected men as men and women as women."[2] These variations grew out of a mixture of political, economic, and biological ideologies.

When I first became immersed in Holocaust research I had little curiosity about gender. At best, my interest in the subject was peripheral. For years I studied the destruction of European Jewry and how cooperation, compassion, altruism, rescue, and resistance played their parts. My research tends to follow a continuous path: findings from one project often suggest additional issues for study and become the next project. It is as if my work has a mind of its own, and I follow its lead. My current research on gender conforms to this pattern, originating in an earlier book, *Defiance: The Bielski Partisans*. Covering the years 1941 to 1944, *Defiance* is a study of various partisan groups situated in the junglelike, dense Belorussian forests. This book pays special attention to a group of Jewish forest dwellers who took on the dual role of fighters and rescuers. In a preliminary examination of my data, I noticed that both Jewish and Gentile women were defined as burdensome by male partisans and treated as an insignificant minority. These unanticipated findings formed the basis of a chapter in the book entitled "The Fate of Women."[3]

Moreover, from my research for *Defiance,* I learned that an estimated 2–3 percent of all Soviet partisans were women. In the forest most women were treated as sex objects and rejected as fighters. Some women were raped, others killed, but most were simply relegated to domestic tasks. Some of the attractive young women became mistresses of partisan officers. Occasionally, however, when a detachment was poorly equipped and in need of partisans, women were asked to take on the role of fighters. These findings stimulated my curiosity. I wanted to explore how women, Jewish women in particular, fared in a variety of Holocaust settings: the ghettos, the camps, the forests. So I embarked on a comparative study of women in diverse Holocaust settings whose working title contained two key words: *Holocaust* and *women.*

Myself a Holocaust survivor, I have for about a quarter of a century been listening to and recording the histories of those who lived through World War II. My current project also relies on direct interviews. While conducting these more recent interviews, I became aware of the survivors' caution, which was more apparent than in earlier interviews. The survivors seemed more concerned about the accuracy of their recollections. I also began noticing the sadness and compassion with which Jewish women spoke about their men's inability to find gainful employment.

I had not expected to come across such a consistent absence of resentment; after all, under "normal" circumstances, women tend to be critical of unemployed men. Even during severe economic depressions, when men are chronically unemployed their families become strained; sometimes there is violence, which can lead to the breakup of the family.[4] Perhaps the Jewish women's supportive comments about the plight of their men grew out of their recognition that German oppression was responsible for what these men had to endure.

Historical evidence shows that in times of upheaval, in extremis, women tend to step in and fulfill the traditional male roles. For example, during World War II, American women kept up the wartime economy, taking over the jobs vacated when the American men went off to fight. The women's smooth entry into the labor force—in particular, their work in jobs geared to wartime production—contributed significantly to the Allies' victory. With the end of the war, the women were expected to quit their newly acquired jobs, and they did.[5]

But women's participation in "men's" work is not always solicited, nor is it necessarily accepted when offered. For example, a less-well-known story of how women tried to make a wartime contribution is that of the more than one thousand women who enlisted in the U.S. Air Force. The initiative for this venture came from Jacqueline Cochran. Herself an accomplished flyer, Cochran wanted to assist American men with the heavy burden of wartime flying. But her plan to train women pilots met with several rejections and only succeeded in part in 1942. The women who were accepted into the program underwent six months of training. A third of them did not pass—equal to the proportion of men who did not pass. However, the women who did pass were allowed to work only as test pilots and instructors. Thirty-eight of them died in the line of duty. Yet female pilots were not considered part of the military. Only in 1977, more than thirty years later, were they officially recognized as veterans.[6]

In contrast, in the Soviet Union women pilots participated in combat; some of them were even decorated with the highest orders. Russian women pilots established three combat regiments of their own, and a few participated with distinction in male regiments as well. The differences between the treatment of women pilots in the United States and the Soviet Union may be due in part to the fact that the Soviet Union had been invaded by the enemy; the country was much more threatened and in more dire need of help. The leaders probably decided that aid from women was better than no help at all. Yet even the highly decorated Soviet women fliers felt that they were neither perceived nor treated as equals to the male pilots.[7]

When I became absorbed in my current research, I realized that to concentrate on women alone would yield skewed results. In effect, knowing how intricately intertwined are the lives of women and men, I recognized that to exclude the male experiences would offer only limited insights, whereas comparisons of the experiences of both sexes would result in a broader understanding. Such comparisons could lead to important generalizations;

eager to come up with more general explanations, I opened the project to include the experiences of Jewish men, interviewing male survivors and collecting data about them from the same sources I had used for my study of women. Because men were included in this study at a later date, my sample of survivors has more women than men. Since this research is based on qualitative data, claiming no representative samples, the higher proportion of women does not affect the validity of the findings.

This book relies on data collected in Poland, France, Switzerland, the United States, and Israel. Although part of my evidence comes from western European countries — France, Germany, Holland, and Belgium — I focus on eastern Europe, particularly on the area that made up Poland from 1939 to 1945. This special emphasis is dictated by two facts. First, prewar Poland and the other East European countries had the largest concentration of Jews, and second, under the German occupation East European countries became the center of Jewish annihilation. Most Jews from western Europe were sent to their deaths in eastern Europe. Some were sent to the ghettos, others to various concentration camps. The experiences of these refugees appear throughout this book.

As the center for Jewish annihilation, and as the place where the Holocaust programs were instituted the earliest and conducted the most ruthlessly, eastern Europe provides the key to an understanding of the Holocaust in general, and of gender-related issues in particular. But although my research focuses on eastern Europe, whenever possible I compare findings from this area to findings from West European countries. I compare the histories of Jews from East and West to see whether the experiences in western Europe correspond to those in eastern Europe. These comparisons serve as informal tests for the rest of my findings. Together they offer generalizations that may apply to all European Jews.

For this project I conducted interviews intermittently over a period of ten years that explored a range of issues dealing with the Holocaust and gender. The bulk of these interviews were with Jewish survivors, although I also spoke with a few Gentiles. The interviews lasted anywhere from two to six hours, and I met with some respondents several times. My familiarity with several languages facilitated communication: in addition to English, I conducted interviews in French, German, Hebrew, Polish, and Yiddish. I personally transcribed each taped interview and translated it into English. For my earlier publications (from 1975 on) I had studied the accounts of hundreds of Jewish Holocaust survivors and some Christians. For this book, I have also drawn on the evidence collected for my earlier research, especially the parts that contained information about gender.

When collecting direct evidence from survivors one may legitimately ask how much credence can be given to recollections given more than fifty years after the events. Memory may disappoint. In all interviews we must be concerned about the trustworthiness of the respondents' accounts; however, we must be particularly careful when the information is collected after such a lapse of time. Usually the greater the time gap between the actual experiences and their narration, the more suspicious we become about the validity of these recollections.[8]

One way to check the validity of the information is to compare the stories told by a particular person at different times. Some of those I interviewed had previously given oral testimonies that were deposited in archival collections. Others had published articles or books about their experiences. Whenever possible I would compare these narratives. Those that remained consistent seem likely to be more reliable. Nevertheless, it is also true that inasmuch as this consistency appears in the testimony of the same individual, it may simply reflect this individual's consistent distortion. Another way of checking the validity or trustworthiness of the material is to compare it with information from several independent sources. The greater the number of sources containing similar information, the more we can trust their validity.[9]

Despite these efforts, testimony given at such a late date remains problematic. Shortcomings or gaps in respondents' memories tend to reappear in certain patterns. Many of those I spoke to had a hard time remembering specific dates and chronologies. Some could not recall names but came up with descriptions of events that they associated with those whose names they had forgotten. Comparisons over time may yield varied answers, although some of these probably reflect a change in perceptions rather than an inability or unwillingness to tell the truth. And it is important to note that different versions of the same events, described either by one individual at different times or by several individuals, may enrich rather than call into doubt the validity of the data. Different responses do not always represent distortions. Through direct interviews, especially by asking the same question in different ways at different points in the interview, the interviewer may uncover nuances within events, nuances that can help her or him recognize errors. The Holocaust took place in a series of complex, unprecedented upheavals that carried their own built-in contradictions. Awareness of these complexities can reduce errors. Finally, faced with the absence of valuable materials, researchers may be forced to choose between getting no data or using data tainted by time. Usually I chose in favor of the latter.[10]

When analyzing their findings, social scientists are often tempted to use quantitative, statistical measures. Quantitative presentations of data seem to add respectability. But with qualitative data, quantitative, statistical measures tend to be inappropriate. Applying quantitative measures to qualitative materials promises something the researcher cannot deliver. For example, when dealing with evidence about gender and the Holocaust some have been determined to show that women were more oppressed than men or that more women perished than men. In fact, systematic data to support or refute these assertions do not exist. Unrepresentative figures about deportations or mass killings cannot prove whether more women perished than men. At best, they indicate that in specific places, at specific times, either men or women were more likely to be deported, that in particular environments either men or women may have had a better chance to survive. Evidence about the death rates of men and women is so scattered, so incomplete, that definitive answers are impossible. The most we can say is that we don't know: the exact figures are missing.[11] Moreover, I am convinced that knowing whether more women died than men is less important than knowing how women and men fared in different Holocaust settings, and how they responded to their circumstances and to each other.

Finally, too, the qualitative nature of Holocaust data imposes certain methodological limitations. In Holocaust research we cannot take random samples because the universe from which the samples would be drawn does not exist. Many of the people we want to know about have died. Some refuse to be identified. Others may be alive, but we don't know their names or we cannot find them. Still others, because of their advanced age, find it difficult to sustain an interview. This absence of random samples and the gaps in our knowledge should caution researchers against misusing statistics or offering premature generalizations.[12]

The inductive research method thus seems most appropriate for an analysis of qualitative Holocaust data. In a way, the inductive method and the qualitative nature of the data ask the evidence to speak for itself and expect the researchers to listen to what they hear. Throughout my Holocaust research I have relied on the inductive approach, although I shall be revisiting methodological issues throughout this book.

Concentrating on both collective and individual gender comparisons, my research is guided by a set of interdependent hypotheses. I encouraged my respondents to tell their personal stories, but I also used a set of core questions as a guideline for each interview. I started with the basic assumption that in times of upheaval, in societies dominated by oppressive and coercive demands, compassion, mutual cooperation, and self-sacrifice are rare. Nevertheless the appearance of such positive features in coercive and oppressive societies tends to improve the quality of life for the oppressed and may even increase their chances of survival.

Additionally, oppressive political systems are often accompanied by strong patriarchal ideologies. Patriarchal principles, which are inherent in gender-based power structures, promote gender-related reactions to societal upheavals. Borrowing from Max Weber, I view power as an ability to impose one's will on people regardless of their wishes.[13]

Comparative cross-cultural studies show that most people live in patriarchal — male-dominated, male-identified, and male-centered — societies. In such societies, including Jewish communities, men are traditionally defined as dominant, competitive, and rational. In contrast, women are viewed as submissive, cooperative, emotional, and nurturing.[14] These distinct role models often create asymmetrical female-male relationships, in which men officially wield more power. In general, in relationships of inequality the subordinate partner is more likely to give in, more likely to adjust to the demands of the powerful one.[15] Therefore, as the subordinate partners in male-female relationships, women tend to react rather than initiate actions. And because they are responding to rather than initiating behavior, women are more likely to satisfy their needs and wishes in indirect ways. Ironically then, because of their consistently subordinate roles, women may have an easier time adapting to traumatic changes than men.

Like the rest of Europe, Germany was governed by patriarchal principles. With the establishment of the Third Reich the country's patriarchal ideology became stronger; eventually it was transformed into a virtual caricature of its former self. Thus, theoretically, under Hitler's rule German men who adhered to the Nazi ideology could acquire unlimited power. In contrast, German women were relegated to subordinate positions outside the political sphere. Hitler himself opposed women's participation in politics, claiming that such involvement would both demean them and corrupt their "true" nature. He saw German men as productive, German women as reproductive. In line with this ideology women were to be mothers, wives, and homemakers. They were to play no significant roles in public life—in the executive branch of the government, the legislature, the judiciary, or the armed forces. At a 1939 party rally, Hitler declared, "What man sacrifices in his nation's struggle, woman sacrifices in the struggle to preserve that nation on the individual plane. What man contributes in his heroic courage on the battlefield, woman contributes in her patient devotion, in ever-patient suffering and endurance. Every child she brings into the world is a battle which she wages for the survival or extinction of her people." Hitler had consistently argued that "men were creative while women were intuitive. Woman's position in Nazi society would be such as to allow her to exhibit her natural qualities, sympathy, self-sacrifice, and comradeship, rather than demand of her the 'unnatural' attributes of independence, intellectual ability, or a competitive spirit."[16]

These ideas had far-reaching consequences. German women in the Third Reich were excluded from higher education, civil service jobs, free participation in the labor market, and all important political positions. Denied intellectually demanding participation, women found themselves relegated to less important spheres. However, when he appeared in public before female audiences, Hitler would praise women's contributions to society, particularly at the early stages of his rule, when he wanted their support.[17] And Hitler received the support he sought from the majority of German women; few opposed their Führer. Most German women and men exalted the virtues of male domination.[18]

In pursuing the goal of Jewish annihilation, the Germans relied in roundabout ways on these patriarchal principles, which praised men's unique capacity to think and act rationally and aggressively. From these accepted ideas it followed that men could more easily assume and exercise power than women. In line with this ideology, Jewish men were viewed as a potentially greater threat to the Nazi political system than Jewish women. Inspired by this kind of reasoning, the Nazis set out to eliminate Jewish men first.[19] Relying on strong patriarchal perceptions, the Third Reich focused first and more vigorously on the degradation and murder of Jewish men, rather than women.

From the Nazi perspective these anti-Jewish gender policies served two basic aims. First, the Nazis felt that by attacking Jewish men they were preventing political opposition. Second, since the Nazi measures of Jewish annihilation contained an important subgoal of Jewish degradation, by rendering Jewish men powerless and humiliating them the Germans fulfilled this aim as well. The Nazis probably assumed that the humiliation of Jewish men neutralized them as political opponents and eased their subsequent murder.[20]

This special degradation and murder of Jewish men had additional, unanticipated consequences. The early, more vigorous assaults upon men suggested to the Jews that women were less threatened. Once established, the idea that men were in greater danger than women persisted, and most

Jews seemed to have continued to act upon it even after different policies regarding women emerged. In general, even when faced with unprecedented attacks and terror, some Jews had a hard time grasping that the Germans intended to murder them all. And because certain anti-Jewish policies originally differed for women and men, many Jews saw in these differences guidelines for the way they should behave. For example, from the start of the war, Jewish women made themselves more visible than men. Women were more likely to search outside their homes for food. They were more likely to appeal directly to the authorities.

In part, the way women and men coped with their respective circumstances was contingent upon what social and economic position they had held before the German occupation. But regardless of whether the Jews guessed what was in store for them, and regardless of their social position, the accelerating pace of Jewish annihilation inevitably transformed their lives. Some of the ways they dealt with those transformations were based on gender.

Relying on these assumptions, then, I shall explore two broad issues: whether and how the temporarily different treatment of Jewish men and women led to diverse, gender-related responses; and how their prewar roles affected the coping strategies of Jewish women and men. We shall see that even though the Germans were committed to sending all Jews to their deaths, for a variety of reasons women and men traveled toward that destination on distinct roads.

But how did the Jewish people react to the German invasion in general? One recurring finding is that under the German rule most Jews were preoccupied with the preservation of contemporary history. This interest was especially pervasive in eastern Europe, and resulted in the accumulation of data about every aspect of contemporary Jewish life. The danger inherent in gathering illegal materials failed to deter the professional and amateur historians from amassing this wealth of information.

Outstanding among these wartime chroniclers was the eminent Jewish historian and social activist Emanuel Ringelblum. Shortly after the outbreak of the 1939 German-Polish war, Ringelblum initiated and directed the most extensive collection of contemporary historical materials compiled. Known as *Oneg Shabath* (the pleasure of the Sabbath), or simply the Ringelblum Archives, this ambitious project sought to gather information about every possible aspect of contemporary Jewish life throughout eastern Europe. Eventually this archival collection included systematic data about Jews of different ages, male and female — about traditional and emergent social classes; about smugglers, beggars, and refugees; about the Jewish police and the Judenräte (Jewish councils), and much, much more. Specifically, too, among these materials was a valuable study concerning the wartime experiences of Jewish women. Initiated by Ringelblum and conducted by Cecylia Ślepak, a historian and translator, this research was interrupted in 1942, when Ślepak was deported to the death camp Treblinka.[21]

Interest in the categorization of Jews and in Jews as a single category stopped with the end of the war. Around 1945–1946, at the International Military Tribunal, the Jews were not even discussed as a distinct entity.[22] At the subsequent Nuremberg Trials (1947–1948), they were not considered a special category of victims. Jews were mentioned only in individual documents and only when specific charges were made against the German occupation.

In the 1950s postwar historians who examined the destruction of European Jewry concentrated on the perpetrators rather than the Jewish victims. Later, when some attention was paid to the persecuted Jews, they were identified simply as Jews. Few if any discussions about the different fates of Jews according to age, sex, or nationality followed. Perhaps this inattention to categories of Jewish victims should not come as a surprise. The Holocaust was dominated by extreme cruelty and devastation. The diverse experiences of various kinds of Jews were overshadowed by the enormity of the wartime crimes. Perhaps, too, it should not come as a surprise that early historians of that period were interested in learning about the forces that brought on such unprecedented destruction. Only after the basic outlines of the processes of Jewish annihilation were examined could scholars even begin to notice the less-visible parts to the puzzle, namely, the different categories and subcategories of victims.

The first postwar conference that called for the study of gender, emphasizing the fate of women during the Holocaust, took place at Stern College in New York City in 1983. A collection of papers stressing the need for the study of women in the Holocaust appeared in a volume of the proceedings.[23] Since then special conferences and conference sessions have been devoted to this topic. Most publications on women during the Holocaust have appeared as collections of articles, as chapters in longer studies, or as personal memoirs of female survivors. Several book-length studies based on historical research concerning the fate of women have also been published. A number of these books deal with the Third Reich, concentrating on the fate of German rather than Jewish women. Among the notable exceptions is Marion Kaplan's *Between Dignity and Despair*. More recently there has been an increase of books and articles about the Holocaust with the word *women* or *sisters* in their titles.[24]

Absent from these numerous publications are systematic, cross-cultural comparisons of the fate of Jewish women and Jewish men. Moreover, parallel to this special interest in women in the Holocaust is a mounting opposition to such studies, with objections coming from a variety of groups: scholars, journalists, and Holocaust survivors.[25]

When I began this research I knew that some scholars and Holocaust survivors objected to the study of the Holocaust and gender. Some of the survivors I was interviewing had conveyed their reservations to gender analysis. Many were reluctant to compare the ways Jewish men and women had fared in and coped with the oppression of the Holocaust. When I asked them to make general gender comparisons their discomfort grew. Some felt that there were no differences in the experiences and reactions of men and women. My continued probing into these comparisons only increased their uneasiness. If I was unable to dispel their resistance I would move on to other topics.

After a while I would return to these unresolved issues, keeping in mind a set of gendered pairs that would be relevant to whomever I was talking: mother/father, brother/sister, male friend/female friend. I would invite the interviewee to describe what had happened to one of these individuals during the Holocaust and discuss how this person reacted to various situations. First I would inquire about several persons of the same sex: father, brother, male friend. Then I would switch to the other sex, asking similar questions. I would thus avoid overt gender comparisons by asking more specifically about the experiences and reactions of individuals to whom the respondents were personally connected.

To this new set of queries most respondents would offer vivid descriptions of fathers whose public humiliation had led to serious depression, feelings of apathy that were often followed by illness or death. When our attention turned to mothers, the survivors would portray them as hardworking. These mothers were usually described as struggling to keep their starving families away from death. Other accounts would include uncles who, to save themselves, had escaped into the Russian part of Poland while their wives stayed behind and searched for ways to feed the family. Some survivors spoke about brothers who emigrated while their sisters stayed on with the parents, only to perish later. Consistently different coping strategies emerged for the two sexes.

After the interviews were completed, I would present this new information to the respondents together with their earlier reactions to questions about gender differences and ask them to comment. I wanted them to explain the discrepancies between their initial denial of gender variations and these subsequent vivid descriptions of gender-specific experiences and coping strategies. If a respondent said that he or she saw no discrepancy, I would ask why. Some argued that because the Germans had intended the annihilation of all Jews, both women and men, in the long run, differences or discrepancies between the experiences of the sexes did not matter. The respondents were correct that the Nazi goal was to annihilate all Jews. But this still left my question unanswered. I still wondered what was behind the inclination of some to avoid making gender-based comparisons of experiences during the Holocaust.

Through further probing of survivors and discussion with Holocaust scholars I came to realize that the concern about gender-focused research is based on the fear that such research might shift attention from the Jewishness of the victims to their sex. In turn, an undue emphasis on gender could lead to historical distortion and trivialization.

Clearly the history of the Third Reich attests to the centrality of the victims' Jewishness and not their sex: whether a person was Jewish was the key factor in what determined the fate the Nazis planned for him or her. It is also possible that an undue focus on gender to the exclusion of the victims' Jewishness could distort and ultimately trivialize the history of the Holocaust.[26] Yet when the research is guided by proper methodology and clearly defined concepts this will not occur.

To reiterate, the survivors and others are correct in asserting that in the Third Reich and the countries under its control whether an individual was Jewish was the most significant factor in determining how he or she would be identified and what would be his or her ultimate destiny. The sociological analysis of the individual in terms of his or her associations clarifies this issue. Thus, a person can be a Jew, a mother, a professional, a lover, and many other things at once. Each of these labels is referred to as a "status," or a position in a system of interactions. The different statuses of individuals are ranked in terms of their relative importance. Under the German occupation the most important status was the individual's ethnic or "racial" affliation. This was the so-called master status, and all other associations were subservient to it. Next in importance came political affiliation. A Communist was doomed, a Social Democrat less so, while a Fascist was highly valued.

Under a variety of circumstances one's sex could make a difference, but this distinction was not as central as whether one was a Jew or an "Aryan." Nonetheless, variations in the experiences of Jewish women and men and the different ways they reacted to the German assaults cannot be traced to the Jewishness they all shared. These variations need to be examined in terms of other factors that differentiate Jews from one another. One of these characteristics is gender — a society's shared definitions, meanings, and expectations about females and males.

Anthropologists and sociologists who pursue comparative studies of societies agree that gender distinctions are universal and important features of every society.[27] They also agree that gender is one of the basic, distinguishing characteristics that in significant ways affects peoples' lives. Given the universality and importance of gender, objections, denials and hesitancy about its effects during the Holocaust demand some attention. We need to be sensitive to the issues the objectors raise. But the universality of gender experiences demands attention as well. By neglecting to consider the distinct experiences and coping strategies of men and women we miss an opportunity to broaden our knowledge about the Holocaust. Inevitably, too, by avoiding the study of gender during the Holocaust, we miss a chance to widen our understanding about life in extremis.

Armed with some version of the above arguments, I once more turned to those respondents who insisted on denying differences in the experiences of women and men while at the same time offering vivid descriptions of those different experiences and coping strategies. In the light of my arguments and faced with their own inconsistent accounts most of these interviewees reconsidered. They now agreed that awareness and knowledge about gender-related differences do not in themselves result in distortion and trivialization of the Holocaust. Actually, it was not I but the survivors' personal observations and reconstructed memories that convinced them that the experiences and coping strategies of Jewish women and men were distinct. Once these survivors had overcome their initial reluctance to deal with male-female differences, they offered a range of rich gender-specific comparisons that led to new understandings about the complex and vital relations of gender to class, power, cooperation, bonding, and much more.

I believe that by questioning these survivors I helped their dormant memories to resurface. That is, by asking them to make gender comparisons, and by listening attentively to their answers, I was signaling to them that these distinct experiences deserved further study. What happened during these interviews resembles what happened to me, as I described at the opening of this chapter, when Gruber reminded me of my mother's visits to the sick POWs. He was helping me resurrect a part of my past. But I was not ready to attend to these memories until I became involved in research on the

Holocaust and gender. Probably, in similar ways, the survivors in my study reconsidered their memories because they became involved in the events they were being questioned about.

Although central, my direct interviews with survivors are not the sole source of data. Additional information for this book comes from archival collections, unpublished and published wartime diaries, postwar memoirs, and secondary sources. Unlike the evidence collected during my interviews, information about gender in these additional sources was rarely the result of specific questions on the issue. This probably explains why the additional data contain fewer male-female comparisons than my direct interviews.[28] Nonetheless, the evidence in these sources is complex and rich. In addition to offering answers to specific questions, the information contained in these sources guided me toward further fascinating, unexpected, and unexplored areas of study.

The German destruction of European Jewry proceeded along the stages of identification, expropriation, removal from gainful employment, isolation, and annihilation. Complex and often overlapping, these stages were intended to secure the victims' degradation before their murder. To facilitate the process of destruction, the Germans established special settings for the Jews. The Nazi-created ghettos were established to accelerate the stage of isolation, while the concentration camps facilitated the final stage of Jewish murder. Faced with a system of ruthless destruction some Jews created their own, new settings: undergrounds and resistance cells, forest havens, hiding places, and new identities as Christians in the forbidden "Aryan" sectors. Such arrangements represented semi-autonomous reactions to the Nazi process of annihilation. Collectively they reflect Jewish efforts to retain a semblance of humanity. Inevitably, under the German occupation Jews were threatened regardless of their settings or their sex. But the kind of threats directed at them and how they subjectively experienced them depended partly on their particular settings and in part on other factors, among them gender.

How did it all begin? What did the perpetrators do? How did the prospective victims—the women and men—react to the assaults? What coping strategies did the Jews devise and what impacts and implications did these have? What in addition to gender made for distinct experiences and diverse coping strategies among the oppressed Jews? By listening carefully to the voices of the oppressed this book contains a multitude of answers, some predicted, some unanticipated, all throwing some light on the Holocaust and more generally on life in extremis.

In the Beginning

September 1939. In a suburb of Warsaw called Prague, a group of tenants finds shelter in the cellar of their building. They anxiously listen to the roar of German planes. The passage of time and the intermittent explosions only increase their apprehension. One notable exception is Shlomo Peltel, the Jewish owner of a modest haberdashery and the father of two daughters and a son. His older daughter, Vladka Meed, remembers him as a lover of books, an idealist, and a man sensitive to the suffering of others. In World War I Shlomo had met German soldiers during the occupation, and he had liked them. These friendly encounters had convinced him that the Germans were good people. Now, as the bombs drop, he shares his impressions with his neighbors. Eager to calm them, Peltel argues that civilians have no reason to feel threatened, that none of the German soldiers will harm them.

Days later, when the German takeover has brought severe food shortages, Peltel joins one of the breadlines. The Poles around him accuse him of being a Jew, and a German soldier comes over. Without explanation, he pulls Shlomo out of the crowd and beats him with fury. For Peltel, as for countless other Jews, this kind of episode presages the unimaginable future.[1]

In Poland, from the start of the 1939 campaign, five German Security

Police (SS) and Security Service (SD) task forces—the Einsatzgruppen—operated behind the front lines. Their main task was to secure and "pacify" the occupied area. In so doing they, along with some German army units, assaulted and murdered Jewish civilians. The majority of the victims were men, a small minority women and children. On September 21, 1939, Reinhard Heydrich, head of the Reich Security Main Office, ordered that "[a] Council of Jewish Elders is to be established in every Jewish community which as far as possible is to be created from the leading persons and rabbis. Up to 24 male Jews (depending on the size of the Jewish community) are to belong to the Council of Elders. It is to be made entirely responsible, within the meaning of the word, for the exact and prompt fulfillment of all instructions which have been or will be given."[2]

Shortly after the establishment of these councils (*Judenräte*), each was ordered to conduct a census of the Jewish population of its city. (Adam Czerniakow, the head of the newly appointed Warsaw Judenrat, mentions the census in several of his diary entries.)[3] When they were complying with this demand, Jewish officials had no idea how the Germans intended to use the censuses. No explanations accompanied the rapidly expanding number of anti-Jewish orders, decrees, and laws issued by the occupiers.

Officially the Nazis defined all Jews as fitting into a racial category distinguishable by specific physical, social, and psychological characteristics. Yet undermining this myth was the fact that in the freshly occupied territories of Eastern Europe, the conquerors often had difficulty separating Jews from the rest of the population. An official decree requiring Jews to wear a Star of David helped, but it took a while before it went into effect. Therefore, at the start, the Germans relied on collaborators to identify the Jews and their property. To gain the cooperation of the local populations the Germans poured virulent anti-Semitic propaganda into the newly conquered territories. Not only did this propaganda describe the Jews as subhuman, vermin to be exterminated, but it also blamed them for every conceivable ill, including the start of the war. These ideas often fell on fertile ground, and anti-Semitic mobs sprang up, encouraged by the official attitude.[4]

Commenting on the ensuing anti-Jewish violence in Poland, the his-

21

torian Emanuel Ringelblum suggested that from the moment Polish anti-Semites helped Germans drive hungry Jews away from food lines the "street" became a link between these anti-Semites and the Germans; for this was where both victors and collaborators found their Jewish prey.[5]

The chronicler Chaim Kapłan described Warsaw in an entry of October 1939: "Every public place shows hatred and loathing against Jews. Isolated incidents of violence against Jews have grown too numerous to count. Eyewitnesses tell horrifying stories, and they are not exaggerations." Half a year later the situation had worsened: "Gangs of young toughs, Polish youths (you won't find one adult among them), armed with clubs, sticks and all kinds of harmful weapons, make pogroms against the Jews. They break into stores and empty their goods into their own pockets. The Jews they encounter on the way are beaten and wounded. The Jewish quarter has been abandoned to toughs and killers who were organized for this purpose by some invisible hand."[6]

Eager to see the Jews degraded and tortured before their deaths, the Germans followed each territorial conquest with assaults designed to debase and humiliate. Numerous photographs show gleefully laughing German soldiers looking on while their comrades cut off the beards of orthodox Jews. Often such encounters involved brutal beatings, with the victims forced to kneel, pray, dance, and sing.[7]

Some Jews reacted by running away. From what used to be Poland, an estimated 250,000–300,000 escaped. Most went to what was then Soviet territory. It is estimated that the majority—about two-thirds—of these escapees were men. For most of the men who remained, the anti-Jewish assaults continued. In addition to the street violence against them, Jewish men were rounded up and forced to clear rubble, fill anti-tank ditches, shovel snow, and perform other physically demanding and degrading tasks.[8]

By October 1939, the Germans had issued a special decree that made work by Jewish males mandatory. Yet random street roundups of Jewish men, many of whom were unfit for hard labor, continued. And whenever the abductors managed to seize rabbis or men who seemed prominent, intellectual, or rich, they assigned them to the most degrading and debilitating jobs, such as cleaning toilets or road work. Because these captures involved men rather than women they seemed to send a message that Jewish men were in special danger.

In the face of these widespread, abusive raids, the Judenräte volunteered to become the official suppliers of Jewish labor, hoping that such cooperation would calm the situation. Once again, these work transactions seemed to apply mainly to men.[9] Depending in part on the kind of job they were made to perform, these Jews were labeled "useful" or "useless." Those designated useful were supposedly exempt from the haphazard roundups, whose victims were still forced to do the most debilitating work and might even be transferred into the unknown. Jewish men thus tried desperately to avoid being labeled useless. But the criteria for making these distinctions kept changing in unpredictable ways.

Even for those who managed to remain in the "useful" category the situation grew increasingly bad. Jewish laborers were not entitled to regular wages. Most were forced to work without pay or for earnings that were too small to avert hunger; usually payment took the form of meager food allotments.[10] Regardless of their social backgrounds and occupational skills, Jewish men found themselves deprived of freedom, authority, and the ability to earn a living. These deprivations in turn stripped them of their traditional roles as family protectors and providers.

There were exceptions. Occasionally, a few members of a Jewish council or men who had been part of the underclass before the war would gain a temporary semblance of power. Some Judenrat members may have deluded themselves that their work would allow them to shield themselves and their families — even some of their fellow Jews — from destruction. Similarly, smugglers and collaborators, with their extra earnings, may have temporarily felt protected.

However, for most Jews the war created a blurring of class distinctions. In part this blurring of social and occupational differences was caused by the low economic value that the Germans attached to all Jewish labor. The potential and real economic advantages the Nazis might have gained from Jewish labor gave way to their goal of Jewish destruction. Within the different Nazi government branches one can discern a tension between those who emphasized the advantages of slave labor and those who felt that Jewish destruction should proceed regardless of economic cost. Depending on who had the upper hand, Jews were either kept alive for economic reasons or destroyed despite their economic value. In the end, those who favored Jewish annihilation regardless of economic advantages prevailed.[11] For Jews, therefore, work served only as a temporary respite on their road to death.

Parallel to these developments, from the start of the German takeover, Jewish communities had been continuously bombarded with a barrage of new laws, decrees, and orders. Given the strangeness and the large number of these demands it was inevitable that Jews would miss hearing about some edict or another, or fail to grasp its meaning. But failure to comply with any of the new orders met with severe punishment. For Jews who survived the initial Nazi assaults, the continuously multiplying hardships led to the emergence of new living patterns and coping strategies. Women and men seemed to be affected differently by these conditions and coped in different ways.

Shlomo Peltel illustrates both the effects of the initial assaults and how they might have influenced his coping strategies. At the start of the German occupation Shlomo was severely beaten by a German soldier. His daughter Vladka thinks that this incident triggered an emotional decline. The public beating undermined his dignity and shattered his trust in the German people. Perhaps this humiliating beginning made it harder to deal with subsequent hardships.

A German bomb hit the Peltels' haberdashery just before the fall of Warsaw. The family salvaged a part of the merchandise. No store meant no income. But the rescued goods came in handy; they could be converted into cash. This, however, required a trip to the sector the Germans had declared off-limits to Jews. Vladka volunteered for this job because, unlike the rest of her family, she could pass for a Polish Gentile. She took off the armband that identified her as a Jew and went to the "Aryan" side to sell some of the merchandise.

When she recalls this period, Vladka refers to her father as "a broken man." With much compassion she explains that after the German takeover, "he had nothing to lean on. He could not in any practical way help the family, as he used to in the past. He could not act as the provider, as the protector."[12] Quite naturally, because she felt that she was now best suited for the role of provider, Vladka stepped in and helped support the family.

Similar changes occurred in other Jewish communities. Eva Galer's experiences during the initial stages of the German occupation resemble the Peltels'. One of the authorities' first acts in Olszyce, a small town close to Kraków, Eva's birthplace, was to order the Jews to collect prayer books and other religious objects for a public burning. After the fire had started, old orthodox Jewish men were forced to sing and dance around the burning books. Shortly after this, German soldiers seized Eva's father, Israel Vogel, and unceremoniously cut off his beard in front of a crowd. It quickly became clear that Vogel, a prominent and respected businessman, had lost his fortune and all prospects of gainful employment. As Eva explains, "Before the war, my father was an important man in the community; he was highly respected and very active. He traveled all over the world, spoke German and Hungarian. People would consult him when they had problems . . . Once he stopped being the provider, he sat at home depressed. He did not try to do anything else . . . He gave up . . . My father did not budge . . . He did nothing, nothing, just sat home."[13]

Israel Vogel's abdication of authority spilled into other areas of family life. This was shown during the evening visits of Eva's boyfriend. The two would laugh, tell jokes, and openly flirt in front of Eva's father. Before the war this parent, an orthodox Jew, would not even have tolerated her having a boyfriend in the house. Open flirtation would have been out of the question. After the Nazi takeover, he stopped reacting to such provocation. Painfully, Eva concludes that her father had stopped behaving as the head of the household.[14]

Reflecting more generally upon these changes Eva says, "I think that men lost their spirit; the women were more likely to withstand hunger. To me it looked as if men were more resigned . . . Women were looking for ways to live, to cope; they tried harder than men. I saw it happen to my father. When he could not be the provider, he just did nothing. He gave up. My mother, my sister, and I would sell things from our home, exchange them for food; we went out to find food so that the rest of us would have something to eat."

About her mother, Ita Princ-Vogel, Eva spoke with admiration rather than pain. The mother of two children and stepmother of six, she is remembered as active, perpetually on the lookout for options. As the oldest child, Eva formed a partnership with her mother. Both stepped into the role of family food suppliers. Eva felt that her father's dejection could be traced to the enormous distance between what he had had and what he had lost, and perhaps in part to his advanced age; Ita was much younger than Israel. However, regardless of age their different reactions matched those of many women and men.

In many Jewish families children and wives were eager to ease the sense of powerlessness of their fathers and husbands. In the early days of the occupation, some of the teenage daughters and sons managed to reduce their families' burdens by working for local peasants. Their earnings consisted of farm products that helped feed their families. It was by no means unusual to hear of young sons and daughters who were eagerly working to aid their families. Most often, however, wives and mothers would step in and take over the roles of the disempowered fathers and husbands. Sometimes the efforts of these special helpers took unusual twists.

Tonia Rotkopf-Blair was fourteen when the Germans occupied Łódź, her native city. She described her father as an "intellectual and a rebel, a high class weaver." Both parents were well-educated and politically active; they belonged to the Jewish socialist party, the Bund. Tonia sees her background as rich in culture but poor in money.

Her father's first encounter with the authorities occurred at the start of the occupation, close to the curfew hour. An aunt, the owner of a grocery store, had promised the Rotkopfs flour. Because Tonia looked the least Jewish, she accompanied her father to collect this treasure. Before they reached the store, Tonia noticed a group of German soldiers approaching from around the corner.

[They were] coming towards us; with those ugly voices they screamed at my father, who looked very Jewish. They knocked him down. It was a horrible, horrible feeling for a child, to see her father fall, defenseless. He was very tall. They shoved him like he was some kind of a bundle. They kicked him and covered him with heavy blows . . . these horrors were taking place and I was watching, knowing that I could not help, sure that they were killing him. Eventually when he was still, they left . . . Only when he moved I realized that he was alive. I was humiliated; I felt horrible . . . Jews were not supposed to use the sidewalk. The Germans had just passed this law. We didn't even know it. I think that they announced it, but we missed the news.

The attackers probably knew that Tonia was Jewish, yet they chose not to bother her. This raises the question of how spontaneous the anti-Jewish terror was.[15]

Tonia describes how quickly the fate of her family changed.

Soon enough, my father was dismissed from his work; no work, no income. We didn't have any money. There was no food. Father smoked, and no cigarettes, a terrible blow for him. My little brother who was about ten went to collect cigarette butts. He would re-roll them into cigarettes and sell them. One day, he came back all bloodied . . . Some anti-Semitic youths had beaten him up. It was a real shock when this child came home all bloody . . . a terrible change had happened to my father; he really couldn't do anything, mother had to take charge of things.

To ease the family's burden, Tonia took a job in the Jewish hospital that stood at the edge of the future ghetto area. The fourteen-year-old was an assistant nurse, caring for infants. This work entitled Tonia to food, lodgings, and the promise that she would be trained as a nurse. How did her family react?

I don't remember them arguing. There was a sadness in the house, but I don't remember much else . . . When I think of my father, all I know is that my heart is breaking. He was so defeated; he was so down. Because he immediately lost his old job; he could not support us; later he worked but could not provide for us because they did not pay him. We had a little bit of food left. My mother was the one who managed the little we had.[16]

Despite these changes, her father seemed able to retain a measure of his former independence. He refused to obey the Nazi order to relocate to what later became the Łódź ghetto. Rotkopf's disobedience was probably a matter of principle; the family's modest apartment was only a short distance from the designated ghetto area.

One day at work Tonia heard that the Germans were forcing out the few remaining Jews who had failed to vacate their homes. She ran to join her family, but when she got to the apartment she found only an eerie silence and an emptiness. The silent surroundings told her that something dreadful must have happened. On the front door she noticed a sign, an official seal warning against entry. What could she do? As a child, she felt particularly helpless and went back to the hospital. The next day she heard that the Germans were about to deport those whom they had removed from the apartments. Once more she ran to meet her family.

She saw a large group of Jews being led down the middle of the road, surrounded by German soldiers with rifles in hand, as if ready for action. Tonia caught sight of her parents, her brother, and her sister. Even now she can see her mother's bewildered eyes. Tonia noticed, amazed and saddened, that each family member carried a chair, a pillow, a towel . . . They must have been ordered to hurry, no doubt roughly, and had grabbed these useless objects. Mr. Rotkopf was on the outside of the crowd. Tonia remembers:

Father noticed me. I saw his hand waving close to the side of his body, in a gesture that told me to disappear, not to approach him. He kept making the same gesture, a discreet, uninterrupted movement. Despite his signal I came closer. Walking toward them I noticed a Volksdeutscher, a boy I used to play with in the streets of our neighborhood; my older sister went to school with him. Dressed in a Nazi uniform he looked distant, self-important. As I was about to reach my people, he kicked me with his boot in the stomach. This threw me against the building, my head hit the wall, and I was bleeding. It all happened so quickly . . .

people carried me to a janitor's house; I was probably half-conscious. This is the last time I saw my family; I saw them being led away. Now I think that the reason this boy kicked me and made me hit the wall was to save me. I don't really know. It could be . . . I think that someone washed my face, but I don't remember what I did after that, if I went home or not. I was all alone.

Letters came to Tonia telling her that her family had been taken to Mszana Dolna, where they lived in deplorable conditions. She found some people who had relatives there and through them sent whatever money she could collect. The last mail she received was a postcard. It was written in pencil, and Tonia could not decipher what it said—most of the writing had been erased. Nor could she tell how long it had been in transit. Such was Tonia's final farewell from her family.

Mr. Rotkopf's defiance had resulted in deportation rather than execution. It was one of those German "exceptions," a variation on a theme. The ever-expanding range of German penalties led to uncertainty, undermining Jewish morale. This incident, like so many others, also shows how a father's inability to support the family created a void that was filled by other family members, the mother and children. Tonia wanted to share her family's fate but was prevented from doing it. For a while she might have eased their suffering by sharing with them what little money she had.

Time and the emergent political, military, and economic circumstances would occasionally alter the ever-expanding course of Jewish destruction. In the absence of other evidence, most historians agree that the plan for Jewish annihilation—the "Final Solution"—crystallized after the start of the Russian-German war in June 1941. As the Germans moved East, they searched for more efficient methods of Jewish destruction. The capture of Russian-held territories coincided with the mass murder of Jews, most of which was accomplished by SS and police troops like the Einsatzgruppen, with the cooperation of the German army.[17]

Official orders connected to this war, known as Operation Barbarossa, stress the important role played by the Jewish male intelligentsia in creating and maintaining international communism in the fight against the Nazis. Some official directives insisted upon "ruthless and vigorous measures against the Bolshevik inciters, guerrillas, saboteurs, Jews and the complete elimination of all active and passive resistance."[18] Nazi documents consistently blamed Jewish male elites for the very existence of the Communist system. These accusations often appear as justifications for the mass killings of Jewish men. The Nazi patriarchal ideology appears to be linked to the German assaults that specifically aimed at the degradation and destruction of Jewish men. Seen through patriarchal lenses, the Jewish male elite were a serious political threat. If carried to their logical conclusions such perceptions meant that Jewish men who qualified as potential leaders would be the first to be eliminated, followed by the remaining Jewish males.

And yet in the newly conquered eastern territories German documents dating from July 1941 on report the murder of Jewish women and children as well. These murders continued throughout the summer and into November. Unlike the executions of Jewish men, mass killings of Jewish women and children appear to have been less coordinated. Probably initiated by local Nazi functionaries, these murders are described in some reports as a way to reduce the population and thereby improve the area's food supplies.[19]

In addition to the mass killings behind the front lines, the Germans upon entering a community would collect the Jewish male elites and murder them. Surprise and secrecy were part of these operations. For example, in Stołpce, in western Belorussia, the Germans rounded up eighteen of the most prominent Jewish men before a new administrative power was even in place. Riva Kantorowicz-Reich's first husband, Harkawi, was among them. Harkawi belonged to one of the richest families in town. When the police came to arrest him, his mother showed them to his room. Harkawi was still asleep, as were Riva and their infant daughter. The police took him away in his pajamas. Riva rushed to the police station with clothes and food. The policeman on duty would not accept the package, assuring her that the prisoner lacked nothing.

Among those arrested were a few non-Jews — an error. They were promptly released, and they told Riva that Harkawi had been tortured and was in bad shape. In an effort to free him, Riva made the rounds of officials. From some she heard that Harkawi was well. Others told her that he was ill. Still others promised to free him. To some she gave Harkawi's clothes, to others large sums of money. She also heard that her husband had been executed in a nearby forest. It was years before she learned the truth.[20]

Similarly, in Białystok, sixteen-year-old Eva Kracowski lost her father in one of the early assaults upon the Jewish male elites and less prominent men. Dr. Samuel Kracowski, a physician, perished along with about eight hundred to a thousand Jewish men in the flames of a burning synagogue. To this day Eva does not know whether or when her mother fully realized that her husband had been murdered. Possibly, to Eva's mother, as to so many others, the truth came slowly, through a myriad of strange, contradictory rumors. The killers themselves probably planted some of the bizarre stories that circulated about the fate of these men in order to further confuse and demoralize the population.[21]

The murder of the Jewish male elites of Słonim, another town in western Belorussia, on July 17, 1941, was conducted more openly. First an SS division arrived in trucks to collect physicians, architects, political figures, and other prominent men. The selection proceeded according to lists, but no one knew who provided them. When the SS had assembled fifteen hundred men, they herded them into a public building. There three hundred of the men were let go, for no apparent reason. The remainder had to turn in their personal identification documents. They were then made to write letters to their families, without dates or any place description. Then trucks transported them to a forest, a distance of some twenty kilometers.

News about the fate of these men reached Słonim before the letters. Not far from the place to which the SS men brought them lived a forester and his wife. They were good, pious people. After the German takeover, the woman brought food to her Jewish friends the Shepetinskis. Zvi Shefet (Shepetinski) remembers, "Two days after the killing of the 1,200 Jews, the woman visited us . . . I can see it all, she came in, embraced us, but could not utter a word, all she did was cry." When the woman regained her composure, she told how upon hearing shots she and her husband had gone to investigate. Walking in the direction of the sounds, they came upon a fresh mass grave. The soil was still moving.[22]

The news spread fast. Many people refused to believe it, and some women went in search of their husbands. Scattered pieces of familiar clothing directed them to the burial site. Yet most of these women said nothing of what they found there. Was their silence dictated by fear, by disbelief of what they saw, or by some other, unknown motive?

In Słonim, as in other communities of the freshly occupied territories, the Jewish men who survived the initial assaults were subjected to humiliating experiences. Following the usual pattern Zvi's father had lost his profitable business as a wood merchant. Without the possibility of an income he became depressed. But like all Jewish adult men Zvi's father was required to register for work with the newly established Judenrat. Those who failed to comply were not entitled to food rations, and they had to hide out.

When the authorities needed men for work they would take them from among those who were registered. Each day these men had to come to a designated place, put their name on a list, and wait for their work orders. While they were waiting, they would often be harassed and beaten. The men generally fell into two groups: steady and casual laborers. Zvi's father was one of the casual workers. But he still had to appear every day. To shield his father from the humiliations connected to the work detail, Zvi would register in his place; when his father's name was called for work, Zvi would go instead. The rest of the family agreed that this was the proper way to deal with the difficult situation. Zvi's case reconfirms that help extended to families by teenage children came from both sexes.

About his mother Zvi recalls: "Mother had a way of creating good feelings around her. She tried to be in good spirits, at least outwardly; this is the impression she gave. She was lively, people loved her and she kept up their morale . . . Father was tense, very worried."

Despite the documentation now available concerning the early mass murders of Jewish women and children, it appears that most Jews were ignorant of these special crimes. Unfamiliar with the ideological intricacies of the Third Reich, Jews based their conclusions about what was happening on what they heard, saw, and experienced. Assaults directed against men were more visible and more common, as were roundups of men for forceful, debilitating labor, usually accompanied by public abuses. Thus, Jewish communities were aware of the rumors or even the hard evidence about the selective mass killings of elite Jewish men, but less aware of the murders of women. Perhaps too, the Jews could not understand the reason for the killings of women and children, particularly at the beginning. All these factors led Jews to the seemingly logical conclusion that men rather than women were in special danger.[23] And so, regardless of occasional evidence to the contrary, the conviction that Jewish men were particularly threatened was common.

Acting upon these ideas, some community leaders sought out women's help. One such request came after the Germans agreed to transfer an additional part of Poland to their then allies, the Soviets. As a rule, whenever they would vacate an area for the Russians the Germans would burn the local synagogues. Niemirów, a small community in southern Poland, was one of these temporarily Nazi-occupied towns. The Jewish elders learned that the Germans were to leave within a day and had reason to believe that their synagogue would go up in flames. In fact, rumor had it that in preparation for their departure, the Germans had already poured gasoline all over it. Eager to save their place of worship, a delegation of the Jewish community leaders approached Sandra Brand, an attractive young woman known for her courage, her independence, and her fluency in German. Though she was the daughter of a respected Hasid, Sandra looked like a Polish gentile. She had recently married a lawyer, a secular Jew twice her age. The couple had eloped, which in itself was seen as scandalous and put the young woman into the category of an adventurous outcast. Nevertheless, in this hour of need, the Jewish leaders pleaded with Sandra to go to the German authorities and beg them to spare the synagogue.

Sandra insists, "I am not so good-natured, not a goody, goody, but I was very flattered that these prominent men, who in the past [had] criticized me for what they saw as my outrageous undisciplined behavior, needed my help. So I wanted to show them how capable I really was!" She agreed to see the German officer in charge, a colonel. There was a security guard walking a beat around the building, but he let her in. Inside Sandra found the officer relaxing in an easy chair. She began by explaining that as a Christian, she did not care about the Jews and their place of worship. She had come to plead on behalf of her fellow Christians, who were very poor and lived near the synagogue. If the Germans burned it down the surrounding homes of the poor Christians would also burn down. Surely the colonel did not want these innocent people to lose their homes.

"Is [the synagogue] far from here?" the colonel asked. When Sandra assured him that it was close by, he put on his shiny boots and followed her there. He inspected the place, said goodnight, and left. It was already after curfew, and all she could do was run quickly home.

Sandra had no idea whether she had succeeded or not. To the many questions that came her way, she would answer with a shrug. Only the next morning, after the Germans had departed Niemirów leaving the synagogue intact, did she realize that she had accomplished her mission. Sandra became a hero. From then on, her Hasid father would introduce her proudly as "the daughter who saved the synagogue."[24]

In our conversation, Sandra described some new habits that developed because of the belief that men rather than women were in danger:

If there was a knock at the door, I went to the door, not my husband,
or if I was in my father's house, I went to the door, not my father or my
brother. When there was a knock at the door, my father, my brother, my
husband ran to the attic, to some back room, some other hiding place,
and I went to the door. We women went shopping, we went to look for
food. In some way, we knew that when we went to the store anybody
could hit us, anybody could grab us . . . Here and there this did
happen . . . You see, if I take the word *hero* loosely, very loosely, during
the war every Jewish woman was a hero. The women went out to provide their families with food, some went to work to earn money . . .
They exposed themselves to dangers.

Sandra's observations are supported by Emanuel Ringelblum, who was impressed by the special wartime contributions of Jewish wives and mothers. A diary entry of January 1940 reads, "The Jewish woman sustains the family by standing for hours in dangerous food lines, by intervening with the authorities—German soldiers and the Gestapo—by accepting jobs, jobs that promise only meager benefits. Gone is the elegant lady with the fancy hats. We see instead simply dressed women with kerchiefs on their heads constantly searching for ways to support their families."[25] Even at the early stages of the German occupation, Jewish women had added to their traditional family duties the making of special contacts within their threatening surroundings. Young daughters and sons often shared these extra duties. Evidence of this change comes repeatedly from direct interviews, archival materials, and published memoirs.

Though they were not at first as openly or as directly attacked as the men, women and children nonetheless experienced painful losses as their husbands, fathers, and other men they valued or loved were forced to run away or were taken away, abused, or killed. The men who remained saw their traditional world shattered, and with it lost important sources of their masculine identification and pride. Unable to fulfill their traditional roles as providers and protectors, many broke down; others suffered from just watching these changes. Women and children were also deprived of their freedom, rights, and property. And in addition to their direct suffering, women were stripped of the traditional emotional support they had come to expect from men. Inevitably, Jewish women knew about and often witnessed the abuses of their men. This knowledge took its toll.

Anti-Jewish policies were sometimes less ruthless and more subject to delay in satellite countries and in western Europe. Yet in retrospect, historians have shown that whenever anti-Jewish policies were implemented they resembled the basic Nazi stages of Jewish annihilation. How did prospective victims respond to these delayed and only slightly different anti-Jewish measures? Slovakia, a newly created country that followed a different path from the rest of Nazi-occupied eastern Europe, may serve as an additional test of my findings of how experiences were shaped by gender.

In 1939 Slovakia became a German satellite state, with Jozef Tiso, a Roman Catholic priest, as its president. Tiso implemented various anti-

Jewish policies inspired by Nazi Germany, forcing Jews to live in specially designated areas. Eager to acquire Jewish assets, in 1942 Tiso paid the Germans 500 Reichsmarks per Jew to transfer them. As a result, between thirteen and fourteen thousand Jews were captured in special roundups and deportations, most of whom perished in Auschwitz.[26]

The Benau family lived in Bratislava, the capital of the newly created state. The family had three children, all around the age of twenty. Before the war Mr. Benau had been a strict disciplinarian who made all the important decisions. Mrs. Benau, an intelligent woman, was permissive, gentle, and giving. Their daughter Berta describes the changes that took place in her parents:

> Mother wanted us to leave . . . When this did not happen, she urged us not to look at the dark side of life, that it could be worse . . . Father was crying all the time . . . Mother was stronger than he, definitely stronger. When they took his store away it hurt him a lot. It broke him . . . At first, we thought that men, especially young men, were in greater danger. My brother wanted to go to Palestine. My parents agreed because they thought that it was most important to protect him. He left in an illegal boat, . . . and reached Palestine.[27]

The belief that only men were in danger was similar to the prevailing ideas in most other Nazi-controlled countries. And this belief was based on a somewhat realistic assessment of the situation.[28] Although Jews in Slovakia realized after a while that women were also threatened, few apparently acted upon this understanding. Berta's father refused to part from his daughters, even though their mother wanted them to leave. They stayed on.

Berta tells what happened:

> In March 1942 the Hlinka Guard came to take us to the station. My sister and I were to go. They did not take my parents. They were collecting only young Jewish women . . . They took 1,000 of us . . . Mother accompanied us to the train station. My father did not come. I never saw her after that, nor him. I heard that my parents, with an older sister and her children, had been sent to Auschwitz and upon arrival were all taken to the crematoria.

Both the conditions imposed upon the Slovakian Jews and their reactions to them resemble earlier findings of this chapter. As in occupied eastern Europe, Jews in Slovakia were deprived of their freedom and property. Mr. Benau's loss of livelihood made him feel powerless, depriving him of his spirit, while Mrs. Benau rose to the occasion. Ready to act, she took on additional burdens and tried to lift the spirits of her family. Slovakia did differ from the rest of eastern Europe in one unusual aspect: in 1942, orders came that women, rather than men, now had to register for "work." These unexpected orders contradicted the established belief that men were at greater risk;[29] nonetheless, with this one exception, the patterns common in Nazi-occupied eastern European countries were apparent also in Slovakia.

In a shaky environment, without guidelines or predictable directives, it is difficult to live. People look for patterns, for a way to make their lives conform to some sort of expectations. They depend on rumors, hearsay, bits of information, and on this basis make predictions for the future. Once they have become used to their new ideas, they resist change, even when confronted with new information, for there is comfort in habits, which by their very nature suggest continuity, predictability. Initially, Jewish women, accustomed to performing nurturing roles, rose to their new situations and offered support to their husbands. Some took on traditionally male roles, filling the gaps left by their husbands' inability to fulfill these roles. Thus as Jewish women continued to protect their men and provide for their families they had to adjust to new situations, sometimes without being aware of the change. And yet because they were in part guided by what they had learned at the beginning of the occupation, they didn't recognize that their new roles exposed them to the increasing German threats. With the appearance of a new environment, the Nazi ghetto, an important step was added to the process of Jewish annihilation. In this alien setting, Jewish women and men had to devise new strategies to cope with everyday life.

3

Life in the Ghetto

A mother of two little children who was married to an unemployed laborer, Mrs. F. continued her modest blackmarket operations after she moved into the Warsaw ghetto. Neither Mrs. F.'s unexpected pregnancy nor the birth of a third child interrupted her efforts to support her family.

In the fall of 1941, the Germans introduced a law forbidding all unauthorized crossings between the ghetto and the "Aryan" sector of Warsaw. Apprehension meant death. But Mrs. F.'s husband had been incapacitated by a severe case of typhus; she had to disregard this threat.

Even though Mrs. F.'s appearance did not betray her Jewish background, a Polish policeman stopped her.

"You are Jewish," he said.

Her automatic "No, no, I'm Polish" met with, "Let me see your papers."

But Mrs. F. had no papers to show. The man told her to follow. On the way, she offered him a bribe of 50 zlotys; the policeman demanded 100. All she had was 50. He refused. After her arrest, Mrs. F. was transferred to the ghetto prison. She was among the first Jews executed for crossing illegally to the Aryan side.[1]

Mrs. F.'s murder took place during the early stages of the ghetto, signaling the accelerated pace of Jewish destruction. The Nazis had designed the ghetto as a temporary Jewish quarter to serve as a prelude for the final stage of Jewish annihilation. Before the ghettos were built, Jews had heard only rumors that contained no clear-cut information about the character and purpose of these quarters. The conflicting ghetto stories increased the apprehension of a people who were continuously exposed to terror, although here and there among the grim predictions a hopeful note was struck. Perhaps these future Jewish quarters would be autonomous communities in which Jews would have free access to their surroundings. These rare positive notes failed to calm people.[2]

Responding to the mounting tensions, Adam Czerniakow, the head of the Warsaw Judenrat, petitioned the German authorities to stop the building of the Warsaw ghetto. They responded by establishing two ghettos, one in Łódź and one in Warsaw. This action was followed in 1941 by a spate of ghetto building; the number of new ghettos in eastern Europe eventually reached an estimated four hundred.[3] Because the characteristics these Nazi-created quarters shared by far outweigh the differences, I will concentrate on their basic similarities rather than the occasional variations.

All the ghettos were located in the most dilapidated parts of urban centers, where there was no running water and no electricity. In their excessively overcrowded living quarters, several families would be assigned to a single room. The inevitable accumulation of filth resulted in epidemics and many other calamities. Death could come from a variety of sources: starvation, sporadic killings, epidemics, and less directly from forced removals, the so-called deportations that led to the concentration camps.

Although the Nazis had utilized Jewish labor from the start of the occupation, more systematic economic exploitation followed the establishment of ghettos. Eventually compulsory employment applied to women as well. Some women, particularly those who had no husbands or whose husbands could not support them, were glad to work, even for the inadequate rewards. Usually the larger ghettos would have two kinds of work force; a municipal labor system and a private enterprise system. The municipal labor system was more common, and it was arranged via the Judenräte, who were under pressure to exploit the Jewish work force. The Judenräte were allotted payments — starvation wages — for the inmates' work. The occupational authorities closely supervised all labor transactions. The private enterprises were owned by German firms, and they had the freedom to exploit their work force; low payment for Jewish workers translated into enormous profits for German businessmen. The Jews themselves were motivated to work hard because many of them equated economic contribution with survival.

More basically, survival of the ghetto inmates depended on food supply. By controlling the ghettos' food deliveries the Germans turned these closed quarters into death traps. In Poland, an estimated 20 percent of the ghetto populations died of hunger. Yet for the Germans even this death rate was not fast enough; around 1942 the German rulers became more determined to do away with "useless" ghetto Jews. Unproductive people — the old, the sick, children — were murdered.[4]

The Germans were probably eager to speed up the process of Jewish destruction because time no longer favored them. After the Germans' initial spectacular advances at the eastern front, the Soviets had stiffened their opposition. Hitler's army began to incur losses. Then the year 1943 brought defeat at Stalingrad. A turning point in the conduct of the war, this setback made German victory less certain. As the prospects of military conquests continued to dwindle, the Nazis began to concentrate on winning a different war: the one against the Jews. The need to win this war, in turn, heightened the Nazis' awareness that women were a vehicle for the perpetuation of the Jewish race. Among the weapons directed against Jewish women were forced labor and assaults and prohibitions against motherhood, pregnancy, childbirth, and child care. German laws and directives poured into the Jewish communities, and severe punishment, usually death, followed disobedience of any one of them. Attached to these punitive measures was the principle of collective responsibility: relatives, friends, or even other ghetto inmates were held responsible for transgressions committed by the "guilty" party.

The Nazis had already created the Judenräte as special administrative bodies to transmit their orders. At first they had tried to recruit into these

Jewish councils prewar communal leaders. But some of the leaders managed to escape while others refused to become involved with the German authorities. The history of the Nazi-appointed Judenräte is filled with many unsettled debates, in part because their character, function, and fate were in a continual flux.[5] Displeased by any sign of independence, the Germans would often execute a part of a Judenrat, or they would even murder the whole council and replace it with a new one.

With one notable exception, these Nazi-appointed councils consisted of men; the few female employees held clerical jobs. The exception was the council of Wieliczka, a small town near Kraków. Here the initial German takeover had been marked by the brutal execution of many prominent Jewish men. These murders shook up the community, and all the surviving men refused to become part of a Judenrat. The Germans insisted, threatening reprisals. When still no men responded and the threats grew, women volunteered to take their place. The first Judenrat in Wieliczka consisted of women—a response that conformed to the emerging pattern of women filling the gaps created by the absence of men. The Wieliczka Judenrat changed in 1941, when two male refugees from Kraków took over.[6]

Isolated from the world around them, deprived of facts, inmates of the ghettos based their opinions on subjective observations and experience. From the start of the occupation, they tended to view the Judenräte with suspicion. Over time, this suspicion turned into accusations of betrayal. Perhaps these attitudes sprang from the direct contacts that Judenrat members had with the enemy. Perhaps, too, the relative advantages that the Judenrat members and their families seemed to have and the growing deprivation of the rest of the population fueled resentment. And, inevitably, the corruption of some Judenrat members contributed to the accusations. Yet within the ghetto, the Judenrat was by no means the sole source of dissension. Nazi-built ghettos were fragmented communities, with cleavages and conflicts that came from many directions and fed on many prejudices.[7]

The ghetto was a community in which the traditional social order was shattered and the new one "kept in a perpetual state of flux. Class distinctions in the ghetto were based . . . on factors related directly to survival under the new conditions: shrewdness, audacity, indifference to the plight of others, physical strength, manual dexterity, and the external factors such as access to the German authorities."[8]

A large proportion of the ghetto inmates had come from the adjacent smaller communities. The Germans fomented strife by pouring into the ghettos potential antagonists: converts to Catholicism known for their anti-Semitism; Gypsies who shared with the Jews only a range of mutual suspicions; Jews from western Europe who looked upon eastern European Jewry with contempt.[9] The ghetto was thus a highly fragmented community, with blocks of strangers who shared only their mutual distrust and hostility. Poorly integrated, composed of some hostile and competitive subgroups, the ghetto was a community threatened by extinction, led by powerless, disillusioned men, once prominent, who were now a source of disillusionment for the rest of the population.

The ghetto was a community ravaged by hunger, disease, and terror; a sealed-off community, isolated from the world.

It was a community about whose fate no one seemed to bother or care.

It was a community left (within limits) to its own resources that had no resources.

And yet, despite the ghettos' cleavages and limited cohesion, some inmates rose above their personal sufferings and engaged in cooperative, communal efforts. Women became a growing force, in both numbers and influence, among the workers dedicated to the welfare of the ghetto.

In eastern Europe the increasing deterioration of ghetto conditions made it clear that the majority of the inmates required aid. In itself the growing proportion of impoverished members in the ghetto populations functioned as a serious obstacle to any ability to help. Nevertheless, despite the mounting hardships, or perhaps because of them, all kinds of organizations devoted to social and health services, and to educational and cultural pursuits, proliferated in the ghettos.[10]

Officially, inside the ghetto the Judenrat was in charge. The council was entrusted with keeping order and with the care of incoming refugees. In most places Jewish ghetto councils had expanded their operations to include public kitchens, health care, hygiene, and educational and cultural pursuits. But the councils had support from a number of outside aid groups.

Unlike most other prewar organizations, the American Jewish Joint Distribution Committee, known as the JDC or Joint, continued to function in Poland after the German invasion. Until the United States entered the war the Joint operated legally. After December 1941 it continued its activities illegally. Headed by David Guzik, the Joint retained many other dedicated prewar leaders. Welfare activities included the sheltering of Jewish refugees, aid to hospitals, educational programs, the establishment of kitchens, help to children, and much more. It has been estimated that by 1941 about six hundred thousand Jews in Poland were receiving aid from the Joint.[11]

Also an important presence in the Warsaw ghetto were the newly created house committees. Each building had such a unit, bringing the total to about two thousand. As did most other ghetto organizations the house committees performed a variety of functions. They created public kitchens, offered health care, collected and distributed clothing to the poor, and attended to the educational and cultural needs of the population.[12]

Over time ghetto organizations mushroomed. Sometimes their legal operations served as covers for illicit activities. Collectively and individually, occasionally in tandem, at other times in competition with one another, the different organizations promoted social welfare and a range of cultural and educational goals. Central among them were soup kitchens for the poor, procedures to combat the spread of epidemics, lectures, theatrical presentations, and libraries. In the ghettos of Poland, Lithuania, Latvia, and Estonia illegal schools flourished.[13]

The historians Emanuel Ringelblum and Cecylia Ślepak were particularly impressed by the contributions of Jewish women to the welfare of others. Ringelblum had commissioned Ślepak to conduct a survey about the fate of Jewish woman during the war that would be part of the *Oneg Shabath* archive. Her research showed that ghetto women tended to fall into two categories. On the one hand were those who struggled for life because they were convinced that it was their duty to do so in order to take care of themselves and their families. Such a woman was Mrs. F., described at the opening of this chapter.

But there were also women who rose to the challenge posed by life-threatening disasters on a broader scale. The upheavals of the war had pushed these women into activities that reached beyond self-preservation and the preservation of their families. Some as independent, private individuals, others as employees of welfare organizations, these women devoted themselves to helping wide circles of people. Ślepak believed that such women had the will and ability to identify with the suffering of strangers and the community at large.[14]

A professional librarian, identified in Ślepak's survey as Mrs. B., serves as an example of this second type of woman. In the Warsaw ghetto, Mrs. B.'s paid job barely satisfied her needs. Yet she ignored her own difficulties and devoted herself to creating a children's lending library. She began by collecting books and contacting potential helpers. Despite seemingly impossible obstacles she persevered. Eventually her dream came true, and Mrs. B. became the director of the Children's Lending Library.

She shared her feelings about this accomplishment with Ślepak: "My library job has a wonderful psychological effect on me. It gives me life. I believe in the importance of this kind of work for the present and for the future. Before, when I used to sort clothes under much better physical conditions, and I also had then more strength, I frequently felt exhausted and sick. With my library work, although what I do is physically more taxing, and the surroundings are less agreeable . . . and even though I am now undernourished, I feel healthy and invigorated. I feel fulfilled. My feeling of self-fulfillment must be strengthening my immune system."[15]

Independent of Ślepak's research, a 1942 Ringelblum diary entry arrives at similar conclusions: "Recently we have observed an interesting development. The men, exhausted by the strenuous labor, make room for women. Some house committees are run by women. For our expanding welfare operations, we need new people. It is both fortunate and important that we can rely on these new sources of strength."[16]

Around this time, Ringelblum paid a special tribute to two activists whose work on house committees had expanded into other important community needs. One of them, Eliahu Kahn, established the first house committee that tried to ease the suffering of the needy and promote educational and cultural activities in the ghetto. The other distinguished person, whose aid was noted for its innovation, was a woman, a Mrs. Mokrska from Łódź, who started several house committees.

Mrs. Mokrska had a gift for finding women who were ready to make sacrifices. Many of her co-workers became patrons of boarding schools, refugee centers, and public kitchens. The tireless Mokrska seemed to be everywhere, spreading her effectiveness in most unexpected ways. During the height of the 1942 deportations, she discovered a workshop that accepted laborers without asking for anything in return. At that point, people were convinced that employment would shield them from deportation, although in reality, work offered either a temporary respite or an outright illusion. In the end, Mrs. Mokrska herself fell victim to the 1942 deportations.[17]

Efforts on behalf of others were not limited to adults. Teenage boys and girls also participated in activities related to the house committees. The fourteen-year-old Roma Nutkiewicz-Benatar was one of those youthful Warsaw ghetto helpers. Roma's father, an only child, had benefited from his wealthy parents' generosity. Despite substantial financial losses, her grandparents had managed to hold on to a part of their property and jewelry. For a while these had shielded them from excessive deprivation.

Roma's paternal grandmother was convinced that war and food shortages went hand in hand. As the rumors of war had increased, she began stockpiling flour, cereal, beans, and fuel. Because the family owned the building they lived in, which became part of the Warsaw ghetto, these provisions were saved. Although their accumulated foods included no vegetables, fruits, meats, sugar, or fats, what they had could feed a large family for years.

Since no one knew how long the war would last, Roma's parents and grandparents felt that they had to use their supplies sparingly; they took only one major meal in the middle of the day. It consisted simply of a thick soup and a slice of bread, but it was more than most ghetto inmates had. Aware of the pervasive hunger, they shared some of their food with the less fortunate.

Concern for the plight of the truly needy pushed Roma into charity work. She explains:

> In every house, there was a house committee. We, the young people, belonged to a special committee for the young. I was thirteen, fourteen, and I was a part of this group, some kind of a board member. Our house had three entrances. The front entrance was where people lived who were well off. Another entrance had middling wealthy people, and the third one was the entrance for the poor. It was extremely hard for the poor. They had no reserves whatsoever, no means of subsistence.
>
> There were always poor children in the back of our house, but I was never allowed to play with them. I had to go to the park to play.
>
> I was always curious about those poor children; some of them were wonderful. In the ghetto, we would go to their homes . . . Each of us would collect whatever he or she could. Each of us would give this food to a child, whom we helped with schoolwork. Every morning we would give them some food. We each selected a child, and we taught and fed this particular child, separately. You see, in the ghetto I went to school. But the school I attended cost money. These children could not afford my kind of school. So, we gave them instructions and we also fed them.[18]

Eventually, for greater safety, Roma's parents sent her to work on a nearby estate. This interrupted her charity work. When Roma returned to the ghetto in the fall of 1942, her family and their provisions had disappeared during the massive summer deportations.

Also active in practically all East European ghettos were youth organizations. Before the war these were a part of both Zionist and non-Zionist movements that covered a wide political spectrum. At the beginning, most of these politically minded youths saw the war as a passing phase. They concentrated on their own education, hoping to diminish the demoralizing effects of the ghetto. They studied illegally in preparation for a better future.[19]

With the deterioration of ghetto conditions, many of these young people switched from a preoccupation with self to concern for others. They devoted themselves to teaching needy children. Soon their work spilled into other areas, covering a wide variety of welfare and cultural activities. Taking their cue from current developments, they expanded their aid to the needy. Moreover, more realistic than members of the older generation, most leaders of the political youth organizations had recognized by 1942 that the Germans aimed at the biological annihilation of the Jewish people. As a result, to their social welfare and cultural pursuits ghetto youth movements added underground operations to prepare them for armed resistance.[20] Both sexes cooperated in these illegal ventures, which led to many joint efforts and eventually to open armed resistance. And over time the underground operations spread into a variety of settings outside the ghetto.

Towering over ghetto existence and affecting all aspects of its life were food shortages. The vast majority of the ghetto population was severely undernourished; only a handful of inhabitants had escaped hunger. With few exceptions, the hardest hit were the refugees.[21] Coming from the adjacent smaller communities or from western Europe, most refugees were penniless, friendless, and without prospects for earning a living. Many of them were forced to join the ever-increasing ranks of beggars. Often the majority of ghetto inmates were refugees, who were usually the first to be deported to the camps. Themselves heterogeneous, as a category the refugees stood out because of their special suffering.

The Szajewicz family could be described as "self-made" refugees. Before the war, Mr. Szajewicz's managerial position in a Łódź bank gave the family a comfortable life. Karla Szajewicz-Frist, the younger of the two daughters, was five when her mother died. When her father remarried she became attached to her stepmother and had no trouble calling her Mother.

At the start of the occupation, German friends had urged Mr. Szajewicz to leave the city. They argued that as an area annexed to the Reich, Łódź would be more hostile to Jews than other places. And so, before the establishment of the Łódź ghetto, the fifty-year-old Szajewicz settled his family in

Radom. In 1940 the Jews of Radom still lived in their prewar homes. But the new arrivals were automatically refugees. Szajewicz had difficulty finding employment. After many disappointments, he accepted work as a night watchman. The family could afford only one room. With the establishment of the Radom ghetto, they were forced to relocate to even more crowded quarters.

Karla Szajewicz-Frist describes the effects these changes had upon her father:

> He was a broken man . . . for him, life in Radom, especially in the ghetto, was so different from what it was before! He felt that he ought to support the family but could not.[22]

What did being "broken" mean?

> It was expressed in a terrible depression, with bad mood swings. He became very pessimistic. He was not the same man. My father, before, was very open, cheerful, most of the time. We had a big house, with many people, all the time. There was a great feeling of giving to people, embracing them. Here, the fact that he could not afford things, and his fear for all of us, really shattered him.

And what about the stepmother, whom Karla called Mother and to whom she was close?

> Mother was much less affected than father. She was not in a happy frame of mind, to be sure, but she did not feel the same responsibility, the same pressure that he felt . . . Mother was in charge of food, and she was very busy cooking. She did what she could.

The jobs the father and the two daughters found could not feed them properly. They had to sell some of their belongings—jewelry and household items—to supplement their meager diet. But even this extra food did not banish hunger. Karla remembers the family around the table, each pretending not to be hungry, so that the rest would eat more. To my question about whether her stepmother ate as much as others comes a quick answer:

No. None of us ate enough. Food was extremely expensive. I remember
I would say that I had enough even though I was hungry. Others wanted
to give me more because I was growing, but I didn't think it fair. My
stepmother was a very good woman; she also wanted to give me more.
All of us took a little and left the rest because we wanted the others to
eat. We would give to each other and share with each other.

Karla explains that even though they were hungry and cheerless, relationships within the family did not deteriorate. No one blamed their father
for not earning enough. They were aware that the Germans alone were responsible for their plight. Then came the worst day in Karla's life. She and
her older sister returned home to find that their father and stepmother were
gone. As refugees they had fallen victim to an early deportation and disappeared without a trace.

Chava Grinberg-Brown, her parents, a younger brother, and a sister
were transferred to the Warsaw ghetto from a small town called Wiśkitki,
near Żyrardów. Before the war, the father had worked as a porter and occasionally as a coachman, but he was often unemployed. The mother had tried
to help her family by cleaning other people's houses and doing their laundry. Recalling the prewar period Chava says,

I used to dream about a tomato but did not have it; this was always so.
We were very poor. In our home we had no electricity. The only light
that did come in was from the staircase.[23]

Despite their abject prewar poverty, after the move to the Warsaw ghetto
the Grinbergs' circumstances worsened. Almost immediately upon arrival,
the father was captured and sent to a work camp. His letters painted a desperate picture: he was forced to perform exhausting work that kept him immersed
in water for hours. His powerless family could not ease his burden.

Chava's recollections of the ghetto were colored by her personal experiences of an absent father and chronic hunger. She remembers that in the
ghetto,

Most men were taken away and the rest would usually be in hiding . . .
I was moving around in the streets of the ghetto all day long. I would see

people die of hunger. I saw women, children, and also men die of hunger. I felt that I, too, was on the way to death. I was swollen and starving.

Chava's mother had spent much energy searching for work, any work. Occasionally she was able to find domestic jobs. From time to time she would sell one of their personal belongings—a pot, a pillow, a cherished mirror, but there was little to sell. To supplement their income the children would join street singers and earn a few coins or some bread. Once a day each received a bowl of soup from the public kitchen.

Asked how her mother reacted to the situation, Chava says,

I remember when someone gave her food, any food, she would divide it, she gave it to us. No matter how poor we were, when a person came in mother shared the little soup we had.

Chava carries an image of a sad, a very sad, mother who never stopped worrying about her children. She is convinced that for her mother,

It would have been easier if she were dead. To see your children starve without being able to help was terrible. Death was better than life, under these circumstances.[24]

Eventually death claimed Chava's entire family. Chava shared with me many of her wartime experiences, which will reappear throughout this book. But she could not tell me how her family perished.

Coming from different backgrounds, Mrs. Mokrska, Karla Frist, and Chava Brown, three refugee females, were variously preoccupied with themselves, with their families, and with helping others. Sharing their meager resources was often mentioned by refugees and nonrefugees alike, both women and men. Such reports support my earlier generalization that the more deprived people are, the more their lives depend on cooperative efforts. But people's ability and willingness to help others may in turn depend on the kind of deprivation they are experiencing and on how their past has conditioned them for compassion and cooperation. Many of those I studied saw cooperation and sharing as positive, valuable activities. But it is impossible to compare those who were able to reach out beyond their families and those who could not. Considering the terrible plight of the ghetto inhabitants, it must have required special fortitude to share with others and to care about them. Throughout this book I shall offer discussion and illustrations that touch on these complex issues.

In the ghetto, the acquisition of food and the preparation and distribution of meals were obviously critical. By making food shortages a central means of humiliating and ultimately annihilating the Jews, the Germans inadvertently created conditions that gave women a chance to make the most of their traditional domestic and nurturing skills. But the contributions of women went beyond cooking and domestic chores. The deprivations of ghetto life created a situation that suited women's traditional nurturing roles and satisfied their need to ease the burdens of those who had even fewer resources than they.

Men's coping skills were also affected by their past habits. Traditionally men took no part in domestic chores. The increased value given to domestic skills in the ghetto might have added to men's feelings of inadequacy. Obviously, men who were forcefully separated from their families — and many were — could not even try to help. But even those who stayed in the ghetto could not fulfill their traditional roles of protector and provider. This inability to meet accepted male obligations often had an emotionally paralyzing effect.

Alexandra Sołowejczyk-Guter captures certain differences between the way men and women handled the new situation:

> In the ghetto, when the men got something, a bone . . . the woman made soup out of it . . . The woman contributed so that life would continue somehow in an accustomed way. The woman was the one who washed something in the dirty water. These were common, simple jobs that were necessary for living. Just to comb a child['s hair] to get the lice out, the woman did it. The men sort of gave up . . . I am specifically talking about men who were a part of the upper class . . . Common men, from lower classes, were more flexible, and they were getting used to the situation. But when it came to the intellectuals, the higher classes, the men did not adjust.[25]

Allowing for exceptions, Alexandra thinks that women's reactions were different from men's:

Women of all classes were more able and more likely to concentrate on everyday, little things. They were not trying to get so deeply into all those other things, as men do. When somebody brought a piece of meat, the woman was happy to cook it for the family. The man would eat it, but this did not lift his spirits or gratify him. The woman was very busy with everyday, little things, not concentrating so much on the war and what was really happening.

She argues,

One consequence of women's preoccupations with everyday things . . . was the feeling that they [the women] were necessary. They felt needed . . . Men who could *not* bring the loaf of bread home felt horrible, it depressed them. But especially men who were intellectuals . . . the upper-class men didn't know how to smuggle . . . Women could always adjust, somehow.

The satisfaction of contributing to the family's welfare extended to young unmarried women as well. Lidia (Itke) Brown-Abramson, who was a teenager at the time, relates that she stayed home, cooked for the family, and took care of her little sister. She was glad that they relied on her, and it gave her the incentive to do more. Nonetheless, after dwelling on the positive, she continues,

I remember once when I cooked for father; I cooked all the time, but I remember a particular incident. I fried onions and told him that I prepared food for him and he said, "That's all?" What he said stayed with me, but I don't know what it meant.

Lidia refused to elaborate, perhaps because the pain of his failure to appreciate her efforts was still strong.[26]

The reaction of Lidia's father fits Alexandra Sołowejczyk-Guter's perception that men were less adaptable than women. Thinking aloud, trying to explain the women's conduct, Alexandra muses,

Maybe the fact that a woman is a mother, maybe that stimulated in her the tendency of doing so much for others . . . It was important for women to really concentrate on seemingly little things. Everyday things . . .

For example, when we first came to the ghetto, I got the apartment, not my husband. One day I had decided to buy something new, and I ordered a hat. But there was something wrong with the edge of the hat, and I was walking around in the ghetto, distraught, very upset that the hat didn't have the proper shape. *Can you understand that!* And suddenly I stood in the middle of the street, and I slapped myself in the face. And I said to myself, 'If now you can worry that the hat is not cut the proper way, then you really should be slapped in the face.' I was so preoccupied with the shape of that hat! You could not find a man who would give a thought to his hat![27]

For men, the ghetto created a more definite rupture between their prewar and wartime roles. The discontinuity between their prewar positions and their slavelike ghetto existence meant that most men experienced ghetto life as a constant reminder of their failure to live up to their traditional masculine roles. In contrast, women's roles retained a semblance of continuity, for their ghetto activities allowed them to fulfill their traditional nurturing roles. And their preoccupation with the mundane everyday things of life may have energized women, allowed them to go on, at least for a while.

As a central unit the family can serve as a testing ground for comparisons between female and male coping skills in the ghetto. Several of my questions concerned how mothers behaved at mealtime. I asked, for example, whether my respondents could recall seeing their mothers eat. I was especially curious to know whether mothers would eat as much as other members of the family and whether they shared food with people who did not belong to the family.

Most of my respondents could not recall ever seeing their mothers eat. Of those who did, some were reluctant to discuss it or could not remember whether their mothers ate as much as the rest of the family. When questioned more closely, a few of the respondents became evasive, annoyed, apologetic, or hurt. They were never indifferent. Their answers often included comparisons of the way their fathers and mothers behaved. Not all of these memories were related to food.

Vladka Meed, who had been a teenager at the time, talks first about the deteriorating effect the Warsaw ghetto had upon her father.

> He was not only helpless but a broken, dejected man who could not take care of his family. He was undernourished, run down; he got pneumonia and died. In contrast, my mother was someone who did not give up. Internally she was a strong person. Somehow she had the strength to keep our home spotless without soap. By keeping the place clean, she was fighting diseases, especially typhus.[28]

But Vladka is puzzled because she cannot remember seeing her mother eat.

Searching hard for an image of her mother eating, she came up with a picture of an old aunt who used to visit them to whom her mother gave food:

> This aunt would sit at the table and fall asleep, she was a lonely woman, no doubt hungry. Occasionally I recall seeing my mother drink tea with this old aunt. At that point I might have seen mother take something into her mouth . . . But my eyes do not recall an eating mother. My eyes see a very worried mother. I remember her as someone who was on the run, who was protecting, doing things for others. She was always busy with something . . .
>
> How did we cook? We sometimes broke up a chair, we would buy a little wood, and in the early "good times of the ghetto" a little coal. She would occasionally buy some potatoes. A smuggler, a child, would come to us from time to time and bring potatoes. [My mother] would give him things to sell on the Aryan side. But later on he stopped coming. Neighbors told us that he was shot close to the ghetto wall.

Vladka thinks of her mother as someone who "knew instinctively what to do for her children":

> When my brother was almost thirteen, this mother, though she was hungry, there was a swelling under her eyes from hunger, would hide a slice

of bread for the rabbi who would come to teach my brother for his bar mitzvah. She herself would not eat the bread but pay with it for the lessons. We knew where she kept the bread. It was hidden under her pillow. She had no money . . . For the slice of bread the rabbi would give bar mitzvah lessons to my brother . . . How much strength a woman needed! To be able in those days to think about my brother's preparation for bar mitzvah!

For Vladka, as for most ghetto inmates, hunger was a constant companion. More than fifty years later, she still marvels at her preoccupation with food. She would daydream about potatoes—just plain, boiled potatoes. She tried to chase away these images by reading, but the visions of potatoes would stubbornly reappear. One day Vladka could not put on her shoes because her feet were swollen from hunger. She skipped work. It was a fateful move. That day everyone at her workshop was deported.

The very different reactions of women and men to the issues of eating and feeding the family follow a similar pattern in every ghetto. To recall, Eva Galer and her large family were transferred from their hometown of Olszyce to the small ghetto in Lubaczów. Their initial experiences had conformed to the wider pattern: after Eva's father, a respected businessman before the war, lost his fortune and all prospects of gainful employment, he practically gave up on life. The transfer to the Lubaczów ghetto accelerated her father's loss of spirit, making him apathetic and listless.

After the move to the ghetto made feeding a large family more difficult, Eva would sneak out of the ghetto, take off her armband with its Star of David, and start walking toward her hometown. She used side roads, carefully avoiding human encounters. Her destination was the home of a former neighbor, a Christian woman with whom they had left some of their belongings. The neighbor would greet Eva warmly and give her as many provisions as she could spare, mostly potatoes, flour, milk, and, if she had any, bread. Each trip was fraught with danger and the possibility that there would be nothing to spare. Eva's benefactor was poor. Since the woman could not afford to part with much, Eva could not make too many requests of her.

The family's hunger continued. Eva still carries the haunting images:

I remember my father dividing the bread I once brought into equal
parts. When a few crumbs fell, my youngest brother bent down and
licked the crumbs off the floor. We had rations but hunger was great.
People would eat grass; stomachs were distended. People died not only
from hunger but also from dysentery or typhus. It was very dirty and we
did not have enough water to bathe. We could not wash the laundry.
Every day people died; there were many funerals.[29]

But the fathers and husbands were not equally depressed. Nor were the
mothers all enterprising and energetic. I came across a few exceptions, which
are relevant to the emerging behavior patterns discussed here. The father of
Ita Shapiro, for example, continued to be active and enterprising even after
the German invasion. Ita was twelve in 1941 when the Germans occupied
Vilna. Before the war, her father had enjoyed a comfortable income as the
manager of a furniture store. The war brought the usual changes: loss of a
job, shortages of money. Ita says that her mother was always concerned with
helping people, yet because at first her family had little to spare, all she could
offer was emotional support. Ita's father, on the other hand, was sure that
"he would somehow find a way; that's why he was constantly on the lookout for hiding places, how to save us, what to do. We always had hideouts
within the ghetto."[30]

For the Shapiro family, the move into the Vilna ghetto coincided with
Ita's father and brother finding employment on the Aryan side. These jobs
made it possible for them to smuggle goods in and out of the ghetto. Profits
from these exchanges yielded more food for the family and enabled the father to contact his Christian friends. These contacts almost paid off; as Ita
describes it:

There was a Christian who wanted to hide my father and brother.
We talked about it. In the end, my father decided not to accept the offer
because he did not want to separate the family. He said, "If this man
wants to take the four of us, we will go. Otherwise, no." [My father]
couldn't find another place for my mother and me. We didn't have any

money. This Christian wasn't doing it for money. He knew my father well. People loved Father, and this man probably liked him as well. He must have made this offer out of friendship.

Mr. Shapiro refused to abandon any of his family and continued to search for more acceptable solutions. In the meantime, the smuggling brought in more food and gave Ita's mother a chance to do what she loved most—help others:

Whenever she met a friend or relative, she would invite them to eat with us. People felt very depressed that they needed the food she gave them . . . grateful, but they also felt humiliated by it. In the ghetto, I studied English privately, because my mother met her former French teacher. The teacher's husband was an economic attaché in England. In the ghetto they were starving. My mother had me take English lessons from him so they could buy food with the money. She wanted to help them. Sometimes she would send me with a package of food. She would pretend, "Oh, I cooked something very good." . . . She would do it in a way that it wouldn't embarrass them. She even found for them two more students for English . . . There was a boy in our school who became sick with typhus. So my job was to go every day to the hospital and bring him food. My mother said I had to do it. This boy had no parents; his parents had been taken away. I was embarrassed, partly because I liked him. He was much older than I, but I liked him and was in awe of him. My mother insisted that I go. I went.

Shortly before the liquidation of the Vilna ghetto Mr. Shapiro and his son lost their jobs. This meant less food. Now the menu consisted of thin soup, based on something that was in part barley but not as tasty as barley. Their income depended on occasional sales of clothing or household items.

The family would still eat together in the evening. To my question about whether her mother would eat and if so, how much, Ita hesitantly answers, "I think that she did. She was a heavy woman, but she never had a big appetite; she never ate a lot. Toward the end it was very difficult; we had very little food . . . My mother insisted that I eat her part, because she said I was the smallest and I needed to grow."

"And did you?" I asked.

"Yes, I ate. It was terrible."

My probes about how much her mother ate upset Ita. First she talked around the issue. Eventually, she offered, "My mother ate, but I don't know how much, I didn't look and I don't know. She would put the food on the table and divide it for all of us. And everyone ate what was given to him or her." But why had Ita said earlier that she felt "terrible" if she didn't know how much her mother ate? Was she signaling me to stop? Since I already had the information I needed, I switched to another subject.

Those who spent time in the Białystok ghetto also experienced hunger, yet they consistently say that death from starvation was unknown. Naomi Zeif's family came to Białystok in 1939, when the city was under Soviet occupation. Here they owned a pharmacy, which was later confiscated by the Soviet authorities. Naomi was impressed by how unaffected her father was by the loss; he simply shrugged it off. He continued to work hard to support his family, wife, and six daughters. After the German takeover and the creation of the ghetto, Naomi's father tried to adjust by learning carpentry. His new skills led to employment outside the ghetto. Her mother stayed home while other members of the family, including a brother-in-law, found jobs on the Aryan side. Naomi explains,

> Because my father and my brother-in-law were working outside the
> ghetto . . . people would bring things to sell. My mother would receive
> the goods and then give them to my father and brother-in-law for sale,
> and they made a little profit. One had to go and take the material and
> bring it back and get the money, etc. Sometimes I would help them.
> Everything had to be done in secret, of course. We went individually
> with these things. We didn't want too many people coming to our
> house.[31]

These transactions helped, but the family still suffered from hunger.

> We didn't have much food. We were hungry, but somehow we managed.
> All the time we were working, some of us were outside the ghetto, and
> everybody shared what we could get.

Although her father worked diligently to cope with the situation, he had no illusions about what might come, and he was ready for any eventuality. Naomi recalls,

> My father always said that he had hidden some poison; in case life should become impossible, each of us should commit suicide. At the end I was not with them, so I don't know what happened.

When I raised the issue of her mother's eating habits, Naomi too was uncertain. She thinks that the entire family would be together at mealtimes; therefore her mother must have been with them. But did her mother eat as much as the others at the table? Here hesitation was followed by

> Well, I don't know . . . she even invited an old woman from an old-age home to eat with us. And she said that if each of us would give up one spoonful of the soup, the old woman would have one bowl. We did this. Every day this old woman would come and she would get a bowl of soup. She (my mother) loved to give; she loved to feed people. This woman was not even a relative—she was just a poor person who needed the food, a stranger. I think that my mother probably ate as we did; I don't remember that she didn't.
>
> I remember once she got hold of some mildewed flour. Mother baked rolls out of it. Everybody got one roll. And after I finished, I asked her, "Mom, maybe I could have another roll?" And she started crying. She said, "I thought that no one would be able to eat it with the terrible taste it had."

Now, as Naomi talks about it, she weeps. Silently, I wait. She stops and on her own resumes the conversation. Neither of us mention her tears.

Like Naomi's father, Mr. Kizelstein was able to provide more food for his family than was officially allotted. He also took advantage of the opportunities created by an outside job to smuggle all kinds of goods in and out of the ghetto. Again, these black-market transactions reduced but did not do away with hunger. Nor did the extra earnings stop Mrs. Kizelstein's preoccupation with food. She would join seemingly endless food lines, try any and all provisions she could afford: bones, vegetables at various stages of decay—anything that promised even a remote nutritional value. Continuously improvising with dishes, she never stopped worrying that her family might not have enough.

With sadness her daughter Mina Kizelstein-Dorn admits that she cannot remember whether her mother would eat. After this she becomes irritated by my questions about the amount of food her mother might have eaten. She argues,

> I didn't notice that she ate less. Anyway, she always ate less. What should I tell you? I did not pay attention to this. I did not see. I worried about my own plate . . . She would always share, she would give. Before the war we had a very open house. Whoever came was asked to eat. This remained so in the ghetto, too. We did not actually give bread because each got very little of it. If there was soup in the pot, we would share it.[32]

Mina saw her father as someone who was in charge, whose spirits did not break. When I met with Mina's brother, Shamay Kizelstein, at a different time, in a different place, he, like his sister, appreciated his father's resourcefulness and was eager to tell me how he organized groups of workers.

> He would take them outside to the factory where he worked, to give them employment. Later on, after a factory fire, my father was also very active. He went to the burned-out place and collected what was left. This was important, because we had to have coal or fuel for cooking. And when the factory was being rebuilt, he was not exactly in charge of it, but he was helping, trying to organize work groups to rebuild the place.[33]

To a question about his father's spirits, Shamay answers,

> In our family, we didn't lose the will to live, or the spirit. We always believed that somehow we would overcome the difficulties and that we would live. Both my mother and my father believed that. My mother always used to say, "What can they do to me, take my skin and bones away?" (She was very skinny.)

And yet Shamay admits that with time he noticed a difference, a decline. In this case, the mother was more pessimistic, feeling that she had no chance to survive. Their father was realistic, thinking that at his age (he was in his fifties), he was not likely to survive. But although he became physically weaker, he remained strong psychologically. Shamay explains,

> Toward the end, my father was not able to do much. He was physically drained . . . When my friends would come to visit, he would tell them, "Young people, you should know that you will survive. I will not, but you will."

In my interviews, I noticed that my questions about food distribution, specifically about whether mothers would deprive themselves of their share, sometimes led to irritation. Occasionally this irritation meant that the respondent, who had been a child at the time, had accepted a part of the mother's food. Perhaps this touchiness may also have signaled regret or guilt that the respondent had not cared enough at the time to be able to remember. How much each family member ate *was* important, and images of food consumption continue to haunt many survivors.

In the few reports where children talk about fathers who were able to bring home extra earnings these fathers are not described as depressed. These same children would also gloss over differences between their parents' reactions to ghetto conditions. In the three cases mentioned above, the fathers and mothers were perceived as equally aware of the dangers, each trying hard to improve the family's situation. Thus, Ita stressed her father's energy, the efforts he made on behalf of the family, and his selflessness. Naomi praised her father's talent and resourcefulness. She was impressed by his newly acquired carpentry skills and was convinced that they helped him get better jobs.

The fathers of Naomi and the Kizelsteins continued to provide for their families in the ghetto. By contrast, the ability of Ita's father to support his family in the ghetto lasted only a short time. Nevertheless, the three, at least for a while, had been able to provide for their families, and this had lifted the families' spirits. In this the three differed from most of the other fathers described. It is clear that a father's ability to support his family was contingent on outside forces over which he had little control. Given the German determination to destroy all the fathers, few men were able to escape. Those who succeeded usually did so for only a short time, before they were caught up again by the deathly policy.

And yet these exceptions suggest that the ability to fulfill the traditional male roles of provider and protector improved the family's situation. At the same time, they also tell us that success was rare, sporadic, and subject to sudden change. These exceptions show that mothers tended to react to events in matter-of-fact ways. Women tried to adapt and adjust. Finally, too, although they were enterprising and energetic, all the parents in these three cases had perished. The destructive forces were overpowering, and energy and resourcefulness offered only a temporary slowdown of disaster.

How much hunger the population had to endure varied from ghetto to ghetto, although as a rule the level of starvation in every ghetto increased over time. Chronic starvation, in turn, seemed to accentuate gender differences. The extensively documented Łódź ghetto was distinguished by its hermetic closure, long history (1940–1944), and slow death through starvation, disease, and brutal deportations.[34] Dawid Sierakowiak's diary provides an important document of life in the Łódź ghetto.

For many pages, the teenager watched the physical decline of his beloved mother, which he long blamed on his father's selfishness. One entry reads, "Poor broken dear unhappy creature. She has had enough trouble in the ghetto already . . . quarrels and conflicts at home . . . may we be able to save her! . . . Feeling worse, mom decided this week to give him [father] only 25 dkg [a quarter-kilo] out of each loaf of her bread [instead of the former 50 dkg]. He does not like this idea, but he calculated if there is no mom, he will get even less." Sierakowiak then describes how his father moved from accepting a smaller portion of his wife's bread to stealing from his son's and daughter's rations.[35]

As Dawid's hunger grew, so did his worries about mother's health. He deplores her sacrifices. "I am very worried about mother, because she is terribly emaciated, shrunk and weak. Nevertheless, she still works in the garden most of the time, is not sick, and even cooks, cleans, and if there is need, does laundry." Sierakowiak's concern was justified. The day after he made this entry, during a house raid to root out the "unfit for work," his mother was taken away. Distraught, Dawid describes their parting:

> With heartbreaking, maddening logic, she spoke to us about her fate. She kind of admitted that I was right when I told her that she had given her life by lending and giving away provisions, but she admitted it with such a bitter smile that I could see she didn't regret her conduct at all, and, although she loved her life so greatly, for her there are values even more important than life, like God, family, etc.
>
> She kissed each one of us good-bye, took a bag with her bread and a few potatoes that I forced on her, and left quickly to her horrible fate. I couldn't muster the willpower to look through the window after her or to cry. I walked around, talked, and finally sat as though I had turned to stone . . . nervous spasms took hold of my heart, hands, mouth, and throat, so that I thought my heart was breaking. It didn't break, though, and it let me eat, think, speak, and go to sleep.

The son believed that his mother had no regrets about the sacrifices that hastened her death. In sharp contrast to this giving woman, he sees his father as selfish.[36]

Fathers who stole their family's food are rarely mentioned, and when they are, the reports depict such conduct as an aberration. I found no stories of mothers who stole the family food. However, just because an action is not reported does not mean that it did not happen. Infrequent or no mention of such an event may reflect a reluctance to dwell on a painful subject. The occasional references to men who accepted or stole food from their families come with uneasiness, suggesting that the speaker has broken a taboo. Dawid Sierakowiak's direct accusation of his own father as a food thief is exceptional. Most such stories are portrayed as experiences told to the speaker by others.

Sara Zyskind, who was a teenager in the Łódź ghetto, heard about several men who stole or extorted extra food from family members. One woman, a co-worker in Sara's workshop, complained that her husband could not make his bread last out the day but would eat it as soon as he got it. Later he would steal his wife's or his daughter's bread. He even justified his theft; as a grown man, he needed the food more than they. Similarly, one of Sara's friends confided that since her father could not make his bread last, she and her mother would give him a portion of their rations. (Even this sacrifice did not stop his violent temper fits.)[37]

In contrast, many survivors spoke spontaneously about mothers and wives who gave away portions of their rations. Yet they also describe men's special sensitivity to hunger, explaining that women who were close to these men tried to step in and help. In the Łódź ghetto Sara Zyskind saw this in her own family. Before the war Sara's father had been a successful business-man. After the German takeover deprived him of his ability to earn a living, a debilitating depression set in. As her father became emotionally incapaci-tated, Sara's mother first became an inventive cook and later turned herself into a creative businesswoman. She supplemented the family income by selling hot coffee to ghetto inmates who had to pass close to their house in the early morning hours. At first embarrassed, the daughter's attitude soon changed to one of admiration. She explains, "Though selling coffee was not profitable, it did make it possible for us to buy an additional ration of bread for father, acquired at the black market, and an adequate supply of coal. Now our room was well heated, greatly lessening the fear of the winter . . . My weak and ailing mother was never once heard to complain about the de-plorable conditions of our lives."[38] In fact, Sara's mother passed away after a short while.

Zyskind's comments show how her father benefited from his wife's en-terprise. Sara specifically states that "the profits bought bread for father." She also thinks that her father needed the extra bread more than she or her mother. In fact, after her mother's death Sara tried to step into her mother's role, occasionally giving her father some of her own bread. Her donations stopped only with her father's death, brought on by malnutrition.[39]

Next to the continuous preoccupation with food, ghetto occupants con-cerned themselves with devising a number of social, cultural, educational, and political activities. In fact, these pastimes bore some relation to the con-stant hunger. Dawid Sierakowiak's diary entry for May 21, 1941, reads, "There are no new food allocations at all, and the soup in the communal kitchens is becoming thinner and thinner. There is no barley or potatoes at all, and we are already running out of vegetables in the ghetto." The entry continues, "We've had another meeting of a unit of lecturers. We discussed the difference between a proletariat revolution and a bourgeois-democratic one."[40]

Eighteen months later, on December 30, 1942, his diary entry reads, "We have had our last potato in a watery soup. As usual in times of hunger, I have to turn to forced, intensive reading to drive away the sense of deprivation with this 'opiate.' My brain seems to have become much too exhausted."[41]

The connection between hunger and intellectual pursuits recurs throughout the ghetto narratives. Oskar Rosenfeld, a well-known writer whom the Germans had deported to the Łódź ghetto from Prague, noted in his diary, "Terrible diarrhea. Ghetto illness for the second time . . . Tomorrow, Saturday, I will give a public reading of my novella, *The Secret of the Ghetto,* that is, *Prague to Łódź.* I am pleased about this."[42]

Hunger even invaded public events. Concerts, occasionally featuring contemporary ghetto composers, were among the favorite pastimes. These well-attended concerts also served as platforms for public announcements and speeches. After one musical event in the Łódź ghetto, the head of the Judenrat, Chaim Rumkowski, announced that the next week there would be no potato deliveries. This news was followed by Rumkowski's plea for help for the ghetto's homeless children.[43]

A comment by Sierakowiak about a meeting on resistance specifically relates chronic hunger to involvement with intellectual and cultural pursuits: "I quickly wrote down the most important thoughts about my theory about pure egoism and the sanctity of human life so that I would have an outline for our next discussion. If I had something to eat, maybe something more substantial would grow out of my notes." Like other observers, Sierakowiak recognized that chronic hunger reduces the capacity to think.[44]

Additional observations also suggest that passive exposure to the intellectual and cultural activities of the ghetto could also ease the pain created by starvation. Sierakowiak describes a theatrical revue he attended, a revue that he thought had little artistic merit. But he finishes his critique with this observation: "The most important thing is that for two hours I could stop thinking about food or hunger." Thousands of ghetto inmates attended these variety shows, probably as much to ease the agony of hunger as to stimulate their minds. By May 1942, Revue Number Three had been presented twenty times; eventually, it was attended by ten thousand people.[45]

Cultural and intellectual pursuits were an integral part of ghetto life, particularly in large ghettos like Białystok, Kraków, Łódź, Vilna, Warsaw, Kovno, and others. In Warsaw, under Emanuel Ringelblum's supervision, intensive instruction in history, philosophy, and literature was offered to various political youth groups. Graduates of these courses would in turn teach children and lecture to adults on a range of topics. Often the audience was made up of the tenants of a particular building. If the lecturer was not a tenant, he or she would spend the night in the building; usually, the host of the event supplied a bed. These arrangements were dictated by the curfew.

One of the instructors, Vladka Meed, described an evening devoted to a lecture on Boncze Szveig, a character created by I. L. Peretz. She explained that this was one of the many illegal cultural evenings, a permanent and important part of Warsaw ghetto life. The event took place in a large room, filled with mature listeners. The windows were securely covered. By the gate of the building, in a secluded corner, stood a lookout. Vladka was younger than the members of her attentive audience. People were accustomed to such young and passionate lecturers. The air was filled with tension, which lasted until the very end of the presentation. Then came a question period. Animated, eager to learn, to explore, audience and lecturer were locked in an intense, heated exchange of ideas.[46]

This special evening, like other cultural events, had the power to transport the inmates away from the poverty, the hunger, and the devastation of the ghetto into a more meaningful, dignified world. What happened in this and similar rooms was real, in some ways perhaps more real than what inevitably greeted each Jew on the outside, in the ghetto streets. Those who were a part of these gatherings concur that it was comforting just to be present.

Some of the events were benefits, with proceeds going to various welfare programs. Often these gatherings were free. All cultural, educational, and political pursuits included voices from the prewar past. Created and propelled by memories of what had been, these events may have served as attempts at reasserting the inmates' humanity. By clinging to things that had been, by embracing the past, Jews may have tried to deny the unbearable present and with it the Nazi definition of Jews as vermin. As suggested by Sierakowiak, these cultural and theatrical pursuits, by connecting the inmates to the past, made it possible for them to bear the present.

Thus, in the Vilna ghetto, a few months before the community ceased to exist, the teenaged Yitskhok Rudashevski noted, "In the evening I attended an interesting literary circle. The young poet, A. Sutskever, told us about the Yiddish poet Yehoash. Read his poems. Yehoash's poems, his descriptions of nature truly inspired us. The predominant idea of Yehoash, that of sunshine and mists, beauty, is indeed so pleasant. As you read Yehoash, you unite with beauty. In his poems Yehoash celebrates nature and all its splendor. We decided to arrange a Yehoash evening and a Yehoash exhibition." This literary gathering represented more than a return to the past and an effort to deal with the present. It was also a look toward the future. Inherent in these activities was the insistence that there would be a future. The legal and illegal ghetto pastimes created by and for the imprisoned populations bound the past, the present, and the future. And essential to that vision was the education of the young.[47]

Children represent the future. Women in the ghettos, because of their special ties to children as well as their traditional nurturing roles and their conviction that there would be a future for their families, gravitated toward activities related to children. But precisely because children promised a Jewish future, the Germans targeted them for annihilation. Significantly, Jewish children did not contribute to the wartime economy through labor, so they were not even temporarily exempt from Nazi destruction. In fact, the Germans attacked both the Jewish children who were already in the ghettos and those who had not yet been born.

The severity of Nazi opposition to Jewish children and to procreation varied with time and place, although humiliation, starvation, and the accompanying oppressions in themselves reduced the chances of successful births. When occasionally pregnancies occurred, the mothers would usually abort the fetuses to avert punishment.

Dobka Freund-Waldhorn was one of those women caught in a web of conflicting demands: the prohibition against Jewish pregnancies battled with her desire to have a baby. Dobka came from a wealthy orthodox family of nine children. Dobka's father, in particular, saw her as an independent rebel; even in her 1939 marriage to Julek Fröhlich, a man with whom she was deeply in love, her father saw a form of resistance. Handsome, intelligent, and from a respectable family, Julek was nonetheless deemed unsuitable because he was not orthodox. The war and the opposition to Dobka's marriage pushed the young couple to Vilna and from there into the Vilna ghetto.

In Israel, in 1995, at the end of a long interview in Dobka's comfortable home, she invited me to come again because she wanted to share a secret she had never talked about: a wartime pregnancy. Since I was leaving Israel the next day, the interview took place a year later. I learned then that when Dobka was transferred from the Vilna ghetto to a nearby estate, she realized that she was pregnant. Jewish women were prohibited from having babies. Dobka's husband and a Polish doctor at the estate pleaded with her to discontinue the pregnancy. She refused. In love with Julek, she wanted his child.

When she was seven months pregnant, as a concession to her husband, Dobka went to the ghetto hospital to learn firsthand about her options. Although sympathetic, the doctor urged her to give birth and then "dispose" of the baby. Under the existing laws, unless she followed that advice, she would die as well as the baby. The doctor accepted Dobka into the ghetto hospital and tried to induce delivery.

In a restrained, almost artificial voice, Dobka continues the story.

I stayed in the hospital, for a long time, maybe a month. They gave me medication to break the water, but there was no birth. They increased the dosage. They did all kinds of things, but the child refused to be born. Eventually, I got a fever, high fever. I think that it was already the eighth month. Only then it happened. She was alive. They showed me the little girl. She was so beautiful. She looked just like my husband, and we were so much in love! Then, they took her away . . . The doctor tried to console me, that I was young, that I will have other children, that this had to be . . .

My husband came to the hospital. He knelt next to my bed . . . He took my hands into his, and he cried . . . terribly, terribly. "You will see, we will have children, there will be children."

For Julek Fröhlich, there were no more children. He died in Klooga concentration camp. After the war, Dobka remarried and had two sons.[48]

In the same constrained voice, Dobka goes on.

After the birth of my second son, with my second husband, I dreamt that my first husband, Julek, came to me. He looked very neglected, not shaved. "Where were you?" I asked, "so many years? I have a husband and children." He answered, "Yes, but you will come back to me." In the dream I thought, How could I go back to him? But to him I said, "I will come back to you." I woke up and found my pillow soaking wet from my tears.

I remember the day, I think about it. I think about my first husband, I dream that I went back to him. I did not forget and I do not want to. I love even the suffering because it is a part of me.

Efforts to protect and help Jewish children were born out of the battle between those who wanted to kill and those who wanted to save. It was an uneven struggle, a war that left many child victims and only a few survivors.[49] Yet all the ghettos had organizations devoted to helping children.

The head of the Łódź Judenrat, Chaim Rumkowski, was known for his special affection for children. Among his past jobs was the directorship of a Jewish orphanage. Yet this man, who felt particularly close to children, was compelled to ask his fellow Jews to sacrifice the very young and the old so that the rest could live. The Germans had demanded that thirteen thousand elderly inmates and eight thousand children aged ten and under be delivered for deportation in order to save the remaining 80 percent of the ghetto population.[50]

In a speech given on September 4, 1942, to his fellow ghetto inmates, Rumkowski tried to convince parents to deliver up their children: "A broken Jew stands before you. Do not envy me. This is the most difficult of all the orders I had to carry out at any time . . . I reach out to you with my broken, trembling hands, and I beg you: give into my hands the victims, so that we can avoid having further victims. A population of 100,000 can be preserved . . . the part that can be saved is much larger than the part that must be given away."[51]

No one volunteered to give up their children. Nor did the sick and the elderly submit passively. Descriptions of deportations are filled with vivid images of resistance: mothers and fathers who defied the orders, parents who begged to be killed instead of their children because they could not bear the loss. Targeted for these deportations were the very young, the old, and the sick. Many ambulatory hospital patients escaped. Jewish policemen, joined by Germans and their collaborators, dashed about searching for patients, for the very young, for the old. The entire ghetto population was in a state of desperate agitation. Chaos reigned. Relying on brutality and force, the Germans reached their required quota of victims.[52]

The massive deportations of 1942 affected all the East European ghettos.[53] In Warsaw, these deportations lasted from July to September. Just as in Łódź, their aim was to collect the "unproductive": children, the elderly, the sick. Children were rounded up from orphanages, families, and hospitals.

The liquidation of the children's institutions started in August. Dr. Janusz Korczak, a noted educator and pediatrician, was the head of the best-known orphanage in the Warsaw ghetto. Korczak's Polish friends offered to hide him on the Aryan side, but he refused because he would not abandon the orphanage children and staff.

On the designated day, August 8, Korczak, nine staff members (eight women and one man), and the two hundred orphans were ready. The children, washed and dressed in clean clothes, each held a little bag containing bread and a flask of water. They arranged themselves in rows. Hatless, Korczak led the procession, with a child holding onto each hand. No one cried; no one tried to run away. As they proceeded calmly toward the waiting freight cars, the Jewish police, forming a cordon to make a path for them, saluted instinctively. Nachum Remba, a Judenrat official and a member of the ghetto underground, was present, looking for ways to ease the pain of the victims. A German pointed to Korczak and asked who he was. Remba burst into tears. As Korczak continued to walk, head held high, with a fixed, intense gaze, as if he were gazing at something in the distance, a wail went up from the Jews assembled on the square.

At the Umschlagplatz, the place of assembly for deportations, Remba urged Korczak to go to the Judenrat and negotiate for a postponement. But the doctor refused to leave his charges, even for a moment. Instead, silently, together, they boarded the cattle car that was to take them to the Treblinka death camp.[54]

The fate of the children in the Bernson and Bauman hospital, which was staffed and directed largely by women, was different. Dr. Anna Brande-Heller was the head. Among the physicians who played a special role during the deportation was Dr. Adina Szwajger, the young assistant—barely out of medical school—of Dr. Anna Margolis, a pediatrician in charge of the children's tuberculosis ward.

At the height of the deportations each hospital director received a pass that exempted him or her from deportation, along with a few additional passes to distribute among members of the staff. Such passes were scarce, accounting for only a few of the hospital employees. The directors were thus burdened with the decision of whom to select for exemption. At that point people correctly equated deportation with death.

At first, Dr. Brande-Heller refused to take on this responsibility. But her staff urged her to distribute the passes. They argued that if she declined, the passes would go to other hospital directors, who would be glad to give them away to their own staff. In the end, Dr. Brande-Heller went along with these arguments. Yet she still vacillated, waiting until the day her hospital was to be emptied of most of its people.

With the deportations in full swing, everyone at Bernson and Bauman expected their hospital to be targeted soon. When Dr. Szwajger reached the building on that fateful September morning, she discovered that except for the very young children and patients who could not walk, everyone seemed to have disappeared. Soon, however, from different directions, older children patients reemerged from their hiding places and surrounded Dr. Szwajger. One of the youngsters stepped forward to act as a representative for the others: "Doctor, we all know that we have no mamas and no papas any more. And that we are not going to live through [the deportation] either. But will you stay with us to the end?"

Without much thought, Szwajger assured them that she would "stay to the end." At that point, no one knew who would be given a pass, who would be spared from the deportation.

Now events began to move quickly. That morning Dr. Heller decided to give the five passes to the younger staff members: Dr. Margolis and her daughter Ala, who worked as a nurse; two young women doctors who were barely out of medical school (Dr. Szwajger was one of these); and Marek Edelman, a hospital employee and leader in the underground. After Szwajger received the news, she returned to the ward, where a young nurse was administering an injection. This nurse abruptly turned to Szwajger: "Doctor, please give my mother an injection! I can't do it. I beg you, please. I don't want them to shoot her in the bed and she can't walk." With a nod, Szwajger agreed. Coming closer to the nurse's mother, with the injection of morphine in hand, the doctor saw a smile on the old woman's face as she eagerly offered her arm.

Afterward, Szwajger turned to the nurse and asked her whether there was a big supply of morphine. There was enough, replied the nurse. She added, "Help them, surely." There was no need to say more. They understood.

Szwajger went to see Dr. Margolis and told her of her plan to give morphine to the children. Margolis agreed. Soon the two doctors were moving among the youngest children and the babies, pouring a morphine solution into their open mouths. Next they turned to the older children and told them that they had a medicine for them that would make all the pain disappear. Trustingly, the children drank from their glasses. When they were told to undress and go to bed, they obeyed quietly. Outside the door, the commotion told a different story. There restless people shoved and pushed. The noise was coming closer, but the children in the ward seemed unaware of it.

When the children had all been given morphine, Szwajger left in a daze, with the pass pinned to her white coat. From total silence she moved into nervous chaos, bumping into a teacher she knew (a patient?). With obvious bitterness in her voice, the older woman inquired whether Szwajger had a pass. Ashamed, the doctor kept silent and moved on.

The few who were saved met in their lodgings. From there several times they sent their passes back to the hospital in the hope that a few more lives could be saved. The next day Ala Margolis returned to the hospital. About to enter the room she and her mother shared, she saw her mother sitting on her cot while a nurse knelt in front of her kissing her mother's hands. This nurse, the mother of a four-year-old patient, was thanking Dr. Margolis for causing her child's painless death.

Szwajger was active in the ghetto resistance and subsequently worked as an underground courier on the Aryan side of the ghetto. After the war she stayed in Warsaw, where she became a well-known pediatrician. For fifty years Szwajger told no one about the day she had helped give the children a quick, painless death. These experiences, deeply buried inside her, made her feel like an outsider for the rest of her life.[55]

When the deportations ended, the population of the Warsaw ghetto had been reduced by about 85 percent. Exact figures are elusive; the estimates of the number of Jews who remained in the ghetto range from fifty-five to sixty thousand. Within this small population were several underground groups. The histories of these Jewish resistance groups, closely intertwined with the fate of the rest of the Jewish people, will be resurfacing throughout this book.

Inside the East European ghettos, the fate of Jewish women and men was dictated by the Nazi measures of destruction. The majority of the adult men who survived the initial Nazi onslaughts were prevented from fulfilling their main traditional roles of provider and protector. Equating these roles with masculinity many men became depressed and apathetic when they found themselves unable to meet these obligations. Upper-class Jewish men may have been particularly distressed by the wartime deprivations: having more to begin with, they had more to lose. Thus they seemed to have had a harder time adjusting to the humiliations and hardships than working-class men.

For all Jewish men, of their two main roles, that of protector was totally obliterated, while the role of the breadwinner, although severely limited, was occasionally still open to them. Most Jewish men were forced to work for no payment or for earnings too small to allay hunger. Others were rounded up and forced into work camps or murdered. Still others were able to escape the areas occupied by the Germans.

In contrast women were able to use their traditional domestic and nurturing skills to fill the gaps vacated by men. Equally barred from becoming protectors, women concentrated on being providers, caregivers, and nurturers. Trying to adapt to the new, constantly changing situations, women expanded their activities, moving from helping only the immediate family to aiding friends and the community at large.

When I interviewed the survivors and read their memoirs, I noticed that the women would speak about the changes in their husbands and fathers with pain and compassion. None blamed the men for their plight. On the contrary, the stories they told show consistent efforts to understand and find ways to reduce the suffering of their men. When survivors discussed women in the ghettos, especially mothers, they did so with praise and admiration. Most focused on self-sacrifices and inventiveness. A frequent assumption in their accounts is that it was the flexibility of the women that allowed them to cope with the unprecedented upheavals.

There were a few exceptions to this trend. Jewish men sometimes found loopholes in the Nazi system, which they exploited to boost their earnings. These men tended to be less depressed. And when a man had found a way to earn a little more, the women in the family would see this as an invitation to help those less fortunate than they. From a variety of sources, then, the image of the ghetto woman emerges as that of a person who tried to adjust to ever-changing conditions, who was concerned about the welfare of others, and who tried to act in ways that benefited others.

But Jewish women, the bearers and chief rearers of children, had a burden they did not share with men, and one that created further divisions between the women themselves. In the Third Reich the attitudes toward procreation and motherhood and the policies used to implement them were diametrically opposed when applied to "Aryan"-Germans from those applied to Jews. For Aryan-German women, childbearing and childcare were highly valued, promising not only intangible but quite concrete rewards. In sharp contrast, Jewish procreation was defined as a political threat. The Nazis felt that by giving birth to Jewish children and rearing them, Jewish women interfered with the establishment of a racially pure, Aryan world. As the victories on the battlefield became less frequent, the Germans began introducing special measures for racial purification. Among these were prohibitions against Jewish pregnancy, which became a crime punishable by death.

Because childbearing and caring for future generations are universally cherished traditions, these Nazi prohibitions created havoc within Jewish communities, especially among potential and actual parents. In particular, the intricately close mother-child connection took a heavy toll on potential and actual mothers. Inevitably, these oppressive German measures resulted in differences between single and married women, who either were or were more likely to become mothers. Beyond facing the direct Nazi threat of murder—as we have seen, mothers and their young children were targeted—Jewish mothers had often to experience the unimaginable pain of watching their children starve to death. Many reports about parents, in particular mothers, praise the ingenuity and courage with which they tried to protect their children, in and out of the womb.

The increasing Nazi assaults, particularly against mothers and children, led to greater Jewish efforts to defend themselves. Oppressors and oppressed were locked in an uneven battle waged wherever Jewish children and their mothers could be found. By early 1943 the Germans had liquidated most of the East European ghettos. Jews who lived through this phase of destruction continued their struggle, in the concentration camps, in hiding and passing as Christians in the Aryan sectors, and in the forests. How the Jews had left the ghettos and the kind of settings they reached shaped the ways men and women dealt with their situations.

Leaving the Ghetto

Lidia (Itke) Brown-Abramson threw herself into the pile of straw next to the attic wall. The eleven-year-old understood why she was up there but wanted to know more about what was going on. The cracks between the wooden boards revealed several figures below them, each moving tensely. Then they were gone. Silence took over. Soon heavy smoke began pouring in from all directions. Fumes crept through the spaces in the attic walls. Breathing was becoming difficult. With a nod, Lidia's parents agreed: they had to leave. Outside, bullets immediately found Lidia's father and one of her sisters. Before their bodies hit the ground, Lidia's mother was calling out to the other children to stay down. In response, a German soldier appeared at her side and pointed the gun in his hand.

"My mother collapsed," continues Lidia. "She said something but I don't know what . . . from all over people rushed out, turning into a frantically screaming crowd. They too wanted to get away."[1]

Death followed after them. All alone, the girl ran. Her feet brought her close to her parents' bodies; then her feet continued to move in circles, as if they had no destination. In the evening, she was somehow able to meet up with her brother:

> My brother, I, and a few other people tried to keep away from the bullets. Together we reached huge water containers, prepared for the coming Sabbath. This was Friday. The ghetto had no running water, and the containers were filled with well water. We climbed into these huge containers so that the fire should not reach us . . . Later, my brother and I came to the wall of the ghetto. Lying close, we heard the Germans talk. My brother said, "Go see where they are." I left, but I never came back . . . Why? I don't know to this very day. I only know that in my dreams my brother appears all the time.

The liquidation of the Głębokie ghetto, in western Belorussia, occurred in the summer of 1943. Lidia watched both her parents fall, hit by bullets; she kept moving.

> I went to where my father told us we should meet, where he used to work. It was a field. When I came there, even though I had seen my parents die before, I shouted, "Father! Mother!" . . . I thought that they were somewhere, I called for them. Only the echo of the forest answered me. Maybe I did not grasp . . . no one was there.

She entered a half-burned house, collected a few items of clothing, gathered them into a bundle, and left. Outside she met a German soldier, who asked her who she was. She explained that she was a Polish orphan who had come to gather a few Jewish belongings, and he let her go. Later on, with the help of Belorussian peasants, Lidia was accepted into a Soviet partisan unit. Lidia Abramson belongs to a minority of Jews who successfully defied the destruction that accompanied the dismantling of the ghettos.

When, how, and which inmates left the ghettos depended on a wide range of circumstances that were intricately connected, often in unknown ways. But almost all originated in one of three actions: direct action by the Germans and their collaborators; the urging of various family members; or the instigation of underground ghetto movements. The majority of the inmates left during ghetto liquidations. Usually these "official" departures ended in mass execution or deportation to concentration camps. An unknown minority managed to escape during these forced deportations. Of this minority some survived until the end of the war.

The dismantling of ghettos began in 1942, and by the end of 1943 most were empty. Forceful removals during ghetto deportations and liquidation constituted "legal" departures. Through these measures the Germans continued to pursue their goal of Jewish annihilation. But a few inmates also managed to exit illegally. Some of these escapes were spontaneous, someone seizing a chance during an Aktion (roundup, mass murder, deportation). Others were planned, not necessarily in conjunction with ghetto Aktions. Sometimes single individuals escaped, other times groups of various sizes. If planned ahead these escapes usually called for intricate arrangements. Inevitably, all such departures were marked by danger and unpredictability, making cooperation and mutual aid indispensable. Depending on a wide range of circumstances, women and men contributed in different ways to these illegal exits.

Most ghetto inmates were officially removed from the Nazi-created quarters. Rumors about ghetto assaults, the coming Aktion, would warn the Jews that their official removal was imminent. Inadvertently, such rumors also enabled them to make illegal escapes. Determined to do away with all illegal departures, the Germans relied on surprise and speed. Dates about official ghetto liquidation, whether partial or total, were kept secret. When information about an impending Aktion leaked out, the authorities would deny it. Along with the denials, officials would assure the Jews that the future would be more secure. It seems that the closer the rumors were to the truth, the more vehemently they were denied, and the stronger were the German pledges about future improvements.

A deportation or Aktion had several steps. First extra guards and other officials—SS, soldiers, police—as well as special collaborators would arrive. These new arrivals would tighten the security around the ghetto. Next would come public announcements, usually over loudspeakers, that reported that the Jews were going to be transferred to a better place and urg-

ing the inmates to come out for the roundups while at the same time threatening anyone who disobeyed. A search would follow. The interlude between the coming of the new arrivals and the search, no matter how brief,
was crucial. This was the period when people could try to find or reach their
hideouts. Of course, if the ghetto was going to be physically dismantled, all
hiding places became useless.

The actual transfer of inmates also proceeded in steps. It would begin
with the general collection of all the people and move on to various sorting
procedures. Usually, if only a partial liquidation was intended, the "productive" Jews would be immediately separated from the rest. These were usually the young, who were employed in valued jobs. During the final breakup
of the ghetto the remainder were assembled and divided into special groups.

Because Jewish children were particularly targeted for destruction,
ghetto deportations created special anxieties for parents. Eventually, the
Germans began equating Jewish mothers of young children with children,
marking them also for death. While exact figures are elusive, historians tend
to agree that only a small minority of women abandoned their children during deportations. Most mothers and fathers tried to protect their offspring,
often in ingenious ways. When their efforts proved ineffective, the mothers
and, less frequently, the fathers would go with their children. During ghetto
liquidations, the Germans insisted on keeping mothers and young children
together to ensure more orderly procedures.

The final liquidation of the Vilna ghetto began on September 23, 1943.
What happened on that day followed an established pattern. First the assembled population was divided by age and sex. There were exceptions:
occasionally, invalid males were thrown in with the group of older women
and women with children. Dina Abramovicz, who was young, watched from
afar as her weak, elderly mother struggled with her heavy bundles. Then
Dina spotted a teacher whom she and her mother knew. He was paralyzed
from the waist down, walking on crutches. Because he was an invalid, he was
pushed into the group of older women and women with children. Dina
realized that he would be expected to climb a hill along with the crowd.

He looked around imploringly, as if asking for help. Dina tells what happened next:

> There was someone — my mother . . . she put down all her bundles and
> took the arm of the crippled man, who leaned heavily on her. As they
> walked toward the steep hill together, the tall, crippled man and the
> elderly, frail woman, their faces glowed with a sublime light — the light of
> compassion and humanity that overcame the horror of their destiny.
> This is the light in which I see my mother and which will not disappear
> from my memory as long as I live.[2]

Dina's mother came to the rescue of a person in need, an action that was often associated with women's nurturing role. Later Dina was able to jump off the moving freight train that was taking her to a concentration camp. Miraculously, she managed to join a group of partisans and survive the war.

In another part of the Vilna ghetto Dobka Freund-Waldhorn, along with the rest of women and children, was separated from the men in the customary shoving and pushing. Then the SS men began to divide Dobka's group into two. One side consisted of mothers with children and older women. The other contained only young, healthy-looking women. As she waited for the segregation to be finished, Dobka caught sight of her friend Mira Salomon, standing with her two children. She remembers:

> I still see how the two little girls clung to her . . . I stopped next to them.
> From her pocket Mira took out rouge and gently put some on my
> cheeks. She wanted me to look healthy, so I would have a better chance.
> With my eyes on her beautiful girls, I asked, "Mira, and you?" She said,
> "I go with my children." Standing there, she only wanted to part from
> friends. She was young, bright, courageous . . . Mira would not leave her
> children. She knew that her decision meant death. With a child a woman
> had no chance, none.
>
> A few mothers had left their children. Later they were with me in the
> camps. I heard them cry at night . . . On that last day some of us were
> made to stand on the right side . . . We saw the tragedy and how some
> tried to switch sides, for life.
>
> Then I see a beautiful little girl walking with an SS man, and she is

looking among us for her mother. But her mother is hiding behind us so that the child should not find her. I witnessed this. These are not things from books; they don't write about it. This woman succeeded. I hear the German say, "The cow; she hid herself!" He was outraged. And he took the child to the left side, to her death.

Now I am a mother of two sons and a grandmother of five grandchildren, and when someone tells me, "I would not have done this," I don't want to hear it. At that point I was not a mother of a child, and so I don't know. It's good that God did not test me. I don't know what I would have done. I don't know . . .

Why do I tell you this? Because I want people to understand what it meant to have a drive for life. How strong the need for self-preservation was for some of the mothers. Only a few.[3]

With a group of two hundred young healthy women Dobka was transferred to the Kaiserwald camp in Riga, Latvia. Most of the men ended up in Klooga camp, in Estonia. One of these was Dobka's husband. The roundup was the last time they saw each other. Although she was independent and enterprising, Dobka was unable to find any loopholes in the deportation procedures.

Many others who fell victim to official deportations would search, unsuccessfully, for a way out up until the last minute. When Roma Nutkiewicz-Benatar lost her parents at the end of 1942, an aunt tried to fill the void. In the ghetto Roma shared a room with her aunt and the aunt's family. After the armed confrontation between the Jewish Warsaw ghetto resisters and the Germans on January 18, 1943, the ghetto population expected a bigger uprising to follow.[4] In preparation they built ingenious hideouts, tunnels, and passages.

Roma's family had prepared a special bunker, which became home to some seventy people between April 18 and May 5. Roma describes how they lived:

When we went down to the hideout, the table was set for Passover, everything was prepared. In every courtyard there were secret bunkers. The Germans didn't find the entrance to ours. The entrance was well camouflaged. When you stand on steps, you usually don't think that an entrance would be below you; one usually looks ahead. But our entrance was below the steps.

During the uprising, even though they did not find it, the Germans knew that there was a bunker because people had disappeared. They would put bombs and grenades into courtyards where they suspected hideouts.[5]

On May 5 a stray bullet entered Roma's hideout. It pierced a medical box, shattering a bottle filled with ether. The air became unbearable. The strong odor made some people push to the outside, where they were seen, giving away the location of the bunker. The Germans poured gas into the opening, and some of those still inside became ill. Overcome by the ether and gas, Roma began to feel that life was coming to an end. Lying on the floor, she refused to get up. She did not care, wanted it all to end.

What happened next?

My aunt slapped me and forced me to move, shouting, "If anybody has a chance, it is you. Get up!" There was a small hole, and through it the Germans grabbed us . . . They pulled a few of us up, including my aunt's son-in-law. They ordered him to show them where other hideouts were. He said that he didn't know. So they shot him on the spot.

After that Roma, her aunt, and others were pushed into cattle cars. From inside the moving car they heard shots; people were trying to escape. They realized that this meant that doors could be opened. In Roma's car people began to work on the door, and it seemed to yield.

At that point, my aunt asked me to remember the address of her daughter who lived on the Aryan side, so that if I succeeded in running away, I had a place to go. With great difficulty, we opened the door: we realized that we were approaching a station. So, we quickly shut it. The train came to a stop, and we thought that this was the end of the road. But it wasn't. The train stayed for a little while, and then moved on. The road between this particular station and where we were going was too short for us to escape. By the time we opened the door for the second time, we had arrived in Majdanek.

Chance, that elusive force, had prevented the prisoners from jumping. Was this a missed opportunity or protection from a bullet?[6]

Efforts to care for others, often members of the family, kept some individuals from trying to make their escape. Many teenagers, both male and female, were eager to help parents and other relatives and refused to leave them. In the Białystok ghetto, the teenaged Shamay Kizelstein knew that his parents wanted him to escape into the forest. He was aware that some Jewish men were doing just that. But Shamay refused to go. When he was telling me about this, he explained that after a while he began noticing a marked decline in his parents. They became distraught and physically weak. Shamay felt that by staying with his parents he could lift some of their burdens. He wanted to ease their suffering by supplying them with food; as long as the ghetto lasted, he managed to gather extra provisions. But with the liquidation of the Białystok ghetto came the inevitable separation. Shamay does not remember whether his mother or his father was more eager to see him leave for the forest. Shamay survived to the end of the war as an inmate of various concentration camps. Both parents disappeared without a trace.[7]

Occasionally in the course of an official ghetto liquidation, a number of inmates would succeed in escaping from the enemy. These escapes involved cooperative efforts among a number of people. The story of how Zvi Shefet (Shepetinski) escaped is both similar to and different from that of Shamay. When the Germans invaded Słonim, Zvi was sixteen. Blue-eyed and fluent in Polish, he was a good candidate for passing himself off on the Aryan side. One day Zvi overheard his parents broach the idea to a Polish woman. "They spoke to the Polish woman about how she would take me to Warsaw as a Pole. I was very hurt that they wanted to get rid of me. I was sure that I had to stay, to protect the family. My sister looked very Jewish. She could not go out of the ghetto. I could do that and help."[8]

Because Zvi insisted on having his way, the plan to send him to the Aryan side was dropped. Zvi speaks with pride about his mother's involvement in finding ways for family and friends to get away. Once when he was caught and sent to a work camp, she orchestrated an escape. She hired a Belorussian peasant to transport Zvi in a hay-filled wagon to the ghetto gate.

From there his mother, escorted by a bribed guard, brought Zvi home. Paying special tribute to his mother, Zvi felt that this incident showed her core character: "My mother . . . managed to make documents for friends . . . She knew how to arrange everything better than my father. In those days, women had greater responsibilities, family responsibilities."

By June 1942 the Słonim ghetto was filled with nervous anticipation. This anxiety reached a special pitch after the arrival of a large group of SS men, who placed heavy guns around the place. As in most other Jewish quarters, the inmates had built ingenious hideouts. At this point practically all of them had disappeared into their shelters. When the Germans and their collaborators reached the Jewish homes, the people were gone. Frustrated, the raiders searched with no success.

Zvi and his family had moved into a well-camouflaged part of the house. He describes their preparations:

> There were about twelve of us. Before we went into the hiding place we made a mess of our place to make the enemy think that somebody had been in a rush when being taken away by force.
>
> But it seems that they had exact lists of how many people they had taken out of each place. They knew who was hiding by the number of people that were missing. In our apartment, they didn't find a soul. They stayed close and watched the building. Some of the Jews they found passed next to our house. They seemed to know what was in store for them. We heard the cries . . .
>
> Because they had caught so few they waited for two weeks . . .
>
> My mother, my father, my sister, and I were together in our hideout.

One day toward evening, Lithuanian policemen set fire to the house. With the ashes still smoldering, but protected by darkness, Zvi's family left the ghetto. On the outside they met an acquaintance, a Belorussian peasant. The teenage son was shocked by his father's reaction. "The peasant took a slice of bread out of his sack and gave it to my father. For the first time I saw tears in my father's eyes. Then he openly cried."

Zvi's family were eventually separated by forces beyond their control.

Few forest partisan groups welcomed Jewish civilians; of the entire family only Zvi made it to the end of the war.[9]

Shamay and Zvi both refused to follow their parents' wishes. To this day each justifies his refusal to leave by his desire to be of help. Each felt capable of supporting the family and for a while was able to. In both cases this usefulness did not last. But their actions suggest that male teenagers might have been considered immune to German attacks upon Jewish men. Like their mothers and teenaged sisters, teenaged men stepped in, trying to fill an existing gap.

Like Zvi and his family, the Garfunks ran into the surrounding forest during an official ghetto liquidation. As a family they had benefited from the help of others in a most unexpected way. The Garfunks lived in the Lida ghetto, in western Belorussia, an area surrounded by thick forests. Luba Garfunk, the mother of a two-year-old boy, had lost most of her relatives, including her parents, during the early Aktions, and she had no illusions. The majority of Jews in western Belorussia were executed in areas that were only a short distance from their dwellings. Shaken by her family losses, Luba stopped caring about the future. Her husband pleaded with her to prepare for an escape from the ghetto. At a considerable sacrifice he bought a gun. But Luba was only going through the motions, detached from these preparations.

On September 17, at five o'clock in the morning, news spread that the ghetto had been sealed more tightly. In the confusion that followed, Mr. Garfunk could not get to his gun. The official voice over the loudspeaker announced that the Jews were about to be transferred to a secure working place. In reality, the cattle cars were waiting to take them to the Majdanek concentration camp. Luba, her husband, and her son dressed, putting on several layers of clothes. They knew enough not to bother with luggage. Then, along with a large group of inmates, they were escorted toward the cars by two soldiers. Luba continues,

As we were led away, one of the Germans came over to us and said,
"I advise you to run away. Don't believe the Germans. You are being

taken to a concentration camp, not a work camp. There cold and hunger wait for you." I asked why he was telling us this. He answered that he was from Alsace and did not approve of what the Germans were doing. He was half-German and half-French. He was young. He looked strange, like drunk. He kept urging us, "Now go! Go!" As we moved on, this soldier took off my Star of David, and he pushed me and my son to the side, telling the other German that he was taking us to get some water for the child. The rest of the Jews murmured under their breath, "This is how a Jewish woman behaves? She leaves her husband?" It was an impulse. My husband urged me, "Go! You must go!"[10]

The soldier brought Luba and her son to a Belorussian peasant and ordered the woman to take good care of them. Before he left he promised to return. The woman, unhappy about this intrusion, did not dare disobey a request from a German. Danger of discovery was real. Not only was the little boy circumcised, but he spoke only Yiddish. In no time the word had spread that two Jews were being kept in the village. Now everybody was anxious, Luba as well.

Before they had parted, husband and wife had agreed on a few possible meeting places. Luba begged her host to tell her how to get to these places. Soon the mother and son began traveling from one Christian home to another. Everyone was afraid; only a few people would take her in for a brief stay. One woman, a stranger, who saw Luba and the boy on the road, invited them in. But here, too, they could not remain. The next day a kind neighbor warned them that the entire village was aware of their presence. This time, before parting, the hostess sent along her teenaged grandson with instructions to return only after Luba was reunited with her husband.

In the meantime, the soldier went back to fulfill his promise and found Mr. Garfunk beaten up and bleeding. The German whisked him away. When they were near a field the German, making sure that no one was watching, urged Mr. Garfunk to disappear.

The Belorussian youth helped Luba locate her husband, and within a week the Garfunk family had been accepted into the Bielski partisan detachment, a Jewish partisan group known for its willingness to take in all Jewish fugitives. The three of them stayed in the forest until the arrival of the Red Army, in the summer of 1944.

The Garfunks' escape was exceptional in several ways. First, a German soldier who was participating in Jewish murder initiated their flight. After this important, completely unexpected offer of help the husband encouraged his wife to go. The husband's strength gave his wife the necessary push. Mr. Garfunk was young; perhaps this is why he refused to give in. Perhaps he was drawn to the surrounding forests, to the implied promise of safety and a partisan life.

More predictable escape efforts included slipping away from the trains destined for Nazi concentration camps. Eva Galer, whose father had lost his zest for life and seemed uninterested in even his family's welfare in the ghetto, managed to get away in this manner. At the same time her father regained some of his former self-assurance on the way to death.

As 1942 was coming to an end, most inmates in the Lubaczów ghetto, including Eva, knew that death was imminent. Earlier a Jewish escapee from the Bełżec death camp had hidden out in Lubaczów, and he told them what deportation meant. In response, people redoubled their efforts to build hideouts. Eva's family installed an extra wall in the attic. In anticipation of previous ghetto raids, Eva and her family had successfully disappeared into this camouflaged shelter. Now, with the end nearing, they knew that no matter how ingenious their hideout was, it could not shield them, for the ghetto was going to be dismantled.

It happened on a cold day, January 4. This time the trucks that arrived were too numerous for a mere shrinkage of the population. Perhaps out of habit Eva's family ran to their hiding place in the attic. But the Germans, using greater zeal than usual, were successful in ferreting out their victims. Eva's hiding place was discovered. She describes what came next:

> It was terrible. Chaotic screams. People were caught, found in different places. They brought us to the station where cattle cars were standing. They hit us, shouted . . . If anyone fell, they would kick and rush them.

They treated us worse than animals. Each family tried to stay together. We were packed tightly into the wagons and the doors were shut. The cars had small, barred windows.[11]

Despite their bewilderment and horror, a few young men started cutting the window bars, which came out. As the train moved on, they pushed one another out of the opening, one at a time.

Everyone wanted to jump. We knew that we were going to die. The older people felt that they could not leave, nor could the children. We stood nearby, and my father said, "Save yourselves, save yourselves." First went my brother, sixteen, sister, seventeen, and I, eighteen. The younger ones must have stayed, but I don't know what happened after me. My little brother cried, "I also want to live." He was the youngest, three years old; he cried and cried. When on the outside I fell, I heard shots. They were sitting on the roofs of the wagons.

What was she thinking about?

I was not thinking at all. There was no thought. Emptiness . . . I fell into a hole filled with snow. I did not hurt. Once the train passed, I got up and went back to look for my sister and my brother. I only found dead bodies.

Did she recognize them?

Yes, definitely. Brother, for sure. It was snowing. So there were no people around. The first thing I did was to tear off the armband. I went back to Olszyce, I walked in the snow. I went to the woman where we had left our belongings.

The woman felt sorry for the fugitive, but she was afraid. She let Eva stay the night, fed her, and gave her 20 zlotys and a warm shawl, but told her she would have to leave early in the morning. Eva's next stop was the house of a peasant from whom she used to buy milk. This woman refused to let her in, so Eva sneaked into the barn. When the woman came in the evening to feed the animals, she found the shivering girl. She, too, took the unwanted guest into the house but told her to leave early in the morning. Afraid to be recognized in these familiar surroundings, Eva walked to a nearby train station.

From there, she left for Kraków, to her a strange city. The station in Kraków provided her with a bench and a bathroom. She ate some of the bread she had with her, and with part of the 20 zlotys she treated herself to a glass of hot, brown liquid called tea. Eva knew that by staying too long in one place she would arouse suspicion. Although she was afraid to venture out of this place, which had already become a little familiar, she moved on a small distance from the station. Nearby she discovered an open vegetable market. Inconspicuously, Eva picked up discarded leaves and bits of rotten vegetables. Then she returned to her bench at the station.

For two days or so this routine continued. Eva would scrutinize faces, looking for a Jew who could direct her to a nearby ghetto. Was there a ghetto? She was not sure. But she never found out. Instead,

> One day I went again to the marketplace. I was just looking; I had no
> money to buy anything. Germans came. They blocked off the street.
> It was a raid. But I didn't know what it was. They grabbed young men
> and women and pushed them into a truck. They took me also. They
> were catching people for forced labor in Germany. These young Poles
> were only shopping; they did not have papers, just like me. We came
> there . . . They asked names and where we were born. There were doc-
> tors, and there was a place for disinfection. I was hoping that I would
> pass the doctor's inspection. They noticed my lice.

But the lice were not an impediment. Eva ended up in Austria and worked as a farmhand until the end of the war.[12]

Eva Galer's illegal exit from the ghetto was a spontaneous occurrence, coming at the last moment but still within the context of an official ghetto dismantling. By cutting the bars of the train window the young men had made the escapes possible. Eva's father had helped by encouraging his children to jump out, leaving him behind. He had given them the green light for this risky step. Men, especially her father, had facilitated Eva's escape.

Eva Kracowski's escape also took place within the context of an official ghetto breakup. It was planned in part by the Jewish ghetto underground and further facilitated by the strong urgings of her mother, who pushed Eva away with her blessing.

We saw that Eva's father, the respected physician Dr. Samuel Kracowski, had burned to death when the Germans torched the local synagogue immediately after the invasion of Białystok, in the summer of 1941. In deference to his memory, his wife and children were offered a room and employment in the ghetto hospital.

In Białystok, as in many other ghettos, the young people who before the war had belonged to a wide range of political movements recognized early on that the Germans intended the biological annihilation of the Jewish people. This knowledge led them to initiate underground activities that supported armed resistance. While eager to fight the Germans, most ghetto resisters were realistic about the outcome of all armed encounters. They knew that they were not strong enough to stop the Jewish destruction. But through armed resistance they hoped to assert their autonomy and at least decide how they would die. Among the issues involved in these preparations were questions of the timing and location of future confrontations. In 1942 rumors about forest partisans began to circulate. Particularly in ghettos close to wooded areas this news offered inmates options: they could resist inside the ghetto or escape into the forest, where they could fight as partisans. Most underground resisters were reluctant to leave the ghettos. Many felt responsible for their imprisoned communities and knew that by running away they would be endangering those left behind.[13]

Sometimes it was the attitude of the rest of the ghetto population toward the rebels that tipped the scale in favor of staying or leaving. Older, more traditional ghetto inmates, often including members of the Judenrat, were suspicious of the underground. Many felt that Jewish contributions to the German war economy could save if not all the Jews then at least those who worked. For some the prospect of a ghetto uprising or a mass escape into the forest meant the death of the entire community.

By 1942 Eva, like many others, had heard about both Treblinka and the ghetto underground. Determined not to end up as a victim of gassing, she tried to make contact with the Białystok resistance movement. A close friend, a co-worker and member of the underground, told her that she had two strikes against her. First, she was unlikely to be accepted because she had been a member of the prewar elite, the so-called golden youths. Second, her strictly apolitical past worked against her. Eva refused to accept defeat. In the end her friendship with the young male co-worker helped her gain entry into the underground.

In 1943, three months before the liquidation of the ghetto, Eva became a member of the Jewish underground. As she explains, "I belonged to the Communist group, which is a little bit strange because I was always an anti-Communist . . . I knew about others, but I had no access to any of them except the Communists."[14] Her first task was to find safe places for illegal goods: documents, weapons, and parts of weapons, stolen SS uniforms, and other items. Eva's brother, who was not yet thirteen, helped her hide these items in inaccessible nooks and closets.

In most underground groups plans about the place, form, and timing of resistance changed often. Some leaders would compromise and accommodate to vacillating Judenrat leaders. This happened in the Białystok ghetto. After considerable soul-searching and consultations with Ephraim Barasz, the acting Judenrat head, the resistance decided to attack the Germans during the final phase of the liquidation. They had hoped that their attack would be followed by a mass escape into the forest. But the liquidation of the ghetto began unexpectedly, on August 16, 1943. A desperate, predictably uneven, battle ensued. In the end, only a few fighters reached either the Aryan side or the forest.

Throughout their stay in the ghetto Eva had tried to protect her mother by mentioning neither her interest in becoming a member of the underground nor her actual affiliation after she joined. Eva thinks that her highly intelligent, well-educated mother suspected the truth. Perhaps because she was wise, she asked no questions.

When at the start of the liquidation Eva told her mother that she would be hiding with her friend, Mrs. Kracowski's reaction was immediate:

"Go, because I cannot help you at all." She added with special emphasis, "Wherever you want to go, go, but promise me not to stay with me." You have to understand the situation, she already knew that she was going to die. Older people and children had the least chance. Mother was afraid that if I stayed with her I would be stuck. My mother demanded that I leave her . . . She wanted to stay with my brother who was still a child . . . for them, there was no way out.

Eva and her friend reached the area to which they were assigned by the underground. According to the plan, at a prearranged time the resistance would set fire to a fence close to a particular ghetto gate. The resisters thought that by burning down the fence they could give the inmates an opportunity to escape.

Eva describes what she saw at her post:

Nobody could really leave, even though the fence was burned, because the Germans were standing behind it. We were throwing Molotov cocktails, we were shooting . . . most of us perished. There were German victims, Germans fell, but we were falling like flies. We were just dying . . . I am talking only about the particular place where I was . . . After a terrible commotion, the shooting almost stopped because there were hardly any of us left. I don't know how many.

Then they surrounded us in the Barasz garden. All of it was very near. This was the only place that had a garden in the ghetto; Barasz . . . lived there . . . Around us were people assembled for deportations. They had to go through the gates. There was commotion, chaos, many dead and wounded lying around . . . Syrota, a partisan who had recently returned from the forest, stood next to us.

He actually pushed us out of this encirclement. He found a way to get out and dragged the two of us with him. And we managed to get through the fence that was burned, and my close friend who was with me had a hiding place and he brought us there.

There were some very good camouflaged places in the ghetto, but the one we came to was not one of them. It could hardly be called a hideout. It was a part of an attic in a three-level house. One part of this attic was never used before. The attic had two slopes at each end, and inside the attic they sort of divided it, made two walls. If you were outside, you could see that there was something missing. If you were inside, you thought that this was the end of the attic.

Even though the Białystok ghetto was officially liquidated, Eva continued to make sporadic visits to their primitive hideout, along with a group
that gradually decreased from six to three. Eva's friend, the young man who
had helped her join the resistance, died from an infection caused by a bullet. Other close calls and painful losses followed. After two and a half months
of being hunted, the group had shrunk to three people. These were Eva, Syrota (the man who had pushed her and her friend out of the encirclement
during the final Aktion), and another brave and capable young man named
Szyjka. Now the three decided to leave the guarded ghetto and head for the
forest Suprasl, some 20 kilometers from Białystok. There they hoped to join
other partisans. In fact, Syrota had belonged to the Jewish partisan detachment they wished to join before he returned to Białystok. On the way to
Suprasl, the three faced several life-threatening obstacles; more dangers
confronted them when they reached their destination.

To my question of who or what had been responsible for her ghetto escape, Eva had a ready answer, an answer she repeated several times,

> If my mother had not told me, "Don't stay with me; it does not matter,"
> had she not approved of my leaving her, I would have stayed. I was very
> attached to her. My mother knew that this was the end. She wanted me
> to live. Her push did it . . . Women behaved in such courageous and
> supportive ways!

Eva credits her ghetto escape and her ultimate survival to her mother's
love and support. In reality, the mother's role was symbolic and at best indirect. Eva herself was responsible for her connection to the resistance movement. And it was this connection that made Eva's departure possible.

Not all illegal ghetto departures occurred during or because of official
deportations. Some of the escapes were planned well in advance, and they
relied heavily on aid from a number of sources. Probably these prearranged
escapes were less frequent than other kinds. In my sample of 308 Jews who
managed to live illegally on the Aryan side, the majority (76 percent) had received aid in response to a crisis, rather than as part of a plan.[15] Both women
and men participated in these organized ghetto escapes.

One of these women was Sandra Brand, the energetic, vivacious, and attractive woman who had saved the Niemirów synagogue from being burned. Those who liked Sandra called her courageous and independent. Those who disapproved of her referred to her as a reckless risk-taker and an adventurer. The German occupation found Sandra in Lvov, where she shared her modest apartment with her four-year-old son, Bruno. From time to time her husband would visit them. He divided his time between the small town of Złoczów, where his sister lived, and Lvov, where his wife and son stayed.

Sandra had a reputation as a devoted, giving friend. During the Soviet occupation, she had worked as a supervisor in a government-owned department store. When her close friend Julius Silberbusch had been in trouble with the higher echelons of the firm, Sandra had successfully intervened on his behalf. Julius, a Jewish-German refugee, was grateful. Before the war, he had married a Christian German, with whom he had two daughters. Political changes led to the couple's separation. When the German-Soviet war broke out, Julius disappeared. Sandra thought that he had left with the Red Army.

In Lvov the hasty retreat of the Red Army created a political vacuum. Ukrainian nationalists, with the tacit approval of the German army, filled the void by committing violence against the Jews. Some Jews lost their lives, others were severely beaten, still others ended up in jail.[16]

Sandra's father was imprisoned. In an unexpected gesture of kindness, several German officers helped to free the old man. This led to a brief friendship between one of the officers and Sandra. To repay this officer, Sandra gave him a tour of the city. During their walk the German painted a bleak picture of the Jewish future. Cautiously, feeling his way, he hinted at a solution. He described how the Jewish girlfriend of a friend of his had moved to a different town, where people didn't know her. There she lived under an assumed name and was protected from anti-Jewish measures. With this story, the German planted a seed in Sandra's mind. And even though the officer soon disappeared, probably sent to the Russian front, the idea lingered on.

Confronted by continuously worsening conditions, Sandra decided to obtain Christian documents. She had the proper looks and knowledge of the Polish language, both important for passing as Aryan. One of her Polish friends supplied her with a copy of her own birth certificate, on condition that Sandra not use it in and around Lvov. But even with a Christian birth certificate, Sandra had no idea how to proceed. She explored various possibilities. Her husband felt that entering the forbidden Christian world was too risky. He disapproved of her efforts.

Then, seemingly out of nowhere, Julius Silberbusch reappeared. He now told Sandra that he was a Volksdeutscher, an ethnic German, and Sandra did not challenge his new identity. Intuitively she sensed that some questions were best left unasked; there was danger in knowing. Julius looked self-assured and prosperous. He was working as a principal buyer for several German stores, a job that involved trips to Warsaw.[17]

A grateful friend, Julius was concerned about Sandra's future. Her Christian birth certificate, he felt, would allow her to move into the Aryan sector. He offered to bring her to Warsaw on his next trip. He also promised to help her settle in under her assumed name of Cecylia Szarek. Sandra was torn between staying close to her family and leaving. She was particularly concerned about her son, Bruno, and her husband. She wanted them to come with her, yet she was aware that moving with them could be more dangerous than going by herself. Besides, her husband was reluctant to go. As Julius continued to pressure her to make the change, Sandra compromised. She decided to take just Bruno first.

But her husband and his sister argued that it would be more beneficial for everyone if she first went alone with Silberbusch. Once settled in Warsaw, she could find a job for herself and her husband, and make a home for Bruno. In the meantime, her husband would take Bruno to Złoczów, where they would wait until Sandra had made the proper arrangements. This suggestion made sense. It reduced Sandra's anxieties and gave her more freedom. It also pleased Julius, which helped assure his aid in Warsaw, a strange city.

True to his promise, Silberbusch had made the preparations. First came the trip to Warsaw in a luxurious official car. There Julius found employment for Sandra as a Polish-German interpreter in a German firm with which he was conducting business. Sandra received special work documents that confirmed her Christian background and shielded her from forced deportation to Germany.

Sandra was able to find a job for her husband in the accounting office of her firm. He was to pose as a casual acquaintance. She also located a Polish woman who was willing to care for Bruno. All these arrangements happened faster than expected. Still, Sandra was anxious. She had heard no news from her husband. Rather than send someone else, she herself went to Złoczów, where she learned that her son and husband were gone. Both had been victims of a roundup that ended in deportation. She never heard from them again.

Sandra benefited from Julius's aid, even though she herself had initiated the process before his appearance. Her entrance into the Christian world was the result of a cooperative effort between Sandra and Julius. Years later, reflecting on her move to the Aryan side, Sandra felt that had it not been for Julius's pressure and help, she would not have made the move. Comparing him to other men she had known then, she said, "He made me do it. He gave me moral support and actual help . . . Other men gave me ideas, but they did not act upon them. Julius was involved in all the arrangements."[18]

Julius was in a special situation. Unlike most Jewish men, he had relative freedom and was still able to discharge a masculine role. In contrast, Sandra's husband, who at first discouraged her from entering the Aryan world, was in the position of most Jewish men at that time, unable to protect and support his family. His unwillingness to take risks was also based on realistic assessments of the situation. Still, his reaction reflects a feeling of powerlessness shared by many Jewish males.

Alexandra Sołowejczyk-Guter resembles Sandra Brand in enterprising spirit and energy. When the war broke out Alexandra organized the escape of her husband and herself from the advancing German army. But the occupation caught up with them, and they ended up in the Vilna ghetto. Here

Alexandra's husband, who was employed as a surgeon, resigned himself to a prolonged stay. But Alexandra had other plans. She wanted to reunite with her family and friends, all of whom were in the Warsaw ghetto. After she convinced her husband, Alexandra organized the trip.[19]

When they were settled in Warsaw, Alexandra became eager to escape to the Aryan side. In 1942 she approached Wacek Pietruszka, a loyal pre-war Gentile employee of one of her husband's clinics. Wacek and his wife were known for their generous aid to Jews. In fact, it was no secret that the couple's modest dwelling served as a shelter for many ghetto escapees. Unfortunately, this reputation in itself exposed all those who found a haven there to the danger of denouncement. Therefore, before Alexandra and four others prepared to leave the ghetto in a group, she asked her Polish rescuer to find them a safer home. Wacek had many contacts and knew exactly whom to approach, and how. He orchestrated their escape to the Aryan side at the height of the ghetto deportations.

Alexandra's group of escapees was in some ways exceptional. They had money, which they were willing to share. (By the time they got to the Aryan side, most Jews were penniless.)[20] But neither Wacek nor the Poles he found as helpers wanted to profit from saving Jews. And so these fugitives paid only their own living expenses — and this only because they had the means. The group's experience was also exceptional because, unlike most other Jews, the fugitives benefited from a network of Poles ready to help them make the move to and then survive within the forbidden Christian world.

Alexandra's husband had no problem with relying on her arrangements. Unlike Sandra's husband he was glad to follow his wife's suggestions and trusted her judgment. The difference between these two cases may have been due to the kind of marriage they had. Alexandra and her husband were close friends before and during the war. Sandra's relations with her husband seemed to lack closeness; they did not always live together and their marriage was filled with tension and distrust.

In western Belorussia, the Słonim ghetto, with its surrounding forests, promised the possibility of successful escape to its inmates. Mina Volkowiski arrived there from Paris, where her husband had recently completed his medical studies. The young couple intended to stay close to Mina's family for a little while.

Mina resented the German occupation and their ghetto confinement more strongly than her husband. Curious and daring, she was continually looking for a way out. She recalls,

> A few months after the Germans came I noticed that something unusual was taking place . . . people were leaving the ghetto and not returning. I wanted to know how this could be done. My family felt that I would bring disaster on all of us, particularly after I had approached certain Communists about it. In my circles, Communists were seen as very dangerous . . . It was they who told me that some Jews were running into the forests to join partisans. They also told me that my husband and I would not fit into forest life. We were too bourgeois. Besides, they had their own people who had to be taken out.[21]

Mina's husband worked in the ghetto hospital. He was very busy but felt frustrated because he could not do much to help. He became dejected and overwhelmed by the plight of the Jews and showed no interest in his wife's restless inquiries. But she refused to take no for an answer:

> I got in touch with a policeman I knew. He advised us to join the partisans and offered to help locate them . . . My family was again angry with me, sure that this policeman would denounce us . . . I did not agree with them. Not to upset them I did not pursue this lead. But only knowing that there were partisans did not get me out.

Eventually Mina met more people who were eager to leave. She tried to arrange an escape for a group of them. Reluctantly, her husband went along with her plans. A Russian doctor promised that a peasant would pick them up in a designated place in the forest and lead them to the Soviet partisans.

> On the outside, we waited for the peasant . . . He did not show up. It was getting dark. We did not want to go back and went on foot to the Andrejewskie Forest. We knew the way. There were seven of us, two women and five men. These were young people who worked in the hos-

pital. We searched the forest but found no one. Then we saw two men approach on bicycles . . . I was in the habit of running fast. So I ran away. When we heard no noises, we returned . . . These Belorussian partisans were local and they knew my husband. They belonged to the Chapajev brigade, a Soviet fighting partisan unit. They were ready to take me and my husband to Chapajev but first had to make sure that we would be accepted. The rest of the people they advised to go to a registration center set up by the partisans in the forest. For one night they took me and my husband to a hut, close to the forest. Next morning they returned and led us to the Chapajev group.

Initiated by young, married, enterprising women, some of these escapes relied on other ghetto inmates or involved the help of Christians. This cooperation improved the chances of success. The nature of these cooperative efforts varied, and occasionally a planned flight never took place because of unanticipated circumstances.

Chava Grinberg-Brown, about whom I spoke earlier concerning her mother's eating habits, received hardly any support in her escape plans.[22] In 1941, when she was eleven, Chava told her mother that she wanted to run away from the Warsaw ghetto. Mrs. Grinberg asked her to take her younger brother or sister with her.

Chava refused.

With a child to take care of, I would not make it either. "Look," I said, "my stomach is swollen from hunger, I am about to die, too. I cannot lose much. I must run away." So my poor mother took the last pillow, she sold it and she gave me a few zlotys . . . It was very hard . . . I could never talk about it . . . [*She cries.*] . . . As I was leaving I told her that maybe we will meet. To this she said, "A mountain does not meet with another mountain but a forest meets with a forest. If we survive the war we will meet."

The departure is engraved on Chava's memory.

My mother cried terribly. They were accompanying me, and she spoke about my birthmark. "This is your sign that you belong to us. If we meet later, show it." . . . The will to live was so strong. I loved my family, but my life I was not willing to sacrifice for them. I was very independent. I refused to give in, to die. I heard about all kinds of people who were running away, and I was determined to live. I was not afraid. I did not dwell on the difficulties.

Chava never saw her family again. She does not remember how she felt at the time; after she left she was preoccupied with the move beyond the ghetto:

I heard that one can pass through the wall at one particular place. One boy said that he was smuggling children out for money. I showed him the money I had. I told him that I would give him only a part because I would need money to go by train or to buy food. He took it and brought me to a special place where people went out to work. He only showed me the way. I got through once but a policeman sent me back into the ghetto. I was not discouraged. I went a second time and was not caught.

When I came out I saw a coffee shop and young smugglers were sitting there. One of them said, pointing at me, "Look, this is a Jewish girl. She will survive, she is not afraid, what guts she has to leave in the middle of the day!" This gave me a good feeling. Then I asked for directions to Żyrardów.

Chava headed for the world that was familiar to her, the place of her birth. Occasionally she would meet a peasant with a horse-drawn wagon who agreed to give her a lift.

Chava's prearranged exit was unusual because it was initiated by someone so young. The illegal ghetto departures of young teenagers were usually arranged by parents and involved close parent-child cooperation. Such undertakings were unpredictable. Even though most parents were eager to save their children, the young who were to benefit from these efforts sometimes would not cooperate: family attachments and loyalty worked both ways. We have already seen that some parents and children found it hard, even impossible, to part.

For a variety of reasons a number of Jewish families had lost their male heads. When this happened, the widows would usually encourage their children to save themselves. Eva Kracowski had such a mother, as did Ania Rud. Ania was not yet twenty when the Germans occupied Grodno, a town in western Belorussia. Several days after the German takeover her father suffered a heart attack and died. Shortly afterward, the Rud family, consisting of her mother, herself, and her sister, moved to the Grodno ghetto. The usual hardships began. Ania and her sister were forced to clean houses outside the ghetto, work that, ironically, gave them a chance to exchange some of their belongings for food. But they remained hungry. Ania watched her mother struggle against the food shortages. Even facing these deprivations, however, Ania's mother shared with those she saw as less fortunate. Like most of the others I interviewed, Ania could not remember seeing her mother eat her share. When I raised the question, she ventured a guess that her mother probably used to give away some of her food.

Before the war Ania had been active in a leftist youth organization. In the ghetto this group formed an underground in cooperation with others. Through special couriers they established contact with outside resistance groups, both Jewish and non-Jewish. Couriers from other ghettos would come to Grodno. Most of them advised the young people to transfer to Białystok, where conditions seemed to be better and the underground was better organized. Ania explains the situation:

> Only at the very end of 1942, when we read and heard the news, did we realize that the Russians would not come back soon. That's when we really decided that we ought to run away. At first we had contact with the Jews from Białystok. Some people escaped from Grodno to Białystok. They felt that it might be safer there. I was twenty-one at the time.
>
> Mother wanted us to go, but my sister refused. She would not leave Mother. My mother was forty-five years old and didn't think that she was capable of escaping. Mother thought that she would be a burden to us if she did . . . that she would slow us down and make it harder. But she begged me and my sister to go. She wanted us to live.[23]

Ania's friends all left. Among them was her commonlaw husband, Grisha Czapnik. But Ania hesitated. It was hard for her to leave her mother and sister. From Białystok, Grisha and others sent messages urging her to come. The underground supplied her with papers that identified her as a Belorussian Christian, and one of her non-Jewish friends offered to help. Ania's mother continued to pressure her to leave. Ania finally left in the winter of 1942.

This Polish friend of mine, Janina Picz . . . went with me on the train when I left Grodno for Białystok, because my mother insisted she had to know what happened to me. Janina came with me, but we were not sitting together on the train . . . She saw that I arrived safely and told my mother about it. My sister continued to stay with our mother.

Did Ania say good-bye to her mother?

I didn't, because I couldn't. She wanted me to go [*Ania cries.*] . . . I was a very active person, sort of the sporty type. I was in different sport groups before the war. I could not just sit around.

Shortly after Ania left, the Grodno ghetto was liquidated. Not a trace remained of Ania's mother and sister. As a member of the Białystok underground, Ania became a courier and eventually established a permanent residence on the Aryan side. She is convinced that were it not for her mother's love and insistence that she leave she would have shared her family's fate.

Family ties to more distant relatives also acted as powerful catalysts for ghetto escapes. In the city of Lvov tragedy hit thirteen-year-old Lusia Grosman and her sixteen-year-old brother Asher, even before the German takeover, when the Soviet authorities sent their father, Natan, to Siberia. Communication between Natan and his family stopped after a single letter. Next their mother, Dora, was killed during a bombardment just before the Germans entered the city. Lusia and Asher were not told about her death. "Mother left" was all the information they got. The children would search for their mother, walking the streets of the now-occupied city. Their grandmother and two aunts, Sala and Clara, looked after them. Soon the family was forced into the Lvov ghetto.

Lusia recalls,

We would get one loaf of bread for five people. The bread was heavy, as if made out of glue. My grandmother would hide the bread for the next day. She divided it fairly. I was so hungry that occasionally I would steal a little slice of bread. I still feel guilty about it. Also, once my Aunt Sala made pancakes from potato peels. She gave them to me and asked me to go into the street to sell them. I don't remember whether I ate them all up or sold them. It was just horrible.[24]

Asher worked as an unskilled laborer at the train station. The job gave him documents that entitled the family to stay in the ghetto. One day Asher returned home in a deplorable state, hardly able to move, and took to his bed. He had received twenty-five lashes because he and the other Jewish laborers had been accused of stealing lunches from the Polish co-workers. Within days he was dead, at the age of seventeen. Lusia was devastated by this loss. She could not even attend the funeral. She was in a daze. Her memory left her; she doesn't know for how long.

Lusia picks up the story.

I know that one of our neighbors remembered that my aunt Andzia was married, well-to-do, and childless. Somebody wrote to her about us. My aunt lived in Stryj, where it was still not so bad. One day, this aunt and her husband, Leon Fiskal, sent a Polish woman to bring me to them . . . My aunt did everything for me. She dressed me, she fed me, she engaged a private teacher for me, she couldn't do enough . . . She was in charge of a kitchen for the poor that was established by a Jewish man. Eventually, the authorities took away my aunt's job — threw her out of the house, and me with her. We had to go to the ghetto, but my aunt had a friend, Jurko Dun, who was Ukrainian and was recognized by Yad Vashem as a Righteous Among the Nations. He was a neighbor of my aunt's and he would do anything for her.

Determined to save her niece, the aunt spoke to Lusia about settling on the Aryan side. But Lusia disapproved of the plan.

I said that I would not go because I didn't want to leave her. When she showed me the false papers, I ran away. They found me and almost by force dressed me to look like a Christian girl, and a man came to take me away.

I got papers based on someone else, who was alive, but older. I was born in 1925. She was supposed to go on a transport to Germany as a slave laborer, so they probably arranged it with the authorities, and they put me on this transport with her name.

My uncle Leon took me to the train station and everything had been taken care of. They sent me on this transport to Germany. My first name was Sława, [so] I became Sława Sikora. My uncle's last words were, "When you arrive, write to Jurko Dun, the Ukrainian, 11 Krzywa Street. Write and say that you have arrived."

Though hesitant and afraid, she lived in Germany as a Polish Christian until the end of the war.

Lusia moved from tragic circumstances to a protective, loving family. Her aunt's care and her uncle's help saved Lusia's life. Even though Lusia mainly discussed her aunt, the narrative leaves no doubt that her uncle was also protective and giving. In the end, their combined efforts paid off. Lusia survived the war; the rest of her family was murdered, including her aunt and uncle.

But a prearranged, successful escape did not necessarily lead to a prolonged stay in the Christian world. Often special circumstances would push the escapee back into the ghetto. Sometimes those who had safely reached the Christian world would turn back for various reasons and were later pushed down the Nazi-designed road toward death.

Miriam Akavia was one such case. Miriam came from a warm, well-to-do family in Kraków. Her family suffered the usual heavy financial losses, which were made worse by extortion and her father's public beatings. Miriam explains the effect of these humiliations on her parents:

My father was an independent man who made all the decisions. He was at ease with himself. But at the start of the war he broke down . . . This is when my mother took hold of things. She took control. He was a broken man — he who had been so decisive could not do it any more . . . My mother was wonderful. As a rule, before the war she was pampered and lived in luxury. She was often weak and sick . . . Then she got the strength to assert herself and did whatever was necessary . . . Still, we had many, many problems . . . felt very powerless.[25]

After the family moved to the Kraków ghetto things got worse. Close relatives left several small children with them, who both gave them comfort and added to their burdens. With dwindling physical and emotional resources, Miriam's father "had no more strength":

He even suggested that we should all commit suicide. My mother would not allow it. She said, "We have our children, and children of other people—we cannot do it. We are obligated to wait until the last minute." . . .

I looked like a Christian and so did my brother, who was tall and blond, with blue eyes. My father got Aryan papers for me and my brother. First my brother went to Lvov. Why there, I don't know, and how he got the papers, I don't know . . . At the end of 1942, there was another Aktion, and we were hidden with the children . . . A few days later, I left the ghetto.

I was bewildered, as in a dream. I didn't know what was happening to me. I went to a certain woman in Kraków and she told me not to worry, that she would take care of things. This woman's husband helped. He took me to the train, and I joined my brother in Lvov.

For brother and sister, life in Lvov meant horrible living quarters, blackmail, near-denunciations, and continuous uncertainty. Then disaster struck. Her brother was caught trying to help a Jewish woman enter the ghetto. Miriam is still haunted by the telephone conversation she had with her father immediately after this happened:

Father started to cry on the phone, and he said, "Come home. Come to Kraków." I felt so horrible . . . I said yes. I wanted to be with them. Whatever would be, I wanted to be with them.

Leaving her belongings behind, Miriam boarded a train. As promised, her father was waiting for her.

When I saw him I realized that he looked worse than before. He took me back to the ghetto. I cared for the small children. I cleaned them from lice . . . But I became hysterical when a letter arrived from my brother. He wrote that he had been caught and taken to prison.

After escaping and searching unsuccessfully for shelter, he had reentered the Lvov ghetto.

The family wanted Miriam to return to Lvov to help him. Miriam refused; she did not think that she would even know how to find him. After the one letter, they never heard from Miriam's brother again. Meanwhile, the family's troubles mounted.

There was a denouncement in the ghetto. They came and searched for my Aryan document and found it. They wanted to know who was its owner. My mother did not tell. So they took my sister instead, and a neighbor girl. My fingerprints were on the document . . . we had to bribe people to release the two girls . . . I felt so guilty that I had left Lvov but my brother hadn't. I felt extremely guilty that my sister had been arrested instead of me. I was so depressed.

Miriam could not face the prospect of returning to the Aryan side. Her family, particularly her energetic mother, wanted her to try again. In the end, Miriam was deported to a series of concentration camps. Of the entire family, only she and her sister survived.

The fate of another young girl, Ruth Hudes-Tartako, resembled Miriam's in some aspects. Ruth began the war with special advantages. Born in Chrubieszów to a close-knit family, Ruth grew up amid affection and care. Immediately after the 1941 German takeover, a Polish teacher, Mr. Szydłowski, paid a visit to the Hudes family. Ruth had been his pupil, and now he was concerned about her well-being. Szydłowski explained that because the Germans had shifted around the student populations, Ruth could safely enter the school as a non-Jew. She could come to live with him and his wife, who were childless. There was even an unspoken inference that they would like to adopt her. The teacher was clearly fond of Ruth, and the Hudes family gratefully accepted his offer.

How did the arrangement look from Ruth's perspective?

The teacher's wife was a cold woman, but treated me correctly. She was polite and all that, but it was difficult to like her. He was a good person. I liked him a lot, and he also liked me very much. Among the subjects he taught was mathematics. Sometimes he would take me to his math classes, and if they didn't know the answers he would say, "This little girl knows." And I knew. He was very proud of me. He arranged for me a birth certificate according to which I was a relative of his . . . I lived with him and his wife, but from time to time I would go to see my parents. The Jewish neighbors did not recognize me because they didn't know me, so it wasn't very dangerous. Each time I visited my family I brought them some of my food. I didn't do it that often. To this teacher, I would bring all kinds of things. I think it was jewelry of some kind. My parents wanted to thank them for keeping me.[26]

Ruth was aware that changes were taking place:

My parents suffered from food shortages. Basic staples were missing. There were Aktions, and the Jewish population was getting smaller and smaller. They were also killing people . . . Father became a different person . . . He hardly talked. He was not conversing; he was saying things, briefly communicating with us. As a child, earlier, I remember when my parents had guests, they talked, they played bridge, I was sent to sleep, but I heard them laughing and joking. Now I did not hear my father talk to anyone or discuss anything. He only told. He said, "Go there, do this, I'm coming," no conversation, just telling.

To Ruth, such behavior indicated "total depression . . . It was as if the people became detached from life. They were living in terrible fear, a fear of hiding and of not exposing themselves."

And the mother? How did she fit into this?

My mother was from a very good home. I always used to laugh that my mother never left the house without a hat. During the war, instead of a hat, she wore a kerchief, which was quite a change. She had a whole collection of hats. From the hats she made for us house slippers, and this was a tremendous change, too. We had no maid at home. I am not sure if she was as depressed as father or not. But there was tension in our home. It was so quiet, so depressing. It was not nice to be at home.

But these transformations did not change Ruth's longing for her family, and she visited them often. On these visits, she was fortunate enough to miss two raids by the Germans. But during the third, last Aktion, Ruth was at home. This time her father brought the news. He asked Ruth to hide with them because the ghetto was surrounded and any attempt to escape would end in disaster.

Ruth remembers the hideout:

> It was somewhere close to their home . . . There was straw in this attic, and we sort of hid under it. Only my father, my mother, my brother, and I. We didn't even take water with us, nothing. We didn't imagine it would take that long . . . I cannot tell you how many days it took, but I know that it was horrible. My mother tried to wet my brother's lips with his urine. He was so dried out . . . I wanted so much to get out of there, but my father was afraid for me. Outside, was a deathly silence.
>
> Then one morning we heard over the loudspeakers that the Jews who were hidden should get out of their hideouts . . . The Jews would be moved to better communities. So my mother told me, "Go to the house; there is a package there; take this package and run away to your teacher."

Ruth went. On the outside she saw a man with a horse, a pail of water next to them. She went down on her knees to drink. Then she turned in the direction of their home. On the steps she met her father, who must have left the hideout shortly after she did. He told her that this was the end. Sadly, regretfully, her father apologized for not having any money.

What stands out in her mind? "The last words he spoke were, 'Save yourself.' He gave me my mother's ring and a package." She never saw her father again, or any of the rest of her family.

Ruth returned to her teacher's home, but circumstances had changed. It was now too dangerous to go to school. She had to stay hidden in a specially camouflaged space behind a movable wardrobe. One day Ruth realized from her hosts' conversation that a handful of Jews still remained in a camp on Jadkowa Street. She could not stop thinking about them. Once, when the teacher and his wife were out, she went to find the camp. There Ruth met some of her parents' friends and an aunt. This was 1943, when the German army was already retreating. The camp inmates urged Ruth to join them. The war, they told her, would soon be over, and if she stayed with them she could remain a Jew. But if she continued living in a Christian environment, she might become Christian.

Ruth remembers,

> When I came back to the teacher's house, they were extremely angry with me. The wife was so furious she shook with fury, and said, "Once more, if you leave the threshold of this place, do not come back again." Now I know that she was right. But as a child, I didn't understand. Who knows—maybe I got offended? . . . The teacher was also angry with me. He explained that this was very dangerous. They were right.

In the end, Ruth left, never to return. Much later, she heard that the teacher and his wife had moved away.

The camp inmates probably made Ruth feel connected to her family, and this seemed more important to her than escape. She was glad that she had made the move—but not for long. It turned out that the prisoners had been brought there for a specific purpose: to sort out the belongings left by ghetto inmates. Once this job was finished, they were scattered to a number of concentration camps. Ruth herself was sent from camp to camp.

For Ruth the longing for the familiar and for family attachments had undermined what her parents and the Christian rescuers had so carefully constructed.[27] More important, for both Miriam and Ruth, circumstances mainly beyond their control prevented their escape, despite parental efforts to save them. Like other teenage daughters and sons, these girls were nurturing and giving.

Mutual family support of various kinds was often triggered by changing needs. These needs were sometimes urgent and real, sometimes illusory, based on misunderstanding of the circumstances. In ghettos surrounded by forests the inmates tended to think about large-scale escapes. Some ingeniously organized breakouts did take place, including the mass escape from the Nowogródek ghetto. Here the ghetto underground first explored a number of flight options. After several trials they decided to build a tunnel big enough to move the entire ghetto population of about 250 inmates. Without engineers but with great determination, after months of hard, secret work and many close calls, they finished the tunnel, which extended for more than two hundred meters. It came out of a ghetto barrack and ended close to the forest.

Before departure the organizers asked the inmates to supply the names of those with whom they wanted to leave. On the basis of these preferences, the inmates were told to arrive at the tunnel opening at specified times. Many escapees were impressed not only with the organization of the break-out but also with the warm, caring attitude of those in charge. As the Jews left the tunnel some held hands and some tied themselves to each other. Everyone followed the orders quietly.

The total exodus took more than two hours. At the end, something went wrong, and a fire broke out at the mouth of the tunnel inside the ghetto. Guards spotted the fire and called out for help. When no one appeared, they guessed that the place was empty and started to shoot haphazardly. But by then everyone who had planned to escape through the tunnel had left. As the fugitives came out of the lighted tunnel into the night, some lost their way; others began to move in circles. The chase and the shooting continued. It is estimated that 100 to 150 escapees survived. In the Nowogródek break-out and other similar large-scale ghetto flights men were in charge rather than women.[28]

German anti-Jewish policies shared the basic goal of the biological de-struction of a people. Measures for meeting this goal were applied at differ-ent times to different places with different degrees of ruthlessness. These differences occasionally slowed up the Nazi death machinery. Jewish de-struction came later to western European countries than to the East, and at first the methods varied slightly. In western Europe there were no Nazi-designed ghettos. Instead, Jews were confined to special houses and transit camps. Only later were these Jews transferred to Eastern ghettos and con-centration camps. By looking at how West European Jewish women and men responded to the various policies we can better understand the re-sponses of the Jewish women and men in Eastern Europe. The similarities and differences between East and West European Jews will help us assess the part gender played in these coping strategies.

Although Germany had instituted anti-Jewish measures before the war, the Germans first implemented their policy of total annihilation in the East, in the occupied countries. Jewish fugitives from the East who managed to reach the West spoke about the German atrocities, and some West European Jews listened. But not everyone absorbed what these fugitives were trying to tell them. Because the Ackermans, a young couple in Belgium, had relatives in Poland, they were probably more sensitive to the implications of what they had heard than those who had no personal connections to the East. They took the news seriously. From the beginning of the German occupation, Mr. Ackerman distrusted all requests for Jews to register with the Nazi-appointed Jewish councils. Similarly, he avoided wearing the yellow star and fought the flood of economic restrictions. As a Romanian citizen, Mr. Ackerman was exempt from some of the new orders. Nonetheless, anticipating more serious oppression, he, his wife, and their two-year-old son moved to the provinces.[29]

A Belgian policeman who was a casual friend rented an apartment for them, and the Ackermans moved in under assumed names. The policeman sent his teenaged daughter to stay with them, to be a link between the Ackermans and the outside community. She took care of the family's errands so that they wouldn't be exposed to inquisitive eyes. The mere presence in the household of someone who looked so much like a Gentile and who was clearly at ease at the local church added legitimacy to the household. It helped Mr. Ackerman, an engineer, to pass for a Christian and find employment. He was able to support his family. He also joined the Belgian resistance movement, something his wife, Amiora, discovered only after the war. But the Ackermans were an exception. They had escaped early and thus avoided exposure to anti-Jewish persecutions.

When talking about her husband, Amiora Ackerman emphasized that throughout the war he was in charge of the family affairs. He had no bouts of depression, nor did he lapse into inaction. Unlike most married Jewish men in eastern Europe, Mr. Ackerman was able to discharge his family duties, providing financial support and protection for his wife and child. With no serious disruptions in his life, he continued to behave in his accustomed ways.

The fate of another Belgian Jewish family took a slightly different turn. When the Germans attacked Belgium, many Jews fled the country, often to France. Some of them had to return, but others stayed on. The Einhorns came to Paris with a group of Belgian refugees. But the French authorities ordered the refugees to leave the capital. The Einhorns were sent to the mountains, in an undeveloped part of the country in the Free Zone administered by the Vichy government, which quickly began collaborating with the Germans. The place was a transit camp for Jewish and Christian refugees.

Mr. Einhorn disliked the accommodations and rented a two-room apartment. Shulamit, his teenaged daughter, talks about those experiences:

There were all kinds of berries and stuff. The whole family would go into the forest and collect them and my mother would cook wonderful things. We were getting some money from my father's brothers in America and other sources, but I did not bother to find out. We had food and ate well. My mother was a very busy person, very energetic and brave; she was never down. Wherever she was, she found some things to do and did them.[30]

Soon the Jews were separated from the rest of the refugees and sent to another transit camp, Agde.

This was a transit camp for Jews only. We didn't know what it meant. We heard that from there they were sending people to work in Germany. We did not know about concentration camps. When the policemen came to take us to Agde, my mother had all the wash hanging. She told them that she wasn't going without the wash.

My father and my brother had already left. Mother and the rest of the children were supposed to join them, but she was lying on the floor and said, "You can't take me." We children were very embarrassed because she was making such a scene. We begged her to get up. So finally she did, and we went on a truck and we took all the stuff. They brought us to Agde, a place surrounded by sand.

In Poland, such an incident would have ended differently, probably with the death of one or more people. But although Agde was the first stop on the trip to East European concentration camps, it was practically unguarded. In fact, a relative of the Einhorns came to visit them there. Displeased with what he saw, he was even able to arrange their transfer to a small community close to Montpellier, where their life changed.

In this new place my father conducted some business. We lived about twenty minutes from Montpellier. It was very primitive. My mother was always busy cooking—you couldn't come to her house without being served food. You had to eat. There were many Jews around; they would come to visit. People knew that we were Jewish; this was not a problem.

Then there was an order that the Jews were supposed to go to a camp. But my mother got a letter from a doctor saying that she was pregnant so we didn't have to go. My father pretended to be sick and registered himself in the hospital. We children were again embarrassed that he pretended to be sick. For us, father rented a room in the hospital. We stayed there temporarily. OSE [Oeuvre de Secours aux Enfants; the Children's Aid Society] brought us food and fed us.[31]

After they left the hospital, the family resettled in Grenoble. Here Shulamit and her sister joined the Jewish resistance. Shulamit's work involved the manufacture, smuggling, and distribution of illegal documents. Her sister worked as a guide, bringing Jewish children across the border into Switzerland.

One day when the Einhorns were out, several SS men came to pick them up. This near-miss had a terrible effect on Shulamit's father. He became depressed. The family had to change living quarters and endured a succession of close calls. Shulamit watched her father's depression grow with each change. In contrast, her mother seemed to be full of spirit. Eventually, as a concession to her distraught husband and her younger children, whom she wanted to save, Shulamit's mother agreed to leave for Switzerland. Shulamit and her sister remained behind. Like most teenaged children in eastern Europe, Shulamit insists that her father was much more affected by the growing persecution than her mother.

Different in terms of specifics, in many ways the fate of the sisters Edith and Rose Margolis points to similar changes and consequences of Nazi anti-Jewish policies. Born in Poland, the sisters were in France when war broke out. Rose had gone to Paris to study, and Edith had followed in 1939 to get an ear operation from a French specialist. After the war, separated from their parents, who had returned to Poland, the sisters moved to the south of France. Because they were Jewish they were ordered into the small community of Bollene, whose population eventually grew from about six thousand inhabitants to about ten thousand. Most of the newcomers were Jewish refugees, and the locals, even some of the French gendarmes, were friendly toward them.

One day two of the gendarmes paid a social visit to the house where the Margolis sisters lived along with a number of other refugees. After several drinks, the guests departed, but they came back at 2:30 the next morning. This time, they had orders to pick up the Jews. The Christian landlady, realizing what this visit meant, pushed two young women into a nearby closet but didn't have time to hide the rest. Still visible were a Mrs. Safir, her sixteen-year-old son, and Edith Margolis. As soon as Mrs. Safir saw the gendarmes, she collapsed on the floor, screaming, as if in pain, calling out in Yiddish. To protect herself Edith showed the gendarmes a letter describing her recent appendix operation.

Edith tells what happened then.

> Mrs. Safir was screaming so much that the gendarmes didn't know what to do . . . They decided to get a doctor . . . In fact, they called for a doctor. In walked a lady doctor. She looked at my paper and said, "You cannot touch her; she has just had surgery." And pointing to Mrs. Safir, she said, "And this woman must go to the hospital. Both must go to the hospital." Little did they know that this doctor was a Jewess working for the underground . . . Her name was Dr. Bache.[32]

The gendarmes brought the two women to the hospital. Everyone else remained in the house, presumably only for the night. The next morning, a local peasant who had heard about the raid offered to find other quarters for the remaining Jews and for those who would be leaving the hospital.

Later on, owing to an unusual set of circumstances, Edith and Rose Margolis, together with Mrs. Safir's husband, were transferred to a transit camp. Here Edith and Rose became aware of marked differences in the reactions of women and men. They felt that the women adjusted better to the camp. They believe that this was due to the women's nurturing skills and their special strength to endure misfortune. But they were cautious about their initial observations:

> This does not mean that men are indifferent to others. Only that women have the responsibility of caring for others. Actually, the male 'macho' attitudes do not mean much. Men break down more easily. When they cannot be in control, they give up.

While the sisters concurred in these ideas, each was hesitant about them. They tried to explain:

> We had each other in the camp. We had first the responsibility to take care of each other. When we were with Mr. Safir, people thought that we were his daughters. We took care of him. He was sick, he could not walk, he could not eat, he broke down completely. He was not any more the family man who had earned money as he did when he was on the outside. In the camp he simply could not go on . . .
>
> Both of us somehow adapted to the camp, but he could not. We had the strength to go on. We had each other, and we still hoped. But once he was taken to the camp, he was a broken man, maybe because he was older, and he was smarter and knew what was coming and we didn't. In a way, he fell from the top to the bottom and thought that there was no hope.

Mr. Safir seemed to have given up on life. He ended up in Auschwitz and never came back.

What happened to the Margolis sisters and Mr. Safir supports my findings about eastern Jewish women and men. When the men lost their freedom and with it their ability to discharge their duties as providers and protectors of the family, they lost their spirit, became depressed and apathetic. Women's roles changed as well but because these changes placed a higher value on their traditional roles of caring for and helping others, they were not as adversely affected.

The fate of the Prowizur family similarly resembles that of the Jewish women and men in the East. When Belgium was attacked, the Prowizurs were too poor to leave. Claire, the oldest daughter, had just been married, to a Phillip Szyper, and both were active members of the Trotskyite underground.

In 1942, when the occupational forces stepped up their anti-Jewish assaults, Claire's nineteen-year-old sister Edith received official notification that she had to register for work in Germany. The letter stated that failure to show up would lead to serious repercussions for her and the rest of her family. If Edith refused to register, the entire family would have had to change its living quarters. The family was willing to move. Claire and Phillip felt that Edith's official notice contained a serious threat.

In part Edith wanted to leave because her boyfriend was also ordered to Germany, and she wanted to be with him. Neither pleas nor warnings had any effect, and she left with her boyfriend. Everyone who complied with the order ended up in Auschwitz. Almost none of them survived. Edith Prowizur was one of the victims.

Meanwhile, Edith's parents went into hiding, and two of their sons crossed into Switzerland. One day, when he was taking a walk, Mr. Prowizur discovered that he had been denounced; he was arrested, and sent to the transit camp Melines. Claire and her husband were also picked up by the Gestapo. The three were reunited in Melines, from which they were scheduled to be deported to Auschwitz.

A day before the transfer, Mr. Prowizur became ill with high fever. With Claire and her husband accompanying him, the semi-conscious man was loaded onto one of the waiting cattle cars. As the train headed East, people managed to cut open the window bars and began jumping from the moving train. But Mr. Prowizur was still semi-conscious, and Claire refused to leave her father. Her husband did not want to desert her and also stayed.

Sitting next to her father, Claire dozed off. She describes what happened next:

> I had a dream in which my mother said to me, "I gave you life; I want you to save yourself." Of course, I saw what I wanted to see . . . I opened

my eyes, and said, "Phillip, I want to jump right now." And I jumped
and he came right after me. If I had thought about it, I might not have
done it. We were both very fortunate, did not break any bones, and the
bullets did not get us. Walking, we saw one person lying there dead.

From this camp there were twenty-seven transports; ours was number
twenty. After Number twenty, it was impossible to jump. They went during the day, not at night. Jumping during the day was more risky.[33]

For the rest of the war, Claire and Phillip continued their underground activities in Belgian provinces. Along with Mrs. Prowizur, they survived the war.

But Claire blamed herself for abandoning her father. She was sensitive
to any mention of the train jump. Her feelings of guilt lingered for more than
twenty years. Then, by chance, she met a woman who had shared their cattle
car. This woman told Claire that after she had jumped, her father opened his
eyes and whispered, "I'm the happiest man because my daughter left and is
free." By the time the train reached Auschwitz, Mr. Prowizur was dead.

Claire escaped because she imagined that her mother had urged her to.
Her case resembles that of other Jewish children of various ages, who relied
strongly on mothers' guidance. Often that guidance was symbolic or imagined, but still it had the power of pushing them toward the "right" move,
toward life. Such maternal influences continued to affect the children in a
variety of settings, in unexpected ways. Discussions about these symbolic,
often mystical effects will reappear again.

Findings from both western and eastern Europe show that just as Jewish women had stepped in and substituted for their men in traditionally
male roles, so they later became involved in efforts to escape. Especially when
there was no longer a father present, mothers would insist that their children
save themselves. Sometimes the children only imagined that their mothers
had urged them to escape. Real or not, the conviction that a mother had ordered them to fight for life, was a powerful incentive for children to take
steps toward safety. Mothers' urgings also helped their children endure the
pain of separations.

The stories of western European Jews serve to validate the findings
from the evidence of the eastern European Jews. From these findings it is

clear that the most common way Jews moved from one phase of the Nazi process of Jewish destruction to the next was through official channels. They also show that both men and women were active in promoting illegal departures. When the men were apathetic or absent, women were more likely to push. It appears that prearranged illegal departures, particularly of children and small groups of family and friends, more often relied on women. Men were more likely to be charged with collective, large-scale illegal escapes. Regardless of their sex, the young were more receptive to risk taking and probably more ready to make escapes.

The trains destined for East European concentration camps were efficient. No matter where they originated, they were able to deliver most of their human cargo. Few escaped by jumping. The next, crucial phase of Jewish destruction was played out in the thousands of Nazi concentration and death camps.

The Concentration Camps

In 1944 a freight train with a cargo of Hungarian Jews arrived at Auschwitz in the middle of the night. None of the passengers knew where they were or why they had stopped. Some hoped that, as promised, they had come to a work camp. Cramped into a tiny corner of one of the cattle cars were a seventeen-year-old girl named Rita, her older sister, and her sister's two children: a boy of five and a girl of ten. Rita's sister was convinced that a woman of twenty would be considered of greater economic value to the Germans than a seventeen-year-old girl. Now, guessing that they had reached their destination, she whispered to Rita, "You must tell them that you are twenty, you must!" Rita promised by squeezing the sister's hand. As yet, there was no need to speak. The train stood still. As if afraid to arouse the evil spirits, most of the passengers were silent. Here and there a few communicated in short, muted murmurs.

After what seemed like an endless wait, the doors were flung open without any warning. Outside Rita saw strange-looking men in striped pajamas, moving rapidly up and down the train, screaming, "Schnell, Schnell" (quickly, quickly). Soon Rita and her family were part of a pushing crowd, and Rita heard her sister reminding her to stay close, to hold on to the boy, to remember that she was twenty.

She recalls:

The four of us were shoved to the left. I was glad that we "passed" the inspection. I see one of those striped pajama men take an infant from the arms of a young mother. He gives it to an old woman. The mother is running because she wants the baby back, but she is hit and prevented from getting it. She keeps going back. An SS man beats her. Dogs try to keep her away . . . Suddenly I feel a hand on my shoulder and hear a voice: "How old are you?" I see those blue, snakelike eyes. I am not able to lie. I say nothing . . . Then, with difficulty, I say "Seventeen." He asks, "So what are you doing here?!" Hands push me to the right. I am separated from my sister, from my nephew. From a distance I see the boy alone among all those people. He screams, "Mama! Mama!" I hope that he found her. That they went together. I meet my sister's eyes from afar. Maybe she was angry with me that I could not lie, that I was not with them? . . . I find myself on the other side and we begin to walk. We come to a place filled with people who look crazy. They have no hair, strange clothes. They make all kinds of gestures toward us, screaming in different languages. Have they collected crazy people here? All are women. They were making signs. If we have clothes we should give them to them . . . We just walk on and on and on.[1]

Another transport of Hungarian Jews reached Auschwitz on a sunny day, right after the male passengers had finished their morning prayers. Here, too, they were first confronted by men in striped pajamas moving rapidly up and down beside the train, shouting, "Heraus, schnell!" (Out, quickly). Jehudith Rubinstein remembers,

My father called me to the side and said, "My child, wherever they take you now, be very careful and listen to me carefully. They will separate the old and the children from the young and the healthy ones. They will send you to work. I am asking you two things: when they call you to work you should be the first one to go, and eat everything they give you,

you will need energy to survive," and he blessed me. And that was the last time I saw him.[2]

Around her, just as her father had predicted, people were being sorted into groups: women with children were one group; women were divided from men; the young were separated from the old. Jehudith remained with her mother and a younger brother. The boy stood between them, holding on to a hand of each. In front of them were four young women with whom they had shared a ghetto apartment. With these four sisters were three little children who belonged to another sister, who had managed to hide out in Budapest. Jehudith recalls,

> The men in the striped pajamas yelled, "Five to each row, five to a row, fast, fast!" I see my mother looking around, maybe trying to take it all in? Then I see her pull these three little children next to her. Now my mother, the three children, and my brother make five. She pushes me toward the four girls who were right in front of us. I become the fifth one in their row. As she does this, Mother says, "I will take care of the little ones, and you take care of Jehudith" . . . So that is how I survived. She took the children, and before I had a chance to turn back, she wasn't there any more. And that "Schnell, schnell" sent us to the left or right — I can't remember . . . to the bath house.

Most of the victims knew little about the concentration camps, and many thought that they had been sent to a labor camp. For all, entrance into the camp was a shock, an entrance into another world, another planet. For these late arrivals, as for the Jews who came before them, the transfer to a concentration camp was the final stage in the chain of destruction. Most Hungarian Jews were sent to Auschwitz. Of those who survived the initial selections some were redistributed into other camps. As the Germans divided them into more distinct groups, some slated for new camps, some for death, families suffered further breakups and losses.

Since 1933 the Nazi concentration camps had functioned as ever-expanding systems of terror and destruction. The number and organization of these camps were continually modified in accordance with the official

Nazi ideology, the external and internal rivalries and alliances, the conduct of the war, and other, emerging economic needs. As systems of terror, oppression, and mass murder, the Nazi camps, often identified by the German word *Lager*,[3] appeared under a multiplicity of guises. Yet for all their diversity they had several common characteristics, and prisoners who passed through a variety of camps report similar experiences. Most prisoner accounts I have studied support Wolfgang Sofsky's conclusion that "a relatively small number of reports from various camps is enough to arrive at a typifying description. Despite all local and temporal differences, there was a high level of standardization of terror."[4] The fact that the Nazi camps shared many common characteristics facilitates the comparative study of life in the concentration camp world.

Initially designed as containment centers for political prisoners, Nazi camps became transformed after the start of the war into places of brutal domination, economic exploitation, and destruction. One of them, Auschwitz, evolved into a place with special features, at the same time resembling all the other camps within the vast Nazi network.

Through the expanding Lager system the Germans sought to achieve several goals. First was the neutralization or elimination of political adversaries. Later some of these places became training grounds for the future Nazi leaders, the SS. Other camps contained "laboratories" in which "scientific" experiments were conducted. In addition, they became a significant source of slave labor: factories were constructed near camps that exploited prisoners, who received no pay and were in no position to make demands. From 1942 on most camps operated as centers for the destruction of the so-called inferior races, mainly Jews. Frequently these goals were pursued in concert, reinforcing one another.

The first prisoners at Auschwitz were members of the Polish male elite. Some were overt political opponents of the Nazi regime, others potential or perceived rebels. But over time the prison populations and camp structure changed, and Auschwitz became "the largest and most lethal of the Nazi death camps . . . It was three camps in one: a killing center, a concentration camp, and a series of slave labor camps." Eventually, about fifty satellite camps clustered around the three main Auschwitz structures: Auschwitz I, Auschwitz II-Birkenau, and Auschwitz III-Monowitz.[5]

Once the political opponents were neutralized, a new kind of power emerged in the camps, one that "shattered all previous conceptions of despotism of dictatorial brutality." All Nazi camps were places of extreme coercion, degradation, economic exploitation, and murder. But now began a systematic destruction by means of violence, starvation, and labor: the businesslike annihilation of human beings. Between 1933 and 1945 the camp system changed from a means "of terror to a universe of horror."[6] Some, such as Treblinka, Sobibór, and Bełżec, were built for the sole purpose of putting Jews to death, although occasionally others who seemed to fit the Nazi definition of the racially "inferior" or otherwise undesirable were also killed there.[7]

By the end of the war the Third Reich had erected and was maintaining more than ten thousand camps. In Poland alone, a country the Germans transformed into a center for human destruction, there were about 5,800.[8] These camps were an extreme example of what sociologists refer to as total institutions: inmates have no direct contact with the outside, and their lives are controlled by specially designated "managers." In such environments, inmates must be resocialized; the greater the discrepancy between the past and present, the more intense must be the resocialization of incoming members. Typically, such resocialization relies on stripping newcomers of their previous identities, through removal or change of clothes, the confiscation of possessions that could remind them of their past, even renaming. Inmates are isolated, humiliated, and mortified through measures designed to make them more likely to submit to the complete control of the managers.[9]

But starting in about 1942 the management policy in the Nazi camps changed from that of other total institutions in one significant respect: now mainly Jewish inmates were brought in primarily to be killed, not to be controlled or used for economic advantage. From the middle of 1942, the vast majority (an estimated 90 percent) of Jewish arrivals to most of the camps — not just the designated death camps — were murdered upon entry. Most were not even registered. Those who were not immediately killed were forced into a horrendous existence in which practically all perished. Even in the work camps, the aim was to murder inmates more gradually, through work. Jewish annihilation took precedence over economic demands, a policy that gradually deprived the SS of millions of Jewish slave laborers.[10]

The concentration camps, then, were the last stage in the process of annihilation that had begun in the ghettos and transit camps. Here, Jews from the East were joined by Jews from the West, coming from the various occupied European countries. Of those few Jews who passed the initial selections some were transferred into a number of camps, perhaps as many as eight. But for all the camps were the ultimate destination, the place in which the only distinction made between inmates was whether they were Jews or not. Regardless of their country of origin, the Jews were all treated the same way.

This treatment resembled that found in other kinds of total institutions, with one significant difference. As in other total institutions prisoners were humiliated and degraded, but in the Nazi camps the degradation was as much an aim in itself as a tool of control. In pursuit of the Final Solution, the Germans excelled in inventing diabolical tortures, varying only in degree of subtlety. These policies were propelled by the idea that "the 'enemy' must not only die, he must die in torment." To degrade the Jews before killing them was an important Nazi objective, close to the main goal of biological elimination, and SS and other camp personnel were rewarded for inventing practices that dehumanized Jews.[11]

Jewish arrivals who were admitted into a camp faced abuses in every aspect of their existence. Although all concentration camp prisoners experienced some form of humiliation and dehumanization, Jewish prisoners (and Gypsies)[12] were singled out within the Lager universe. Jews faced the most vigorous, systematic assaults against their dignity and their lives. Some of these forms of debasement were created by official or unofficial orders, others evolved spontaneously within a particular camp. These many and varied measures of debasement defy classification, but they were designed to engender devastating feelings of degradation.

The humiliations began from the minute the Jews arrived. Upon entering the camp Jews had to undress in public and leave all their personal belongings behind. In many camps, the arms of the incoming prisoners were tattooed with a number. With the exception of some of the work camps, this was followed by the forceful removal of body hair from men and women both. Fourteen-year-old Zahava Ziskowicz-Adam, who had been separated from her parents during the liquidation of the Vilna ghetto, was sent with her sister to Kaiserwald concentration camp in Riga.

After the customary shoving, pushing, and screaming that accompanied all arrivals at the camps, Zahava recalls,

> They led us to the showers and shaved our hair. The shaving itself was an ordeal . . . When it was over, I did not want to look at anyone. What my sister thought, I don't know. We were only embracing each other. We did not talk. No words could tell what we felt . . . But we were not given time to mourn, to cry. We had to move on . . . As we were approaching what turned out to be our barrack, we saw a group of women leaving it. They were unreal . . . Dressed in black, they seemed like out of some fairy tale. Why they wore black I don't know.

Later she learned that these women had been sent to the crematorium; her group was taking their place in the barrack.[13]

The reaction of a woman to having her head shaved transcends national boundaries. All the inmates were deeply shamed by this procedure. When their hair grew out, they would be shaved again, and again, although the later hair losses were no longer as traumatic. There were exceptions: Jewish women who worked in the munitions factory were exempt. And six months before Auschwitz stopped operating as a camp, the haircuts were discontinued. But all knew that the rationalization that hair removal was dictated by hygienic considerations did not hold: except as a punitive measure, non-Jewish women did not have their heads shaved.[14]

All the male camp prisoners were forcefully shaved, Jew and non-Jew alike. But for the men the loss of hair did not seem to be as traumatic. Some of my male respondents did not even bother to mention it. Others, when questioned about the shaving, shrugged indifferently. A few hastened to add that the forced haircuts were just one of the many dehumanizing measures aimed at torturing the prisoners. But even these negative comments seemed devoid of affect. In contrast, for the women the loss of hair was a highly emotional, humiliating experience. The experiences of public nudity and head-shaving were closely tied to their feelings of femininity and sexual identification and were felt as a blow to both.[15]

Additional Nazi efforts to debase were expressed in the physical accommodations allotted to the prisoners. It is clear from the Auschwitz architectural plans that prisoners were crammed into confined quarters with inadequate washing facilities and latrines. Compared to the spaces allotted to guards, those assigned to inmates underscore the systematic, deliberate efforts to dehumanize and debase. The records also consistently show that prisoners were exposed to filth and a range of other dehumanizing elements. Although the inmates lived in dirty surroundings, they themselves were expected to be clean. It is significant, too, that the prisoners' access to toilets was not only rigidly controlled but often nonexistent. The day after Ester Margolis-Joffee was brought to Auschwitz II-Birkenau, she was assigned to Lager A, Block 15, where she and the women in her block were not allowed to use any of the toilet facilities. Instead, the women received bowls for drinking water, which they used as toilets.[16]

Official policy in all camps decreed the separation of sexes, which effectively ensured that the family as a unit ceased to exist. The Germans did not explain the reason for this rule, although an obvious practical explanation might have been to prevent pregnancies. Scholar Claudia Koonz notes that this rule also "eroded emotional bonds, leaving individuals bereft in a horrifying world." The forced division of the sexes thus served as yet another means to dehumanize the inmates.[17]

When I asked former concentration camp inmates about the effect of the separation of the sexes, most would hesitate, then explain that the separation itself interfered with valid assessments of those effects. Nevertheless, most concurred that the arrangement was one of many Nazi efforts to debase. Agreeing with this common view, a few added specific, personal interpretations.

Helen Spitzer-Tichauer, better known as Zippi, came to Auschwitz-

Birkenau in 1942, part of a transport of a thousand Jewish Slovakian women, and remained there until 1945. She remembers how shaken and saddened she and other women were by chance encounters with groups of male prisoners. Zippi told me that the mere sight of these men, reduced to a robotlike existence, made her shudder. She mused that her reaction was probably due to the inevitable comparisons she would make between these male prisoners and the Jewish men she had known before the war. All the prewar images of strength, self-assurance, dominance, and pride had disappeared: just looking at these dispirited, exhausted, chronically hungry men caused her pain.[18]

Tonia Rotkopf-Blair, a veteran of the Łódź ghetto and several concentration camps, was also bewildered and upset by the sight of the Jewish male inmates. She muses,

Maybe it was just as well that we women were separated from the men. To see men in their concentration camp state was more hurtful than to miss seeing them. I am talking about it as of that time. Now, we are a little more equal to men. Even though I come from a liberal socialist home, I am a product of my society. I inherited the idea about a woman's place in society. I don't agree with all of it, but I did inherit the basics. It is interesting that one doesn't remember one's own problems so much: hunger, etc. But I do remember the others' hunger and pain much better . . . I don't know what I was then, but I know how I see it now. I see it from afar now. I think that seeing a man so denigrated, so degraded, was more painful than seeing a woman in that state at that time.[19]

Then she adds, "Maybe even now. A man is a man, you know?"

For Zippi, Tonia, and other women, the accepted image of men as strong and independent was far removed from the sight of the helpless and degraded male prisoners they met in the camps. What they saw depressed them. Perhaps seeing this transformation moved them toward a fuller realization that the world they knew was gone. Perhaps, too, in the transformation of these men they saw what they themselves were or might soon become.

Knowing in the abstract that horrible changes have occurred is less hurtful than actually being confronted by reality, and many prisoners avoided face-to-face encounters with members of the opposite sex. One young woman received a message from her fiancé urging her to meet him; he longed to see her once more. The woman refused, explaining that she did not want him to see her in her present state, without hair, her spirit gone, completely unlike her old self. She knew that she would die soon and wanted him to remember her as she had been. The woman perished, her fiancé survived.[20]

In spite of the pain caused by these transformations, the forced separation of the sexes did allow some prisoners to keep up the hope that those they loved were still alive. Indeed, Viktor Frankl, a psychiatrist and himself a concentration camp inmate, refused to entertain the idea that his wife might have died. He thinks that the idea that she was alive helped him survive; he learned about his wife's death only after the war. Alexander Donat during his imprisonment kept the memory of his son and wife alive and was comforted by it. More fortunate than Frankl, Donat was reunited with both of them after the war.[21]

But the officially enforced separation of the sexes did not stop all contacts between men and women. Because such connections were illegal, they tended to occur sporadically. Usually physical encounters were limited to a man or woman seeing the other from a distance, as part of a group. Probably the bulk of the communications took the form of letters, which were also forbidden. If discovered, their writers — and sometimes the people close to them — would be severely punished.[22] Fleeting and rare, contacts with the opposite sex, regardless of their particular form, were highly valued.

Naomi Zeif, a laborer in the munitions factory in Auschwitz, describes her correspondence with a man, a physician, whom she had not met.

> One of the girls in the factory told me that she knew a guy who worked in the bakery who used to live in my hometown. I asked her to give him my regards, and after that he sent me bread and a letter . . . I got from him beautiful letters, but I didn't see him, I never met him. He was trying to keep up my spirits, telling me that one should be strong, not give in, and in a short while everything would be all right, that the war would

be over and we'd all be fine. I kept those letters . . . Even as I was being selected for the death march, I wanted to leave the letters somewhere so that they would survive. I didn't see him in the camp or later . . . He did not make it . . .

I would also answer him. Sometimes I was able to give letters to men who were working not far from us, and they smuggled them to the doctor. He was in Auschwitz, and I was in Birkenau. Others also exchanged letters, especially if they knew someone from home; this someone might try to help them a little, or make contact for them with somebody else.[23]

Despite the severe limitations on such contacts, the hope that they might be possible and concern about their danger, were a constant presence in prisoners' lives. Often the hope of meetings that never happened hovered over the barriers between men and women. When such encounters did occur, they were cherished.

Tola Szwarc-Chudin spent almost three months in Majdanek. During that time from a distance she twice caught a glimpse of one of her brothers. Then, just before Tola was transferred to Auschwitz, she heard that he had been shot. In Auschwitz, as a member of an outside commando (work group), Tola recognized a cousin in a men's work detail and called out his name. When he turned toward her, the guard beat him. After that "encounter," Tola never again saw a man she knew.[24]

Probably the difficulties in making contacts with the opposite sex added to their value. Emphasizing how rare such experiences were, Zahava Ziskowicz-Adam describes some of them:

Behind a wall there were Soviet prisoners of war. I remember when we were in the yard, there was some communication between us. We tried to talk a little. One of the prisoners threw me a book, a Russian book . . . This was quite an event. And I remember telling him, "You are here and you know why. I don't." He fought for a reason. I don't remember how we started talking in the first place. This was not allowed.

Later, in 1944, they put us, together with men on a boat that went to Torun [then part of Germany]. Our situation was horrible. We passed through Stutthof, and from there to Torun and to the factory we had to work in. This was my only other contact with men; there is nothing that stayed in my mind about it.[25]

This last encounter took place within the context of life-threatening circumstances. The fear of death probably blocked any potential pleasure that might have come from such meetings. Nonetheless, on balance, most prisoners valued the rare and fleeting contacts they had with the opposite sex.

I have also asked these former camp prisoners to compare the fates of the Jewish men and women who passed the initial inspection and were admitted into the Lager. I discovered that their answers were both varied and surprisingly consistent. Most of my respondents were cautious, prefacing their answers by saying that because of the enforced separation they had few contacts with the opposite sex. When their stories unfolded it became clear that both women and men perceived the experiences of the two sexes as different, though not always for the same reasons.

Thus, Berta Benau-Hutzler, who came to Auschwitz in 1942 with a group of Slovakian women, responded without hesitation that men had a harder life in the camps than women. When I ask why, she offers:

I don't know why. They worked harder. But of course it depended on the Kapo or the SS. Work at the beginning was impossible. I was lucky; people were good to me. I did not argue. I smiled. I did not complain. People always helped me. The SS and the Kapo were more cruel to men than to women. The men prisoners were also weaker than the women were. There were men who let themselves go . . . more than the women. But of course there were exceptions and differences. For example, the Dutch women who came to Auschwitz had no strength. They let themselves go so quickly. They were not used to this work; somehow they broke down right away. To this day I don't know how I made it. Maybe it was just luck.[26]

Curious, I looked further into the fate of the Dutch inmates. The Dutch historian, Holocaust survivor, and Auschwitz inmate Louis de Jong discussed the high death rate of Dutch Jewish prisoners, both women and men, in his study of the Netherlands during the war. He attributed their collapse to the fact that before their arrival at the camps Dutch Jews had been exposed to less degradation and suffering than East European Jews. For them Auschwitz came as a greater shock than for the Jews coming from the eastern ghettos. The Dutch Jews were completely unprepared for the ferocious life of the camps. De Jong concluded that the Dutch Jews were "victims of their own past."[27]

Zippi, a keen observer of life in Auschwitz-Birkenau, echoed de Jong's conclusion, noting that the Jewish Dutch prisoners, both women and men, were unprepared for the concentration camp world. She then described the similar fate of a transport of French Jews who were sent to Auschwitz via the transit camp Drancy. Zippi observed that the French women prisoners who entered Birkenau appeared strikingly beautiful, elegant, and well-fed. But they, too, deteriorated rapidly. Soon they were all dead. On the other hand, Polish Jews who reached the Lager had experienced a prolonged exposure to the ghetto degradations and to chronic starvation and were more likely to survive than the Jews from the West because they had already experienced some of the deprivations and degradations that they would undergo in the concentration camps.[28]

Sometimes the sudden rather than continual confrontation with horror can be a more effective way to destroy. The greater the discrepancy between the past and present the more efficient were the newly introduced measures of oppression. Thus, the effectiveness of the Nazi terror varied not only with how strongly it was applied but also with whether it came as a sudden onslaught or as part of an escalating series of assaults.

To elaborate I ask Berta who she thinks was more afraid, men or women. Again without hesitation, she replies, "Men." When I probe for her reasons, she becomes less certain:

I don't really know. Superficially, men are strong, but not really. Emotionally, men are not as strong as women. When something happens, men fall apart. They are used to having things go well for them. There is a difference between men and women. I see this among our friends.

When something happens, the men fall apart right away. Women are strong and they stand on their feet . . . but of course there are exceptions.

Berta Benau-Hutzler and Shoshana Kahn might appear to have little in common: Berta came from Slovakia and was sent to Auschwitz; Shoshana, a Latvian, was sent to the Kaiserwald work camp in Riga. Yet their answers about the relative experiences of women and men are similar; like Berta, Shoshana thinks that men had a more difficult time. She explains,

There was a lot of beating of men. I don't think they aroused the sympathy of others; they didn't have as much support as the women; people didn't feel so much pity for them . . . It was easier to survive for a woman than for a man.[29]

Comparing women and men, Bracha Winger-Ghilai first prefaces her answer with "I was not with men, you know," but then offers her observations: "But anyway, I do think that they had less strength than we had. They had no will to live as much as we did. This is what they told me about my brother-in-law, that he lost his will to live."

To my more general question, "For whom was it harder to stay alive, men or women?" the answer comes: "I'm convinced it was much harder for men."

"Why?"

I don't really know why, but I think that the man in general is a boy, a child, much more of a child than a woman. A man needs to be pampered, taken care of. It is evident that more women stayed alive than men. Two of my brothers-in-law died. I think that a man is weaker emotionally than a woman. Not physically, but emotionally. I think that there is information showing that many more women stayed alive than men. You can check it out, but I am sure that this is so. I think that emotional strength is very important, and men are not as strong emotionally.[30]

Hadassa Moldinger, who was transferred to Auschwitz from the Łódź ghetto, echoes Bracha's comments. She, too, starts with the disclaimer that in the camp she had few contacts with men. But she thinks that probably more women survived than men. A long-time Yad Vashem employee, Hadassa correctly assumes that no exact figures are available to back up her assertion. But when asked to compare the plight of women and men, she concurs with the others: women had an easier time than men because "women can stand suffering much more readily than men . . . Men would give up, much more than women."[31]

Gerda Nothmann-Luner, a German Jew, came via Holland to several camps as a skilled laborer in one of the Phillips factories. When asked to compare the fate of women and men, Gerda also warns that her camp contacts with men were practically nonexistent. Then she adds,

> I know that when we passed men on our way out of Birkenau, for example, the men looked even worse than we did. But that was about it . . .
> I think that men needed more food but didn't get more, and I think that maybe men are not as strong as women are under difficult circumstances.[32]

Another veteran of several camps, Dobka Freund-Waldhorn, validates what so many have said: "I think that if we had statistics, we would find that proportionately more women than men survived."

"Why?"

"The will to survive is probably stronger for women than men."

"What do you think gave women a greater likelihood of surviving than men?"

"Men need special conditions for living. A woman is ready to be satisfied with less than a man. A man breaks down when he does not have the conditions he is accustomed to. But a woman is more flexible. A woman is also able to suffer more than a man."[33]

Naomi Zeif concurs: "I think it was much harder for men."

"Why?"

"The Germans were much crueler to the men. I also believe that women are much stronger than men. Maybe they are stronger only emotionally. Women know how to suffer. In a way, the men gave up; they were much more devastated. Their spirits were broken much more than ours."

"Where and how did you notice that?"

"Wherever I saw them, at work or somewhere else, the men were very depressed, down . . . I think it is in the nature of men to give up. I don't know why. This is what I observed. The character of the men was much weaker. Emotionally, a woman is stronger and can stand much more . . . Maybe the men were getting less food. They were probably hungrier, and they needed more food. They were more starved than we were. Their bodies demanded more food than our bodies."[34]

Karla Szajewicz-Frist's comments about female-male differences vacillate. First she says that the fates of men and women depended on the particular circumstances they faced. Sometimes the women's lot was harder. But she adds that women who had passed the initial entry selections had an easier time of it. She explains that her initial hesitation had been motivated by memories of women who came with young children or visibly pregnant women, all of whom were immediately killed. She elaborates: "From the point of view of physical work, men and women were different. After all, for women physically it was not so hard. And I think that women can survive suffering better than men. So it was easier for a woman, because she could take the suffering from hunger. She could take all kinds of emotional problems much more easily, and so forth."

She adds, "I also think that today a woman is much more resilient . . . even today."

I ask, "Is a woman stronger, or is it that she can adjust more easily to difficulties?"

Karla nods, as if approving of this distinction: "I think that she can adjust more easily."[35]

Karla is not the only one who gives a different answer once she begins thinking about the issue. Miriam Rubyn started out by denying differences: "The fate of men and women prisoners was the same, there were no differences among them." Then comes, "But the men were more likely to die. Women somehow could withstand suffering. Men were thinner than women, and they didn't fight as much. I think it was easier for women, and they were able to fight. Men were more depressed; they did not have the same resources that women have."

"Did you have contact with men?"

"Yes, in the camp Geislinger. We worked together with men, but only at work we had contact. Otherwise we were separated. We were divided by barbed wire. Sometimes the men would stand on the other side and throw us a present or something. Some women were so beautiful that the men would fall in love with them across the wires. They would say, 'I love you,' and give gifts to them. But this was only in the work camp, not in Auschwitz."[36]

Some work camps were not as rigid in their separation of the sexes. Skarżysko Kamienna, established in 1942, was a forced-labor camp for Jews, located next to a large munitions factory. The factory consisted of three separate units, A, B and C, with a camp attached to each. Camp C produced underwater mines filled with piric acid, a chemical substance that caused the laborers' skin, hair, and nails to turn a yellowish-red color. All who were unfortunate enough to work in Camp C agree that after a short while they began to resemble phantoms. Workers in Camp C had a life expectancy of approximately three months.[37]

Working conditions in the two other camps, although difficult, were less debilitating. Nonetheless, in all three camps the official food allotment for a prisoner was 200 grams of bread and a half-liter of watery soup twice a day. Epidemics of dysentery, typhus, and other diseases caused by overall weakness raged, killing many of the prisoners. Selections and executions were common. Out of an estimated 30,000 laborers, about 23,000 perished.[38]

Perhaps because the Jewish prisoners in these camps were performing a number of internal administrative functions, the separation of the sexes was less rigidly enforced.[39] But even here Felicja Karay thinks that men were more likely to succumb than women to the overall murderous conditions. Asked why, she explains,

Men had much harder work, and they simply could not survive on the food they got. They were given more strenuous jobs, and received the same amount and kind of food that we had . . . They perished very quickly. For them, maximum survival time there was three months . . . Women could withstand hunger more easily, perhaps their work was not as hard and not so demanding . . . Women are biologically stronger, and they live longer.[40]

Another prisoner at this camp, Ida Buszmicz, also thinks that men had a higher mortality rate. From this she concludes that women were more resilient. She then moves on, describing the horrendous camp circumstances: work that lasted twelve to fourteen hours, constant exposure to poisonous chemicals. People would simply faint and die. There was no medical care. Only the contacts with the Polish laborers from the outside offered a chance for extra food. Once Ida's mother pulled out a few of her gold teeth and sold them to buy food from the Polish workers.

In Skarżysko Kamienna men and women lived in different barracks, but some of them still managed to become lovers. Ida recalls several couples openly having sex in the hallway, without any embarrassment. If a men had contact with the outside world or held an official position that entitled him to special rations, the woman who was his lover would consider herself fortunate. A special song immortalized these relationships. One line, in a loose translation from the Polish, comments, "For soup and for a slice of bread, she gives him this and that."[41]

Karay concludes,

Men were more likely to die than women. This was true for other camps as well. I have some statistics to confirm this, some special German documents. And when you compare the deaths of men and women, two-thirds of the dead were men, and one-third were women. So basically those who died were mostly men. Mostly they died from starvation. It was not so much that the men died from the heavy work, but they died from starvation. A man can withstand heavy work; he is physically strong. But a man cannot survive hunger, and the men got much less help from Poles and from others. If there was a woman receiving things from a Pole, she paid it back with her body. But what could a man do?[42]

Yet another witness from Skarżysko Kamienna who had the misfortune of being placed in Camp C ascribes a different reason to what she too sees as women's greater chance of survival:

I have a feeling that men had it much more difficult than women. This is just my impression, that there were many more *Musulmann* [walking dead] among men than women. I think that a woman could somehow arrange the situation better for herself; she was more resourceful. I think so, anyway . . . Men just couldn't help themselves. It was harder for men. They broke down under the burdens, not necessarily from hunger.[43]

Bela Chazan-Yaari, a Jewish courier in the underground who ended up in Auschwitz as a Polish political prisoner, agrees with what others had assumed, that "it was easier for women."

A woman could approach a German and ask him for something, and he might do it or not. But if it were a man, he would shoot him without a question . . . You see, the Germans would bring women to a horrible state, make Musulmann out of them, but they were less likely to shoot them just like that.[44]

Other prisoners echo these observations. A political prisoner, who was not a Jew, thinks that "compared with the average treatment of male prisoners, the sadistic maltreatment of individual women prisoners did play a *minor* role, but for all that, it existed in an official as well as in an unofficial form."[45]

Aronek Kierszkowski (now Arnold Kerr), a male veteran of several concentration camps, prefaced his comments about the differences between what happened to men and women with: "The camp was a mess." A "mess" meant that there were no options. Nonetheless, he feels that "good-looking women had it easier."

Guards treated such women differently, even if they had nothing to do with them. It was like seeing a piece of art. But with men, you cannot do this. With men, it was a major battle . . . Good-looking women were luckier.[46]

Like several others, Shamay Kizelstein placed the burden of the different experiences on men's greater need for food:

Women did not give up. For them it was both easier and more difficult. The women didn't need so much food as we did. The men needed more. It is not that they worked harder, but they just needed more. I, for instance, I could never leave my bread from one day to the next. I think that women were able to do that.[47]

These independently voiced opinions, offered by both men and women, are surprisingly consistent. A statement from a yet another Hungarian inmate, Rita Weiss-Jamboger, suggests a connecting link between some of the comparisons.

Men would break down much faster . . . I saw this in Stutthof. Most of the inmates were men. They suffered maybe more than we did . . . But the pride of the male . . . that they came to this kind of a situation, this humiliated them. The men were beaten with whips, they were forced to lie on benches, awaiting their punishment, exposing the bottom part of their bodies. We women were not as much abused as they . . . And the men suffered for a number of special reasons. First of all the hunger . . . In their case it was much stronger. Maybe a woman does not have such a terrible need for food . . . The men worked hard and the food was not enough . . . also they felt more the humiliation.[48]

The evidence from the former inmates shows that the overall experiences of women and men in the concentration camps were perceived as different. All agreed that the men had a harder time coping with the life there; many think that their physical sufferings were also greater. If we now turn to specific issues of daily life in the camps we can see more clearly how being a man or a woman affected the lives of the concentration camp inmates.

Food and Work

In the camps separate living accommodations were assigned to women and men. They were equally inadequate. Overcrowding and cramped sleeping arrangements did away with privacy. The inmates had to share single sleeping bunks and learn to accommodate to bunk partners, many of whom were strangers. Having to share insufficient sleeping spaces was only the first link in a chain of ever-growing abuses and demands. Theft was a serious and immediate problem. Under the Lager conditions, losing one's ration of bread or shoes could spell the difference between life and death. To reduce thefts, the inmates would pool their resources and keep guard on one another. Sleeping partners could also keep watch.

Inadvertently, most prisoners benefited from the fact that a transport would include people from the same locality. This meant that new arrivals shared a common language and perhaps similar habits and values. It also meant that despite the immediate separation of the sexes both women and men might find relatives, friends, and acquaintances.

These unanticipated "advantages" notwithstanding, Jews who passed the initial selections and humiliating initiation into the camps were daily assaulted by horrendous experiences that tested their endurance. The appalling accommodations and lack of privacy were constant ordeals, but in addition to these their lives centered around food and work, both of which were used by the Germans as degradation devices and murder weapons. Separately and together, the two became means to kill rather than sustain.

At the core of prisoner accounts are reports about hunger and debilitating work. Eating and working permeated all aspects of the inmates' existence. The first month in a concentration camp, with its constant emotional shocks and sudden onslaught of hunger and hard physical labor, was particularly difficult. The longer prisoners could last, the better would be their chances to stay alive. More time could mean the chance for prisoners to acquire skills that would ease the adjustment to the Lager's endless challenges.[49]

Officially, men and women received the same food rations. But only a portion of the allotted provisions reached the prisoners. The discrepancy between what the inmates were supposed to get and what they actually obtained had to do with the quantity and quality of rations. Food was apportioned according to status. Jews had the least access to extra food. In camps with mixed prisoner populations they were outcasts, set apart from the rest, prohibited contacts with the outside world. They were not only given the least amount of food, it was of the poorest quality. But at the same time they were assigned to the hardest, most humiliating jobs. With less food, of poorer quality, the physical hardship of their jobs increased the Jews' death rate. Although there are no precise measures of the discrepancies in the food allotted and received, the photographs of the undernourished prisoners speak of their chronic hunger. Although the majority of camp inmates suffered from hunger, historians agree that the Jewish inmates were the hungriest. One report about Birkenau concludes that "the camp food was so inadequate in both quantity and quality that inmates who worked very hard soon became starved, utterly exhausted physically, and in consequence died rapidly." Or as Primo Levi put it, "The Lager is hunger: we ourselves are hunger: living hunger."[50]

Zippi, a three-year veteran of Birkenau, thinks that it was to the inmates' advantage to eat the provisions officially allotted to them. Exchanging bread for soup, say, disturbed whatever nutritional balance there was. However, food trading was rarely based on rational considerations. Sometimes these transactions would speed up rather than stave off death.[51]

Even just eating what was allotted could be a challenge. Frequently, prisoners had no utensils. Without a spoon, a prisoner would have to lap up the soup in the bowl, doglike, a degrading experience in itself. Prisoners quickly learned that a spoon could be bought with a ration of bread. But it was hard for a starving inmate to forgo the daily portion of bread. Ironically, when Auschwitz was dismantled, thousands of new spoons were discovered in the warehouses.[52]

Spoons meant more to the prisoners than simply a chance to restore some dignity to their lives; they could also be the means of restoring some equality to the ration allotments. Ada Wiener came to Auschwitz in 1944. On her first morning she received bread and a brew called coffee, just as the others did. But in the afternoon, one pot of soup was allotted to five women — without a spoon. The first woman to reach the container swallowed half of the soup. The second also got enough, and the third woman took the remainder. The fourth and fifth women were left with nothing. Every day the women had to fight their way close to the container. Ada remained in Auschwitz for three days. Not once did she taste the soup.[53]

In Mittelsteine, Ada's next stop, she was confronted with a different problem. Here her barrack housed about fifty women. In the evening several round loaves of bread were delivered. Each loaf had to be divided among eight prisoners. There was no scale, there was no way of measuring the bread, and there was only one knife. As soon as the bread was delivered, the women would surround the person who was doing the cutting. The women would assign this task to one person. Usually they tried to select someone they considered fair, who would also be capable of doing a decent job of cutting. But no matter who was chosen, accusations and counter-accusations were an inevitable part of the bread-cutting ceremony.

Because of the pervasive shortages, prisoners who believed that they were about to be gassed would often offer their utensils as a going-away gift to those who were closest to them. A father to a son. A friend to a friend.[54]

Beyond shortages of utensils and fairness in distributions, the prisoners were faced with an array of decisions about food: when to eat, what to eat, how to obtain more food, and so forth. "When to eat" usually applied to bread. Often distributed in the evening, the bread had to last twenty-four hours. Inmates thus faced a dilemma: whether to eat it all at once and thus temporarily stop their hunger or to divide it into several portions that would last until the next ration, reducing the severity of their hunger without elimi-nating it. It was a choice between a short-lived, one-time gratification or an incomplete satisfaction that lasted longer. Chronic hunger made waiting difficult. Many devoured the entire portion at once.

Eating one's bread at once had another advantage: it prevented thieves from stealing it. Bracha Winger-Ghilai describes what happened when a group of Jewish Greek women were assigned to her barrack in Birkenau. At first, Bracha felt sorry for the inexperienced women whose inability to speak any language but Greek made life particularly hard for them. Soon, however, her sympathy was mixed with resentment. The newcomers were effective thieves. Bracha was in the habit of saving some of her bread. Yet no matter how ingeniously she hid it, the Greek women would find it. None of them was ever caught.[55]

Most prisoners felt that men were more sensitive to hunger than women. Women were also perceived as being more efficient at dividing their bread and saving some for later. "As homemakers women had it easier . . .

They knew how to divide food, how to ration it. This was very important." Men tended to argue that "you had to eat your food right away": "If you didn't, someone would steal it, so you were sure to finish it."[56] Whatever the reason, those who ate their bread right away were forced to begin the new day with only a little watery brew.

Because they had traditionally been the selectors and preparers of food, women tended to be more knowledgeable about food in general. In survivor accounts they seem to have been better-equipped to deal with the initial eating hurdles. In Kaiserwald, Ita Shapiro was first detailed to dig potatoes. During her first week she learned several valuable lessons.

> I worked in the fields with a woman from Germany who had been in several camps. Soup was brought to us to the fields. Once, I started eating and noticed a louse in my bowl. I was about to spill out the soup, but this Jewish-German woman said, "What are you doing?" She was very intelligent and refined, highly educated. With her spoon she took out the louse and finished eating my soup. When she ate uncooked potatoes from the field, she explained, "It is a vegetable; it doesn't need to be cooked."[57]

Paralleling these rational approaches to nourishment were reactions that strayed from the logical path. Some women could not overcome their aversion to the Lager cooking. Ina Weiss was one of them. Born in Germany, she came to Auschwitz via Theresienstadt. Although she realized that the midday soup was the only warm meal she would get, she could not eat it. As soon as the huge soup container would appear, the smell would make her ill. She insists that she simply had to retreat "like a sick dog."[58] Men, on the other hand, were more likely to complain about food shortages than the taste.

Other women often had seemingly irrational reasons for failing to take advantage of opportunities for extra nourishment. Tola Szwarc-Chudin was one of these. After her stay in Majdanek, she was transferred to the deadly Camp C of Skarżysko Kamienna. There she met a man who had known her family in Warsaw. He invited her to come to his place for soup. After her first visit, he asked her to come again. He was generous. However, Tola was embarrassed to eat the soup there. Each time she went, she felt like running away. Finally, although she was very hungry, Tola stopped going.[59]

Curious about her reaction, I ask whether the man expected some favors in return, sexual favors. She emphatically denies this. Trying to understand her own reaction, she muses,

> From this man I was ashamed to take food, but not from a close friend. Maybe because we were equal, maybe because my friend was a woman like me. Because he knew who I was, he knew my father? I felt terrible, but I don't really know how to explain it. I always tried to do what I thought was right.

The inequality of their relationship seems to have prevented Tola from accepting his gift.

Then, more for her own benefit than mine, Tola tells another story:

> I remember once in Skarżysko I was on night duty. Next to one of my machines sat a Christian woman. She took out a sandwich and ate it. Then she ate cherries. One of the cherries fell to the floor. I fought with myself not to pick it up. I was trying not to lose the human part of me, not to pick up from the ground and [put] into my mouth. I did not touch the cherry.

Because of her successive imprisonments in the Warsaw ghetto, Majdanek, and Skarżysko Kamienna, Tola had been deprived of fruit for years. Cherries were an exceptional luxury. She knew this. Still, her reaction to the man's offer and her decision not to pick up the cherry were connected to her past—to her self-image, to her life before the occupation. For Tola the refusal to accept the soup, may have diminished her physical chances, but it supported her emotional, perhaps even her moral well-being.

Other prisoners were prevented from eating by religious dietary commitments. Renée Hofland lost her parents as soon as they arrived at Auschwitz; only she and her younger teenaged sister were spared. The sister became particularly dejected: she stopped eating and began losing weight. Renée worried that she might have lost the will to live. One of the Hungarian women who had been on their transport wanted to help. She thought that if the sister were given more appealing food, it would improve the girl's appetite and lift her spirits. This woman knew of a Jewish man who offered to throw food across the barbed-wire fence just for the pleasure of seeing a young and pretty Jewish woman on the other side. She suggested that Renée take him up on it. Renée found the offer strange and refused. A few more days of watching her sister's deteriorating condition changed her mind.

One day, feeling like "a cow on display," Renée came to the fence and waited. As promised, a man on the other side threw over a small package wrapped in paper. It contained a slice of bread and raw bacon. Renée ran happily with this gift to her sister. But the girl flew into a rage. She threw the bread and bacon to the ground, jumped on it, and screamed that their parents had hardly reached Heaven and she, Renée, was already tempting her with forbidden food! Didn't she know any better? The sister continued destroying the bread and bacon, screaming at the top of her voice. Renée just stood there, watching the waste.

Renée then tried to get a kitchen job, hoping for a little extra food. She was lucky, but the new job required her to transfer to a kitchen far away from her barrack and thus from her younger sister. Through a friend Renée heard that the sister had accused her of abandoning her. The two never met again, and Renée alone survived the war.[60]

In addition to illustrating how complicated the seemingly basic need to eat could be, this incident also shows the part sex played. A man paid Renée with his valuable provisions just for the privilege of looking at a young and attractive woman: male prisoners were less likely to be as "fortunate." Probably no such painless opportunities as this to acquire extra food were available to any man.

How food could become entangled with sex in unusual ways is illustrated by Shoshana Kahn's experience. The attractive Latvian teenager had been transferred from the ghetto to Kaiserwald camp. Here, like the majority of the prisoners, she suffered chronic hunger. She tells the story:

> One Sunday, in comes one of the political guys . . . ancient, I thought;
> he was forty years old or so. I noticed a bulge and was fascinated with

what could be hidden under the jacket. I stood and watched and heard him say, "Come here, little one." Yah, he was from Rhineland, and with his "Come here, see what I have for you," he opened the jacket and out came a big slice of bread with butter. So I ran [with it] to my mom, and we had a ball. Next Sunday, this man, Jacob, came again, and then again. I was already like a dog, waiting for the bread. And here I got this bread, big bread, always something on it, a piece of meat, whatever. It was heaven. After a while I took a liking to Jacob.

This is the first time I talk about this. I shouldn't have been ashamed. You shouldn't be ashamed to tell it to people; these were unusual circumstances. This man turned into my daddy. He was the age of my father, more or less. Most of his life he spent in prison because of his politics; he was a Communist. He had read every library book in Germany! You know, and I was thirsty, very thirsty for school and for knowledge. So he taught me astronomy, German history, math; it was like going to school. In a concentration camp! As a matter of fact he brought me the book by Stefan Zweig, *Marie Antoinette;* he found it somewhere; I don't know where. He really took care of me.

I didn't sleep with him. Sadly. I'll tell you what: today I feel bad. I should at least have given something to the poor man. It would have been a good deed. He never asked, and I never knew. I didn't know what sex was . . . I was idiotic, and that was that. He never asked. All he wanted was to feed me. He was not a good-looking man. Maybe he wanted a good-looking girlfriend so all those other big shots should think that he also had a girlfriend. I don't know. He was extremely kind. Once he asked me if he could possibly masturbate in front of me. That was the only sexual thing that had happened. And that scared me, so much! The whole procedure. I didn't know what was going on, what he wanted, but I would have, I should have . . . well . . .

I had to hold him and he did it on his own. Scary! Scary! He did it only once, maybe because I was so scared. I was crying. I was scared. The whole thing took a different character after that. I didn't trust him as much. To me, a penis was a scary thing. I was a seventeen-year-old girl from Kurland, very innocent. That was once. That was once, and I never told it to anybody. I feel kind of embarrassed, but I shouldn't. There is nothing to be embarrassed about. He gave me life, more or less. So at least I could have . . . he enjoyed that. I should have been nicer to Jacob. Toward the end, the Germans took many prisoners to Sachsenhausen and on the way they killed so many! Jacob was one of those who died.[61]

Shoshana is grateful to Jacob for alleviating her chronic hunger and possibly saving her life. Shoshana's experience with Jacob, which is unusual in its specifics, reflects the general pattern: women were more likely to receive additional nourishment than men. Earlier I described the sexual encounters that took place in the work camp Skarżysko Kamienna. An obvious consequence of these affairs was that the female partner would receive better nourishment. And getting better and more food meant staying alive longer. Of course, such sexual liaisons were more likely to occur in work camps, where the separation of sexes was less rigidly enforced.

No one knows how frequent such affairs were. It seems that usually male partners were camp functionaries or prisoners who for other reasons did not suffer from chronic hunger and therefore retained their sexual drive. (It is generally agreed that chronic hunger extinguished the prisoners' sex drive.)[62] This included only a minuscule portion of the Jewish population. Most likely, Jewish women prisoners who responded to sexual advances were motivated by the promise of food.

Chronic hunger took its toll on more than the prisoners' sex drive. Starvation leads to a marked reduction of energy. Chronically hungry inmates often became forgetful and irritable. These reactions, in turn, were followed by indifference and apathy. A psychiatrist and Auschwitz survivor explains that in the Nazi camps "the last phase of starvation is known as the Musulmann state, when all mental processes are retarded and normal reactions cease . . . In many cases death follows." Most prisoners agree that hunger robbed them of energy, made them forgetful and apathetic. "The so-called Mussulman, as the camp language termed the prisoner who was giving up and was given up by his comrades, no longer had room in his consciousness for the contrasts good or bad, noble or base, intellectual or unintellectual. He was a staggering corpse, a bundle of physical functions in its last convulsions."[63]

Prisoners would marvel at how these starved, apathetic creatures, incapacitated and almost dead, would change when confronted with a promise of food. For many anticipation of nourishment acted like shock treatment, bringing them back to life. The very idea that food might be forthcoming could energize them. Some think that this recapture of energy was propelled by the need for self-preservation, which could also explain why most people did not break down when they lost those they loved. Similarly, the drive for self-preservation may have prevented prisoners from irrationally pursuing revenge. Not only did the will to live help them to live, but it may also have warned them: "Be careful, hold on, hold on so you will survive." Perhaps they had an unconscious feeling of satisfaction that they had succeeded in making it when others were swept away. Perhaps the need to keep watch over one's life gave them the strength to overcome disaster? Was it egoism? Selfishness?[64]

Yet whatever kept them going was eventually overpowered by starvation. In the words of Rachel Aronowicz:

Later on, something burst inside us and continued to break from day to day. Horrible internal changes became visible inside us. There were moments when we did not understand what was said to us. The words failed to reach us. They passed us by, our brains doubted; our past memories became slowly erased. We were approaching a strange kind of state. All that was human continued to disappear, slowly. Only the hunger, this primary, strong drive, refused to be dulled. It demanded attention, its rights, even more forcefully as it grew stronger. And so the chronic hunger, together with a continuous fear of persecution and the murder of those who were dearest to us, transformed us into different beings. There were moments when, like animals, we feared death only when faced directly with a gun. Before and after this visible threat, we had stopped thinking about it. We became robotlike. We became automatons who only listened to the German orders.

The process Rachel describes was the Musulmann's move toward death. The horror of the camps was not just that the inmates were killed but that before their deaths they were destroyed in stages. The production of living dead was "one of the true inventions of the concentration camps . . . The leading figure in the cast of mass dying was the Musulmann . . . the human being in the process of dissolution."[65]

Yet even though the Musulmann were victims of the circumstances, inmates admit that as a group they were abused, despised, and finally avoided by the rest of the prisoners. Perhaps the Musulmann acted for other inmates as a mirror of their future selves: "To watch the Musulmann die was to preview one's own dying, a dying which was more frightening than death." Most of the starving prisoners were preoccupied with self-preservation, struggling for their lives. But what happened inside the dying individuals only the dead know. Those who watched the Musulmann die saw only what was on the outside; they remained shut off from the internal transformations. As Primo Levi notes, inevitably knowledge about the deaths of concentration camp inmates is indirect and incomplete.[66]

All the Jewish prisoners were journeying toward death. For women, the trip was probably a little slower because of their food-handling skills and the rare offers of a little extra food. Hunger was closely tied to work. Women were excluded from some jobs that were traditionally assigned to men: mining, carpentry, electrical work. Yet despite some perceptions to the contrary, this does not mean that women's work was always easier. Both men and women worked on the roads. Both worked in quarries, carrying huge stones, which few of them were able to move. Many were murdered while trying. As a rule, no women worked at Buna, part of the Auschwitz complex, where Germans were trying to produce synthetic rubber. It seems that no laborers could last there longer than two months; the work was designed to kill.[67]

Knowing how linked work and food were, women and men tried to manipulate each, hoping to make the connection of the two work to their advantage. Usually their exertions led to disappointment. For the prisoners, the Lager was an unpredictable, life-threatening world. Yet most of them wanted to make sense out of a senseless universe. Perhaps these efforts in themselves, regardless of their outcome, may have prolonged some prisoners' lives.

One such prisoner, Roma Nutkiewicz-Benatar, came to Majdanek with her favorite aunt. When the women were ordered to undress, what she had dreaded happened:

A German came over and grabbed my aunt by the hair and dragged her out. At the last moment, as she was leaving me, she pushed into my hand a gold watch she had received from her father on her wedding day. I placed it in my shoe. This was my introduction to Majdanek. I never saw my aunt again. I was inexperienced. All alone. I was timid, but I learned quickly.[68]

Roma was assigned to a job that required her to break up and move large stones, in a work detail of Jewish women guarded by a Ukrainian man and a German woman. The work was exhausting, unnecessary, interrupted by senseless beatings; the food was sparse and of poor quality. One day, the two Kapos (foremen) quarreled, and the workers had to pay a price. Roma recalls,

The German woman stood with her legs apart and we had to pass through her legs and he [the Ukrainian guard] hit us with a rubber club. We were to get twenty-five blows on our bottoms, as we moved by. I don't think I got twenty-five because I fainted. It was terrible, I couldn't walk and I couldn't sit. I am sure that I had fever. I decided that no matter what happened I had to get out of Majdanek.

It wasn't long before Roma had witnessed a selection of young, healthy-looking women. She heard that these women were being transferred out of Majdanek. After watching two more of these selections, Roma concluded that since those destined for departure were young and fit for work, those who stayed behind were going to be killed. Therefore, when she saw another assembly of women being processed, she attached herself to them.

Roma recalls,

A few German officers ordered us to undress, and they studied us. One of them looked at me and asked "How old are you?" I said, "Sixteen."

He pushed me out saying, "Too young." So I went into the back, hoping that he would not remember me. I went to the end of the line. The second time, he stopped me and asked again how old I was. I said "Twenty," and he passed me. I had nothing to lose, actually.

She ended up in Auschwitz. Strange as it seems, for Roma this was an improvement: more food, better work.

Men also tried to manipulate a system that was rarely manipulable. Arieh Eitani, a teenager in the work camp Kaufering, searched for ways to reduce hunger through work. An indirect contact with a rabbi landed him a choice job, supplying the kitchen with firewood. Proximity to food promised extra nourishment. Arieh explains,

> One evening as I was working in the kitchen I saw a potato on the floor. As soon as I took it, a German pounced on me. It was as if they had put the potato there to tempt me. He started beating me. Then he placed me between two wire fences with a potato in my mouth. All night I had to stand there between the two fences. There were many people in our camp who ran to the fences to commit suicide. I could have finished my life then, but somehow I was not ready for that. Next morning they took me out."[69]

Arieh sees himself as "nothing special." Yet his conduct shows much resourcefulness, most of which focused on finding work that could bring him more food. One day he thought that he had gotten a lucky break:

> I found an apple. I was so excited. Who am I, a Jew, to have an apple? I kept it with me all night. I smelled it, I polished it, I couldn't sleep because I had it. I thought of changing it for food. [Apples were a great luxury and exchanging it for bread—perhaps even more than one slice—would have been a good move.] Kapos had boys to polish their shoes and to do all kinds of services. Sometimes a boy like this slept with the Kapo. These boys were called Pipels. As long as a Kapo liked him, the boy had more food. I worked with a doctor whose brother was a Kapo who had a boy like this. When I heard that the boy had disappeared, I decided to give my apple to this Kapo hoping that he would make me his Pipel. Maybe I also felt that after all, who am I to deserve

an apple? So I gave him the apple and waited for him to arrange for me the job as his Pipel. With my luck, this Kapo also disappeared. I lost the apple, and I lost the job.[70]

Even Arieh, who had the capacity to bounce back, faced circumstances that were stronger than he.

I had diarrhea and couldn't stop running to the bathroom. My clothes would not dry from the previous night. I had no shoes . . . I knew that a shoemaker in the camp, a Jew, had extra shoes, but he wouldn't give me any . . . It was raining, it was cold. I had enough. I thought that I was finished. I wanted to die and stopped working . . . just stood there. A Kapo saw this and started beating me. Blood was streaming down my head.

A German guard, a soldier, came over, and asked the Kapo, "Why are you hitting him? What's going on?"

The Kapo said, "He doesn't want to live; he wants to give up. He doesn't want to work or do anything. He wants to die."

The German said, "Release him to me."

I thought to myself, "Well, at least the end will come."

The soldier took me to his place. He put me next to the stove so my clothes would dry. He gave me his sandwich and he asked, "Tell me, what is the problem?" I told him. I told him everything, everything, explaining that I just didn't want to live any more. He said, "All this will soon be over." [This was the winter of 1944.] Then he talked about himself. "Look, when I was in Russia at the front, it was also very difficult. I also had diarrhea, and we cut our pants in the back and wore them like this." I can't remember all he said . . . he talked about himself a lot . . . what was important was the heat, the sandwich, the fact that I wasn't working . . . Who knows? . . . All this did something to me.

Next day, after work, this German came over, took me to his barrack. He gave me food and let me sit near the stove. But then after the second day I never saw him again. I don't know what happened. I looked for him, hoping for a sandwich but never saw him . . . We did not always have the same guard."[71]

Help and the glimmer of compassion in a chain of humiliations kept Arieh from suicide.

Perhaps because such incidents of comfort were so rare, they were especially effective. Tonia Rotkopf-Blair describes a similar experience. After the 1944 liquidation of the Łódź ghetto, she was first transferred to Auschwitz and from there with a group of Jewish women to a work camp in Freiburg. In this place food was distributed once a day. It consisted of bread and soup—and the portions of bread kept shrinking. Tonia worked in a plane factory and thought of her work as "horrible":

> We had to cut aluminum, and I didn't know how. They laughed at me . . . The supervisors were German men and women. We were not allowed to go to the toilet; we always had to go in fives. The main supervisor, a Nazi, was a terror. A typical brute . . . Then, from cutting aluminum they assigned me to work with a German, not a Nazi; this German was some kind of a prisoner and was not allowed to talk to me. I would bring the nails and hold them out. He used my hands for the job. I worked with the end part of the airplane. He and I were a team; we had to work together. I had to complete the job because my hands were small. Whenever he wanted to say something to me, he would look in a different direction and mumble under his breath.[72]

Once Tonia went for a drink of water without asking permission. Her absence was noticed:

> When I came back, the Nazi supervisor was there, and he screamed at me, "How the hell can you drink water? You will get sick from it!" Then he slapped me across my face four times. I could see his ring with the Nazi emblem on it. The German prisoner with whom I worked and other co-workers were there. I was ashamed to be hit in the face in front of everybody . . . but then hoped that possibly no one had noticed . . . with the noise and all. When the German master [her co-worker] turned around, I saw one teardrop flow from his eye. One tear, from one eye. This is how I realized that only one of his eyes was real. I also realized that he was my friend . . . Later on he asked me, "Why didn't you tell me that you wanted water?"

Before this incident Tonia had been convinced that a publicly humiliating experience, such as a slap in the face, would push her toward suicide. But when it happened, she just looked around at those present to see how they reacted. Suicide was not an option. From then on Tonia's friendship with this German made hunger, hard work, and humiliation more bearable. For both Arieh and Tonia a crisis on the job was followed by outside help. For them it meant an interruption in a chain of humiliations. The compassion shown by others reestablished a balance, giving each of them some strength to continue.

At times inmates received aid that gave them a push to search for seemingly nonexistent options. Menachem Rubyn came from a small town close to the Carpathian mountains. Known as Carpatoruss, during the war it was occupied by the Hungarian army. Here for a brief period Jews were crowded into ghettos and then shipped to concentration camps in Poland. The sixteen-year-old Menachem reached Auschwitz with his family but lost all of them immediately after arrival. Now alone, he was sent to an Auschwitz subcamp, Jaworzno, a coal mine. He suffered from chronic hunger, reinforced by exhausting work. Menachem offers glimpses of both:

> Every day we walked down into the coal mine, 350 meters down . . . We were laying the rail tracks. From both sides the water ran down the walls. We had to bail the water out or we would have drowned. Before we built the rails, horses dragged the coal loads. These horses knew the difference: if there were 45 kilograms in the load, the horses wouldn't move, if there were 36, they'd move. The horses got food. I would steal food from the horses and eat it. Others did that too. At least we got vitamins.
>
> Our supervisor was a Polish Christian. He brought food for himself and would give some of it to me. He liked me. I was the youngest, and he probably felt sorry for me. Almost every day he put out a part of his lunch for me . . . He didn't hit us, he didn't push us around. He was a fine person.[73]

Menachem saw the extra nourishment as a gift from heaven.

Bergen-Belsen was Ruth Hudes-Tatarko's final stop after a string of six camps. It was 1945. For her, too, there was an experience that touched on the miraculous. The German Reich was coming to an end, but the relentless Jewish destruction continued. Ruth was close to a collapse when she arrived at Bergen-Belsen and remembers little of her arrival, except that the first night she spent in a barn packed with inmates.

The entire night a woman was leaning on me, and I kept telling her, "Move, move!" She was heavy, just resting on me. When morning light came through the cracks of the walls, I once more tried to push her away and realized that she was dead. This was my introduction to Bergen-Belsen.

[When] I came out of the barrack, it was surrealistic . . . There was such a silence, a silence of horror, of pain. Nothing moved. I felt the presence of a horrible death, of horrible smells, it was choking me. It was not the smell of burned bodies, because there was only one crematorium there, and it was farther away from us. Suddenly, from afar, I saw something move. I ran toward the thing. It was a wagon, with women pushing it. On the wagon were vegetables, the sort you give to cows, turnips. I thought that since this was the only thing I could see I should join them. Nobody seemed to expect anything of us, so I began to push the wagon too. They tried to chase me away. When they did, I would join on the other side. I was just touching the wagon. I must have felt that this was the source of life; I didn't know exactly what was happening. The women tried again and again to push me away. Then one of them got a stick and was about to hit me, but the commander of the wagon, a Czech woman, Vera, said, "Why do you hit her? She's such a beautiful child. Leave her alone. Let her join us." Because she said it, they had to listen. So I had a job! We went from kitchen to kitchen delivering the vegetables. I didn't know at the time that these vegetables had vitamins. At least they were food, because there was no other food at all, in Bergen-Belsen. They didn't give us bread at all.

We would stop from time to time. One of the women had a knife. She would take one of those round vegetables, she would peel it and cut it into parts for each of us. This was the only food we ate. And this was my good fortune. After days without nourishment, this was very tasty.

What do you mean tasty? I also remember sometimes cutting up a potato and sharing it, and I thought to myself, "How come I didn't know that a raw potato could be so good?"[74]

Less directly than food, hygiene in important ways affected the prisoners' health, their self-esteem, and ultimately their adjustment to the surrounding horrors. Water was in very short supply, and the prisoners' washing facilities varied only slightly from camp to camp. When asked about sanitary conditions, survivors preface their accounts by describing the difficulties in staying clean. One of them notes that

the only way of washing was when we scooped up some snow . . . We had a stove in the middle of the hut and put the snow into a bucket. We melted the snow and that's how we washed our hands and faces, sometimes in the morning . . . And of course, we had no clothes to change into.[75]

This comment suggests that the chances to wash varied with the season.

Tola Szwarc-Chudin also mentions water shortages:

I washed myself with the little water I had; sometimes I used the tea to wash my face with. I did it to look well during an Appel [roll call], that they should not take me to the crematorium . . . Also, quite simply, I wanted to look human. I thought that if I looked better I'd have a better chance.[76]

Concurring with these remarks, Bracha Winger-Ghilai nonetheless points to the unexpected risks connected with washing:

We didn't have enough water. We tried in a dry way to be clean. Only from time to time they took us for a shower, but when we were under the shower Dr. Mengele would come, and he would check us. This way he could see more easily whether we should be selected to die or not. We were naked. He would stand there and just point to different people, "Get out. Get out. Get out." I was always small and skinny, and I wonder why he did not select me. It was a miracle.[77]

Still, Dvora Rosenbaum-Fogel took advantage of the limited opportunities in Auschwitz to stay clean. For a while she had a job that kept her inside the barracks, and she forced herself to wash every day, regardless of the weather. When she was given new work, washing had to be less frequent. When I ask what being clean meant to her, she says first that it kept the lice away. Then she adds, "Being clean gave me a certain feeling." Dvora cannot explain what this "certain feeling" was. She continues,

> Only very few women were as careful. Many let themselves go. They did not wash. Some of them would even drink [the washing] water, which they shouldn't have, and got sick. Many had diarrhea because of it. I was very careful. I went out of my way to take a shower, just to keep clean, and I never got a cold all winter.[78]

Dvora saw a connection between cleanliness and health, as did Tonia Rotkopf-Blair, who recalls,

> They called me "Tonia the Washing Girl." I was always very clean. Even though we didn't have running water, I was the cleanest around. Maybe because we were called "dirty Jews"—the two always went together. And I wanted to prove that I wasn't dirty. But I really don't know why I did it. In my home, we were very clean. In the camps, of course, I had no towel to dry myself with . . . When I got "coffee" I used it to wash myself with because it was so important to me.[79]

For Tonia, washing was at once a continuation of a habit and a rebuttal of an anti-Semitic stereotype, "the dirty Jew." Others, like Dobka Freund-Waldhorn, washed themselves because they thought that would prevent skin infections. "I washed myself with snow. I did not care that the guards watched. I washed."[80]

Edith Lasman was transferred from Auschwitz to a work camp, Salzwedel, where she had more opportunities to wash:

> Sunday we did not work. In the morning we had coffee and black bread. Then we could wash. We went to a place for watering cows and horses . . . The place probably had enough water, but we were not given enough time. The Germans would not allow us. And so we were pushing each other as we splashed the water. We would wash our things, and until they dried we had to watch so nobody would steal them.[81]

"What did being clean mean?" I wanted to know.

This question receives a long answer.

That one is human. There was a different feeling when one saw oneself in a tiny, broken mirror. The hair started to grow, but it was not the only important thing . . . I don't know how to say it. Before washing, a person felt like nothing, no hair, no dress, but when the bed was clean and the person was clean, and one had a little hair . . . When there was a table and chairs, we began to feel more human. You know that we stroked the table and the chairs as if we had never seen such a thing. It was so important to feel human.

Before that, we were like wild people or something. But because we were a little cleaner here, we felt more like talking . . . When there was frost on the windows, I would write over and over the names of all my brothers and sisters, again and again [Edith had six siblings; only one of her sisters survived] . . . the names of my parents. As I did it, I cried . . . We felt like human beings because we washed and tried to be clean. This way, we somehow acted against them and against what they wanted us to become.

Felicja Karay, from the work camp Skarżysko Kamienna, thinks that cleanliness seemed to matter more to women.

A woman took care of herself much more. I can't explain it more than that. Not that she had better conditions for washing. But she forced herself to be cleaner. When a man became yellow, he became a Musulmann. He stopped shaving, he stopped washing, and he would not take care of himself. He didn't function like a normal person. Women somehow knew how to adjust to the situation. Women were much more resourceful. Germans would not give us clothes to change into until the very end of 1943. But women knew how to comb their hair, how to sew, and they took care of themselves despite everything. The men didn't know how.[82]

Few prisoners were able to explain this emphasis on cleanliness. Even those who tried hard to keep clean were often not quite sure why. The consistently greater inclination toward cleanliness of women may be explained in part by the traditionally high value women place on personal appearance.

For women more than men being clean, well groomed, and healthy were closely related. Somehow the women's past made it more "natural" for them to associate cleanliness with better self-esteem, with health and survival.

Comparisons of female and male attitudes toward cleanliness offer a few consistent conclusions:

The women were more likely to try to keep themselves clean, their spirits were more up, and so on . . . Women were trying to use kerchiefs to look more presentable. Women would pick up a brick and put the pink on their cheeks as rouge, so they would not look so sickly. Men were not paying attention to how they looked or how they kept themselves.

On the other hand, respondents were sensitive to exceptions:

Some women were already tired. They would let themselves go. For me, personally, being clean allowed me to feel human. The men let themselves go. And this had to affect their self-esteem.[83]

Still, while it was usually agreed that men were more likely to give up washing, some men cared a lot about cleanliness. All concurred that under the conditions of the Lager, washing was hard for everyone, women and men. Primo Levi recalls, "I must confess it: after only one week of prison the instinct for cleanliness disappeared in me." During one of Levi's brief visits to the washroom, he met an "older" prisoner who kept washing his body without soap but with much energy. Without any preliminaries, the man wanted to know why Levi was not washing himself. Levi's answer came in a series of questions: "Why should I wash? Would I be better off than I am? Would I please someone more? Would I live a day longer? An hour? I would probably live a shorter time because to wash is an effort, a waste of energy and warmth . . . The more I think about it, the more washing one's face seems a stupid feat, even frivolous; a mechanical habit, or worse a dismal repetition of an extinct rite."[84]

The older man continued his task, at the same time giving Levi a lecture that in essence argued that precisely because the Germans wanted to reduce the prisoners to beasts they must not succumb. They must not become beasts because even in Auschwitz it was possible to survive. The prisoners must

want to survive, to bear witness. But to survive they must force themselves
to save at least a skeleton, the scaffolding, of civilization. The inmates, he
proclaimed, "are slaves, deprived of every right, exposed to every insult,
condemned to certain death. Nevertheless, they still possess one power.
They must defend this power with all their strength, because it is the last—
the power to refuse their consent. So, they certainly must wash their faces,
without soap, in dirty water, and dry themselves with their jacket. They
must polish their shoes not because the Germans want them to, but for dignity and propriety." Levi believed that the man's effort to stay clean was his
attempt to fit into a moral order. Because he could not accept the values of
this order, Levi was confused by them.[85]

Most prisoners understood that washing reduced the chances of contracting one of the widespread diseases. Some saw it but did not choose to
act upon it. Many others saw it but were not in a position to act upon it. The
concentration camp with its substandard living conditions, filth, chronic
hunger, and exhausting work inevitably affected the prisoners' health. Epidemics of all kinds—typhus, lung infections, diarrhea, and an array of skin
conditions—were rampant. Significant too, the camps' "health facilities"
were organized to push patients closer to death. A favored location for
selections for gassing, camp hospitals and clinics offered no medication;
rather, they acted as death traps. Aware of this situation, the inmates avoided
hospitals. Many kept their illnesses secret. Some nonetheless caught the attention of the authorities and were hospitalized. Only a few, who benefited
from the protection of a dedicated staff member, recovered.

Menachem Rubyn, the Jaworzno camp inmate who had received aid
from his Polish supervisor, also received help from the hospital staff. While
he was in the hospital Menachem made himself useful to the staff and to
other patients. People liked him, and they would shield him during hospital
selections. Menachem describes his hospital stay:

Every week there came a special black car, and all those who died in the
hospital and who were Musulmann were also pushed into the car. Then
they took them away. The half-dead together with the dead.

There were two people in this camp from my town: the head of the
Jewish Council and his son. The father was in the hospital and was
scheduled to be sent away in the black car. The day before this was to
happen, I heard a knock at the window, and it was the son.

I asked, "What are you doing here?"

He said, "I know my father is going to be sent out, and I came to
join him."

"Are you crazy? You can't help him."

The son was fifteen years old. I said, "Go and see where your father
is — he is going together with all the dead. What are you going for —
to die?"

And he snooped around and he saw some of the dead lying there. I
persuaded him not to go with his father, and he left.[86]

(More than twenty years later, Menachem met this camp acquaintance in
Israel.)

As the Germans continued to lose the war, the SS began evacuating the
concentration camps, removing the prisoners who could still walk. On what
became known as death marches, prisoners were forced to walk hundreds of
kilometers, further decimating the concentration camp populations. Evacu-
ations of camps were often preceded by executions of patients, sometimes
together with the hospital staff. Occasionally, however, the advance of Allied
armies interfered with these murders.[87]

When preparations for the evacuation of the Jaworzno camp were
under way, Menachem was still a patient. He remembers,

Just before we heard the Russian cannons, the Germans made a big
selection . . . They also came to the hospital and asked, "Who wants to
stay? Who wants to leave?" I chose to stay, but I didn't know which
would be better. Later on, two officers came to the hospital and they told
us that they would come in the evening to take us away.

I spoke to a patient, a friend: "Josef, I think that tonight they will
come and kill all of us in the hospital or they will take us away. You and I
should go and hide together with the dead."

He reacted with, "Oh, my God, that's terrible!" He was afraid. He didn't want to stay there all night . . . I assured him that the dead would do nothing to us . . . He agreed to go down into the cellar, a storage for the dead . . . All night we heard shootings, close by. Then came silence. We waited. Next morning we went upstairs. What we saw was horrible . . . sprawled on the ground were the patients and doctors, dead or seriously wounded. The Germans left, and that day the Russians came.

Menachem and Josef belong to the very few exceptions. For most, the camps' health facilities were deadly. Practically all prisoners who became patients in the camp hospitals were doomed.[88]

Characteristics and Responses of Men and Women

Further examination of the Lager shows distinct ways in which men and women experienced life in the concentration camps. Nowhere were those differences more apparent than in the treatment of the parents (or prospective parents) of young children. Because mothers were identified more strongly with young children than fathers, their fate was more closely tied to their children's. For the Nazis young Jewish children had no economic value. Furthermore, they were considered undesirable because they promised a Jewish future, which automatically transformed them into a threat to the purity of the Aryan race. As a rule then, small children were murdered upon arrival at the camps, and their mothers were killed with them.

Male prisoners assigned to "processing" the incoming people were prohibited from communicating with them. Despite these prohibitions, to save the young mothers, some of these men would urge them to hand over small children to older women, who were slated for immediate gassing. I described such related incidents at the opening of this chapter. Some mothers consented. Others refused to part with their children.

Those who witnessed incoming transports feel that many arrivals did not know what awaited them, but women from East European ghettos were more likely to know or suspect the truth. Nonetheless, although there are isolated reports of mothers who denied their connection to a small child, most remained with their children. It is clear that the Germans insisted on keeping mothers and their young children together, hence "of the concentration camp arrivals, mothers with small children were first to reach the gas chambers."[89] In part, the Germans insisted on herding mothers and young children together because this fit into their patriarchal ideology; also because having mothers remain with their young children made for the more orderly murder of both.

Some of the incoming women were pregnant. Because Jewish women were prohibited from having children, those who were identified as expectant mothers were immediately gassed. The painter Charlotte Salomon and her husband, Alexander Nagler, came to Auschwitz on October 10, 1943. Charlotte, who was five months pregnant, was immediately sent to the crematorium. Her name does not even appear in the camp records.[90]

A few pregnant women were able to conceal their condition, although if the birth was discovered, mother and infant would be murdered. Some physician prisoners performed abortions in secret and assisted with deliveries. But the rules against abortions and deliveries limited access to these physicians.[91]

In Theresienstadt, the ghetto-camp designed by the Germans as a propaganda "show place" for their Jewish policies, Ruth Elias could not find a doctor to terminate her early pregnancy. Later, after she was transferred to Auschwitz, she was still unable to locate such aid. Eventually, Ruth and her friend Berta, each seven months pregnant, were sent to Hamburg with a group of young women detailed to clean up rubble caused by the heavy Allied bombardments. After two months, the two were transferred once more, to the women's concentration camp Ravensbrück. Here they were attached to a group of pregnant Jewish women. Some were in the early stages of pregnancy and had probably been tricked into confessing their condition by promises of a transfer to a better place with more suitable care.

Skeptical about such promises, Ruth and Berta, through complicated maneuvering, detached themselves from the rest of the women who were loaded onto the trucks. Eventually, Ruth and Berta, escorted by a special guard, were brought to the hospital block in Auschwitz II-Birkenau. There they heard that the pregnant women from Ravensbrück had already been gassed.

News about Ruth and Berta's unusual circumstances—that two pregnant women who had been sent away from Auschwitz had now returned—spread throughout the camp. Dr. Josef Mengele himself paid them a visit. Explaining nothing, he left orders that the two women were to be allowed to deliver their babies. He continued to pay daily hospital visits. When Ruth gave birth to a baby girl, Dr. Mengele instructed the staff not to feed the baby and to bind Ruth's breasts.

Berta attended to Ruth and the newborn infant. She violated Dr. Mengele's orders and improvised a baby pacifier—mashed bread mixed with a brew of cold coffee tied with a string—and gave it to the infant to suck. This pacifier was hidden during Dr. Mengele's visits. Soon, such "feeding" proved inadequate. At first the baby cried loudly. But over time, the crying grew weaker and weaker. The infant seemed to be shrinking in size. Within six days, its color "turned into ashen gray." The baby became just a skeleton covered with skin. It suffered soundlessly. That day Dr. Mengele announced that he would return early the next morning to fetch Ruth and the baby. He again explained nothing. The staff and Ruth were convinced that at his next visit he would dispose of the mother and infant.

That evening, Maca Steinberg, a Jewish Czech dentist who worked in another part of the hospital block, came to see Ruth. After she had heard the details of her story, she promised to help. "Help" was a syringe filled with morphine, which she asked Ruth to inject into her baby. She explained that this alone might give the mother a chance to live. Although horrified, Ruth did what she suggested. The morphine worked.

The next morning Dr. Mengele was told that the baby had died. He went to search for the body but could not find it among the many dead. Leaving, he told Ruth that she was very lucky. For a while Ruth stayed in the hospital block. When Berta gave birth to a boy, Maca Steinberg again brought morphine. This time the newborn baby received the injection right away. When Mengele inquired about the baby, he was told that it was still-born. After Ruth and Berta left the hospital, both were transferred to a work camp and survived the war.[92]

The Nazi determination to eliminate Jewish children, combined with the pervasive filth, lack of food, overcrowding, and absence of privacy in the camps, made it impossible to hide infants for long. Prisoners had witnessed the birth of the babies; some had helped deliver them. Prisoner physicians could help pregnant women to abort but were helpless when it came to keeping newborn babies hidden in the barracks. Only mothers who gave up their infants had a chance to escape the death that was the punishment for illegal births. Yet some mothers, despite warnings, refused to have an abortion, convinced that they would find a way to keep their babies.[93]

Time was on the side of women prisoners who reached the camps late in the summer of 1944 and who were in the early stages of pregnancy. Most of them were Hungarian: the last victims. Among them was Dvora Rosenbaum-Fogel. When she reached Auschwitz, Dvora was given a strange, ugly, old-woman's dress. (Depending on when they arrived, some prisoners received clothes brought into the Lager by the incoming transports. Clothes deemed in good condition were shipped to Germany. The discarded garments were redistributed to the incoming inmates.) The only redeeming feature of this horrid garment was its large size. In the future it would hide Dvora's expanding shape. She is convinced that this raglike dress shielded her from evil eyes. The camp authorities never found out about Dvora's pregnancy. After the war, on May 12, 1945, a Soviet physician delivered her baby and announced that she had never seen such a beautiful boy. About the same time, Dvora's close friend also gave birth to a son. Such fortunate endings were rare.[94]

Unlike the younger children, young teenagers who looked fit for work usually passed the initial camp selections. If accompanied by a parent, they could count on his or her attention and care. For mothers, arriving at a camp with young teenagers often translated into an uneven struggle to save any children. Eighteen-year-old Lucy Mandelshtam, who had been born in Vienna, was sensitive to the hardships of motherhood:

I was lucky that I was not a mother with children . . . I would not have made it . . . Even with older children like we were, I was 18 and my sister was 14, it was hard for my mother. My mother had all the worries. She forgot about herself . . . She worried so much about us, mostly about my younger sister who was weak and sickly.

Sometime in August 1944, the camp authorities separated Lucy from her mother and sister. Both mother and sister perished at an unknown time and in an unknown place.[95]

The fate of another family shows the efforts, often futile, that went into the saving of a child. Ania Rubinger's father perished in Dachau in 1942. That year Ania, her younger brother Theo, and her mother were deported from Germany to the Riga ghetto. There Theo, who was not yet eleven, managed to elude the Germans by hiding. One day, however, when his mother and sister were at work, Theo was caught and put into a group scheduled for deportation. The mother volunteered to join him but at the last moment succeeded in persuading the policeman that Theo was fourteen years old and therefore fit for work. Both were freed.

Later, during the liquidation of the Riga ghetto, the mother, Theo, Ania, and her boyfriend Neke were transferred to the work camp Mühlgraben. Here, too, Theo was more vulnerable than the rest of them. One time Ania pretended to be part of a medical team and with Neke's help smuggled the boy out of a large group that was about to be deported.

In 1944 Ania and her family were transferred to Stutthof concentration camp. As soon as mother and daughter had located their barracks, Ania left in search of Theo and Neke. She recalls,

There was a barbed wire, and Neke was there, and he said, "Theo is okay." That was the first day. Next day, I found him again, and he said, "Ania, there is a children's transport going out tomorrow. I don't know if I can hide him." I said, "Neke, you must." The children's transport went out, and my brother went with them. That transport went to Auschwitz.

They never saw Theo again.[96]

Occasionally, the battle for a child took a miraculous turn. Karla, a nurse who worked in the hospital block in Birkenau, never spoke about her children. Rumor had it that her son and daughter were being cared for by a Christian friend. But one day another friend rushed into the hospital block and announced that Karla's children, Krysia and Zbyszek, were in Auschwitz. Their mother pleaded with the German physician on duty, Dr. Koenig, to help her. The doctor intervened, and the thirteen-year-old daughter was registered as sixteen. She received a choice job as a courier (Laufer). The five-year-old Zbyszek was brought to the hospital block. There he stayed illegally, hiding under the mattress at the slightest sign of danger. Although many prisoners knew about him, no one betrayed him to the authorities.[97]

Because of the separation of sexes, whatever child-parent contacts continued beyond camp entry involved mothers and daughters or fathers and sons. Miriam Rubyn, a teenager at the time, cherishes her mother's help: "She would give me some of her food. When I was sick, Mother washed me and fed me. During the selection, she would let me rest and then warn me, 'He's coming; stand up'. . . because I had no strength at all." Other daughters echo these statements. Their memories are filled with moving stories about mutual support of mothers and daughters and their readiness to sacrifice for each other. Some feel that their mothers kept them alive.[98]

Like all relationships, the parent-child ties went both ways. I described earlier how some teenagers in the ghettos became their families' providers and partial protectors. This also happened in the concentration camps. Sometimes a child would decide to share the fate of a parent even if it meant death.[99]

The teenaged Rina Ginsburg was one of these. Rina and her mother were transferred from the Vilna ghetto in a group of two hundred young women to Kaiserwald camp. There they were employed by AEG, a large weapons factory. It soon became an open secret that the German administrator of AEG was in love with the beautiful Rina. In 1944 the AEG factory was moved with a part of its labor force to Torun. The rest of the workers, including Rina and her mother, were transported to Stutthof concentration camp.

Because of his love for Rina, the German administrator of AEG arranged for some of his former workers to be transferred from Stutthof to Torun. Dobka Freud-Waldhorn witnessed this event.

They started calling numbers and names. Some were missing. Then they called Rina's mother. She looked terribly old and frail. When the SS man in charge saw her, he ordered her back to her place, next to her daughter. Close to Rina was also her friend Bela. Once Rina realized that her mother had no chance, she told this friend, "When they call my name, you go instead of me. I am staying with my mother." This is what happened. They called Rina's name, and Bela came forward. I was there, close by. I cannot forget the picture of this sad-looking mother and the beautiful, beautiful Rina . . .

The German responsible for the move was outside asking, "Where is Rina? Where? Where?" There was so much suffering in his face. Someone told him that she had stayed because of her mother. He knew that this was the end. This was his only chance to save her. He was not allowed to enter the camp. As a civilian, he was helpless. Rina and her mother perished in Stutthof.[100]

Considering the ease with which the Germans managed to break up Jewish families, it is impossible to know how many mothers or daughters had the option of staying together, how many chose death over separation, although the literature and unpublished evidence offer many examples of the devotion of children and their parents. Relevant here might be the unusual case of Dr. Aptowicz, a father who devoted himself to saving his nine-year-old son. Miraculously, although the two passed through several camps, they held out until the end of the war.[101]

Efforts to save children met with brutal opposition. And in the struggle between those who wanted to save and those who wanted to kill the killers held all the power. In their war against the Jews the Germans successfully focused on children and mothers. Many mothers who reached the concentration camps with young children suspected what was coming. To diminish their children's fears, mothers would try to stay calm as they went off to be gassed with their children. Inadvertently, then, they helped keep the process of destruction orderly.

In addition to the problems related to the care of their children, which some men also faced, women prisoners had to face problems related to their own biology — especially to menstruation. For as long as they continued to get their monthly periods the experience would be enveloped in a series of humiliations. The prisoners had no way of arresting the flow of blood. A fourteen-year-old prisoner remembers a morning roll call in which she noticed a girl with "a thick red stream of blood on the inner side of each leg . . . I realize she is menstruating. Poor girl. Of course we have no underwear . . . There are no pads . . . The blood simply flows . . . This is horrible. . . I would rather die than have blood flowing down my legs. In full view. Oh, my God!"[102]

The limited access to washing facilities added to the women's feelings of degradation. But nature unexpectedly came to their rescue: within a relatively short time after arriving at the camp, women prisoners would stop menstruating. Many of them thought that the camp authorities had mixed bromide into their soup to halt the menstrual periods, but there is no evidence that this was the case. Rather, today it is generally agreed that poor nourishment and the rundown state of the women's bodies were responsible for the change.[103]

Roma Nutkiewicz-Benatar speaks about the women's general loss of menstrual period in a matter-of-fact way: "We had no period in the concentration camp. I don't know why we lost our period; maybe it's just like here, when girls have anorexia nervosa they too have no period. We didn't talk about it. Actually, we were glad that we did not have it anymore." Also in a detached, matter-of-fact way Miriam Akavia muses about the reasons for the universal loss of the menstrual cycle: "We got some soup; they probably put something into the soup, because we stopped having our periods. Or maybe because I was so worried and upset that is why it stopped. Maybe the tension did it. This happened to all the women in camps." Although many women either welcomed the cessation from monthly humiliation or were in no physical or psychological condition to care, for some women the absence of menstruation created psychological problems. Some felt that it undermined their self-identification as women. Others worried that they would never be able to be mothers. One way or another, each woman had to deal with the issue.[104]

Among the issues that were considered specific to men was smoking. Arieh Eitani describes how important cigarettes were for male inmates:

One day I passed near a train track and found three cigarette butts. I picked them up, and for the three butts I got one portion of bread. Men would take out the tobacco from butts, roll it back into paper from cement bags, and smoke it. Some men were eager to exchange their bread for tobacco. Those who did were the first to die.[105]

After the war Edith Lasman heard that her father had died shortly before the Germans evacuated the camp. She also learned that as a heavy smoker he would exchange his bread rations for cigarettes. His craving for cigarettes had sped up her father's death. Other concentration camp inmates agree that the longing to smoke was a gender difference. Compassionately, they acknowledge, "Many men would give their lives for cigarettes; their suffering was great when they could not smoke." Selling food for cigarettes represented a dangerous cut in already precarious nourishment. The Auschwitz inmate Victor Frankl reports that when an ordinary prisoner, one without special privileges, would smoke, others would correctly assume that he had given up on staying alive and decided to "enjoy" the last moments of his life.[106] Women prisoners are conspicuously absent from these stories.

Woven also into camp experiences of Jewish men are the effects of their prewar social standing. With only a few exceptions, men who had belonged to the upper classes before the war were at a disadvantage in the camps. The Germans continued to target the Jewish male elites, singling them out for the most degrading jobs. But beyond these discriminatory practices, men who had held more privileged positions in the past were least equipped for concentration camp life. The discrepancy between who they had been before the war and what they were forced to become in the Lager was enormous — the shock was correspondingly much greater than for members of the lower classes. Speaking about Jewish prisoners in Auschwitz, Primo Levi argued that those who had a more privileged background faced special problems as they tried to adapt to work and to camp life in general: "At work which was prevalently manual, the cultivated man was much worse off than the uncultivated man. Aside from physical strength he lacked familiarity with the tools and the training which . . . his worker or peasant companion often had; in contrast he . . . was tormented by an acute sense of humiliation and destitution."[107]

Levi also thinks that men from the upper classes were more likely to know and understand what was happening to them. Yet the fact that there was no logic to their predicament undermined their morale. Their efforts to understand inevitably simply underscored how much at a disadvantage they now were. So not only were their efforts to make sense out of their predicament useless but they brought their own suffering and pain. Compared to the Jewish working-class men, who were trained by experience to follow orders without questioning, those who had once been a part of the elite suffered more. In the Lager universe, whatever remnants of male elite habits lingered on had become irrelevant. Jean Améry supports Levi's arguments, pointing out, "Long practice in questioning the phenomena of everyday reality prevented [the elite male] from simply adjusting to the realities of the camp, because these stood in all-too-sharp contrast to everything that he regarded until then as possible and humanly acceptable."[108]

Scattered findings further suggest that men were more affected by their prewar social standing than women. This may be explained in part by the fact that class affiliation is more closely tied to the personal identification of men than women. A man's social class mirrors his personal achievements and failures and helps determine his feelings of self-worth. The saliency of their class affiliation and the impact it had on men's self-esteem affected their adaptation to the horrendous conditions of the camp.[109]

In contrast, women's social position—class—in the past and even now has been determined by the social standing of the men who were important in their lives: fathers and husbands. My interviews with survivors show that in the Lager prewar class background seemed to matter to men and women in different ways. In the Lager, for women, the effect of their prewar class position seemed blurred, receding into the background. No clear-cut association between women's prewar class and their camp adaptation emerges. Perhaps the loss of their social privileges was not as shattering for women as for men because it was not as closely tied to their basic identification as women. In short, it did not undermine their self-esteem as it did for men.

The Lager itself created new social distinctions among prisoners, some of which the Germans instituted or readily endorsed. The camp authorities seemed to be applying to all concentration camp inmates the divide-and-rule principle. Most differences in rank in the camp were determined by access to food and indirectly by the kinds of jobs the prisoners performed. Deprived of their former power, equipped with irrelevant skills and habits, targeted by the SS for destruction, most of the Jewish prewar male elites moved to the bottom of the Lager's social structure. The skilled laborers and men who were used to hard work were more likely to end up with the more desirable jobs. In particular, craftsmen and manual laborers had better jobs than the prewar male elite. But since the non-Jewish prisoners were given practically all the choice administrative positions, only a few Jews became even minor camp officials. This seemed to hold for both men and women.

It was generally assumed that these minor Jewish officials kept their privileged posts by cruelty. Actually, some learned how to fake cruelty. But others grew into the demands of their jobs gradually, and some, seduced by the devastating climate around them, turned into brutes.

For Jewish prisoners the cruelty of these Jewish functionaries was particularly hurtful and demoralizing. Most prisoners, Gentiles and Jews, agree that sufferings inflicted by fellow prisoners pained them more than the blows they received from Germans. Some women remembered vividly how shaken they were when they saw prisoners inflict pain upon other prisoners, or when they themselves were forced to mistreat their comrades.[110]

One woman described a practice imposed by the Mittelsteine camp commandant, a crude and sadistic SS woman:

Our worst suffering came not from the direct beatings by the commandant but when we were made to hit a Jewish woman. This was horrible.

One of those special customs was for the "guilty" one to stand in the middle of a circle of prisoners and each of us was ordered to beat her. Those who had sense only pretended to be hitting hard, but the stupid ones would deliver their blows with vengeance, sometimes even if the victim happened to be her own sister.[111]

Through these practices, the Germans sought to break the prisoners's spirits. Sometimes they were successful.

Menachem Rubyn tells about his exposure to one of these Jewish functionaries in the work camp Jaworzno. This was a Kapo in charge of the dining room who forbade talking during meals. This Kapo would hit all those who dared to break the rule with a rubber club. Menachem recalls,

When he hit you five times, whoever was punished could not even eat that day, it was so painful. The beating was given with such viciousness . . . We were so skinny anyway . . . And once I too was beaten because I offered my spoon to another prisoner.

Jewish prisoners killed the Kapo just before the camp was liberated.[112]

Not all prisoners had a chance to dispose of such brutes or chose to react in this rather uncomplicated way. Miriam Rubyn mentions her experiences with one of these cruel functionaries in Auschwitz.

In charge of one of the wash rooms was a Jewish Kapo, a woman . . . She was from our town . . . My mother liked to wash. Once when everybody had finished, my mother was still washing; this Kapo hit her because she stayed behind. I told the woman, "God will pay you for this. Are you not ashamed to hit an older woman?"

After the war I heard that this Kapo married one of the religious slaughterers. When I met her I reminded her how horrible I thought she was. She wanted to give me stuff and asked me to be quiet about it. I refused her things. Later on she came to Israel with her husband.

Nothing was done against her. Nobody did anything to her. I myself did not talk about it either, I don't know why. People knew what she did but did not do anything about it. She argued that if she hadn't been cruel the Germans would have killed her. It was quite possible, but I don't think it was true.[113]

But other inmates spoke about functionaries who were nice to them. Bracha Winger-Ghilai tells of a woman who would offer her kindness after she heard her sing. When asked how this barrack supervisor behaved in general, the answer is: "She was difficult, but I don't accuse her. I'm not angry at her. I feel that she could not have been different. When we came to Auschwitz, she had been there for two years. She was from Slovakia."[114]

Gerda Nothmann-Luner also had special contacts with a female Jewish Kapo. Gerda had received skilled training at the Phillips electrical company, and the managers protected her for most of the war. This protection was interrupted by a six-week stay in Birkenau. Here Gerda met a sadistic and abusive Kapo, a young and beautiful Polish Jewish woman named Erika. After six weeks Gerda was transferred along with the other Phillips employees to Reichenbach, a camp that had been turned into an electrical factory. She describes her job:

> I was chosen to make a very special radio tube; I don't remember the name, but I was the only one who made that, and because it was an expensive one to make, I was not rushed. And I could take my time, and under pressure I am no good, so I was really very fortunate.[115]

One day the Kapo from Birkenau, Erika, arrived, and Gerda was ordered to teach her how to make the radio tube. The two were supposed to work together. How did Gerda feel about this?

> I didn't hate her. I don't know . . . She started talking to me right away, and said, . . . "I have to explain to you why I behaved the way I did and why I was the way I was . . . I came into the camp with my parents and my sister, brother, and family, and I saw everybody murdered in front of my eyes. And because I was beautiful, I was kept out, and I was made to do all sorts of things there, with German soldiers and what not, and it was all . . . I turned into an animal, from seeing this." I hardly knew what sex was. But I guessed that she had sex with them . . . This is what she said. She continued, . . . "And then all you healthy people came from Holland, and I was going to give you what had been given to me . . . Please forgive me" . . . Here nobody would walk with her, and I walked with her. I worked with her.

The rest of the women hated her. The German head of the camp did not like her:

He took her away and made her scrub toilets. And we all were quite pleased about that. And then he punished her, as he punished many, and he gave her the choice of being beaten or having her hair shaved. And she said she wanted to be beaten, because she had beautiful hair. So he had her beaten and had her hair shaved, and she was distraught about that. But . . . then, toward December 1944, I don't remember exactly, November, December, we were all sent to another camp; they had started bombing the factory; this we enjoyed tremendously, because all the Germans . . . were scared very scared, and we had nothing to be scared about.

Gerda soon lost touch with Erika. Intrigued by Gerda's reactions to Erika I probe further, and she tells me that eventually the rest of the prisoners just ignored her. Gerda, while she did not mind seeing Erika suffer, treated her rather well.

I was unable to ascertain who of the Jewish functionaries was considered crueler, women or men. Nor can I conclude that either women or men were more sensitive to prisoner-induced abuses. And I do not know how pervasive the postwar punishment of Jewish Kapos was. Yet I did find consistently mild reactions to the cruelty of Jewish functionaries. One possible reason for this is that in a real sense inmates saw the Jewish functionaries as simply the means by which the Nazis inflicted their cruelties. Perhaps the reactions of Jewish prisoners were so mild because they recognized that the Germans rather than the Jewish functionaries were responsible for the cruelty and terror of the camps. Assignment of responsibility for inflicting pain on others and forgiveness are intricately connected. Forgiveness, in particlar, has been receiving attention. As yet no clear-cut conclusions have emerged. The debates continue.[116]

Jewish inmates, as the most terrorized and deprived prisoners, rarely had jobs that gave them power. They thus had fewer opportunities than other prisoners to inflict pain on their fellow inmates. However, as a group that was particularly exposed to Lager's abuses, the Jews had an especially great need of mutual cooperation and compassion. Most Jews who passed the initial selection and were registered had participated in mutually cooperative relationships that were an integral part of the camps' informal structures.

Bonding

In the slavelike environment of the camp, inmates established collective support systems and coping strategies. Most of these were the result of cooperative efforts that originated in the barracks. A few of these associations were based on familial ties: mothers and daughters, fathers and sons, and siblings of the same sex. More frequently they included nonrelatives who behaved as surrogate family members. No matter how fleeting these attachments were, they were important to the prisoners' lives.

Felicja Karay believes that prisoners who had a predisposition to keep to themselves or who for any reason were alone had a particularly hard time withstanding camp pressures. Her firsthand observations, reinforced by her work as a historian, fit the assumption of social scientists that under extreme conditions life depends on solidarity and that the need to receive help is as strong as the need to give it. Moreover, under conditions of extreme cruelty and degradation, mutual support and solidarity improve the quality of life and may even aid survival.[117]

Concentration camp prisoners who had been politically active in the past were particularly aware of the advantages of cohesive relationships. One prisoner, Germaine Tillion, noted that the inmates' existence was woven into a series of webs, each bound by surrogate "families" made up of two, three, or four prisoners. By becoming a part of a newly formed unit, inmates were trying to balance two ever-present imperatives: the need to look after oneself and the need to look out for others.[118]

Prisoners cemented their informal camp groupings through reciprocity and mutual aid. Quite often members of these groups were confined to giving one another emotional support rather than sharing goods, simply because there were no goods to share. But no matter what their cooperative efforts were based on, most inmates concur that membership in a group of some sort had the power to keep them from giving up on life. Belonging to these informal units gave comfort to the prisoners. Not belonging moved them closer to death.[119]

Lager conditions themselves pushed prisoners into pooling their resources, although the existence and composition of the groups were often in flux: members might switch groups after a while if they met old friends or relatives. Inmates preferred to forge alliances with relatives and old friends. In most groups the members came from the same geographical area; they may even have known each other before they came to the camp. Thus, those who belonged to a group often shared a common language, customs, and experiences.

In a real sense, however, the existence and duration of these groups lay at the mercy of the SS. The murder and constant shifting of prisoners from one barrack to another or one camp to another interfered with the continuity of these informal associations. Prisoners were powerless. They could not avert breakups and disruptions of their groups.[120] So even though the need and motivation for such cooperative arrangements were present, their existence depended on a range of Lager conditions—including the prisoners' readiness to join.

It is generally assumed that women are more likely to define themselves in relation to others than men and are socialized for more nurturing and cooperative roles.[121] Relying on these ideas, some historians have assumed that women were more likely to form cooperative bonding groups in the Nazi concentration camps. Among the illustrations cited in support of this assumption is the case study of ten Beth Jacov women who, although they were sent to different concentration camps, selflessly offered aid not only to members of their own group but also to outsiders. But the conduct of these Orthodox women, while praiseworthy, does not warrant the conclusion that women rather than men created cooperative groupings.[122]

Another frequently quoted source concludes, without making any actual gender comparisons, that "women shared and pooled their resources better than did men."[123] But unless men are compared to women, it cannot be asserted that more women participated in these groups. At best these statements can serve as hypotheses worthy of study.

Based on her own observations Karay notes, rather ambiguously,

Men, I think, were struggling along for themselves. If they had a wife or a child or a cousin, they would work for him or her. But in general, they were sort of fighting for themselves. Most of the time they fought alone, as a single unit . . . Women always cooperated. Even if women came to the camp alone, they were able to form groups. They created camp families, five women would unite together and they would arrange for themselves some cooperative help. Sometimes a man was included. There were also mixed groups, not necessarily based on sexual attraction. Women always managed to arrange a social group, even if it was a small group of two, three people, a helping group.

Karay suggests that men are less predisposed to bonding, but she nevertheless mentions men who participated in cooperative ventures of their own or joined mixed-sex groups.[124]

Even though systematic comparisons of groupings are not available, the Holocaust literature is filled with examples of male prisoners who formed informal groups of one kind or another. In fact, Claudia Koonz, accepting the idea that women prisoners tended to play out their stereotypical roles as nurturers, goes on to suggest that in the Lager "men learned the skills that women learned . . . as children — nurturing, caring, cleansing, and sharing." Koonz then raises the possibility that life in the camp might have modified some of the patriarchal values the prisoners brought with them. This in turn suggests that extremity may push individuals into cooperative relationships regardless of their sex.[125]

Although women's upbringing may have predisposed them toward cooperation and bonding, this assertion ought to be validated by comparisons of the actual informal relationships of the female and male prisoners. A few comments about cooperative efforts among men suggest that although male prisoners were ready to offer help they might have been reluctant to mix it with open expressions of compassion.[126] But it is easier to find evidence of whether both men and women formed cooperative groups than descriptions of the quality of these associations.

The Holocaust literature, unpublished testimonies of survivors, and the interviews I conducted consistently show that both women and men participated in the various support groups that emerged in the camps. An exploration of these informal groups promises fresh insights into life in extremis in general, and into the coping strategies of men and women in particular.

Modeled upon the traditional family unit, these informal Lager groups varied in the extent to which they resembled the "ideal" family. They were informal, emerging under life-threatening circumstances in response to the need for mutual help and cooperation. The literature variously refers to these relationships as bonding groups, surrogate families, and cooperative units or associations, and I shall use the terms interchangeably. Although most camps had such informal units, not all prisoners had access to them. Some lacked the opportunity to join, others the will, still others both. But even though the groups varied in different ways, inmates who were connected to any such group would be shielded from at least some of the camp terrors, to which loners were more likely to succumb.

Occasionally, inmates would benefit from the support of others without really being aware of it. Some had ambivalent attitudes toward these groups and resisted joining them. When I asked Roma Nutkiewicz-Benatar, the prisoner who had had so many problems at Majdanek that Auschwitz offered her a better life, whether she had been a part of a group, her answer was "Yes and no":

> There were friendships; it all depended. People became friendly with people from the place they had come from. I had it more difficult, though. In Majdanek I felt that I would not make it. So I managed to transfer to Auschwitz.[127]

In Auschwitz, Roma by chance ended up with an excellent job in "Canada," the barrack where clothes brought by the arrivals were sorted out by Jewish inmates and then shipped to Germany. As an employee in Canada, Roma was cautious, stealing only items for which she would not be executed if caught. She stayed there for a month. When I ask whether she shared what she had stolen with friends, Roma picks up on the term *friend:*

> At first, I had no friends. I did not know the people. It took me a while to find a friend, a girl from Grodno. I was with her all the time, until the end of the war. We slept together . . . There were little groups that I saw, cliques. In my block, I was the only one from Warsaw. Usually groups were formed by the place you came from. There were some from Slovakia in my barracks, and they were not always nice . . . Because I was the youngest they sort of looked out for me.
>
> I think that because I was different in the sense that I did not have close ties, I could see that most of them had very close attachments. They would call themselves Lager Sisters. I didn't have close friends, although I did have friends. Maybe I was to blame for that . . . I felt that I was different from the rest. Besides, we did not have much free time, but what we had in free time we usually used for the same things. We talked about what we would eat when we left. They all told stories about what they would do when they got out, what they had done in the past. I was not convinced that these stories were true, and I was bored by them. I felt that some of them were just fantasies. They would tell terrific things about their families, how educated their father was, etc., and I felt these were just tall stories. I created for myself special ways of not being hurt, not to be separated. I preferred to be alone. I came alone, you see; the others came with other people. Therefore, I was really alone in the group.

Roma was friendly with the woman who shared her bunk, but she does not remember her as a special friend. Nevertheless, during her lengthy interview, she talks about experiences that show more than casual friendships. She recalls,

> I remember a Czech girl—her name was Erika—from Auschwitz; she was very pleasant and an interesting person. I don't remember how I met her. She was very beautiful. She worked in the Schreibstube. She would get packages from Czechoslovakia—I don't know how—even

though she was Jewish. One day she came and brought me a can of sardines. This was a fantastic thing for me; you cannot imagine how it was. From time to time she would bring me things.

The biggest help, though, was when I had an infection of the bladder, with terrible pain. I couldn't go to work; I couldn't stand on my feet. I was hiding during the Appel because if I had been outside during the selection they would have taken me because they could see I was in pain. I went to her and I told her that I was afraid to go to the hospital because they would send me to the gas. She brought me some medication; I don't know how she got it; and it really saved my life.

Clearly, despite the fact that she describes herself as isolated, Roma relied on the help and companionship of others.

Gerda Nothmann-Luner fits better into the image of a loner. In 1937, when she was ten, Gerda's parents had sent her from Germany to Holland, where she lived with a Dutch Jewish family. After a while the family refused to keep her, and Gerda was transferred to a more welcoming home. She became much attached to this second adopted family. In 1943 Gerda was taken with this family to the transit camp Vaught. There her adopted mother advised her to take a training course in preparation for a job at the Phillips Company. Gerda passed the course and then waited with the other prospective employees for the company's new factory to be completed. In the meantime, her Dutch family was notified that they would all soon be transferred to the East. As a future Phillips employee, Gerda was exempt from transportation, but she begged the family to let her come with them.

My "mother" would not let me. She said, "I don't know what's going to happen to us, but you be brave and work for Phillips and you will have a chance . . . You have to be strong because you are on your own, and you are going to have to make it, and you are going to make it." And off they went . . . They left. And my life sort of stopped. I think that I became a robot. Just like a robot. I didn't know that they were going to be murdered. Nobody knew that. But I was alone. I was so totally alone. I didn't make friends easily. All the people in the camp were from Amsterdam. I

didn't know anybody. I didn't want to know anybody. Everybody seemed
to know everybody else or had sisters or friends and formed groups; I
was by myself. I didn't want to wash anymore . . . I cared for nothing . . .

And next thing I knew, one young woman from Amsterdam, who
came from Germany years before that . . . she took me under her
wing . . . She was five years older than I. She said to me, "Gerda, now
you have to wash, and you have to wash your sheets. Somehow you must
pull yourself together. You have to snap out of this. You can't let yourself
go because you have to live."

The Phillips factory was still being built. The conditions in the camp
had become better. They were bad enough, but the crowd wasn't there
any more. Then I fell ill, and every two weeks there was a selection.
Those selected were usually sent east . . . I had scarlet fever. This meant
six weeks' quarantine . . .

I'm not sure how it all happened. I was so depressed . . . Just by
chance, shortly after I came out of the hospital, the first factory was
finished. It was a twelve-hour work day. We, the first group who were
trained, became what were called "night cutters." These were dynamo-
operated flashlights, and you pinched them, and we called them "pinch
cats" because they make a noise, "Miaow, miaow."

Then one of the Phillips representatives came and said, "We want to
start a factory of radio tubes, and for that we need a very select group of
girls. They have to be between sixteen and twenty-two years old, they
have to have perfect eyesight, and they have to have perfectly steady
arms and hands." And I was one of those who qualified. I did that work.

In the meantime, this one woman sort of on and off, whenever she
had the energy, did something for me. Once, she even made me a
brassiere; she was a seamstress and a corset maker. We had off on Sun-
days, and she found scraps of material and made a brassiere for me,
because my breasts, even though I was very little and scrawny, were big,
bigger than now. And so she made me this brassiere, and I was so happy
with it. And she continued to tell me, "Gerda, cheer up. You're going to
make it." She always had a friendly word for me.[128]

The Phillips Company was protective of its Jewish laborers. Although Gerda was moved to various factories, she spent the rest of the war with the same group of workers. She muses about her past,

I was really alone there, and I was still under such trauma that I actually didn't notice much. I only learned in 1990, at a reunion, that yes, indeed, everybody belonged to a group, with very few exceptions, of which I was one. The woman who helped me also belonged to a group. She would pat me on the shoulder and tried to give me courage, but not on a regular basis. Still, it certainly helped me.

Although Gerda and Roma saw themselves, at best, as only loosely connected to others, they were not completely isolated. Their comments show that they did have ties to others, which had positive effects on their lives. Both heard about widespread bonding. The tenuousness of Gerda's attachments probably originated in her shyness and lack of social skills. Roma's reluctance to pursue friendships had to do with her anticipation of the pain that would follow the disappearance of a friend.

The Germans stopped many of these close relationships. Tola Szwarc-Chudin was one whose short-lived friendship fell apart abruptly because of German actions. During the Warsaw ghetto uprising, Tola was put into a cattle train that took her to Majdanek. On the way, she and a former neighbor, whom she had known only slightly, became friends. In Majdanek, after a preliminary selection, both were taken to a barrack. There a German with a list in hand called out the names of the arrivals. The women whose names were called had to step forward. Tola explains,

The woman I was with looked very skinny. She was afraid that if they called her name, she might be sent to her death. When her name was called, I came forward. When they called my name, I stepped out again. It turned out that nothing happened. We stayed on.

"You were not afraid?"

I don't know where I got the guts . . . I thought that I was saving her. Actually, in the ghetto, I hardly knew her. I just knew who she was. But the fact that we were together, and she was more distraught than I, made me do it.

After that, there was another selection, a more rigid one. We had to parade naked . . . My friend disappeared after that. I never saw her again.[129]

I sensed that Tola was reluctant to dwell on the effect this loss had on her. Perhaps it hurt too much. Yet it did not prevent her later on from joining forces with a schoolfriend she met. Together with another young woman from home they formed a trio. During a subsequent deportation, the three were transferred to Skarżysko Kamienna. There they lived in the same barrack but worked in different sections of the factory.

One of Tola's friends met a Polish woman, an outside laborer, who brought wool to her Jewish co-workers and asked them to knit sweaters for her. The three girls shared the work:

The three of us would make sweaters, and the woman who gave us the yarn paid us with bread. We divided the bread among us. There were many similar groups. Those who were alone had a terrible time . . . Some were very depressed; some were not able to form any friendships; but as a rule, there were groups of two or more individuals . . . When we had a piece of bread, we divided it; we would not hide it but eat it to prevent it from being stolen.

Practically all prisoner accounts, oral or written, mention such groups. All agree that these clusters of friends made life more bearable. They are also convinced that the groups differed in many ways.

During the liquidation of the Vilna ghetto, the teenaged Ita Shapiro was forcefully separated from the rest of her family. All alone and depressed, she was ready to give up. But then,

A distant relative of ours found me and adopted me. She was always taking care of me in different concentration camps. And she saved me. Her name was Katia. She was a very impressive woman, tall, attractive. I knew her in the ghetto. At that time, my mother had helped her. Katia kept me with her, and we were together in Kaiserwald. We were there a week or so; I don't remember exactly how long. I was very down; I didn't care at all. I thought that I wouldn't live. I made no effort to live. But Katia made an effort for me.[130]

Katia was good-natured and courageous, ready to take risks. At one point, during a selection in Torun, Ita's name was called out for transfer. Without hesitation Katia, who was the *Lagerälteste* (camp supervisor) and respected by all, approached the German in charge. She told him that Ita was her adopted daughter, and she pleaded with him to let her stay in Torun.

The next thing the German did was to slap her in the face. He hit her so hard that she fell. This was because she dared to talk to him and ask him for something. Nevertheless, I did not go. Five hundred and fifteen of us stayed in Torun. Katia saved many more besides me. Young women who came from Vilna helped each other all the time. Our mutual care helped us stay alive. Later on, we had problems with women from Germany, but among ourselves, all we did was help one another. These German women came later on. They were very arrogant. They thought that they were the elite, and there was tension between them and us.

Dobka Freund-Waldhorn was sent from the Vilna ghetto to Kaiserwald, in Riga. From Riga part of the group was transferred to Torun and the rest to Stutthof. Dobka was in the Stutthof group but later was sent on to Torun, where she was reunited with the Vilna group. She explains how important this was.

I was fortunate that I ended up in the elite group of Vilna. There was Flora, older than I by ten years; she was an architect. She gave the tone to the entire group. Thanks to her we remained human beings . . . She was an example for us of how to behave. Most of us were fine women. We did not abuse each other. One of us had hidden some money—gold. She would give the Christian women we worked with the gold in exchange for bread. We divided it . . . We would talk, we would sing, often in Hebrew. Flora was a Communist before the war; she was not enchanted with our Hebrew. But she was great. She would also make things, bags, handmade bags, etc., then we would exchange them for food, which we also shared. I had an admirer among the men. He would throw me an apple from time to time, and we shared that. We would share everything. We did not quarrel.[131]

Irena Lusky, another member of the Vilna group, explains what being part of this group meant to her.

Right away, in Riga, we tried as much as we could to live a group life. Flora Roma was our leader . . . The minute she saw us, my sister and me, she said, "Come, be a part of my group, and I will protect you." She knew our parents. She was in charge of a group of about ten women; it was fantastic. She was helping everybody. What she did, very few people could have done . . . Among other things she taught us. She arranged books for us and she kept up our spirits. She was much older than we were; she was married already. She was a very moral person. She always told us that we should never, never steal, that we must keep certain moral standards. She kept up our spirits, telling us that we would make it. She was trying to keep us always together. Even now, with her gone, we meet at least once a year.[132]

To my question about the things they did for one another she responds,

When any of us had a birthday, we would see to it that the person got an extra slice of bread. Flora kept us going morally. We were also not lonely. We were together supporting each other. Not like the people who lived on the Aryan side and were so alone. Besides, we liked each other. Flora worked in the office. And she was quite influential. She had an exceptional personality. When we became a part of the death march in 1945, she told us, "As soon as you see a little town, run." And we did. Later on, we met again.[133]

Shoshana Kahn, who was also in Kaiserwald, admired the Vilna women but as a Latvian was not a member of their group. Spontaneously, Shoshana spoke about them to me:

The Polish girls were extraordinary. They were extremely loyal to each other. They were extremely helpful to each other . . . They were so close and so protective. When they went to any outside work and brought something back, a piece of bread, anything, it was always divided among them. And there was always lots of talking in Polish, which nobody understood. But there were constantly goings-on. They were also attractive, efficient, and they stuck together, and nobody knew what was going on there, and they gave the impression of being very strong . . . There was an enormous difference between these Polish girls and the Latvian and German women.[134]

Because she was not a part of this group, Shoshana's observation helps validates the assertions of the members. She even echoes their negative views of the German inmates.

Consistently, my findings show that no matter what part of Europe they came from, no matter what camps they were transferred to and when, women formed cooperative groups. Even contacts begun in a casual way could turn into long-lasting bonds. Bracha Winger-Ghilai, who came from Carpatorusse to Auschwitz late in 1944, describes how casual ties became meaningful and enduring:

> Within the camps, we created families among the prisoners. We called each other Camp Mother, Camp Sister, and we really acted upon it. It was very real to us. One day, a friend of mine from my town said to me, "Do you want to be my camp sister?" I said yes. From that day on, we were sisters. And that was accepted. That's how it was. Everybody referred to us as sisters. When we arrived in Auschwitz, we were actually five, a group of five. The Appel was so arranged that in every row there had to be five. So we were five. Four were older than I was. One of them always supported me, watched over me, until this very day . . . She was like a mother to me. Even after I was liberated, she was like a mother.[135]

Occasionally, in the work camps, where the separation of sexes was not rigidly enforced, friendships crossed the gender line. Ruth Hudes-Tatarko's talent in drawing and her quick intelligence helped her find work in the office of the labor camp Budzyń. Her job automatically ensured that she had access to more food. The teenaged Ruth had established ambivalent ties with an older woman, Sara, and the two had managed to stay together through several camps. Ruth tells about another special friendship she formed in this work camp.

> In Budzyń, in front of our barracks, there were two steps. One day, coming back from my office job, I saw a boy sitting there of approximately my own age. I noticed that he was very filthy and covered with sores.

I felt sorry for him. When we came back from work, we would get soup and bread. I gave him my soup and asked him to come again and again. I was sad for him, wanted very much to do things for him. And he would come every day. He did not remember my name . . . I didn't know his name either. We did not know much about each other except that we liked to meet. I would take my soup and give it to him.

One day I also gave him bread. In this camp there was a shortage of bread. When Sara found out about the bread, she was so angry, she screamed at me and dragged me by the hair: "How dare you do such a thing! Bread is so precious!"

"He's also hungry," I argued.

But she shouted, "What do I care that he's hungry; you must worry about us, not him."

There were so many things about her I did not like, and I carried within me a lot of resentment for her. She kept me sort of as a daughter. Who knows, everybody wanted to save themselves. Now I can understand it better. But then I couldn't understand her. After this scene, I would help him secretly without her knowing . . . I asked the German in the office for cream for the sores and gave it to him, and it did help him. This was just a childish venture on my part. I remember that the Germans also gave me some powder, which I also gave to this boy. I would offer him all kinds of good things. I would hide them for him. Once the Germans gave me pudding, and I kept it and I brought it to him.

After the war the boy, Michael, and I met. He looked for me. He found a sister and a mother who had passed as Christian. He brought his mother and sister to the hospital where I was . . . All of them cried. He wanted to show them who saved him . . . At that time I was very ill. He was very handsome. I heard that he went to America, but we never connected after that one time in the hospital.[136]

Ruth and Michael's friendship was beneficial to both of them: Ruth felt better because her gifts made a difference; Michael may have survived because of Ruth's friendship and material help . Sara's resentment underlines her concern with self. Ruth suspected that Sara's attachment to her was self-serving: because Ruth, rather than Sara, was in a position to supply both of them with extra food. Sara probably felt threatened by Michael's potential competition.

Like the women, men from various walks of life and with various degrees of sophistication formed bonding groups. Menachem Rubyn, the sixteen-year-old who worked in the mine of Jaworzno and after the war became a butcher, muses,

> Somehow we had to support each other. This kept our spirits up. We saw that there was no meaning to the camp, to the killing, so whatever we could, we did, to help each other. I come from a family where my father was always ready to help other people. So this was a kind of a tradition for us, for our family, and maybe for me.[137]

At his workplace in the mine, Menachem made eating utensils, which he distributed to those who had none. He was caught by a Kapo and severely beaten for it, but this did not prevent him from continuing to help both the members of his group and others.

Within the universe of the Nazi Lager, the death camp was the ultimate means of human degradation and subjugation. In Poland one of these death camps, Treblinka (completed in July 1942, it stopped operating after the August 1943 Jewish uprising), specialized in the murder of Jews. Occasionally Gypsy victims were sent there as well. Early in 1943 a core of Jewish prisoners began to organize a rebellion to destroy the camp or at least to offer all prisoners an opportunity to escape. Of the estimated 700 Jewish inmates, about 100–150 got away during the uprising. About 70 survived the war.[138]

Richard Glazar, a Jewish youth from Czechoslovakia, was among the escapees who survived. In 1995, in Basel, he spoke to me about Treblinka:

> My friend Karl Unger and I were always together. We were like twins. In this camp you could not survive an hour without someone supporting you and vice versa. We knew that we were destined to die . . . No individual could make it alone. Treblinka was a death camp, where people were brought to die. Here one had to be very cautious, very alert. One had to be always sensitive to signs of danger. We had to know which

direction death might come from. We had to have a sense of how to use someone's weaknesses and how to manipulate. I and my friend Karl survived because we supported each other constantly. We divided absolutely everything, even a small piece of bread.[139]

To my question about why mutual help and the creation of groups were so prevalent, he said,

One felt it. One knew it. This is how it was. It gave us a certain feeling of solidarity. I think this was particularly important because it was a death camp. Egoism and selfishness had no place in this camp. Perhaps in other camps but not here. Mostly these little groups were based on the country of origin. Most of us came from the same country, but not always. Because we were so close to death, we felt very down, we felt very humiliated. We were in a death factory. We were so degraded because we were participating in the creation of death. We were used by the Germans as a part of their death machine.

Given these horrible, degrading, slavelike conditions, we had to get together with somebody else. What kept us going was the idea that we could do something. We always tried to do something to counteract this tremendous helplessness and dependence and our participation in this terrible crime. While I was there, we tried to smuggle out two people, to tell the world what was happening. We wanted them to get in touch with the Polish Underground.

When talking about the Treblinka uprising, Glazar again emphasized the prisoners' ties and their solidarity.

There was a group of rebels, resisters, of about ten people, which in time became organized. These were the ten most important people; all of them had some kind of military skills. My friend Karl and I did not go through military training at all. Because my friend and I were not military men, we were not real members of the resistance group. However, two other Czech men, Zelo Bloch and Rudi Masarek, were an integral part of the resistance. They would inform us about a lot of things. They would also use us to do all kinds of jobs for the underground. Not as a member of the group, but as a marginal member, I knew a great deal.

Many people knew something, but we were very careful not to have much contact with the Germans. It was difficult not to give something away. The plan was to start the uprising in August 1943. All the horrors that happened, that we felt we were a part of, were somehow canceled out by this uprising. This is a very interesting thing. Through this desperate rebellion, we regained our pride. We regained some autonomy, some independence . . . Even though there were few people who participated and planned, the others knew, and it gave them relief. It had a wonderful impact upon the rest of us just knowing about it. All of us knew something about it, and all of us felt a part of it, even though we were not specifically involved with it . . . It gave us the illusion of having some control over our destiny.

There were many, many helpers in this. They were not told exactly what was happening because it would have been dangerous for them. But they had a feeling that they were a part of something. Of course, everybody, in a sense, in some way, contributed to this uprising. You cannot do this without having full cooperation.

Wishing to be sure that I understood him I began asking very specific questions: "You were not afraid that some of the inmates might denounce you?"

"I told you before that there were about three whom we did not really trust. Actually, even about the three, it wasn't that we thought that they would denounce, but we thought that they might not be strong enough, if they were caught, not to talk. There were no explicit denouncers of whom we might have been afraid."

"Are you telling me that there was an overall solidarity among you all?"

"In a sense, yes. I am telling you that among those living there, among those slaves, yes, there was such solidarity. I think that solidarity was much stronger than in other camps because this was a death camp. But I became aware of this when I read about other camps."

"I want to see if I understand what you are telling me. I don't want to put words into your mouth. Are you saying that the solidarity that existed among the prisoners made you feel or gave you the possibility of feeling like a human being?"

"Definitely. Definitely. This was a way of telling them [the Germans] that they could not fully dehumanize us, that we shared this solidarity. This realization happened later on as I looked back and discussed and read and thought about it."

The horrendous environment of Treblinka made bonding indispensable. In his comments, Glazar emphasized, in effect, that the more degrading the life in the camp, the greater the need for cooperation and solidarity. Although they were in some ways life promoting, such cooperative and supportive groups could not in themselves avert death. In fact, most leaders of the Treblinka uprising perished. And of the many others who died, most also belonged to various groups.

Organized, armed Jewish resistance occurred in five major concentration camps and eighteen work camps.[140] But most bonding groups were not as dramatic as those created for armed resistance. Yet they all shared certain characteristics. What were they? The experience of Aronek Kierszkowski (Arnold Kerr) may help us identify some.

Predictably, Aronek and his older brother, Dudek, were very close. For about half a year, the two worked in a coal mine, Vivikond, Estonia. Aronek admired and looked up to Dudek, praised his enterprise and courage. The brothers shared their food, their thoughts, and their leisure time. Aronek's feeling of protection came to an abrupt end when Dudek was shot in the spring of 1944. Aronek, who was sixteen at the time, collapsed. He is not sure how long it was — probably several weeks — that he remained oblivious to his surroundings. He remembers nothing about that period. And he is surprised that in his vulnerable state he was able to survive. Aronek's first memory is of standing in the collection field near Talin harbor hearing his name called out by a cousin. He knew it was his cousin's voice, but he could not see her.

After this he was sent to Burggraben, where he worked the night shift. There Aronek met a young man, Borke, who asked him to join his group of four men. He accepted, becoming the youngest member and the only one who did not speak Yiddish. He is sure that all five of them benefited from their friendship.

"But how?"

We did not help each other with food because hardly anybody had food. If someone was in a group, people would not jump on them. People would not steal from them. You did not want to start trouble with a whole group. Some of these fellows were strong. I was a kid of sixteen-and-a-half or so, but they were twenty-eight or thirty. They were strong physically. Because of them, I was able to survive the last camp.[141]

During the winter of 1944–1945, the death marches were at their height. Aronek recalls that period.

We were about to leave for the march west, from Burggraben. Not far from us a train with goods from Prussia derailed. Our commandant . . . had to send twenty-five strong men to salvage it. It was snowing. We came to the place where the train was turned over, and there were sacks of sugar and sausages from the freight cars. Sometimes before that when I was in Stutthof I was getting bread from a Polish inmate [with] whom I helped distribute bread rations . . . For a few slices of bread I bought military boots . . . At that point, I took some of the sugar and put it inside the boots, and I took the sausage and hid it in my clothes. We were wearing . . . striped outfits.

After marching for a few days we came to camp, Rieben. Horrible! They dumped us in a place with no beds, nothing. My friends and I got a corner, across from the door, and almost barricaded ourselves. We wanted to keep what we had. We knew that the war was almost over. Maybe we had a bowl of watery soup a day, but no bread, nothing else. I made up my mind that I would take a spoon of sugar a day. I thought that this way I might stick it out for six weeks. I made sure that nobody would steal my sugar. I had it with me all the time. I was not afraid of my friends but I was afraid of the others. I think that they each had some food from the same source I had.

Prisoners were powerless against the authorities, but a group could protect its members to some degree, especially if the problem emanated from other prisoners. Not surprisingly, prisoners who were torn away from their groups were eager to reconnect with them. A veteran of several camps, Shamay Kizelstein tells how he and other inmates formed and joined groups.

There were some who knew each other before, and others who met only in the camp. If you were standing in line for something, you could make connections if you thought you liked someone. Later they were called "Lager brothers." They became real friends . . . Of course not all were helping; people would steal from each other. If a thief was caught, he would be beaten up. But there were no special people who were known as thieves . . . and besides, there was usually nothing to steal. We ate the bread right away, so there was nothing to steal.[142]

Both Aronek and Shamay mentioned what others repeatedly said earlier: that a bonding group could serve as protection against stealing. Whereas Shamay emphasized that he immediately ate all the bread, Aronek explained how he had rationed his intake of sugar, one spoonful per day. Aronek was an exception. On balance most observations and reports consistently point to men's inability to ration their food and to women's special ability to apportion and save their food allotments.

In addition to shielding the prisoners from hostile acts of other inmates, the groups played a more direct role in keeping members alive. Toward the end of 1944, Shamay was sent to the work camp Ohrdruf, in southern Germany, close to the Alps. Here Shamay helped build a factory for the production of V-2 rockets. The work involved cutting a tunnel through a mountain in severely cold weather. Hampered by inadequate clothing and meager food allotments, many laborers collapsed. Those who fell were shot.

The nearby Swiss border, with its promise of freedom, acted like a magnet, and two of the laborers, Soviet POWs, talked to Shamay about escape to Switzerland. By January 1945, Shamay had become convinced that he would soon die, so one day, out of sheer desperation, he joined with the two Russian prisoners. Taking advantage of an inattentive guard the three made a run for the border. When nagging cold and exhaustion forced them to look for shelter, they found an abandoned barn on the outskirts of a small town. Soon the three fell asleep on the hay.

Barking and rough voices woke Shamay. Before he realized what had happened, he was dragged out by two SS men to face his two Russian comrades. The three were taken back to the camp, where Shamay discovered that the two Soviet POWs had made an unsuccessful escape before. The POWs were hanged. Shamay received an easier sentence: public flogging. It happened quickly. Shamay was placed on a bench and ordered to count to fifty.

I did count. But I don't know how long. Apparently I lost consciousness and fell into the snow. I lay there with my senses dulled. A sharp pain in my right shoulder and a sticky fluid by my left eye led me to wonder whether I was still alive or whether they had beaten me to death. I felt the cold dry snow beneath me chilling my wounded body . . . Then I heard light footsteps approaching. I thought that it was someone from Barrack 10 coming to collect the dead from the scaffold and from the commandant's field. I was alive, but how could I let them know? I began to move the arm that hurt very much. I was unable to feel the other arm. I tried to make some sound, and I heard myself making noises that were not human. My voice was weak . . . The footsteps stopped, and the man approached me and asked, "Shamay, are you alive?"

I tried with all my might to move my arm and to get some sound to leave my lips so as to answer his question in the affirmative. The footsteps retreated quickly. Again I lay with my face in the snow, at the base of the two scaffolds. I don't know how much time passed, but suddenly I felt hands lifting me from the snow and supporting me gingerly. They led me in the direction of our barracks. I had teeth missing, my head was injured, and my eyes were swollen. (I'd like to add that for a long time after my release, I suffered numerous complications: my urine was bloody, I would lose my balance and fall.) My friend who asked if I was alive saw that indeed I was, and he went to the old man in charge of our barracks and told him . . . The man ordered the others to bring me back . . . and he himself went to the camp commandant to inform him that I was alive.[143]

The man in charge of the barrack was a political prisoner, a Dutchman. He asked the camp commandant to exempt Shamay from heavy work. The German agreed, and Shamay was allowed to "recuperate." But in February 1945, they decided to deport him. Shamay was put into a truck along with a group of prisoners:

In the last moment a friend of mine came running to give me his bread ration, which he had received for the day. I still managed to ask him, "What will you eat?" His answer was, "I am staying here, and you are leaving."

Shamay and the other prisoners were then loaded into trains. Their destination was Oranienburg, near Berlin. On the way heavy bombardments stopped their convoy. For a long time the trains just stood in the middle of a field. No provisions were distributed. After several days an SS man opened the door screaming, "Get out, if you can." Some of the prisoners were dead; others were too weak to walk. Shamay left the train with a handful of prisoners and hid behind a bush, thus avoiding being hit by flying bullets. Shamay is convinced that the bread his friend gave him saved his life.[144]

Throughout all his concentration camp ordeals Shamay managed to form attachments to groups of three or four men. Though the participants changed, the effectiveness of the groups remained the same. In addition to the friend who offered the aid that saved his life, Shamay remembers members of his groups collecting potato peels, washing and cooking them, and sharing them among themselves.[145]

After a lengthy discussion of the horrendous conditions of the camps and the groups that formed there, Eugen Kogon, a former inmate and a student of the Lager universe concludes, "Group allegiance meant joining a small circle of friends or co-religionists, men of like mind, who brought similar attitudes to their discussions and 'club meetings' held in such places as the few privileged rooms of the hospital or even in cellar halls. In such groups men again became human beings, after the humiliations suffered in the toil of the day, after punishment and roll call and barracks life . . . Hope was revived, helping them to be ready to proceed on the appointed path step by step. Membership in such a group was perhaps the finest experience in a concentration camp."[146] Other accounts show how prisoners' cohesive, cooperative groups helped keep them alive, touching on such issues as food, work, cleanliness, and protection during illness. In addition to providing material aid, membership in these bonding units led to feelings of independence and became a source of hope and dreams for the future.

Indeed, certain illusory, intangible, or nonutilitarian ideas and pastimes that were peripheral aspects of these bonding groups had the power to remove prisoners, if not in body, at least in spirit, from the Lager's slavelike existence. Some of these activities were embedded in a variety of art forms: story telling, writing, reading, painting, music, poetry, and theater. These pastimes seemed to create links to life, giving the prisoners a semblance of autonomy.

But not all artistic pastimes were initiated by prisoners. Some originated with the concentration camp administrators. This, for example, was true for the official concentration camp orchestras, such as the orchestra in Auschwitz, which was an administrative invention. In fact, the Germans usually opposed artistic expressions that they could not control. Painting without official sanction was forbidden, and if discovered some painters would be severely punished. On the other hand, the SS favored certain public entertainments, as long as they were in charge. Some of these Nazi-initiated pastimes were simply additional means of humiliating and degrading the prisoners. Public sports activities and artistic shows in Treblinka fell into this category.[147]

Occasionally prisoners were able to balance their own needs for artistic expression with the German demands. However, the more successful the Germans were in pushing their own agenda, the more devalued these activities were for the inmates. The ghetto-camp Theresienstadt had a particularly active cultural life. Its prominent Jewish artists, transported there from Germany and Austria, were largely responsible for the high caliber of the musical and theatrical offerings. As long as the Germans thought that these artistic expressions were politically harmless, they tolerated and even encouraged them. In fact, the Germans expected the official visitors who inspected the camp to see these cultural events as a validation of their claims that they treated the Jews properly.

"Coffee shops" were erected in the center of the ghetto, where prisoners would come after work to listen to concerts. Some of these inmates were convinced that despite constant hunger and degrading work, exposure to these cultural events immunized them against the surrounding horrors.[148]

Most prisoners preferred to engage in the variety of artistic activities that took place within informal settings. Zahava Ziskowicz-Adam notes, "In the camp, in Riga, we would make theater in our barracks. We did it at night, very quietly. We could do it because we were actually not Musulmann. In this place we did not die of hunger. They needed us for the work. We would also be singing a lot, also in the evening." Aronek Kierszkowski and his brother Dudek attended such get-togethers in their sleeping areas when they were working in the Vivikond mine. Aronek thinks that as the German war situation deteriorated so did the prisoners' fate. Chronic starvation, murderous work, and camp transfers finally ended social and musical undertakings.[149]

Others muse about the different camps, comparing how camp conditions affected group-centered pastimes. One woman remembers her Płaszów imprisonment and how in the evening the women would beg an inmate with a beautiful voice to sing. Listening to this voice was "the only escape from the gray reality":

We were on our bunks, it was dark, and we listened, and listened . . .
But in the Lichtenwerden camp, there was nothing like this. There we
felt oppressed, depleted of energy, for so many years . . . We were free on
Sunday, but the commandant would usually find some punitive jobs for
us. In this last place, when we had a little free time we would only sit
and talk. Some of us were intelligent and cultured women. Some would
recite their own poetry . . . Each of us gave to the group whatever
she could.[150]

Reports about informal, spontaneous singing and how it kept up inmates' spirits abound. Bracha Winger-Ghilai recalls,

We were singing a lot. I had a very good voice, and by the way, it helped me greatly. It helped me in that others reacted to me positively. And also from the perspective of food, they gave me a little food. Even the block Älteste gave me a little more food. Of course, I looked after myself; if I hadn't, nobody would have been able to help me if I did not try hard to make it. Just the fact that I was singing a lot kept up my spirits. But when I talk about singing, I'm not thinking about Bergen-Belsen. There was no singing there. It was too horrible a place for singing.[151]

About her group activities, Ita Shapiro emphasizes,

Most of the women would eat their slice of bread and go to bed. But some would sing. They would sing songs from the ghetto, Jewish songs. We would tell stories and fantasize. We would dream about what we would do once the Germans left. It was sort of nice to run away into the world of fantasy.[152]

Miriam Rubyn's experience shows a shaky connection between bonding groups, work, help, and singing:

For the first months in Auschwitz I worked in the kitchen. I was peeling potatoes, cleaning carrots, and so on. It was a good job. I could throw out of the window food to women who were standing out there . . . They liked me at my work . . . I would sing and dance for them. As a reward, they gave me extra food, which I could bring to my group. Then suddenly, all this ended . . . They moved us out from the kitchen to the factory work.

With the loss of this job, Miriam also lost her enthusiasm for singing.[153]

Others, both men and women, mention story telling as an informal pastime. To one woman prisoner, "It was the most important thing . . . Those stories we told each other, they took us out of ourselves. They gave us something bigger than our surroundings." Primo Levi remembers such evenings in Auschwitz: "From the outside door, secretly looking around cautiously, the story-teller comes in . . . At once gathers around him a small, attentive, silent crowd. He chants an indeterminable Yiddish rhapsody, always the same one, in rhymed quatrains, of a resigned and penetrating melancholy . . .

It must be a song that he composed himself, in which he has enclosed all the life of the Lager in minute detail. Some are generous and give the story-teller a pinch of tobacco or a needleful of threads; others listen intently but give nothing."[154]

Groups became a place for voicing original dreams. Irena Lusky recalls,

We would tell stories to each other, about books. We were always dreaming about what we would do when it was over. I said that I was going to have a maid and twelve pairs of panties. Yes, I was thinking about panties. Everyone dreamed about something different.[155]

But some survivors I interviewed refused to dwell on camp entertainments. For some, perhaps their own plight had prevented them from noticing such activities. Others were opposed in principle to talking about camp entertainment, seeing it as disrespectful to the memory of the murdered. When Felicja Karay began her research into the camp where she was imprisoned, Skarżysko Kamienna, she met with opposition from some former prisoners. As she tells me,

I wanted to find out about the different sections, about their informal leisure activities, and our smart Jews didn't want to give me information about it; they didn't want to talk about it. They said, "On the graves, there is no singing." These were people from smaller, provincial places, and this mentality remained with them all their lives. There were many Jews, when I was writing my book, who didn't want to talk to me. And there were some who gave me wonderful testimony . . . When it comes to testimony, everyone has some drawers shut and some drawers open. To make order out of this mess is hard . . . involvement in cultural life really kept us alive. There is no doubt about that.[156]

Like others, Felicja describes the way cultural activities varied from camp to camp, even among the three camps of Skarżysko Kamienna. For example, she mentions that prisoners were only able to give two public concerts in Section C of the camp:

Of the three camps, C was the most debilitating place . . . We were in a small group. There were a few people from the Akiva movement.

I remember when we would get together we did a lot of mutual sharing and mutual giving . . . If not for that, everyone would have died. There was Inberger, a wonderful young man. He was a musicologist. Unfortunately, he did not survive the war. He was organizing choral groups. We would sing in these groups. Many things I forgot, but all the songs I sang in this chorus I do remember.

In August 1944, when Skarżysko Kamienna was liquidated, Felicja was transferred with a group of women prisoners to a Leipzig camp, where she worked in the Hasag ammunition factory. The work force consisted of women only—Jews, Poles, Frenchwomen, and Russians. Felicja describes the changes:

I took a very active part in the cultural life in Leipzig. In Leipzig conditions were not so bad. The Polish women sort of organized the camp, and there was some competition. The supervisor of the camp was a Christian Pole, and they introduced theaters, and so on. The second in command was also a Pole. It was later discovered that she was actually a Jewish woman passing as a Christian.

Bombs were falling on Leipzig; the war was about to end. The commandant, although he was known as a horror, did not interfere so much. Each of the national groups, the Poles, the French, etc., each organized some cultural activities. The Russians were watched more carefully. The Jewish women, too. In the evenings we would recite poetry. There were two women poets with me, Ilona Karmel, who wrote the book *In a State of Memory;* she was a known poet. Another book is *Stefania,* which came out in English. We were really not working together, among the groups, but each group listened to the other. Especially the others listened to us, because our poets were talented. My two older sisters were writers; one wrote beautiful prose . . . On New Year's, 1945, we arranged a concert for the entire camp.

For the first two months, in Leipzig, the food was good, and this put us on our feet. Otherwise, we would not have made it. Later on, we were hungry there too . . . Leipzig was probably most unusual in terms of its artistic productions.

Although women seem to have taken the lead in some of the artistic activities, men were also active in the cultural life of Skarżysko Kamienna. Several men were involved in performing and writing music; others wrote poetry, which many left unsigned. Karay concludes,

The prisoners fought not only to preserve their lives, but also to preserve their identity. They used their manner of resistance available to them: self-help and social and cultural activities . . . A chat, a song or a simple word of encouragement strengthened the prisoners' hope, maintained their solidarity, and added a spark of humanity to their hellish existence.[157]

Former camp prisoners often spoke about their many bonding activities and how these related to survival. Trying to ascertain what else might have touched upon their lives, I would continue to probe. Spontaneously, some would mention their dreams and fantasies. I had not anticipated such comments. Thus, for example, when I casually asked Roma Nutkiewicz-Benatar what helped her overcome the concentration camp horrors, she said, "My mother." Intrigued, I asked how and in what way. I knew that Roma admired her mother's intelligence and courage. I also knew that because of her parents' efforts she had been sent out of the Warsaw ghetto to work on a nearby estate. When she returned to the ghetto in the summer of 1942, her parents were gone, and she never saw them again. Roma was convinced that she had to live up to her parents' expectations, particularly her mother's. She saw her struggle to survive as a tribute to her mother.

Roma knew how complicated her efforts to live were.

First of all, what helped me survive was in part an instinct of every human being that wants to live. Self-preservation. But in my particular case, I made an extra effort because I felt that my parents wanted me to live and that I owed it to them to follow their wishes. My mother was so very important for me! And so, in the most difficult times, I would review in my mind my grandmother's address in Palestine, not to forget that I wanted to go to her. And all the time I sort of tried to talk myself into the fact that when this was over, my parents would be alive, and I would find them. This was so despite the fact that I knew they were dead. I just did not accept it . . . For years after the war, I would walk the streets and think that I would see them, that I would find them. I had a family here in Israel, my grandmother and my mother's brother; it grew into a big family. But I was sure that my parents had to have survived. It made no sense, it wasn't logical . . . Both during the war and later I would daydream of how I would meet them. Even in Auschwitz, I would dream about meeting them.[158]

In part, what seemed to help Roma in the camps was her ability to detach herself from her environment, to deny the reality of the Lager. Roma was not alone in this.

Zahava Ziskowicz-Adam went through several camps with her sister. They had belonged to the group of Vilna women discussed earlier. To my question of what most helped her survive, she answers, "I think that it was my imagination, my fantasies."

"What kind?"

"When I closed my eyes, I threw away all the reality around me. I thought about good things from my past, warmth and friendships, I thought about wonderful things that were, that will be. I was thinking of how marvelous it would be to survive the war."[159]

Remembering those they loved gave many the courage to carry on. Tola Szwarc-Chudin had been particularly close to her father, who died of a lung ailment in the Warsaw ghetto. Tola, a veteran of several concentration camps, including the notorious Skarżysko Kamienna, always thought that she would survive. "I believed that I would make it. Each time I dreamed about my father, I was convinced that I would survive. About my mother, I hardly ever dreamed. My father and I were very close. Before the ghetto was established, I would accompany him on his various business activities."[160]

Spontaneously, without my probing, she adds, "I was touched by his goodness. The night my father died he said to my aunt, an old maid who was helping take care of him, 'If we survive the war, I will take care of you. You will never need to work.'" When she dreamed of her father, it may be that

having him in her mind, with her, helped Tola remove herself from her surroundings. Most daughters and sons emphasize their strong attachments to
their mothers rather than fathers. Tola was an exception.

Dobka Freund-Waldhorn also mentioned dreaming in her comments
about survival. "I know that I built for myself a world of illusions. During
the day, I did what I had to do, and at night I was dreaming. I was dreaming
of what I would do after I left the camp. The reality was so horrible that it
was impossible to live. I think that most of us had to do this. I was not exceptional."[161]

Ruth Hudes-Tatarko compares the different worlds, real and make-
believe, that she lived in. She describes how she dealt with the reality of
Auschwitz.

> I remember one night the whole sky up there was so red like fire and the
> smell was so horrible, so heavy. I couldn't sleep; it was sort of choking
> me. I knew what it meant, and what it was. They were burning people.
> We knew exactly what was happening. At another time, one early morn-
> ing, I went out of our barracks and was sitting outside, I saw birds sit-
> ting on the electrical wires that were surrounding us. You have to realize
> that we did not see any flowers, grass or trees, nothing. I sometimes
> thought, how does a tree look? I didn't remember any more. I did not
> tell you this before, but I had all kinds of fantasies. It was something
> between fantasy and a dream. I thought to myself, I tried to talk to myself
> and say that whatever I see around me is not really real. And that maybe
> I am dreaming, a dream and that this is a nightmare, and it is really not
> happening, I am just dreaming about it. I was pretending that I would
> wake up soon and find out that all of this around me was a dream.
>
> I was inviting these fantasies to myself. So when I was sitting that
> early morning and the sky was so red and the smell was there . . . I
> thought to myself that this is hell. And then I thought to myself that I
> must be dreaming. I talked to myself, If only one of these birds would
> take me out of here, out of this!! These were my fantasies. As I think back,
> I was sort of ordering for myself dreams. I was creating for myself a make-
> believe world. Something that was not part of this hell around me.[162]

These accounts, collected separately and independently, show how each of these prisoners relied on their dreams and fantasies for survival. Because I had not expected such responses, I made no attempt to elicit them. The fact that the comments were spontaneous and consistent increases their validity. Together they emphasize the frequently heard generalization that the more horrendous an environment the harder people try to escape its destructive forces, often in unusual ways. For the Lager prisoners, the world of dreams and fantasies represented one of these special flights.

I had not anticipated such findings because I had read assertions to the contrary, claims that the horrors of concentration camp existence barred inmates from entering the world of fantasies and dreams.[163] My unanticipated findings contradict this assertion. Probably concentration camp inmates who had reached the Musulmann stage were unable to participate in these ephemeral journeys into an unreal world. And yet the more horrendous the environment the greater seemed to be the efforts to escape from the grim reality.

The need for self-preservation, feelings of autonomy, and actual survival are intricately connected in ways that are often unclear. In this chapter I have explored through the collective experiences of concentration camp inmates what *they* thought was responsible for their own survival. At first, each one said simply: luck, chance, fate. Prisoners did not wish to suggest that their survival was contingent on their talent, intelligence, or personal efforts. But as I continued to probe, to search out what other factors they thought were responsible beyond these intangible, elusive things we call luck, chance, and fate, they came up with additional reasons but insisted that these were neither necessary nor sufficient causes for survival. They saw such factors as secondary at best. Most survivors agreed that central among these subsidiary reasons for survival were cooperation and mutual compassion. Most of these prisoners at one time or another belonged to an informal bonding group that involved mutually supportive efforts. Both sexes relied on the relief offered by joining or creating such mutually supportive groups, which, by giving them some autonomy, improved the quality of their lives. For most, being part of these groups gave them a reason to be alive.

6

Hiding and Passing in the Forbidden Christian World

With the arrival of each trolley car the crowd would move forward in a huge wave, only to retreat in disappointment as the train picked up just two or three passengers. The rest remained at the stop, watching the arrival and departure of each overflowing vehicle. This seemingly endless wait, made more agonizing by the approaching curfew, must have added to the frustration of the would-be passengers, for the shoving increased. Ruth belonged to the timid minority of this contracting and expanding mass. After several tentative trials she opted for the long walk home.

Suddenly someone grabbed my hands and pulled me back. First I thought it was perhaps a man trying to get fresh. But no! There were three SS men. They asked me to admit that I was Jewish; I kept saying desperately, "No, no, you are mistaken . . . I am a Roman Catholic, Krystyna Kosina." I produced my passport and a worker's registration card, but to no avail. After beating me up, they dragged me to the nearest Gestapo office . . .

I was kept in jail for a week — a week of physical and mental torture, beaten to unconsciousness, revived with cold water thrown over me,

interrogated again and again. All they wanted me to say was that I was
Jewish . . .
    I was released after my landlady confirmed that I was Catholic and
her tenant. She came to take me home. I was half dead, bruised,
wounded, and terribly frightened.

Ruth never found out what had made the SS men suspect that she was
Jewish.[1]

Ruth had probably been denounced. She had violated a Nazi law that
made an unauthorized Jewish presence on the Aryan side a crime. Judging
by the length of her interrogation, the Gestapo needed more solid evidence.
Ruth was fortunate that the SS men did not act solely upon the information
they had. She was also fortunate that her Christian landlady was willing to
vouch for her as a Catholic Pole. Ruth's experience illustrates several conditions that affected the lives of illegal Jews.

    The danger in being recognized as Jews originated in the initial Nazi
decrees barring them from special areas. In eastern Europe, particularly the
territories that had been part of prewar Poland, such prohibitions were
clear-cut. On October 15, 1941, a new law made any unauthorized Jewish
move outside the ghetto a crime punishable by death. The same punishment applied to Christians who helped Jews enter or live in the forbidden
Christian world.[2]

    This law was widely publicized, and transgressions were promptly fol-
lowed by executions — which were also widely publicized. The Germans
were efficient. As part of their continuous anti-Semitic propaganda, they
offered rewards for those who denounced Jews. The nature of these prizes
varied depending on the locality and the demands for certain goods. They
included rye flour, sugar, vodka, cigarettes, clothing; in some instances the
reward was half the property of the apprehended fugitive. Some native collaborators were lured by the rewards; some came under the influence of the
Nazi propaganda, accepting the definition of Jews as subhuman.[3] Others
made a business out of blackmailing Jews.

    Scattered evidence, based on individual cases and special samples,
underscores the precariousness of the position of illegal Jews. Of the 308

illegal Jews whom I studied, an overwhelming majority (88 percent) were blackmailed, denounced, arrested, or almost arrested.[4] All concur that on the Aryan side Jewish fugitives faced a seemingly inexhaustible array of obstacles and threats. As part of the anti-Jewish campaign, the Nazis continually emphasized the presence of such runaways, urging non-Jews to deliver up the fugitives. The many pressures to apprehend Jews created a virtual Jew-hunt.

Additional dangers arose from the body of German laws designed for local non-Jewish populations. Many of these newly established regulations were more punitive toward men than women. For example, in Poland, in one of their early oppressive measures the Germans targeted the Polish male elite: intellectuals and professionals, clergy and army officers. Some of them were murdered. Others were sent to concentration camps. But the persecution of Poles was not limited to the upper echelons of society. Following the annexation of parts of western Poland to the Reich, the Nazis began to Germanize the region. This involved the removal of large segments of the native population. Such transfers were forcible, without regard to human cost.

In addition to persecuting Poles, the Germans, guided by their own economic needs throughout the war, continued to deport Poles to the Reich to work. Of the estimated 2.5 million who were thus transported, many were worked to death, while others returned in wretched condition. As well, during the German occupation any sign of political opposition brought swift and brutal suppression.[5]

Not only in Poland but in all countries under German occupation, men were more vigorously persecuted than women. The greater distrust of men grew out of the Nazi reliance on patriarchal principles; as I mentioned earlier, men were seen as intelligent, rational, and aggressive, while women were defined as intellectually limited, emotional, and passive. In part these varied gender perceptions were reflected in Nazi laws that required all male adults to work, preferably in jobs that benefited the German economy. Such laws made the presence of young men on the streets automatically suspect. Invariably, the authorities would check the documents of men before they checked those of women. Anyone who violated Nazi employment laws or was engaged in "insignificant" work could be sent to Germany for forced labor. Men who were identified as Jews were executed. Those who were suspected of being members of underground groups were shot or imprisoned.

Because women were considered politically unsophisticated, less intelligent, and more passive, little attention was paid to them. Some Nazi laws excluded non-Jewish mothers and housewives from compulsory employment. Unless non-Jewish women were caught in a raid designed to collect bodies for slave labor in Germany or as a reprisal against the killing of a German, their presence in the streets of towns was ignored.[6]

Jews who lived on the Aryan side were affected by two sets of laws: those that targeted them as Jews and those that applied to native Christian populations. The nature of these laws, with their emphasis on men, added to the precariousness of the situation for the illegal Jewish males. As time went by the search was stepped up for all escaping Jews and their Gentile protectors. But neither the Nazi laws nor the harsh enforcement of them prevented some Jews from entering the Aryan side and some Poles from helping them.[7] Ghetto runaways who came to the illegal Christian world simply substituted one set of dangers for another. Most had known about the lurking perils.

In the course of my interviews with concentration camp survivors a few quite unexpectedly spoke about Jewish life on the Aryan side. Tola Szwarc-Chudin, a Warsaw ghetto dweller and concentration camp inmate, felt that life on the Aryan side, with its continuous threats of discovery, was torture. Convinced that she could not have made it in this kind of surrounding, Tola referred to Jews who stood up to these challenges as heroes.[8] Karla Szajewicz-Frist also spontaneously compared her concentration camp experiences to what the illegal Jews had to endure.

> We were fatalists; we were all together; those who were on the Aryan side didn't have anyone to lean on; they were constantly on guard, constantly afraid they'd be discovered. All the time a person had to think, How do I walk? How do I look? What do they think? And so on. One was always tense. But we in the camp, we became robots. We all wanted to live. Somehow, deep inside us . . . we felt that maybe we had a

chance . . . Perhaps we were more hopeful . . . did not have these continual fears. I did not feel that people wanted to do something bad just to me; I knew that they wanted to do something bad to everybody; I wasn't singled out. I got some comfort from thinking that I was in the same boat as everyone else.[9]

Occasionally a few of those who were on the run would even feel relieved when their efforts came to an abrupt stop. In Hungary, Dvora Rosenbaum-Fogel and her first husband eluded capture by constantly changing addresses. In 1944 they went into hiding at the home of a Hungarian Christian whom they paid. This move coincided with the German takeover of Hungary and the stepped-up persecution of Hungarian Jews. Massive concentration camp deportations began, along with threats against those who harbored Jews. One day the sound of voices invaded the hideout of Dvora and her husband, alerting them that their host had denounced them. Dvora recalls, "When they arrested us . . . I was glad. Why? Because to be in hiding, your heart beats fast all the time. You are always scared. I thought, I'm caught already; whatever will be, will be."[10] Dvora's relief was real. Yet she submitted to her fate only when she was forced to.

Most Jews who managed to survive in the Christian world, however, were convinced that what happened to them was not as horrendous as what the concentration camp survivors had endured. These perceptions may explain the reluctance of some Jews who survived on the Aryan side to confront their wartime past. The idea that they somehow had it "easy" may also account for the inability of some of these Jews to mourn.[11]

The unpredictability and danger that were at the core of the lives of these illegal Jews created a special need for cooperation and mutual aid. In my sample of 308 Jews who lived on the Aryan side, 95 percent say that they received help from others, mostly Christian Poles. When questioned more closely, even the 5 percent who felt that they had been on their own had benefited from some kind of aid. In these cases, a warning about danger or a one-night stay in someone's home sometimes made the difference between life and death. Although this aid did not guarantee survival, failure to locate people who offered it made survival virtually impossible.[12]

Some of those who gave up on the Aryan side did so because they were convinced that they had exhausted all their options. The fate of Tola Szwarc-Chudin's brother illustrates this. In 1943, after the Warsaw ghetto uprising, the teenaged boy was herded into a cattle car destined for Treblinka. On the way, he jumped off the moving train and returned to Warsaw. A penniless fugitive, he made the rounds of his Christian Polish friends and acquaintances asking for help. None was forthcoming. After countless rejections, this homeless youth jumped off a tall building.[13]

The lives of Jewish women and men were also affected by a range of personal characteristics and coping strategies. To begin with, Jewish men were circumcised. A casual examination could thus easily reveal a man's Jewishness. In contrast, "women who were caught could get out of it. A woman could do that but not a man."[14] Inevitably then, the potential consequences of their circumcision dominated the lives of illegal Jewish males, affecting all aspects of their existence.

Other factors also exerted distinct pressures upon the lives of illegal Jews, both women and men. One was physical appearance. Individuals whose features conformed to the stereotypical "Jewish look" were more likely to be caught. Dark curly hair, black eyes, and a long crooked nose were all part of this stereotypical look. In contrast, having straight blond hair, blue eyes, or a short nose tended to protect Jews who came close to this idealized Aryan image.

In reality, the looks of most men and women fell somewhere between these two extremes. For Jewish men, however, having even slightly suspicious features was particularly dangerous, for if they were arrested, their circumcision would betray them. Not surprisingly, therefore, some of those whose appearance was deemed "risky" decided to avoid exposure and preferred to hide. Physical appearance, then, for both men and women, and the fact of circumcision were two major factors in the decision of whether to stay hidden or to try and pass as a Gentile. Even so, to become invisible Jews needed Christian protectors who were ready to take risks. Such protectors were rare.

A Jewish appearance and the lack of a Christian protector led to the murder of Ania Rud's husband. She explains:

> Because he looked very Jewish, he stayed in the ghetto longer than I . . . He tried once to leave. He grew a moustache, but it was very dangerous for him; everybody looked at him. So he went back to the ghetto . . . We decided he should try to reach the Aryan side just before dark, so people wouldn't notice him . . . that he should try again. But the day before he was supposed to leave, the ghetto was closed. We saw it from the outside. Many Ukrainians surrounded the place. At first we didn't know what was happening.

After the war Ania heard that her husband had eluded the main deportation and for a while continued to hide in the almost empty, closely guarded ghetto. She never found out how he died.[15]

For Alexandra Sołowejczyk-Guter's group the disadvantages of their Jewish appearance were outweighed by the unusual readiness of Polish rescuers to protect them. Alexandra recalls, "While in hiding, I only walked into the streets in the evenings, when people couldn't see me, because everybody recognized me as a Jew."[16]

Like Alexandra, the entire Gottesfeld family could be recognized as Jewish by their appearance. The parents, a seventeen-year-old daughter, Fanya, and a ten-year-old son, Arthur, lived in the small town of Skala, in Galicia. Here the majority of the Christians were Ukrainians. The Jews and the other natives lived in separate worlds, untouched by cooperation. The Gottesfelds knew their neighbors well enough to realize that they could not count on them. Besides, their Jewish appearance and shortage of money widened the gap between them and any potential rescuers. But just as the Gottesfelds thought that they had exhausted all options, Jan, a Ukrainian militiaman, appeared, seemingly from nowhere. A shoemaker by trade, this young man had joined the local militia that collaborated with the Nazis. Engaged to be married to a Ukrainian woman, Jan fell in love with Fanya Gottesfeld.

Jan and Mr. Gottesfeld became friends, and Fanya had no idea that she was the reason for the Ukrainian's visits. She was puzzled when her father urged her to be nice to him. After Jan broke off his engagement, his attachment to Fanya became more obvious. Later it dawned on Fanya that her father had agreed to a postwar marriage between her and Jan in exchange for his promise to rescue her family.

Jan's relatives, particularly his mother, were vehemently opposed to the connection. They warned Jan not to bring any Jews near their property and threatened to denounce him if he did. Although he had no home of his own, Jan disregarded these warnings. Cautious yet determined, he secretly built a hideout in the barn next to his family's house.

One day Jan heard at the police station that the Germans were about to make Skala free of Jews (*judenrein*), and he brought Fanya and her brother Arthur to his hideout. The older Gottesfelds were transferred, with the remaining Jews, to a nearby ghetto. As Jan continued to take care of his charges, he also kept in touch with their parents. Later he found a place for them with Ukrainian peasants. Food was becoming scarce for both the Gottesfelds and their protectors. Yet all shared their meager provisions — as well as their continually growing anxieties. Mixed in with serious deprivations were the attachments that became part of the rescuer-rescued existence.

Jan's family and neighbors suspected him of aiding the Gottesfelds. But they had no clue where he had hidden them. Through ridicule and threats they pressured him to reveal the whereabouts of his charges. Jan never caved in. This young Ukrainian, with little formal education, was socially beneath the Jewish family he so courageously shielded. But what Jan lacked in schooling and social standing, he seemed to make up for in sensitivity, an inborn refinement and common sense. It was natural to him to identify himself not only with the woman he loved but also with the rest of her family.

In 1944 the Germans retreated from the advancing Soviet army, abandoning Skala. The Gottesfelds had all survived. It appeared that Jan had not only won the battle against the Germans, he had also won Fanya's love. Then Mr. Gottesfeld disappeared under mysterious circumstances. Shortly afterward, Mrs. Gottesfeld left Skala with their two children, never to return. Before she left, the woman Jan had loved and whose life he had saved married a Jew.

Because Jan was a member of the Ukrainian militia, the Soviets deported him to Siberia. A few years later, he returned, dejected and in poor health. An outcast among his own people, he had become a changed man, and soon Jan committed suicide by hanging himself.

Although a Nazi collaborator, Jan had treated his charges most considerately. His conduct and fate defy conventional expectations, underscoring the complexities of life under the German occupation. In the end Jan became a double victim: of political upheavals and broken promises.[17]

Having a Jewish appearance, although a significant factor, was not the only element in the decision to hide. As a prominent surgeon Alexandra Sołowejczyk-Guter's husband had a wide circle of acquaintances: patients, employees, co-workers, and many others would have recognized him. Rather than risk being denounced, he opted for an invisible existence and stayed hidden. Similarly, Dr. A. Liebesman-Mikulski, after escaping from the Stanisławów ghetto, spent the last part of the war in hiding. For him, too, the decision to become invisible was dictated by the large number of people who knew him. His mother-in-law and wife, both of whom were passing as Christians, protected him. They had rented an apartment in the community where Dr. Liebesman-Mikulski was born.[18]

Unrelated to gender, then, were the dangers of chance encounters with someone from the past. Anita Adler had one such unexpected encounter. In 1938, after the Nazi takeover of Austria, Anita's parents urged her to leave. They felt that Poland, which was still an independent country, would be a safe haven for their only child. The young and adventurous Anita reached her destination, but after several brushes with the Polish authorities, with considerable help from the Jewish community she ended up in Vilna. Here, Anita fell in love with the writer Herman Adler, and they married. Eventually the young couple relocated to Warsaw, where Herman passed as a Czech and Anita as an Italian. Under an assumed name, Anita found employment in a German hospital. Officially she was a secretary. Unofficially, she acted as her boss's administrative assistant.

She describes her job and the threat it brought.

Because I had finished business school, I would help my boss, who didn't know how to run a hospital. As a part of my work I would distribute money to hospitalized German soldiers. One day, as I was handing out the money, one of the sick soldiers asked me, "What are you doing here?"

I said, "What do you mean?" My legs were shaking. I did not recognize him at all. But sure enough, when I checked the files I saw that the two of us were once students in the same acting school . . .

He denounced me to the mean German sergeant, who went to my superior. I guessed he had done this when, through the window, I saw the two of them approach my office. I thought, "Should I jump through the window?" I knew then that something was coming. "Should I warn my husband? What to do?" But instead I sat down near my typewriter with my back to the door, so they wouldn't see my face, and I began to type with fury.

My boss opened the door. He came in, and I heard him say, "There is no trace of it, no evidence at all." He didn't say anything to me. He did not admit it [the possibility that Anita was Jewish]. He rejected it. Because he said there was no evidence, the sergeant had to listen; my boss was his superior.[19]

Also potentially disastrous was one of Ania Rud's chance encounters. It occurred in Białystok when, passing as a Gentile, she went to get a document on the basis of her Aryan birth certificate. Ania recalls,

When I opened the door to this office, I saw a young man, a Pole, a fellow student, with whom I had studied for a teacher's license. I thought, "What should I do?" He noticed me. I knew that. But he seemed to be indifferent, and explained what to do next. He said, "Go and have a picture taken." Then he told me what else to do. I did it. And when I came back, I got the document. Of course he knew who I was. I was fortunate. He was a good person.[20]

No one knows how often an unexpected encounter erased the advantages that came with an Aryan appearance.[21] But the protective shield offered by an Aryan look could disappear in confrontations with strangers as well. Alexandra Sołowejczyk-Guter describes such a case.

We had a friend who looked like a thousand Poles; he had no resemblance to a Jew. But he had to move around town because he had to make a living. Once, he was just walking the streets, and a Pole stopped him with a "Come into the courtyard." He went in. The usual happened: the Pole threatened, made our friend pull down his pants, and then examined his documents. In the end our friend had to bribe the blackmailer.

Before leaving, our friend asked, "How did you ever recognize me?"

"Well, you are the fifth one that I caught today. Some were Jews and some were not. After all, Christmas is coming and I need extra money. This is how I earn it."

You see, once this friend was stopped, the very same day his apartment was suddenly of no use. The blackmailer saw from the documents where he lived. Now this Jew passing as a Christian had no apartment. He was desperately looking for an apartment when the police caught him.[22]

Even though an Aryan appearance could not always provide protection, it usually served as an important asset to both men and women.

Documents that identified a Jew as a Christian offered additional protection. Usually when several members of a family managed to reach the Aryan side, they would prefer to take different names. In case of an arrest, at least some could be spared, claiming not to know one another. Some documents were manufactured illegally and gave fictitious names. Others were duplicates of documents which belonged to real people, both living and dead.[23]

In Poland non-Jewish men and women who were of age were required to carry a special document, a *Kennkarte,* that was issued on the basis of a birth certificate. Non-Jewish civilians had to apply for this new identity card in person. Each Kennkarte gave the owner's name, date and place of birth, present occupation, and religion. Holders of Kennkartes then had to register a second time with the vital records office.[24] The requirement that one appear personally in two offices stopped many Jews from getting such valid documents. Of Jews who passed as Christians only a minority had obtained officially issued papers. Others had a variety of false documents. Still others had no documents at all.

Whether backed by documents or not, a new identity required familiarity with the facts contained in the new identity. It also called for knowledge of the Christian religion and practices. Poland was a country where people took their Catholicism seriously. Ignorance of prayers and customs would have helped confirm a suspected Jewish identity. But familiarity with the new identity and knowledge of Christian practices were only two of the factors that could tip the scale in favor of a Jew who was passing as Christian.

It was especially important that Jews be fluent in the native language of the area in which they were living and be able to blend into the native culture. In eastern Europe Jewish women seem to have had certain advantages over their men. In the Jewish religion women had traditionally been pushed into peripheral positions. They were barred from religious, political, and cultural leadership, confined to the domestic sphere. Women only occasionally earned a living, usually when their husbands devoted themselves to religious study. Because women were excluded from traditional Jewish educational pursuits, they had more freedom to become involved in secular education. In practice this meant that women were more familiar with the common language of the country and were more fully integrated into the native non-Jewish culture.[25]

It is generally agreed that in small prewar Polish towns Jewish women had more contacts with the local population than Jewish men. The women's greater exposure to the secular culture through education and day-to-day contacts with Gentiles gave them a greater ability to blend into the non-Jewish culture. In my sample of 308 Jews who lived illegally in the Christian world, the percentage of those who spoke Polish moderately well was higher for women than for men (90 percent against 71 percent). Greater familiarity with the local language and fitting more easily into the local culture gave Jewish women advantages in making a life in the illegal Christian world.[26]

However, the ability to submerge into the native culture was in part affected by individuals' subjective reactions to their circumstances. Alexandra Sołowejczyk-Guter felt that all Jews on the Aryan side were inevitably fearful. At the same time, she concedes that there were differences:

> Men were more fearful than women and more likely to hide . . . It was harder to find places for men. If somebody took money for protecting Jews, they took more money for men . . . People were less suspicious of women. A woman could much more easily find an apartment. She could walk around town and pass more easily. A woman could dye her hair. Dressed up, she looked more like a Polish woman. Men even if slightly Jewish looking were more exposed. Women were more resourceful. But they were also fearful. I was afraid, very much so.[27]

I ask her to elaborate and she continues,

> Fear is an interesting thing. When I heard steps on the stairs, I would shake. Later on, during the uprising in Warsaw, the roof was burning and we were trying to put out the fire with pails of water and the bombs were dropping and there was crossfire, [but] I was not afraid at all. Because what happened on the roof was for everybody. Those steps on the stairs were for me, concentrated on me.

Tied to fear was depression. Alexandra believes that men were more depressed than women. As I continue to probe, she explains that the men's tendency to be more depressed began in the early stages of the German occupation, when Jewish men were subjected to more severe persecutions, pushed into degrading hard labor, and were more likely to be murdered. This distinction was sustained for those living on the Aryan side; men could be more easily identified through circumcision and because of the stricter laws that applied to Gentile males. And so, realistically, Jewish men had more to fear than women. On the other hand, individual reactions and perceptions of dangers were not necessarily based on reality.

For example, compared to other Jews who were passing as Christians, Sandra Brand had little reason to be anxious. She had what was considered to be a typically Aryan appearance, and she spoke Polish fluently. Immediately after she came to Warsaw she had obtained a secure job in a German firm as a Polish-German interpreter. She also had solid documents, including a duplicate of a real birth certificate given her by a Polish friend. In short, she was an "ideal" candidate for a Christian Gentile. Despite these advantages, Sandra admits to having been extremely frightened. At times she was on the verge of giving up, convinced that her Jewish identity was obvious. Sandra knew that Poles expected Jews to gesticulate with their hands, so she was always on guard when talking. During the winter, she carried a muff and kept both hands inside. She believed that this precaution prevented her from conversing like a Jew, at least during the cool months.

Her fears were expressed in other ways as well. On the street, she would try to make herself inconspicuous by walking close to the walls of buildings, almost hugging them, even though she actually thought that it was safer to walk close to the outer edge of the sidewalk. Being at the edge, she argued, gave a Jew a better chance to run. Sandra was never denounced. But she never lost her fears.[28]

Anxiety, fear, and depression were often expressed in the sadness of Jewish eyes. In fact, Jews were known for—and identified by—the sadness of their eyes. Close calls because of "sad eyes" were common. Vladka Meed describes one such incident.

I always played a role. I tried to fit but was always told about my sad eyes. "These are Jewish eyes," they said. I was once stopped on a tram traveling with a Polish friend from the underground. It was eight in the morning. We were standing on the platform. I noticed a policeman pass. It seems that my eyes rested on him. I was not even aware of it. In a moment, the train stopped, and this man jumped onto the platform. Coming straight to me he asked for my documents. I had with me two kinds of documents, with two different names. He ordered me to come off the tram. He was taking me to the police station to have my papers properly checked. I knew that once I reached the station I would be lost.

I asked him why he was taking me, adding that I had to go to work. I tried to smile at him. He wanted to know if I was afraid. I said, "Why should I be? I cannot understand why you took me off the tram." To this he said, "Maybe I'm making a mistake."

So I asked him what it was all about; I wanted him to explain. His answer was, "You know, you look Polish."

"But I am Polish," I interrupted.

"But you have Jewish eyes," he said.

I started to laugh. "How is this possible?"

He laughed too. I was young; it was a nice morning; so I asked him, "Can you give me my things back; after all, I'm in a rush to get to my job."

He said, "Okay, take it."

Then I asked if I could jump on the tram. "I will stop it," he said. And he did.[29]

When I myself was about to enter the illegal Christian world, my parents kept urging me above all else not to have sad eyes. I was about ten years old, and I wanted to know how this could be done. They told me to pretend that I was happy by thinking about happy things that were and happy things that would be. Their advice invariably ended with "You must try to have happy eyes!" I tried.[30]

The historian Emanuel Ringelblum concurs that Jews on the Aryan side could be recognized by the sadness of their eyes. Such eyes, he said, had a "melancholy . . . pensiveness. The whole suffering of the ghetto, the many years of torment, the loss of family . . . all this was concentrated in their [eyes]." Ringelblum describes one man's solution to the problem. Whenever this man left the ghetto for the Aryan side, "he assumed a grim facial expression and, so he says, his eyes darted angry glances." This was a safer alternative.[31]

The ability to switch from anxiety to a smile and play the part of a non-Jew with assurance could save one's life. Ania Rud, who lived in Białystok passing as a Christian Belorussian, explains how important flexibility and quick reactions were.

We women acted instinctively. We were not thinking. Only after the fact did we think, "Why did I do this, why did I do that?" not at the time.

I was once arrested. A Belorussian took me to the Gestapo. He insisted that I was Jewish and not a Belorussian woman as my papers said. At the Gestapo they checked my documents.

The German who examined them said, "These papers are in order."

But the Belorussian replied, "There are many with papers, but this one is Jewish."

"He doesn't know his job!" I said. "Here I am working, I am busy, he grabs me from the street and brings me in." As I was talking and objecting, a high officer passed with a beautiful woman on his arm. I turned to them. "I don't know what they want. I am busy and I will lose my job because of them. Why don't they look for those they really are after, more of what they want?"

The German at the desk added, "I really don't see anything wrong." So they told me, "Go ahead." I left."[32]

This was the only time Ania was caught. Had she submitted then, she would probably not have survived.

A similar, less dramatic incident happened to the Viennese-born Anita Adler, who in Warsaw pretended be Italian. She describes a brief encounter with Polish blackmailers.

It was not far from the Warsaw ghetto, near Długa Street. I had a kerchief and a man's coat on. I was not dressed well, waiting for someone. Suddenly two men approached me from the left and right, and they said, "This is a Jewess."

I answered them in the German language I knew so well. "What is it that you want!!?"

They said, "Oh, no, this is a German!" and ran away. But my knees were trembling. One had to take in the situation and respond properly.[33]

For Jews who were passing as Christians there was a delicate balance between physical appearance, behavior, and attitudes. Next to appearance, fear and feelings of insecurity could become easy give-aways. Self-assurance and a relaxed posture could tip the scale in favor of a passing Jew. Unlike men, women under suspicion had a better chance of tipping the scale in their own favor. On rare occasions, however, a man's self-assurance could also counteract suspicions.

One such exception was Oswald Rufeisen, who spent part of the war passing as half-German, half-Polish and worked as an interpreter at the police station in Mir, in western Belorussia. Before Oswald took on his police job, he was constantly identified as a Jew. Each time this happened, suspicions would evaporate when Oswald confronted his accusers with self-assured denials. Oswald's speech and his talent for playing the role helped him belay suspicion. When Oswald assumed the official position at the police station, people stopped questioning his background. He was never checked to see whether he had been circumcised.[34]

Gentiles who had special ties to Jewish men might have been reluctant to subject them to a physical examination. It is also likely that Jewish men who were able to blend quickly into the Christian world could more easily avoid being checked for circumcision precisely because of the ease with which they fit in. Their ability to blend into the culture would create a positive attitude toward them. Such an attitude probably barred lingering suspicions.

The experiences of illegal Jews varied greatly. But allowing for vast differences there were nonetheless certain shared patterns. Among them was the frequent need to change living quarters. Often these moves forced Jews to switch from going into hiding to passing and back again. Some of these changes were prompted by real, some by imaginary dangers.[35]

Jews who lived on the Aryan side had to become unobtrusive, invisible. Alexandra Sołowejczyk-Guter describes how she and the group she was with had at one time to live in an archival office:

> We had to be very quiet. We ate very, very early breakfast and we stayed in bed all day long. We read books or soundlessly played cards, bridge. There were five of us. I was with my husband then, another couple, and my girlfriend's husband.

Later, threatened with denouncement, the group dispersed. When August 1944 came and with it the Polish uprising in Warsaw, Alexandra was separated from the others. People could not stay safely in their homes.

> There were centers where you could enlist into the army of the Polish underground, and that's what I did. I did not know that it was a part of NSZ [a fascist section of the Polish underground]. I went to them and

told them that I wanted to join and that I was Jewish. I announced it very loudly; I was so happy that I could tell them. My job was to listen to the radio from England and to translate it into Polish. Because they were counting on the Russians to take over Warsaw, they were very glad to take Jews as a cover.[36]

Eventually the victorious Germans ordered the evacuation of Warsaw civilians, and Alexandra was one of those moved out. Her superior in the Armia Krajowa (Polish Home Army) gave her a certificate stating that she had fought in the Polish uprising. At the same time he cautioned her against admitting to her Jewishness. Alexandra's looks betrayed her. Shortly after she came to the camp, a Polish friend warned her, "There is talk that you are Jewish. When you leave here they will probably arrest you and take you to the Gestapo."

I was already so down and so upset, and I thought that if they interrogated me too much my nerves would snap. I felt like an animal, running from place to place. To pretend all the time . . . Sometimes an expression could give you away . . . Upon hearing that they knew I was Jewish, I fainted. A German doctor came to give me an injection. He said that he liked me very much and that my illness had spread so widely that he had to send me to a very special place, to Wrocław, for a cure. He took my two hands into his, looked into my eyes, and said, "You probably want to leave, right?" So it was obvious that he knew who I was. And he really saved me. At his order, I went to Wrocław, and nobody could get to me; the Gestapo couldn't reach me. This was already at a time when they were not looking so eagerly; it was almost the end of the war.

Alexandra is convinced that she survived because of the physician's help. Her husband, along with a few others, remained in a cellar during the entire Warsaw uprising. He later discovered that he had tuberculosis; he died in a Swiss sanatorium in 1951, at the age of forty-two.

Alexandra belonged to the privileged few who knew Poles ready to risk their lives to save a Jew. She was also a part of the small minority of illegal Jews who had money. Most Jews living on the Aryan side suffered from a shortage of funds. Employment might solve their financial problems, but it automatically increased the danger of discovery. For Jewish men, in particular, mere suspicion about one's identity could have devastating consequences. The men's special vulnerability is reflected in my findings: of the Jewish men I studied 60 percent lived mainly in hiding, compared to 48 percent of women. More important, only 26 percent of the men compared to 48 percent of the women were employed.[37]

The political and economic wartime conditions affected the illegal lives of women and men differently. Jewish men and women found different employment opportunities. Maids, cooks, and governesses—women's work—topped the list of job openings. After this came agricultural work, generally perceived as a masculine occupation. The continual funneling of slave laborers into Germany from the Nazi-occupied countries created agricultural employment opportunities for those who were left behind. In addition, food shortages, uneven distribution of goods, and rigid prohibitions led to a thriving black market in food and other hard-to-get products. Most black marketeers were women; children were also employed to transport goods.

Tradition barred men from domestic jobs. In contrast, Jewish women found such work suitable. Usually domestic work offered food, shelter, and at least the hope of safety. Eva Safszycka, not yet twenty at the time, took advantage of these circumstances. She had been born into a prosperous family in Baranowicze, in western Belorussia. When the Germans occupied this area in 1941, Eva's parents sent her to stay with their wealthy friends in Warsaw. Eventually, Eva moved with these friends into the Warsaw ghetto. In 1942 the situation became more threatening, and Eva's aunt arranged for her to transfer to the ghetto in Siedlce. But there, too, Eva barely escaped deportation, by hiding in a bunker. During the Aktion, the loud sounds of cries, pleas, and shooting on the outside reached Eva's hideout. Then and there, she decided to do everything in her power to avoid future exposure to the experiences voiced in these sounds. But neither her aunt nor anyone else she approached shared her determination to run away from the ghetto. Eva refused to give up.

After I left the bunker I met a Jewish policeman; he helped me get out of the ghetto. I had three small gold pieces. People thought that I looked like a Pole; my speech was also faultless. But I didn't know the area. I just walked and walked. On the outskirts of Siedlce I came upon an empty brick factory and sneaked in. Then a watchman, or someone who herds cows, came in. To me he looked old. He probably understood who I was. Here I was, seventeen and alone in the middle of the night. Roughly he tried to rape me, threatening that if I did not go along, he would denounce me. When I reacted by saying, "Take me to the Germans." He gave up and left. I stayed on.

Next day, a young Polish man passed by. He too must have guessed that I was Jewish. I asked him for help. I told him that I had the three gold pieces and offered these to him in exchange for Polish papers. He agreed and left with my gold. I waited. This Pole returned with the documents of a young Polish woman who had died; she was younger than I. He also bought me a ticket and put me on the train. I arrived at a place where I expected some help.[38]

Eva went to one of her father's business associates. He in turn contacted his friend Zygmunt Chlasko, the owner of an estate. She picks up her story.

I met with so much kindness from the Poles, so many were decent and helpful that it is unbelievable. The estate I came to belonged to very wealthy people. In a way, I passed through the war in an uninteresting way because I had it so good with these people. I had never met them before. At this estate I worked as a chambermaid and a governess. I did work, but they took me in. Nobody except the owner of the estate and his wife, Helena, knew that I was Jewish. I stayed there until the end. I didn't have a penny and had nothing to wear, but I got everything from them, and they also paid me. The attitude toward me was extraordinary . . . They hid other Jews, one of them a girl of eleven. Chlasko was the head of an oil concern.

Not all experiences of those who took domestic jobs were as positive as Eva's. Examples of exposures to anti-Semitic talk and mistreatment abound. Leah Silverstein, for example, worked in a German household where the woman made unreasonable demands and threatened to transfer her to a concentration camp. Leah feared that the woman's husband, a high Nazi official, might follow up on these threats. She escaped to another city.[39]

Even though there was a shortage of agricultural laborers in eastern Europe, the chances of getting such jobs were limited. Peasants who were in dire need of farmhands could not afford them; many could not even feed their own families. Moreover, the Jewish men who reached the countryside tended to come from urban centers and knew little of farmwork. Some of these men would go into hiding instead, paying for their protection. Of the men who found farm employment, only a few had farming backgrounds. Most Jewish farmhands were teenagers, both women and men, who were flexible and willing to do any kind of work.[40]

But even outside the cities, employment opportunities for Jewish men were rare. In the villages, as in the rest of the countryside, people were afraid to employ Jewish men, for they were more conspicuous, more easily identified, and therefore more dangerous to have around than women. Men were also considered less accommodating than women and thought to require more food; as a rule young farmhands, both men and women, received no payment other than food and shelter.

One of the hard-working teenage girls who found work on a farm was Chava Grinberg-Brown. Born in the small town of Wiśkitki, Chava and her family had lived in abject poverty for as long as she remembered. Even before the war her mother had hired her out to local peasants to tend cows, take care of pigs, and perform other farm jobs. For this work, her mother was probably paid in farm products. After the family was transported to the Warsaw ghetto, the eleven-year-old Chava escaped and tried to return to the villages around her former home. The trip took several weeks. Chava recalls,

> I wanted to go to the places I knew. This was an animallike need that I don't quite understand. On the way, at the end of each day, I would beg people to let me come in and sleep. I remember that once someone gave me a place to stay and offered me chicken soup that was very good and fat. But from this I got diarrhea. In another home, one of the women gave me medication for my skin condition. They knew that I was

Jewish; they had to know; I was so run down, starved, it was obvious.
As I wandered from one little place to another, people fed me and let me
sleep in their homes or close to them; in barns, pigstys, etc.[41]

Chava spoke Polish fluently. A few caring individuals advised her not to
admit to her Jewishness. Others warned her against entering her native
town. She soon learned how right they were.

As I was passing close to my town, I met a Polish fellow who recognized
me. He wanted to take me to the Germans, to get money for it. He
caught me, but I ran away. Some peasants who realized what he was after
threatened to give him a beating he would never forget. That stopped
him from bothering me.

I went to the place where I had worked before. I stayed there for a few
days. After that, they sent me away, so I went to another place, and then
another one. I kept moving from one place to another. Some refused me
work. Then a peasant offered me a more stable job. I had to take care of
geese. The geese had to be fed by force. They would bite and run away
from me.[42] Whenever the geese escaped, this peasant would beat me.

I cried, but only at night. I would dream about my mother, that she
was dying. I somehow felt that my mother was dead, that my father was
dead, deep inside myself I felt it . . . I remained with this peasant for most
of the summer. Then I left and went to another village. I went from one
village to another. Even during the summer I would change places. When
the Poles sent me away, I was not angry. I understood that they were
afraid or had not enough food and could not share the little they had.
I did not particularly feel their anti-Semitism; yet I remember one peasant I worked for who threatened to deliver me to the Germans. I argued
with him that I was not Jewish, that I was a Christian. And he didn't.
Most people knew right away when I came in that I was Jewish, but they
did not harm me. Only a few times did I have to run away.

Chava was on the lookout for danger signs and sensed when she would
have to disappear. She saw herself as hard-working and cheerful. When she
was asked to leave and had no special place to go, she would go to a nearby
village.

When I entered a village I would go first to the head of the village, and he would send me to a peasant. Usually they were not afraid if they had a note from the head of the village. Without such a note they would not have accepted me . . . When I entered a hut, I would say, "Blessed is Jesus Christ and Mother Mary. Maybe you have work and food for me?" I would work at whatever they wanted me to.

I have no bad feelings toward the Christians. I survived the war thanks to them. They helped me. But no one did me any favors. I worked very hard for the food. Whenever they did not need me or want me, they sent me away. I supported myself. I had no one who could pay for me. I worked for it . . . No one worried about me. No one comforted me. I went from village to village and stayed a short time. They would feed me during the winter; they had to eat, so I ate too . . . And I didn't actually suffer hunger. But in the winter I also worked. Maybe I don't remember so well, but I think that they fed me. In the winter you feed the animals, the cows, and the pigs, so they gave me food also. I cleaned their houses. These are things I probably did in the winter.

Asked whether she had an urge after the war to visit the families she had worked for, Chava gave an emphatic no.

Why not?

It was not a good time for me. There was nothing good to remember. I felt no gratitude; no one kept me out of pity or compassion. It was a business exchange. I gave them hard work for the food and the permission to sleep.

Of Chava's family, she alone survived. At the time of this interview, in 1992, Chava was living in Israel, on a moshav (farm). She is married and has three children and many grandchildren. Her life centers around her family, all of whom live close by.

Tema Rotman-Weinstock's story resembles Chava's. She was born in a small town to a poor family. As long as she can remember, they lived in a slumlike apartment that threatened to collapse. Tema had only four years of schooling, but her Polish was fluent, and she was familiar with village customs. From the beginning of the Nazi occupation, Tema, dressed as a peasant, smuggled food from the countryside to the town to help support her family. During the last stage of the war she roamed the familiar countryside. She worked hard and had to move from employer to employer, most of whom were hungry themselves and found it hard to feed her. Constantly exposed to raids, cold, and hunger, Tema fought against her feelings of hopelessness.

One winter, while searching in vain for shelter, she suffered frostbite in three of her toes. A peasant woman who could hardly support herself and her retarded daughter took pity on Tema and kept her for three months. But the days when peasants were willing to keep her were coming to an end. Tema's frostbitten toes continued to hurt her, and hunger made her grow thin. Finding solace in prayers, she persevered. For a while she hid out with a few meager provisions in the attic of a small roadside chapel. But hunger drove her out, and she went on until she found a hut. There she met a cousin who had come in from the forest to buy provisions. He told her that he and his wife lived in a bunker in the forest. Tema begged him to let her join them. He refused. She continued to roam the countryside, sick and often starving. When she was on the verge of collapse, kind peasants took her into their home. She describes her stay.

I could not regain my health. I stopped feeling hunger, vomited a lot, and suffered from headaches. I was hardly able to work. And after a month, afraid to keep me, this peasant, Popko, directed me to a woman who lived on a farm with her daughter. This woman had a hard time running the farm, yet she was too poor to hire a farmhand. The village was called Kajtanówka, and the name of the peasant was Niedźwiedzka. Her hut was far from the main road, and the Germans were unlikely to come there . . . She was not afraid to take me in; and I worked for her as much as I could. She fed me mainly potatoes and milk, while she and her daughter ate bread."[43]

The year 1944 brought the Russian front closer. Tema's health continued to deteriorate. She could barely eat, yet she had to work hard. Her employer seemed pleased with her; then somehow the word spread that Tema was Jewish. Fortunately, no bad consequences followed because she found a powerful protector in the local priest. He baptized Tema and defended her against those who still saw her as a Jew. "The priest stood up for me, arguing that conversion was a wonderful Christian deed . . . Slowly I began to feel better, my health improved, and the wounds on my toes healed . . . Then a miracle happened. I saw my mother, dressed the way she had been when we parted. She entered the hut, smiling, and said that we wouldn't be suffering much longer because on the 23rd of July the Soviets would come to liberate us." When Tema reported this vision to her employer and neighbors, they laughed at her. She herself began to doubt her dream or vision. But "the miracle happened — on July 23, 1944, the first Soviet soldiers came to our village and to the next one."

After the Soviets came, a group of women rushed into Tema's house, calling her Santa Teresa. Each wanted her to come and stay. Each brought delicious food, insisting that Tema eat it. Like the people around her, Tema believed in miracles and saw herself as a saint. Eventually, however, Tema decided to return to her Jewish faith. She settled in Haifa, Israel, where she married and became the mother of two children. Unlike Chava, Tema stayed in touch with the peasants who were kind to her.

Tema remembers that when, homeless and desperate, she would sneak into a barn to sleep, it was men rather than women who would hit her and chase her away. And Chava concurs that women were more likely to show compassion than men. A few men went beyond beatings and raped defenseless young women. Understandably, victims had a hard time talking about their sexual experiences. Only toward the end of the interview would a few venture into descriptions of sexual encounters.

One of the women, as our interview was winding down, hinted at a rape. She vacillated, agreeing to talk about it but requesting anonymity. At the time it occurred she was a teenager, wandering around the countryside performing hard labor in return for food and shelter.

I never told this to my children. Why should I? Maybe I don't care? It is very strange. It is very personal . . . It happened on one of my walks in the forest. I had to go from one village to another, and this was often a few kilometers. I would have to cross forests. I did not like to do it alone, so when I saw someone I would try to catch up with him or her, just to be with someone. One day I met the forester. He had three children. He was probably forty or so; I did not know him. He agreed to take me through the forest. In the meantime, he started with me. By force he pushed me to the ground. I asked him what he was doing, complained that it hurt.

"Nothing, nothing," he answered.

I said, "I am afraid of men."

"Now you don't have to be afraid," he assured me.

"Leave me alone; I don't want it," I pleaded.

I didn't know what he did, but I felt bad about it. When he finished with me, it was getting dark. I told him that I could not reach the place I was going to before dark. He said that he would take me to his house if I promised not to tell about what had happened. I agreed. At his home, I noticed that his family felt sorry for me. They pitied me. They must have known what he did to me. Probably I was not the first one. His wife was in the house. The children, sixteen, fourteen, or so . . . they gave me food and a place to sleep. There he did not touch me. But I remember it as if it were today. The entire family was so very sad and so nice to me . . .

The next day, I did not know how to get out of the place. He said that he would take me, and I agreed. Maybe I was afraid. But I had no choice. He tried again when we were in the forest; I objected. I don't think that I allowed him. He tried to make me change my mind, but I did not let him. The second time, no, NO! This time, he did not force me. He brought me out of the forest, and I went away.

This did not leave me with a strong trauma; I don't know why. In 1946, after I met my future husband, I told him about it. In the end . . . after our wedding night, my husband said to me, "What were you telling me? You were a virgin." I'm not preoccupied with it. You asked, so I told you . . . I don't think it made any impression on me.[44]

Emotion, or rather absence of affect, dominated the account of this experience. The speaker's voice and gestures did not match her assertions of indifference. Judging by the hesitation I encountered among interviewees to recount these coercive sexual experiences, I have to assume that most of these stories will die with the victims.

Despite rigid prohibitions, black markets flourished in eastern Europe. Like farmwork, the black market offered earning opportunities for Jews. Most of these illegal activities involved bringing food in from the country-side to urban centers: small towns and cities. Illegal traffic in items like thread, needles, buttons, and used clothes — often left behind by Jews — also moved from towns to villages. Most of these transactions involved a railroad trip, which was particularly dangerous for men. If caught the smugglers faced confiscation of their goods or even arrest. The high visibility and dangers involved in train travel therefore discouraged Jewish men from participat-ing in the black market. And because men rarely transported illegal goods, those who did were conspicuous. However, some Jewish men were active in local black market businesses that required no travel. Women usually dealt with the more visible transactions that called for travel; children were also employed.[45]

Rina Eitani was the daughter of a German Lutheran mother and a Jew-ish father. The family, which included an older brother and a younger sister, came to Poland from Germany in 1936 to elude Nazi persecution and be closer to her father's family. Rina's father died in the Warsaw ghetto; the mother and children stayed on the Aryan side. Next the sixteen-year-old brother was caught in an unexpected street raid and sent to Germany with a group of young Poles. There he contracted tuberculosis and died shortly after the war's end.[46]

Rina's mother kept her German Lutheran background secret, con-vinced that her marriage to a Jew and her former involvement with the Jew-ish community had made her children officially Jewish. Though her Polish was limited, she carried false papers that identified her as a Polish Christian. When they reached the Aryan side, the mother and her two daughters sup-ported themselves by smuggling farm goods from the countryside to War-saw. The mother, eleven-year-old Rina, and her ten-year-old sister worked separately, to lessen the risk of discovery.

While the Germans were ruthless toward smugglers, the natives treated them with kindness. Like some of the young women who roamed about the countryside looking for work, Rina thinks that women were more supportive than men. In this connection, she describes a special incident:

> One day I was buying something in a store. A little girl came in, warning me, "The Gestapo are in the house where you live." Right away, the owner of the store, a woman, put me in the cellar. She wouldn't let me go until the Gestapo left. It would have been safer to leave the apartment, but we had no place to go. So we tried to be at home as little as possible. We stayed a lot in the villages where we bought the produce. The peasants were nice to us. They would feed us and sometimes, in exchange, we worked for them . . . The Germans never came back.[47]

For women, wartime earning opportunities were not exhausted by black market jobs. Another option was to transfer to Germany as a Polish laborer. Throughout the war, the Third Reich tried to boost its economy by bringing in cheap labor from occupied countries. At first, they tried to enlist volunteers, but their slavelike treatment of foreign laborers soon reduced the volunteer workforce. When the demand for more workers grew, the Germans resorted to roundups of able-bodied men and women, who were sent to be slave laborers in the industrial or agricultural sectors of the German economy.

In Poland, work in Germany appeared to be an attractive alternative to the constant terror from Poland's anti-Jewish measures. A move to Germany promised extra safety because Germans could not easily distinguish Christian Poles from Jewish Poles. But this reasoning was only partially correct. Most Jews could not pass the scrutiny of the pretransfer stage. Before being shipped off to Germany, each candidate had to submit to a thorough physical examination. For a Jewish man this meant special dangers. In addition, the documents of those who volunteered were closely scrutinized. Under examination a prospective worker could slip up. In fact, as the number of volunteers dropped, those who did register became more suspect. Although it is unlikely that many Jewish men even tried to transfer to Germany, a few were able to pass the tests and ended up there. Rina Eitani's brother, who was caught on the streets of Warsaw, managed to join the forced transport, his circumcision undetected. He survived the war in Germany.

Zwia Rechtman-Schwarz, who herself became one of these laborers in Germany, agrees that it was much harder for Jewish men to pass the test. Nonetheless, she tells about one exception:

> A neighbor of mine, a Jew, survived in Germany as a worker, and he told me that when he went to bathe with other men, he concentrated all the soap on his genitals. For a man, it was not enough that he should look like a Gentile, have the right speech, but even with these he was in great danger.[48]

In time, however, it became more difficult even for Jewish women to pass the tests for transfer. Still, with most safety routes closed, some women were ready to take the risk. A few of these young women found their way to Germany on their own under seemingly miraculous circumstances. Others received aid from their families and friends, who thought that such a move might save their lives.

Eva Galer, who had jumped off the train that was taking her to Treblinka, next walked to Kraków, where she kept close to the train station and the nearby open market. Without any resources, she was at her wits' end when she was caught in an unexpected raid and after a brief investigation put on a train to Germany. The fact that Eva did not volunteer to go but was caught in a raid may have accounted for the fact that the authorities did not subject her to a thorough check. She had no documents, but the authorities accepted her explanation that she had gone to shop at the market and forgotten her papers.

Eva's good fortune followed her.

> They sent us to Neustadt, on the Austrian-Czech border. Farmers came there to pick up the arrivals. One of the farmers selected me. Only me. At the farm I was so scared. I was afraid to sleep, afraid I would speak Yiddish in my sleep . . . I had a room that was like a closet . . . They had

to teach me how to milk a cow; I knew nothing. They were not bad; of course if they had known that I was Jewish that would have been a different matter.

The husband was far away in Denmark, guarding prisoners of war. He came back for Christmas. Once when his wife was away, he got drunk and started to scream, "Hitler, the murderer!" I shut the windows so that others would not hear. Later I told him what he had said. He thanked me.

I was afraid that somehow I would give myself away. I had terrible dreams, did not know how to behave . . . I told them that I was from a town and that I was in school . . . I tried to learn German from my employers . . . From the surrounding farms, the Poles and the Ukrainians wrote home; they received packages, but I did not. I looked for excuses for why my family did not write.[49]

Eva was lucky to be the sole Polish worker at her farm. She had few direct contacts with other Poles. But life had other complications. Before Easter, her German employer asked whether she was going to confession and communion. Eva knew that the Polish workers in the area went to a Czech church. She also knew that she would feel out of place in any church and was concerned about committing errors. She came up with a partial solution by using the services of the fourteen-year-old daughter of her employer.

I told the young girl that I don't want to go with the Poles, "I would rather go with your family, but tell me how the services are conducted here, because it must be different from the way Poles do it." So the German girl took the prayer book and showed me what kind of prayers they had in the German church. This way I thought that I would avoid mistakes. Also I thought that the German Catholic priest, if I behaved incorrectly, would think that I was Polish and that's why I erred.

I went to the communion. I see everybody sticks out their tongue, and I do the same thing, and the priest comes close to me and I, probably out of fear, see only black in front of my eyes. My employer stood next to me. She asked, "Why are you so pale? What happened to you?" I told her that I just didn't feel well.

So as not to arouse suspicion, in her time off Eva would meet with Poles who worked on surrounding farms. Unlike most other young women, she was not interested in boyfriends. Actually, she had very little time for such amusements. Poles worked six and a half days a week. Eva was glad that she had no leisure to spare. She was also glad that she rarely heard anti-Semitic talk. She suspected that one of the Polish girls she met was Jewish but preferred not to probe. Always on guard, she made no close friends, even though she is a friendly person by nature. At the end of the war she learned that none of her family had survived.

While Eva's transfer to Germany came about by a fortunate accident, most Jewish women relied on cooperative efforts by family members and friends to make the move. Yet no matter how the transfer came about, the prospective laborers learned quickly that a trip to Germany contained special perils. The Christian Poles who were a part of the transport represented a serious threat. They were bringing their anti-Jewish prejudices with them, and some were willing to act upon them. Another indirect but potential danger was the presence of Jewish women who were lonely and eager to attach themselves to fellow Jews. To locate and identify Jews passing as Christians might give comfort but at the same time it could lead to discovery. How these Jews passing as Poles coped with their conflicting needs for making friends and ensuring safety is illustrated by the experiences of several women I interviewed.

In Lvov, twenty-one-year-old Miriam Gold-Kowadło lost her husband during one of the Aktions. In 1942 she decided to move to the Aryan side, and for that purpose she prepared a false Polish birth certificate. But the day she made the actual break from the ghetto, she was caught in a raid. Ukrainian policemen had found several hidden Jews. One of the Ukrainians stopped Miriam and ordered her to join the group of Jews under arrest. She objected loudly, but the man refused to budge. Then she noticed a German gendarme come out of the building. He turned to Miriam and asked, "Why are you shouting?" (He spoke Polish.)

Still angry, Miriam replied, "This man forces me to stay with the Jews.

I'm Polish. I just came from the provinces looking for work. Please tell him to let me go."

The German looked at her closely and then said, "If you are Polish, then let me hear you pray." Under the circumstances Miriam found his request comical. She burst out laughing, unable to control herself. She believes that her extreme tension contributed to her unusual reaction, but she is convinced that her strange behavior saved her life. No one could imagine that a Jew who was facing death could be filled with so much merriment. The gendarme ordered Miriam released.

After several futile attempts to settle in Lvov, Miriam decided to register for work in Germany. Her fluent Polish and high degree of assimilation helped her pass the inspection, and she arrived in Germany with a large transport of women. Upon arrival, they were examined by their prospective employers. The manager of an ammunition factory selected Miriam and fifteen other women. Eventually, Miriam discovered that eleven of the sixteen women were Jewish. Their superior, Willi Grosse, was the son of the factory owner. This factory employed more than three hundred workers: Poles, Lithuanians, Latvians, Czechs, and French. For the first two years they worked ten hours a day, then the load was increased to twelve. They lived in a camp close to the factory. Initially the food was poor, but Miriam thinks that it was improved at the owner's request. Similarly, she considers the working conditions and the overall treatment of the foreign laborers fair.

This tranquillity was interrupted by a tragic event. One of the young Jewish women, Marysia, longed to go back to Poland. In vain her co-workers advised her against it, but she persisted, seizing the first opportunity that came her way. One of the Ukrainian women had mental problems, and the manager decided to send her back to Poland. She was incapable of traveling alone, so Marysia volunteered to accompany her. Yet when they reached Poland, the mentally deranged woman recovered sufficiently to denounce Marysia as a Jew. Marysia was shot on the spot.

This incident created a panic among the rest of the Jewish women. Without saying that they suspected the origin of the Polish women, the managers tried to calm them. Gradually, sometimes by accident, the Jewish women learned about each other's origin. In Miriam's case, she was discovered one evening as she sat on her bed, looking at her husband's photograph. Hela, a young woman who sat next to her, fainted, for she recognized the man in the photo as her former teacher, Eliasz Gold. She thus learned that Stefania Wodzińska was not Miriam's real name. Hela and Miriam, now Stefa, became close friends.

One day Hela came to Miriam, pale and agitated, and whispered, "They know about us, this is the end!"

"In what way? How?" Miriam murmured.

"Hans spoke to a policeman, and I heard him say, 'Doppelte Papiere' [double papers]."

Miriam could not rest. She went to Hans, the head of the camp, and asked casually, "What did the visiting policeman want?"

Hans answered, "He wanted us to get double paper to reduce the escaping light from the windows." (This was a preventive measure against air raids.)[50]

But suspicions would come and go. One Jewish woman, a professional prostitute named Bronka Nowakowska, posed a serious threat. She had been caught by the authorities and as punishment for engaging in prostitution was shipped off to Germany. Her identification as a Polish prostitute eliminated suspicions about her Jewish origin. Bronka knew which of the women was Jewish. She engaged in reckless behavior, returning very late from illegal escapades and then forcing the Jewish women to cover up for her, threatening to denounce them. Bronka argued that the authorities would believe her and not them. Determined to avert a showdown, the Jewish women would give in.

Zwia Rechtman-Schwarz also found her way into Germany. Zwia had been born in a village and was used to country life; she spoke Polish well, had an Aryan appearance, and had a number of friends among local Poles. Yet despite Zwia's willingness to work hard, she was constantly on the move, reduced to begging for shelter. After half a year of seemingly endless efforts that offered only sporadic work stopovers, Zwia decided to go to Germany as a Polish laborer. This idea came to her while she was on a temporary stopover with a Polish woman who was eager to help but was too frightened to keep her for more than a week. The woman encouraged Zwia in her plan.

Not yet fifteen, Zwia invented a fictitious past that could not be checked, for it included a burned village, a large transfer of peasants, and the death of her parents. Her Polish friend persuaded her brother to take Zwia to the next large city and show her where to register. Small, skinny, without papers but with a solid background story, Zwia faced the officials and passed the inspection. After that she waited for the transport. She was cautious and tried to make herself as inconspicuous as possible. Instead of pushing as the others did for food, she divided up the few provisions that the Polish woman had given her and ate those. As she waited for her departure, she was painfully aware of the dangers.

She recalls,

One day I heard them say that they had caught a Jewish woman right there in the office. They sent for dogs, and the dogs tore her into pieces. I was only waiting for the moment to leave for Germany . . . We came to Breslau. In Breslau they examined my head, found lice, and shaved my head. They didn't shave the other people's heads. I was so embarrassed. I felt so terrible. Except for some kind of a rag, I had nothing else to put on my head. I thought that they were laughing at me. Who knows— maybe they were.[51]

Zwia reached a camp with a group of women. First she worked on an estate. The work was extremely hard, and more problems followed.

Instead of food we got some kind of cards, and with these we had to buy provisions . . . I couldn't even reach the stove to cook the things I bought. The others were big and strong. They pushed me out of the line. I was the smallest and the youngest and the skinniest and the palest and the weakest. They stole from me. I asked one woman to buy me shoes with a coupon we got . . . She did, but never gave them to me. I was afraid to complain. Then I got terrible pain in my back.

The job was seasonal, and when it ended Zwia and another girl were sent to a village. She was taken to a different estate, where four other Poles and a Ukrainian worked. They lived together in one room. Life remained hard.

We got up very early and the work was very, very difficult . . . I understood German, but I did not speak it. Only when I caught the words precisely did I use them. Luckily I got the easiest job: I was a housemaid. I had to get up before the others and prepare breakfast. But you know what we ate? Flour with water and a little bit of milk to make it whiter. Then I would feed the chickens and the rabbits, I would wash all the dishes; there was no dish washer . . . At lunch, we ate soup. Once a week we got some kind of a piece of sausage, potatoes, or something. Twice a week we got bread, half a loaf and butter.

I was in the same room with these girls and they never found out that I was Jewish. I would arrange trips to church, and I decorated the Christmas tree. When I went to church, I felt as if someone were watching over me, keeping an eye on me. I was at peace in church. The silence was very good . . . I liked the atmosphere. I tried not to quarrel at all . . . One of them stole bread from me, but I said nothing . . . All kinds of boys came to these girls. Once they brought a handsome boy for me, a Pole, very nice. We would go for walks. Our friendship was platonic; we didn't even hold hands. He was there with his father, who was not happy about our friendship.

Zwia tried to be on good terms with all her co-workers, but she never opened up to anyone. Nor was she willing to learn about anybody else's Jewishness. She explains how she felt. "From the moment I parted from my mother, I was very much alone until the end of the war. I did not trust anybody; I did not talk to anybody; I was not ready to open up for anybody. I had a wall inside me." She survived all alone.

Not all Jewish women who went to Germany were as careful as Zwia. Lusia Grosman-Sternberg was also barely fifteen. Her aunt, uncle, and a loyal Ukrainian friend had made her trip possible. But the wait before they were able to leave left Lusia feeling insecure and lonely. She describes her misery.

As I was sitting there, I saw a German come in with a Pole, and he would point his finger and say, "This is a Jew, this is a Jew," denouncing them. Then I noticed one woman who had to be Jewish. Somehow I wanted very much to be next to her. Unlike me she was not on the list [of those who were to go to Germany]. She was much older than I. Later we realized that we were Jewish. I looked at her; she didn't even talk to me. Whatever she did, I did. There was another girl there, too, Pola, who was with Wanda. I didn't know that they were already friends. We traveled for about a week and arrived at Metz.

They asked, "Who wants to go to the sugar factory? Who wants to go to a peasant farm?" The girls went to the sugar factory, and I went after them; I followed them. They went into one of the barracks, and I went after them; they didn't even notice me. I took a sleeping bunk next to them . . . One day, I became sick. I had an abscess in my throat, and during the night I began to speak Yiddish, which I had never even spoken before in my life. It was fortunate that when I shouted, "Mame" ["Mother" in Yiddish] that only Jewish women were around me. Only Pola heard it, and they took me aside and told me they knew I was Jewish.

The factory burned down after a year or so, and the laborers were sent to different farms. But the manager liked me and arranged for me to work as a maid in his parents' house, in Vienna. When I came to their beautiful home, it took them no time to realize that I knew nothing about housework. Immediately they took me to an employment center for Poles, and from there I was sent to a laundry. This was my luck because Russian women worked with me. They were less likely to see me as a Jew . . . We did the wash for the German army. One day, I found a shirt with a yellow Star of David.[52]

Nobody in Lusia's family survived. She emigrated to Israel, married, and bore two children. She continues to be in close touch with the Jewish women she met working as a Polish laborer in Germany.

Jews who came to Germany as Polish laborers were placed with other Poles, who inevitably brought their anti-Semitism with them. The fact that Christian Poles could easily recognize Jewish Poles increased the danger for those who tried to pass as Christians. Occasionally, Polish and Jewish workers who had actually known one another in Poland would meet. Some Poles would act upon this knowledge. Others would denounce Jews for a mere suspicion. Occasionally, even those who were formally denounced were able to escape.[53] For all Jews who came to Germany, the threat of discovery was ever present, as was the possibility of survival.

Some illegal Jews went to Germany as laborers while others continued to pass in their native countries on the Aryan side. Among those who stayed on and lived in the forbidden Christian world some were members of Jewish underground groups. Many of these underground workers were couriers, carrying messages from one group to another. Most of the couriers were women, for they could more easily blend into their Christian surroundings. As long as the ghettos remained in existence couriers and other ghetto underground members continued to move between ghettos, camps, and Aryan sectors. These passages forced them to switch from Jewish to Gentile identities.[54]

Emanuel Ringelblum saw Jewish couriers as "heroic young women who require the pen of a great writer. These brave and daring women travel back and forth, throughout Polish cities and towns. Their documents identify them as Poles or Ukrainians . . . Day in and day out they face grave dangers. For protection they rely totally on their Aryan features and the kerchiefs that cover their heads . . . undertake the most threatening missions without any objections, without a moment's hesitation . . . They recognize no obstacles." Ringelblum praised the conduct of all Jewish women. But he felt that among them, the couriers stood out for their selfless dedication to the Jewish people.[55]

When they began living in the Christian world, these young couriers continued a wide range of clandestine activities. Some devoted themselves to helping Jews who lived in hiding. Others served as important links between the few remaining ghettos, work camps, and forests. One of them, Leah Silverstein, explains,

> The most urgent task was to find living quarters for Jews who escaped from the ghetto. It was crucial for these escapees to have a place to spend the night before the onset of curfew. Once a place was found . . . the courier also supplied them with their basic needs, buying provisions for them, delivering books and newspapers, sometimes illegal leaflets and letters from other members of the family hidden in other places.[56]

Occasionally too couriers would accompany underground male leaders to meetings. Jewish men felt protected when they were with a woman with an Aryan face; Vladka Meed recalls how inadvertently she assumed this role.

> I had to go to Częstochowa to the train station . . . [and I was] returning to Warsaw, . . . walking very fast. It was in the evening and close to curfew. Suddenly someone took my arm, and I looked around, and it was a man with a very Jewish face.
>
> He said to me, "May I walk with you to the station? I have to buy a ticket."
>
> I asked, "Why did you grab my arm?"
>
> He replied that it [would] be safer for me and him. I thought to myself, God, this is a Jewish face, and if we are stopped I will be through. I had illegal things with me.
>
> Sure enough, when we were close to the station three Germans came over. They looked and looked at me, and I thought that if they stopped me I would be lost. But they left. At the station the man disappeared. I never saw him again. As a woman I probably saved the situation.[57]

Because the Aryan sectors were filled with denouncers vigorously looking for Jews, all illegal Jews had to limit their personal contacts. Violations of this rule often had tragic consequences. But trying to adhere to it left Jews in the Christian world missing their friends and families; all felt lonely. In different ways they concur that

the greatest pain came from loneliness caused by losses. All of us shared
the need to have someone to lean on . . . a craving for warmth and attention. To have someone who cared for you and for whom you cared gave
us strength to continue.[58]

This need helps explain the relationship of Vladka and Ben Meed. The
two met by chance in 1942. She was a courier, and Ben helped her smuggle
a map of Treblinka out of the Warsaw ghetto for the Polish underground.
This single encounter led to a marriage that has lasted until the present.

We continued seeing each other. He would tell me about his place, about
his life. He was hidden on the Aryan side with a mother, father, and sister in a small Russian Orthodox cemetery. At first we were just friends.
If you asked me if it was love from the start, it was not. I had a need for
someone who would think about me. When I went on a mission,
I needed someone who would worry about if I would come back or not.
He knew when I was leaving; he did not know where to; but he knew
when I was supposed to be back. Just the feeling of not being completely alone was important. The fact that someone was interested in
you . . . this in itself helped me develop other feelings for him. He would
sometimes come to my place and stay over. His mother was a sick
woman . . . She knew that he was sleeping in someone's home and she
wanted to meet me.

So I went. We tried to help them. After several months, the mother
took out a ring and gave it to me, saying, "This is my ring and I want you
to wear it. This is the only way I will know that the two of you are
united." I wore it; I still wear parts of it [worked into another piece of
jewelry] . . .

One day, when I was passing Hotel Polski, I met two people who
knew me. I had lilacs in my hand; it was springtime, 1944. When I
stopped to greet them the woman remarked, "How come in such a time
you bought lilacs?"

At a loss, I answered, "I don't really know, but I had an urge to
buy them." I was young, it was a beautiful day, I was walking with a
person who was interested in me. I wanted to have them. Maybe I

tried to convince myself that I was still a part of this world? I wanted to laugh.

Unlike most illegal Jews, couriers and other underground figures would go in and out of the ghettos. As long as they could return to these familiar surroundings, they could regain a sense of belonging. But there came a time when such reentries had to stop. When the Białystok ghetto was being liquidated, Bronka Klibanski and a few other resisters were on the outside, standing close to the edge, watching thousands of inmates being packed into cattle cars. Bronka muses,

> Something pushed me to see our despair. The total helplessness of the Jews. Ignoring threats, perhaps I wanted to justify the fact to myself that even though I was alive, while my people were dying, I was, indeed, helpless to aid them.[59]

In Bronka's case being at the scene had more tangible consequences. Hidden out next to the dying Jewish quarters, she and others had a chance to assist ghetto runaways and lead them to the nearby forests. Exhausted by the flight, disheveled and unarmed, these fugitives were conspicuous. Helping them to a quick disappearance into the forest offered them a better chance of rescue.

Leah Silverstein, for whom the Warsaw ghetto meant home, echoes what others have said:

> With nobody to console you, with nobody to tell you it's okay, it will be better, hold on, you are in total isolation. Total loneliness. You know, you are among people, and you are like an island. You have to make life-threatening decisions all by yourself . . . You never know whether your decision would be beneficial or not. It is like playing Russian roulette with your life. And it is not one incident; it [was] this way from the moment I came to the Aryan side. Day after day.[60]

Like the others, Leah was also drawn to the ghetto during its final stage. She knew that

> danger was always there. I stood, with a smile on the outside and crying on the inside. I went . . . every day. I was driven there by some force.[61]

In Leah's case, one thing driving her was that the man she had fallen in love with and continued to love, Jurek Wilner, was inside the burning ghetto. She explained how their lives touched.

I don't want to claim that I was his fiancé. It was not official at all . . .
It happened on the farm, Żarki, and he was there for a while . . . And in
those days everything was temporary. We didn't know what the next
day would bring. Arieh [Jurek] came to Żarki in the spring of 1942. I
met him and fell in love. Maybe we were ten days or two weeks together;
I don't know. In those days two weeks was a lifetime. Now from a distance . . . I ruminate . . . about those times . . . I search for images of
those who were close to me, boyfriends and girlfriends . . . The face of
Jurek Wilner stands out vividly among them. I see him as young, handsome, with light hair . . . Jurek was on his way to Bendźyń and he
stopped at Żarki for a few days. My enchantment was instantaneous. For
me he expressed all that was beautiful, energetic, and pulsating with life.

I can say this today, that I still smell the grass on which we rested,
close to each other, in the vegetable garden. I see how he chewed on a
blade of grass, smiled, lightly absorbed in an examination of the sky,
sprinkled with scattered clouds. I patted his blond hair, enraptured by
the youthful magic of love. He spoke little, probably determined to
unwind from his many burdens. His eyes contained an overall weari-
ness. With a full open mouth he breathed the country air. This was followed by the incredible sweetness of his kisses. How I longed to stay
with him forever. His smile and caresses meant life, which for me,
pressed so tightly to him, took on a happy glow despite the raging war.[62]

In the early spring of 1943, Wilner was arrested by the Gestapo. He was tortured but divulged no secrets.

When he returned . . . he was in very bad shape and so depressed; had
broken bones all over. He could hardly do anything. Yet he insisted on
staying in the ghetto . . . I entered the ghetto the week before the outbreak of the uprising, left because they felt that I could help them more
on the outside.[63]

Illegal Jews who found reliable and caring protectors on the Aryan side had much to be grateful for. Nevertheless, some had a hard time getting used to the confinement and the precariousness of their situation. In Białystok, Arthur Schade was one of four German industrialists who cooperated to help individual Jews and their underground organizations. In the ghetto Mina Dorn worked as Arthur's housekeeper. When the ghetto was liquidated, Schade offered to hide her with her favorite cousin, Miriam. The German treated both women with especial kindness. He also actively supported remnants of the Jewish underground. He was cautious, admitting to no one that the two cousins were staying with him. Schade's official story, even to his close associates, was that he had sent them to the country. Compared to the plight of most other Jews, the situation of the two cousins was enviable. Yet Mina remembers,

> When we were at Schade's, Miriam would fall into deep depressions and would continually ask, "What do we need all this for; we won't make it . . . We are struggling for nothing. Why didn't I die with my parents?" . . . My mother and her mother were sisters. We were very close. I would try to keep up her spirits, telling her, "You will see, we will make it, this will be our victory, and so forth. There are other people who suffer more than we do; we have food and a roof over our heads." But she would return to her dark thoughts and complaints. I felt that I could not stand it. I was becoming depressed too; I was sure that I was going to die . . . One day, listening to her, I became furious and slapped her face with all my strength and screamed, "If you don't want to live, take a rope and hang yourself! But stop it; I cannot stand it any longer." And this helped. She stopped. She was the weak one; I was the strong one.[64]

Not surprisingly depression was a companion of many illegal Jews, women and men. And yet personal attachments had the power to lift their moods. Arthur Schade protected Mina for about a year and a half. For the last six months she and he became lovers. Arthur was married, but his wife and young son were in Germany. Asked what this relationship meant to her, Mina considers.

Did I like him? Well, I was so grateful to him; he was so good to us. It happened. I don't know. What else? He was very musical; he loved music, and I also loved music. He sang beautifully. For Jews, he did so much. I had warm feelings toward him; I did not see a German in him. I was so grateful for everything he did. In the ghetto, for instance, there was a woman who had no coal. When I told him about it, right away he sent coal to her. He was a very good person. And yet in his soul, somehow, he was a German. But what does it mean? Let me try to explain. For example, if two or three toothbrushes had to lie next to each other in a special way, and somebody moved them, he would walk around upset. Order was so important to him . . . But this was just another part of him. Basically Arthur took care of me; he was attentive and loving. If we had not been separated by circumstances, I would have stayed with him. I was grateful to him, and I liked him, too. I was not so madly in love with him, but I liked his definiteness, his personality. He was a very courageous man; he was never afraid of danger, a very principled man. I respected him greatly. He was handsome. He had beautiful blue eyes . . . He wanted to save anybody he could . . . no matter how he felt about them.

After the war the Soviets sent Schade to Moscow, to head an organization that promoted Soviet-German friendship. Arthur lectured extensively on this topic and settled in East Germany. Many years later, Mina and Arthur established contact by mail. By then Mina was living in Israel with a husband and daughter. Arthur shared a home with a woman in East Germany. He was full of hope that they would meet. But in 1982 he died of cancer. That same year, Yad Vashem bestowed the title of "Righteous Among the Nations" upon him.[65] Despite Mina's total dependence on Arthur Schade, their loving relationship was based on mutual respect and mutual care. She cherishes Arthur's memory and looks back on their life with gratitude.

The love affair of Fanya Gottesfeld and Jan, the Ukrainian militiaman, also involved a rescuer and a hidden Jew. In those days, Jews were completely at the mercy of their Gentile protectors. However, just as with Mina and Arthur, so with Fanya and Jan: despite these inherent inequities, their relationship was free of coercion. In fact, meetings between Fanya and Jan were filled with tender feelings for each other and mutual affection. Their love lessened the impact of the surrounding horrors.[66] Still another relationship began differently but had similar consequences. Sandra Brand, the vivacious and well-liked young woman who moved to the Aryan side in Warsaw and became Cecylia Szarek, had a lasting love affair with Rolf Peschel, a German officer who was an investigator at the criminal police headquarters.

Sandra's job as a Polish-German interpreter in a German firm often took her into the Jewish quarters. Without revealing her identity, Sandra took advantage of the opportunities created by her access to the ghetto. At considerable risk she facilitated transfers to the Aryan side for many ghetto inmates. Once outside some of the Jewish fugitives turned to her for help, which she never refused. She performed these tasks naturally and without fuss.

After Rolf and Sandra became lovers, they cooperated in helping Jews and Poles. On his own, Rolf became active in the Polish underground. Sandra and Rolf's attachment could not remain a secret for long. The Nazis disapproved of close relationships between Germans and Poles and probably knew about his involvement with the Polish underground and his rescue efforts. Sandra thinks that her Jewishness remained a secret. Only Rolf knew her identity; most others around her thought that she was Polish. Shortly before the August 1944 uprising in Warsaw, the Germans murdered Rolf and made it look like a crime committed by the underground.

Sandra's love affair in part helped her overcome her anxieties and gave her much happiness. Over the years, to the present day, she has valued this wartime attachment. Its memory continues to enrich her life. At Sandra's initiative, after a thorough official investigation of historical evidence, Yad Vashem listed Rolf Peschel as one of the Righteous Among the Nations in 1997.[67]

Inevitably, scattered throughout this chapter are stories about male-female relationships and the distinct forms they took, including rape. In complex ways, sexual experiences and love had the power of changing the life of each partner. Just as in most other settings, so in the Aryan sectors pregnancy and motherhood affected women more dramatically than men. I have repeatedly shown how under the German rule Jewish mothers, Jewish children, and Jewish pregnancies were under attack. These assaults varied with time and place. As the war was nearing the end, the persecution became stronger. In East European countries, in particular, opposition to Jewish mothers and children took on perilous forms.[68]

Pregnancy, usually a prelude to life giving, pushed some Jewish women to make life-threatening decisions. This pattern was discernible for those living on the Aryan side as well. For example, when Zwia Rechtman-Schwarz was roaming the countryside alone, she heard about her mother's denouncement and execution. Her mother had been arrested in an office of a Polish gynecologist to whom she had turned for help. Zwia suspected that the doctor had betrayed her mother when she asked him to abort her fetus.[69]

But not all Jewish women were willing to discontinue their pregnancies. Margot Dränger was one of those who was not. Born in Germany, Margot was deported to Poland with her Polish-born parents in 1938. The family relocated to Kraków and then were forced into the Kraków ghetto. There Margot met and married Jurek Dränger. At the end of 1943, the young couple were hiding in a bunker in Bochnia. Jurek was familiar with the area, which was dotted by many forests. Some of the local peasants sheltered Jews, and for a while the young Drängers stayed at a farm owned by a widow, Hanka Berota, who allowed them to stay without paying. The couple shared a small, damp, dark hiding place with Margot's father and uncle. Although they were denounced twice, the police were unable to find their hideout. Still, food and money were scarce, and at night Jurek would sneak out to steal whatever he could find in the fields and unguarded barns. Their protector was barely able to feed her two young children.

Margot seemed to take her pregnancy for granted. When she felt the baby's movements, the couple collected a few rags, cotton, and scissors. Shortly before Easter 1944, Margot's birth pains began. She knew the danger of screaming and kept silent. Only her hands held on forcefully to the ladder next to her bunk. Her husband helped with the delivery, cutting the umbilical cord with scissors. It was a little girl, but the infant lived only a few hours. Margot believed that the baby's death was caused by a poorly tied umbilical cord. She suffered from serious postpartum complications yet had no time to dwell on them. Two days after the delivery, the farm was raided. This time the Germans came instead of the Polish police. Once more they found no trace of the fugitives. But the Drängers' protector had had enough. Fearing for the life of her own two children, she asked her charges to look for another place. In three days, the four had left and entered a bunker prepared by the peasant Bronek Wyrwa.[70]

Jewish mothers with children faced seemingly endless problems that were at once diverse and similar. Most mothers devoted themselves to the children's welfare. Although they preferred to stay with their children, they were ready to part with them if separation promised the child's survival. Often Gentile rescuers agreed to keep a child but not the mother.

Zwia Rechtman-Schwarz describes how she and her mother moved from one peasant home to another, begging for shelter. Rarely were they kept for more than a few days. Then one winter evening, when the two were resting in a cold attic, the peasant, a woman, asked them to leave. Zwia recalls, with pain, how her intelligent and proud mother begged the woman to let Zwia stay. In the end the Polish peasant agreed to keep the half-starved, half-frozen girl. Zwia was not sure whether she did so out of pity or for money or both.

I ask Zwia how she felt about staying.

I don't know whether I wanted to stay or not. The situation was such that if she wanted to keep me, then I should have stayed. Of course, I didn't know that I would never see my mother again. I cannot say good-byes. [*Zwia cries.*] When my mother left, the Christian woman asked me to come into the house, which was . . . one small room. I don't even remember who else was there. I wasn't thinking whether she was nice or not. She was very, very poor . . . But this arrangement did not last.

Similar and yet different was Fela Sztern's experience. Fela and her mother escaped during a ghetto liquidation. After they got out they met a Jewish youth, who joined them. From then on, together, they searched in vain for shelter. Eventually they came to a hut close to some railroad tracks, away from other dwellings. The Poles who lived there seemed more refined than other peasants they had met. The three fugitives were received well. As it turned out later, the man of the house, a carpenter, was deeply involved in underground work. The two-room hut was clean and well furnished.

The couple, Józia and Adolf, explained that because their place was exposed and Germans stopped here often, no Jews could stay safely for more than a night. Fela's mother tried telling them that she would give them the property she owned if only they would agree to shelter them. Appealing to their conscience she described their horrible predicament. Józia interrupted her: "You and the boy I cannot keep, but your girl I can. She does not look Jewish." Mrs. Sztern thanked her for this kind offer. Fela angrily refused, insisting that under no circumstances would she be separated from her mother.

Soon the three went to sleep on a pile of straw spread on the floor. Fela was depressed. Lying close to her mother, she did not say much. With arms wrapped tightly around her, she fell asleep. In the morning Fela woke up next to an empty space. She understood. Mrs. Sztern had left a message with Józia that Fela should not cry and that she would try to come back. This was the last time mother and daughter met.

Later on, Fela heard that her mother, confronted by constant rejections, came to the verge of collapse. One day Mrs. Sztern looked out a window and saw a group of Jewish men being led away by Germans. She simply walked out and joined them.[71]

Painful separations and permanent losses were common. For the one who survived, mother or child, the effects were shattering. In the spring of 1943 Edzia Wilder, her mother, and a young girl who shared their bunker escaped during the liquidation of the Brody ghetto. Despite many recent blows, including the murder of her husband and a daughter, the mother took charge of the two young girls. The three reached the countryside, where they occasionally came across kind peasants who fed them and warned them about bands searching for runaway Jews. The women shared whatever food they got with one another. They usually stayed in the forest during the day and came out in the evening to beg for food.

With the end of the summer came cold weather and shortages of provisions. One peasant, a woman, directed them to an abandoned bunker in the forest. Even though this turned out to be a hole in the ground, it gave them some protection from the cold, especially after they started a fire. One Sunday in the late afternoon, as the three huddled in their bunker warming themselves by the meager flames, they heard suspicious noises, followed by a rough "Heraus!"

Edzia recalls,

Obediently we came out, knowing well that we were going to our deaths. Waiting outside were two German gendarmes, one Ukrainian man, and a young girl. These last two carried pails with mushrooms. They were probably spying on us. Both my mother and our companion cried, pleading with the Germans to let us go. I, in a split second, with all my strength, started to run. Without any thought, I came to a small forest we used to hide in. There, totally exhausted, I collapsed. I must have fainted. When I woke up, I was on the ground. The moon looked down on me. There I was, motionless, stonelike. I craved a peaceful death. Only the trees witnessed my despair.[72]

Aged fourteen at the time, Edzia went back to the place where she had last seen her mother. On the way she asked everyone she met whether they knew what had happened to her mother and her companion. She learned that the two had been murdered in a nearby village. She also heard that as her mother was being led away, she had cried, pleading with the peasants she met to help save her runaway child. In this appeal, there was so much love mixed in with despair that the listeners were moved:

They showed me later some compassion by bringing me food. Some of them saw in me a martyr selected by God. I continued to stay in the forest, and during the night I made fires to warm myself by and during the day, when I was in the forest, I would cough when the peasants brought me food. This was to show them where I was. They tried to keep up my spirits, and some of them gave me warm clothes, so I wouldn't be so cold. I was not afraid of animals, only of people. The trees were my friends.

On snowy or stormy nights, Edzia would go to people's huts. Some would take pity on her and keep her for several days. This is how she escaped death by freezing. Edzia felt that her mother watched over her even after death. With the arrival of the Red Army in 1944, Edzia's wanderings stopped. Eventually she settled in Israel.

Earlier I spoke about Sandra Brand, who passed as a Gentile in Warsaw, and told how she came to Złoczów to pick up her son, Bruno, and her husband only to learn that they had been taken away in a roundup. In our interview Sandra muses,

> Because I lost a child, I pledged never to have children. I did not want to forget my little Bruno. With joy from another child, I could have neglected the memories of Bruno. Without another child to gratify me, I do not forget . . . I kept my promise. I never regretted it. This is the honest truth. It is not because I pledged this and with time was too old and couldn't have any more children. No! I never wanted to have them.
>
> I can always see my child; I close my eyes, and I see Bruno. And he was very cute; he was very, very sweet, and because I don't have other children I can hang on to him.
>
> So life was good to me, with all the troubles. I must say life was very good to me. I must tell you that many survivors have some guilt feelings, thinking about why they remained alive and not their child, and so on . . . Many have it . . . If my boy survived, it could have been only in a Polish family. Maybe he would never remember that he was a Jew . . . And since life was given to me and, not to brag, but through me, through my German friend [Rolf Peschel], many Jewish lives were saved. So this is one reason that I say to myself that maybe I shouldn't have guilt feelings, because otherwise I would go insane. I often feel as if I chose life for myself but not for my Bruno. Perhaps I didn't do enough for my child. These feelings never leave me. They bother me. I tell myself that I should not have let my husband talk me into leaving Bruno with him, not even for a while.

Only during a recent conversation did Sandra mention two postwar pregnancies, which she deliberately aborted. Sandra remains true to Bruno's memory. Sadly she ruminates that even though for her Bruno is very much alive, he never grew beyond the age of four and a half.[73] Sandra's motherhood ended many years ago, but it continues to be a part of her life. It remains, mixed with complex emotions and feelings.

Cyla Menkes-Fast's experiences were very different. A teacher, Cyla was married to an engineer who was arrested at the beginning of the German invasion of Lvov, along with a group of prominent Jews. His wife never found out what happened to him. Expecting their first baby, Cyla had hoped that its father would return. In the fall of 1941, she gave birth to a daughter.

Cyla looked like a Pole and spoke Polish fluently. She escaped during a deportation, with the baby in her arms. A Polish friend helped her buy false papers. For two weeks she stayed in the homes of two Polish friends. One of them located a young unmarried Polish woman who was willing to adopt the six-month-old baby. This required a birth certificate, which the local priest supplied.

At the moment of parting, the baby clung to her mother, crying loudly. There was something so disheartening and sorrowful about the crying baby that the Polish woman who had come for her could not take her. The baby stayed with Cyla, who soon found a job as a cook on an estate. She welcomed the work and the peace that came with it. In her free time she befriended a teacher who was out of work and a Polish woman who was helping Jews from a nearby forest. To these new friends, Cyla gave food. All seemed to run smoothly until a new law was passed requiring Poles to get special working papers. Because of this law, the manager of the estate discovered that Cyla's birth certificate was fake. He asked her to leave immediately.

For a while Cyla and the baby roamed the countryside, hungry and homeless. Things improved after Cyla's friend the teacher found her a job with a German who needed a cook. There she worked until the Red Army came in 1944. In an entry of her diary for that year Cyla wrote, "My little daughter has been the sunshine of my life. To this day she continues to bring me good luck. At dangerous times my child would distract a murderer's attention from me to herself. Occasionally, too, the compassion people felt for her made them invite us both into their homes during our horrible wan-derings."[74]

Wartime experiences of motherhood varied greatly. But happy endings were extremely rare. No matter how the war affected the actual mother-child relationship, its effects continued to linger on. And as time passes they exert continued pressures upon the mother or child. Decades later the intricate mother-child ties remain, still powerful, even beyond the grave.

7

Resistance

Eva Kracowski is convinced that her mother saved her life because before the impending liquidation of the Białystok ghetto, she insisted that Eva not stay with her and Eva's younger brother. Eva is not sure whether her mother knew that she was a member of the ghetto underground, but she understood that her mother was pushing her toward life while she herself watched over her young son, ready to die with him. An upper-class teenager, a member of the ghetto Communist underground, a courier, and a forest partisan, Eva recalls her shaky journey to life: "I did not want to perish in Treblinka. I wanted to die where I was. I wanted to die with a gun in hand." But Eva's membership in the underground did not entitle her to a gun, nor did it make it easier for her to escape to join the forest partisans. The ghetto underground usually sent only young men to the forests. Eventually Eva did escape and joined the forest partisans inadvertently.

The ghetto resistance organization would decide who would go to the forest and who would stay. Such groups were organized by us, from the ghetto, and the young men who left had to build their *ziemlankas* [bunkers] there. They had few arms. Many died; the conditions were horrendous. We think that of the partisans who left from the ghetto about 60 percent perished . . . Of course, only the young men were sent, those who were strong.[1]

Eva agreed with the underground policy of sending men rather than women to the forest. Similarly, she did not mind that weapons were distributed only to men. She felt that the shortage of guns justified this rule. Nonetheless, she waited for a chance to leave. Then came August 16, 1943, the beginning of the liquidation of the Białystok ghetto, which acted as a signal for the start of the ghetto uprising. An uneven, desperate struggle ensued that ended in a Jewish defeat. The majority of the ghetto population were forced into cattle cars destined for concentration camps. Most of the rebels perished. Among them were the two underground leaders, Mordechaj Tenenbaum and Daniel Moszowicz. Today many legends surround their deaths but few facts are known. The actual battle lasted four days, and intermittent shooting continued for more than a month. A small number of inmates, some of them underground members, remained trapped inside the ghetto.[2]

Eva Kracowski and two of her comrades, Syrota and Szyjka, did not escape from the seemingly empty but closely guarded ghetto until November 1. Their destination was the Suprasl Forest, about 20 kilometers distant. Only Syrota knew the way. In the past he had stayed in these forests as a partisan organizer, returning to the ghetto shortly before its liquidation to brief the underground about transferring more fighters to the forest. The deportations and later the uprising prevented him from leaving.

Eva recalls their move to the forest.

We had to cross practically the entire city before coming to a major highway. Close to this highway stood a guard house that served as a clearing point for entry into the forest. Inside we expected to find a guard, but when we entered, we saw a lighted lamp and no guard. The place was empty. I have no idea what would have happened if the guard had been there. His absence simplified our position . . . Syrota knew of three separate partisan bases, each consisting of several bunkers, ziemlankas. The bases were at a considerable distance from each other. It took us two days to come to the first spot.

There they found a still-smoldering ruin, remainder of a previous human presence. None of the partisans were visible. There were no traces of a struggle. Except for a few scattered personal belongings, the place was deserted. The Germans had probably attacked about two days earlier.

The fugitives continued in the direction of the second base. Now they moved even more cautiously, anxious to avoid encounters with Germans, Poles, Belorussians, and Ukrainians. One could not be certain who was a friend and who a foe, and their disheveled appearance could easily betray them. They passed through forests and deserted fields. Here and there, despite the cold weather, they found a few vegetable roots, potatoes, mushrooms, and other food. The peasants must have missed these occasional gifts. The rain was sparse, which further limited the travelers' water supply. Occasionally the edges of the forest roads would be furrowed by wagon wheels. When the three came upon these indentations, they would kneel to lap up the rain that had accumulated there. The worms that infested this murky liquid did not stop them from drinking. In fact, they longed for more of the water.

When the three comrades arrived at the second base, a desolate, lifeless scene also confronted them. As soon as they had made sure that the scattered bodies were beyond help, they moved on. Now they were besieged by doubts. Were there any partisans left? Should they be searching for the third base? Mightn't it be better to settle somewhere by themselves? Adding to their worries, Syrota was not sure of the exact location of the third base. For the time being, they agreed that first they must find some nourishment, and they moved on.

Then at midday on a grayish day, they saw a *hutor*, a single peasant farmhouse, standing across from a big field. Eva's companions thought that she ought to go in and ask for food and water. She consented, and the two assured her that they would wait for her at the edge of the forest.

When I reached the hutor, I had to climb three steep stairs. I knocked at the door and gave the customary greeting, "In the name of Jesus, etc."
I knew all those things . . . Inside were two men, probably a father and a

son. The father was old; the son was around twenty or so. I noticed a pail filled with water; keeping my eyes on it, I told those peasants that I was on the run because the Germans wanted to take me for forced labor to Germany . . . I was returning home but in the meantime I needed some bread and water. The old one said, "Of course," and he carried the pail of water, put me into a room, and placed this big pail of water in front of me . . . Suddenly, the son was gone. I did not like this. I was like a hunted animal, sensing that something was wrong. I felt that they wanted to trap me. The older peasant left the room and shut me in from outside. I can still see the entire scene in front of my eyes. I looked through the window and down; it was like half a flight; I remembered the three steps as I went up. I jumped out of the window and started to run.

When she got to the middle of the field, Eva heard shots. She ran faster and was soon reunited with her two companions. Eva continues,

My only regret was, Why didn't I drink the water? I couldn't understand why I didn't drink it. To this day I sometimes wake up at night, and I think about this pail of water, and I still don't understand why I didn't drink it.

The three rushed deep into the woods, and after what felt like hours they came to a forest clearing, a large, islandlike opening inside the thick growth. At the side of the clearing stood a destroyed tank, and they decided to lie down next to it. The first snow fell; they welcomed its generous moisture. Eva remembers that evening.

According to our calculations, we had been on the road for about a week. This was probably November 7, the anniversary of the [Russian] Revolution . . . These two fellows were sort of Communists. And we spoke about the festivities that probably were taking place in Moscow. Suddenly we heard footsteps on the other side of the tank. Then we heard voices. They could not have been Germans because the Germans would not come at night into the forest; they were afraid. It might have been foresters who worked for the Germans, Belorussians or Ukrainians. They might also have been partisans, or maybe someone stealing wood at night. Who knows? We knew already from the wagon tracks that some people had been coming here, perhaps to collect stuff from the forest.

Again, her two companions felt that Eva should investigate the intruders. As she moved toward the sound, she saw two men, possibly partisans. They seemed to be waiting and listening. Coming closer, she thought that they were probably Jewish partisans. Eva felt more relaxed as she approached them. She began to explain their predicament, how and why they had come.

First the two men talked among themselves in Yiddish. Clearly, they felt that I was lying, that it was impossible that we could have passed a guardhouse without being arrested. It was impossible that we could have passed the entire town without being picked up. They also decided that we could not have stayed for two and a half months in a ghetto that was already liquidated. Most likely somebody had sent us here. They pointed out that we had come right after those recent attacks; and they were suspicious. Finally they debated with each other about whether it would be better to shoot us. This way they would not run the risk of losing the protection of the forest.

At that moment Marylka Różycka arrived. She was some woman! First she stopped to listen to their arguments, which they repeated. Then she came closer to me. She turned my face up toward the moon, and she started cursing, "You idiot! You don't recognize me?" She was a friend of my aunt's daughter. She knew me well, and later I remembered that I knew her very well too. She had brought a shotgun and medicines wrapped up in a newspaper for the partisans. She had walked alone through the forest carrying these things. She looked more Polish than any Pole. She was short and paid no attention to her appearance. She looked like a very common Pole: blond straight hair, blue eyes. When she talked, she cursed a lot. But she was such a heroine! I never met anyone like her.

For a number of Jewish men and women, just as for Eva, opposition to the enemy originated in the ghettos. For some opposition to the Germans began after they had entered the Aryan world. Still others aspired to membership in resistance groups but were unable to get in. Before I turn to an examination of Jewish women and men and their coping strategies within various resistance settings, an introduction to resistance under the Nazi occupation is in order.

First, what did opposition to the Germans mean? Within the myriad definitions of *resistance,* I find especially useful one that sees it as activities motivated by the desire to thwart, limit, undermine, or end the exercise of oppression over the oppressed. The basic ingredient of this definition is the motivation to eliminate or reduce oppression over the oppressed. Additional aspects of this concept are also relevant. In itself the term "underground movement" suggests an organized entity. Most publications on the topic refer to collective, organized resistance groups. As a rule these groups are differentiated as armed or unarmed, spiritual or nonspiritual, urban or rural, and many other forms.[3]

Yet when observed directly, all underground activities are dynamic rather than static, appearing in many guises. Moreover, resisters may simultaneously engage in a variety of illegal activities. This in turn suggests that the many "types" of resistance are not mutually exclusive. The multiplicity of forms of resistance, their transformations and flexibility, underscores the complexity of the subject. Nonetheless, World War II underground movements shared certain basic characteristics.

Most scholars agree that every Nazi-occupied country in Europe had some kind of resistance movement. They also concur that in addition to and beyond the countries' mutual aim to end German oppression, each country evolved its own distinct kinds of underground organizations.[4] They further conclude that the characteristics of the individual underground groups were determined by varying sets of conditions.

Foremost among these were the German policies and attitudes concerning a particular country or groups within that country. Historian Henri Michel argues (and others support his position) that "the best recruiting agents for resistance were the savagery of the SS, the ineptitude of the occupying regime and the severity of the economic exploitation." Stated differently, the type and degree of German oppression against countries or groups largely determined the distinct features of the resistance movements.

The Danes and the Jews represent two extreme examples. Denmark enjoyed a politically privileged position, while the Jews were systematically targeted for biological annihilation.[5]

In addition to the form and degree of German oppression, underground movements were also affected by the social, cultural, economic, and political conditions within a country or of the groups within the country, as well as its physical features. Mountains or forests increased the possibilities for launching opposition; flatlands made it more difficult.[6]

Finally, the attitudes and policies of the Allies toward a country or group mattered as well. The Allies rarely relied on European resistance groups. Here too Jewish groups represent the extreme in a range of responses: to all Jewish pleas for help and offers of cooperative efforts, the Allies responded with silence. On the basis of his wartime experiences, Jan Karski, the prominent Polish emissary, concluded that during World War II the "Jews were abandoned by all world governments." This touches on another frequently made observation, namely, that contrary to some postwar claims, and despite many selfless sacrifices, European resistance did not win the war.[7]

It has been argued that the diversity of national resistance movements together with their need for secrecy blocked any effective integration across national boundaries. There was no such thing as a unified European resistance. Moreover, just as was the case across the continent, so within each country the security concerns of each resistance group, together with the groups' diverse political, social, and economic demands, interfered with the integration of different underground movements. Each European country had several illegal underground organizations.[8]

In all underground movements the amount of secrecy increases with the movement's division into subunits that have minimum contact. Each group's ignorance about the others' illegal activities means greater safety for all. However, in order to function as a unit in order to strive for the fulfillment of its aims, an underground organization must coordinate its activities. These two basic requirements of an underground movement, secrecy and coordination, seem to operate at cross-purposes. Therefore, they have to be reconciled and balanced.

Resistance members who are identified as couriers, liaisons, or emissaries create some of this balance. As an integral part of every underground movement, these resisters help maintain a certain parity between secrecy and coordination by serving as connecting links among subgroups, uniting the discrete parts of the overall movement. Because these liaisons have contacts with many individuals, many people know their identities and how to reach them. In addition, since these couriers travel to many different places, they become more visible. More contacts and greater visibility, in turn, increase their chances of discovery.[9]

During the Holocaust, closely connected to the need for secrecy and integration was the fact that all underground groups had to cope with threats, which forced them to depend on cooperation and mutual assistance for survival. Stated differently, the more threatened an underground group was, the greater was its reliance on cooperation, mutual aid—and couriers, who helped make both possible. But how extensive a particular threat might be to an entire underground movement depended on a number of circumstances. The oppressor's attitudes toward a group would mostly determine the extent and severity of the threat.

In addition to the threats that emanated from the oppressor were those that came from within, generally owing to the newness of the underground movement. That is, initially, some of the threats were created by the ineptitude of the movement leaders and members. It took time to learn the pitfalls inherent in illegal opposition. Often the underground organizations learned their conspiratorial skills through trial and error. At their inception, therefore, illegal organizations were more likely to incur heavy losses.

The resistance groups also had to take their cues from their oppressor; they needed to be alert to the opponent's initiatives. Because these initiatives varied from country to country and by kind of victim, the conspirators needed to be flexible and to learn the special skills required for that flexibility. But special skills and flexibility develop gradually. At the beginning, before they had acquired these conspiratorial skills, the underground movements were more likely to take risks that led to failure. These failures, in turn, created a greater need for couriers who could promote cooperation and mutual aid between movements and among subunits of a single movement.

Implied in the preceding discussion is the idea of time, another crucial factor in the success of the underground movements. It took time to organize a resistance movement. And over time local interest in underground participation could change. When the Germans began to lose the war, toward the end of 1943, resistance became a more attractive option to the native populations of occupied countries. By then, however, most Jews had already been murdered or forced into concentration camps. Compared to the rest of the oppressed peoples, the Jews had very little time.[10] Time was not their ally; until the end the Germans continued to vigorously pursue their policy of biological destruction.

With few exceptions, couriers were women. One of the exceptions, Jan Karski, was aware of the precariousness of these couriers' existence: "The average life of a woman courier did not exceed a few months . . . It can be said that their lot was the most severe, their sacrifices the greatest, and their contributions the least recognized. They were overlooked and doomed. They neither held high rank nor received any great honors for their heroism."[11] And yet it was these couriers, whose work enabled the underground movements to coordinate and integrate their efforts, who did much to keep the movements alive.

I mentioned earlier that under the German occupation, especially in urban environments, women were less likely to be suspected of political transgressions than men. The more extensive persecution of men in all countries under German occupation grew out of the Nazi belief in patriarchal principles, according to which men were seen as intelligent, rational, and dominant, women as intellectually limited, emotional, and submissive. I showed in the preceding chapter that these distinct gender attitudes were reflected in stricter work laws for adult males than for females. These perceptions were also expressed in the consistently lower arrest rates for women. Undoubtedly, such distinct gender policies account for the high percentage of female couriers.[12] Women made up the bulk of couriers in clandestine operations in general and in Jewish resistance groups in particular.

The enforced isolation of the Jews automatically made women more strategic to Jewish underground movements. Because of their circumcision, Jewish males were in much greater danger on the Aryan side—another reason for the higher proportion of female couriers. This situation existed in both the East and the West. In addition, the special precariousness of the Jewish people over other native populations demanded that Jewish resisters develop special flexibility and improvisational skills. The Jewish women's readiness to take on a variety of resistance jobs was coupled with their knowledge of the personal risks and their awareness that these risks were even greater for Jewish men.

When asked to compare the threats faced by women and men, Thea Epstein, a Jewish courier in southern France, replies, "It was harder for men. A man had no right to be in the city, to move around; he was supposed to be employed in work that exempted him from military service, and so forth. Or he had to study or to be in the army."[13]

Another woman, a Jewish courier who had been a teenager in a Communist resistance group in France, at first seems surprised by my question but then responds, "I might say that being a girl helped me. I took advantage of this fact."

"What were these advantages?" I ask.

"Well, for instance when there was a control of the baggage in a bus the Germans had a tendency to pass a smiling young girl; perhaps a pretty girl could use her seductiveness . . . It was simply difficult to imagine that I was doing what I was doing with the way I looked—I didn't look like a scout. It's a good question, but I never before thought about it."[14]

In the beginning most underground groups, both Jewish and non-Jewish, had a higher percentage of women in general, not just women acting as couriers. Sometimes women's resistance spilled from urban settings into different underground operations. Also at the early stages of these movements, women were more likely to take various leadership roles. This, for example, was true of the first Minsk underground organization, established within a few weeks of the German takeover. Over time, as an underground organization became more established, the presence of women, especially among the higher ranking positions, diminished.[15]

A partial exception to this general pattern were Jewish underground movements. The uninterrupted precariousness of the position of the Jewish people probably accounts for a consistently higher proportion of women in their underground movements. This was particularly apparent in various ghetto resistance groups, where women sometimes reached the middle range of the leadership. Two women who attained this rank were Gusta Draenger, in Kraków, and Civia Lubetkin, in Warsaw.[16] The more threatened an underground is, the more receptive it becomes to women and the more likely to offer them at least token leadership roles. Vulnerability tends to make an underground less choosy. But this does not mean that prejudices against women in leadership roles disappear.

The belief that men were entitled to any leadership positions within an underground movement was pervasive. And regardless of location or resistance group, women themselves seemed to accept this view. At the beginning of this chapter I showed that Eva Kracowski agreed that the men should have had special privileges. Many women shared her view. But mixed in with their general acceptance I found some ambivalence. This ambiguity can be illustrated by a partial reproduction of my conversation with the Jewish French courier Thea Epstein. I began by asking about the leadership: "Who was giving the orders?"

"Actually, Toto was the head of the entire organization. And then there was another man who was directing us."

"And women, were they in leadership positions?"

[*Thea hesitates.*] "Well . . . I would say no. But we did not feel it. We didn't expect to be in leadership positions. Even though Toto was the head and someone was under him, we somehow didn't feel that he was the one in charge."

"You did not mind it; that's one thing. But the fact was that he was in charge, the man was in charge; was that correct?"

"Yes. This is a fact; the men were in charge." [*She sounds surprised.*]

I continue, "Do you know, for example, about cases where women were in charge, in as high a position as Toto?"

"No, absolutely not. I don't know of a case like that. But I also didn't think about it. It was obvious that it would be a man."

Similar was my conversation with Shulamit Einhorn-Roitman, a Belgian who as a teenager settled in southern France during the war and became a courier with the Jewish underground group, headed by Toto. Her answer to the question about the differences between the position of men and women in the underground is prefaced by the statement that young women had an easier time than men. Then she asserts, "Except for the leadership position that the men had, there was complete equality."

When I suggest, "But if they were the leaders and you were not, that already shows lack of equality," her response is firm.

No. We had the dangerous tasks and we were in the field, and our jobs were not less dangerous than theirs were. We didn't think that we were unequal. It was not important that they had the leadership positions. What was important was to win and to live . . . Two girls were killed of those who were smuggling children to Switzerland. One was killed straightway, and the other was murdered in a camp . . . Even at these border crossings those who were the organizers and had the power were men . . .

Most of those who were in the resistance and had our kinds of jobs [couriers] were women. Young men were not allowed to move around unless they were special students, because men who did not work were sent to Germany for slave labor. So it was very dangerous for every young man. Even the French Christians . . .

But in the entire resistance movement, there wasn't a woman in a leadership position. The men did all the most important aspects of the work . . . The men did the leadership jobs . . . I knew brave women. I knew women who were really risking their lives, but they were not the leaders. As a girl, I was the one carrying those documents and moving them from place to place . . . I never worked as a social worker; I only worked with documents, making false documents. Some people were very nice to me because I looked very young and I was carrying such a burden, and they would help me more readily.[17]

Toward the end of the interview I pose one of my standard questions: "If you were a man, how would your life have been different?" Without hesitation Shulamit answers,

My big ambition was to be like a man. I wanted to do everything that men were doing. I wanted to be equal to men. If they went on a bike, I only wanted to go on a bike, and only on men's bikes. I was acting. I was not thinking about myself in those days. You don't have time to think about yourself . . . I always tried to be not less than the men. I would imitate them. Once I was going on a mission with a man. As you know, I was afraid of heights, and I had to go down a steep hill— and I fainted. I was taken to the doctor, but I had on me all kinds of documents and papers. So the man who was with me went with me, and I pretended to be romantically involved with him, and the doctor never knew that I had handed him the papers.

Fela Isboutsky-Szmidt, another girl who came to France from Belgium as a young girl and also became a courier, describes her varied duties: "I would transport . . . all kinds of things; I had a special coat sewn in such a way that it had a double lining. When I reached the train station, I would go into the bathroom and take out the illegal things sewn into the coat."

"What kind of things?"

"Usually documents, papers, mostly documents. Most of them were false papers. I put everything in a newspaper and made a package out of it."

"Were you afraid?"

"I was afraid of only one thing. I was very much afraid that if they caught me I wouldn't be able to keep my mouth shut, I wouldn't be able to keep from talking about other people, especially under torture. I was afraid of that . . . I was usually supposed to meet someone at the train station. I had to go to a café there, to a man dressed a certain way, and to sit down next to him."

"Did you have any close calls?"

"No . . . I was actually very free; I behaved very freely; I was only afraid for the future if they should catch me. When I came into this café, he had the same newspaper, but mine had something in it. I would put mine on the table and order a cup of coffee. And then we would talk. Then as we got up, he would take my package, and I would take his package. I didn't know who he was; I didn't know him. It was better not to know."

"He was young?"

"Yes. I think a job like this, one could do [only] if one didn't have a family. When I returned to the hotel, I was again in charge of children . . . When there was need, I would go on a trip."

Then I introduce one of the questions that in slightly different forms I ask all my respondents: "If you were a man, do you think your life would have been different?"

"I think if I were a man I would probably have joined the resistance much earlier, and I would not have worked with children. I would have been in a real resistance group and not, as I mostly was, in a unit that took care of children."

"Do you think it was less likely for a woman to be accepted as a resistance fighter?"

"No, it was a chance. I had friends who were in a resistance with men . . . If they had come to me and said, 'Come to the regular resistance,' I would have gone. But they asked me to work with the children so I went . . . When I was in Montpellier I looked for a youth movement to join . . . If I had been a man, yes, I would have found a way to the regular underground. Many people just couldn't find out how to get to them."

I probe: "Do you think that what the male partisans did is more important than what you did?"

"No, I don't think that they did more important things. If we were able to save the children, it was very important. The group I worked in was doing wonderful things. They helped Jewish children whose mothers were taken away. Showed the children where to hide and how to survive."

"If you could, would you have liked to fight with a gun?"

"I don't know . . . The fighting part of the resistance, only the men had guns, not women. I don't know any women who were in the fighting unit and had a gun. Maybe an exceptional woman had a gun. Otherwise, it was the men who had the guns not the women . . . Courier work was done by women."[18]

Throughout my interviews women consistently conveyed the idea that their participation in the underground was different from men's and perhaps not as fully approved of as the work men did. But they and other women seemed to have accepted these differences.

Because of the constant persecution of the Jews and the lack of outside aid, Jews were in special need of cooperative partners. Occasionally such partners came from the least expected quarters. The German-Russian war became an opportunity for Jewish-Russian alliances.

From 1939 to 1941, because of the Soviet-German nonagression treaty, Communists had had to refrain from criticism of the Third Reich. But when Germany attacked the Soviet Union on June 22, 1941, the situation changed. Immediately after the start of the war entire Red Army divisions collapsed. Thousands of Soviet soldiers fled into the wooded areas to avoid being captured by the Germans.[19] Others, the overwhelming majority, surrendered to the enemy and became prisoners of war. German treatment of these prisoners was ruthless. Many fell victim to mass executions; others died a slower death, as concentration camp slave laborers. Estimates of the number of Russians who perished in German captivity run into the millions. The mistreatment of these Soviet soldiers served as an incentive for escapes into the forest and the formation of partisan resistance groups.[20]

Thousands of Soviet soldiers fled into the Belorussian forests, which belonged to the Soviet Union (until 1939 a portion of Belorussia had belonged to Poland). Huge, inaccessible, junglelike woods cover much of this area, now known as Belorus. The men who fled there organized themselves into many small splinter groups. Although they referred to themselves as partisans, they lacked weapons, leaders, and discipline. In the beginning they avoided confrontations with the superior enemy, limiting their activities to finding food and shelter. They would attack Germans only if confronted by an easy target. The main inducement for these attacks was the capture of weapons.

Indeed, instead of fighting Germans, these early Soviet partisans would sometimes rob one another, seizing arms and anything else they considered of value. Group rivalry and greed could also lead to the murder of unarmed civilians. Partisans made contact with local peasants only to acquire food; when the peasants were reluctant to supply the provisions, they were robbed.

By 1942 other young Belorussian men were escaping into the forest to avoid being shipped to Germany as slave laborers. They too joined the partisans. The haphazard military actions mounted by these early partisans led to exaggerated ideas about their power, and rumors about their heroism grew. To Jews in need of refuge these heroic stories promised protection from Nazi persecution. In part because of these rumors, Jewish ghetto inmates began heading for the forests in the summer of 1942.

With the exception of a few young men, most of these Jewish fugitives were unarmed civilians: older people, women, and children. It is also significant that in prewar Poland more than 75 percent of the Jews lived in towns and cities. These urban refugees found adjustment to forest life difficult. Inevitably, many of these unarmed civilians became easy targets. Some of them were abused, robbed, and murdered.[21] Occasionally, the young men among them were accepted into the Soviet groups. For Jews, German terror loomed everywhere. It was this terror that had pushed them into the woods in the first place. And so, regardless of the multiplying dangers, the Jews continued to seek refuge inside the forests.

At the early stages of the German-Soviet war, as the German tanks rolled in virtually unopposed, the weakened, humiliated Soviet Union was short of allies. The Jews of eastern Europe were also in need of allies. And their precarious situation made them receptive to any offer of help. The Jews usually were careful to refrain from making what might appear to be unreasonable demands on their prospective allies. To some of the Communists the Jews thus looked like appropriate allies for anti-German opposition.

With the Red Army in disarray, with portions scattered throughout eastern Europe, the Soviet Union could hardly offer much concrete aid.

Further, not all the forests of eastern Europe were suitable for guerrilla warfare. Nor were these forests equally capable of offering protection to the fugitives who reached them.

However, the Soviet government was quick to recognize the benefits that could accrue from the resistance efforts of their former soldiers. These men could help the Soviet Union fight the enemy from within. As early as July 1941 the Central Committee of the Soviet Communist Party was urging the formation of an anti-German partisan movement. In the spring of 1942 Marshal Clement Efremovich Voroshilov became commander in chief and Pantileimon Ponomarenko, first secretary of the Communist Party in Western Belorussia, chief of staff of the new organization.[22] Headquartered in Moscow, the organization quickly established a school for saboteurs.

But the situation in most forests was shaky, and Moscow's control over its partisans limited. The Russian partisans who looked to Moscow for guidance that was not always forthcoming were more likely to see themselves as vulnerable and therefore become more conciliatory toward anyone who seemed to promise cooperation. The more vulnerable the Russian partisans felt, the more likely they were to cooperate with ethnically diverse partisan groups, including Jews. Their tolerance extended to women, whom they were also more likely than other partisan groups to treat as colleagues. Cooperation went hand in hand with tolerance. However, when the Soviet partisans became better organized and felt themselves stronger, they insisted on breaking up ethnic- and religion-based detachments. They also became more likely to bar women from positions as leaders and fighters.

I mentioned that in some locations Jewish-Soviet cooperation began in the ghettos, from which it would move into the forest. Most Jewish-Soviet contacts began inside the forests. Jewish-Soviet cooperation was more likely to occur in areas that had few Russian partisans and where the conditions for waging guerrilla warfare were unfavorable. This was the case with the woods around Białystok. Contacts between the Białystok ghetto underground and the local Communists began in 1942. The nature and extent of this cooperation were limited because the forests never became a viable partisan center. Only a few Soviet partisan groups stayed in and around these forests. The Soviets' limited numbers, poor organization, and often-unpredictable attitudes toward Jews also blurred the effectiveness of the cooperation between the Communist underground and Jewish ghetto resistance.

Ghetto escapees who reached the forests around Białystok were thus largely on their own. Only a few had been members of the ghetto resistance. As Eva Kracowski explained, before the liquidation of the Białystok ghetto the underground had been exploring the possibility of establishing a forest partisan base. In fact, one ghetto group reached the woods at the end of 1942. Several weeks later they were attacked by the Germans, and most died fighting. After their commander fell, the unit disintegrated. The few survivors returned to the Białystok ghetto, blaming inadequate arms and lack of reinforcement for the defeat.

Another group of ghetto resisters reached the woods in March 1943. By September, this group too had almost been destroyed. Remnants of the detachment contacted the courier Marylka Różycka. Although born in Łódź, Marylka had come to the then Soviet-occupied Białystok during the German occupation. A politically active Communist, she was instrumental in helping establish contacts between the ghetto underground and the city's non-Jewish Communists. From September 1943 on, Marylka served as one of the key links between the Jewish and Communist underground in Białystok.[23]

Most agree that Marylka Różycka stands out as a model courier. The tireless dedication of Marylka and other Jewish couriers like her helped carry the ghetto underground movements into the Aryan sectors and the forests.[24] Throughout occupied Europe, Jewish couriers, mainly women, continued their resistance. The growing precariousness of the Jewish people demanded from these women flexibility and improvisational skills. And it is evident from the accounts of many Jewish women resisters that gender roles frequently became blurred.

We recall that when Eva and her friends encountered the partisan unit, the fighters at first refused to believe that they were colleagues. After Marylka recognized Eva the rest followed naturally. In November 1943, Eva and her two companions joined a Jewish partisan group of eight, with Eva as the only woman. Eva describes their life.

We lived in the forest ziemlanka . . . We had four or maybe five shotguns . . . One was a French make, another Romanian; for several of these guns the bullets did not fit. For food we went to surrounding villages. Whenever we came close to a peasant's hut, we would make a lot of noise, talking, from the outside: "Surround the house! Stand in rows" — we used all kinds of names of people who did not exist. We did this to give the impression that there were many of us . . . Two people would go inside the hut. Seeing the guns, the peasants would have no choice and would hand over their provisions. Besides, if we took one pig, the next day they would tell the Germans that we had stolen two pigs, and [the peasants] would kill one for themselves. Otherwise they were not allowed to do that [because they had to deliver their animals to the Germans]. We also confiscated wagons with horses. We would only take food. We came to the edge of the forest with the wagons, the horses, and the provisions. The horses and the wagons would then return empty to their homes. There was never a case when the horse did not return to its proper home. And then each of us would carry, on our backs, our supplies back to our ziemlanka. Actually, we were the poorest group in the area, with the least amount of provisions. We were hungry, sometimes extremely hungry.

One day the Germans discovered our ziemlanka. Probably, they saw our tracks in the snow. We ran away, leaving everything. But we had to return; we had no choice . . . The weather was bad, we had nothing to eat.

Our contact was a Belorussian man, a Communist, from a nearby village. The Germans wanted to kill him, so he ran into the forest. He told us which village to go to; whenever we engaged in some military action we cooperated with him — cutting the telegraph poles, or mining a certain road.[25]

To my question about who was in charge, Eva replies, "Our boys did it. It was not a big deal . . . actually, there was no commander, no head of the group." I wanted to know how it felt being the only woman. Her answer is casual: "They didn't bother me. There was another group of Jews there whom we called 'the bourgeois.' It was a family unit. It had contacts with a Polish woman. They had money; they paid this woman for getting them provisions. And so they didn't have to go on expeditions for food. They were just sitting there and waiting."

Unlike the family group, Eva's was a partisan detachment, an *otriad*, with very limited resources. At one point Eva fainted from hunger. When the Jewish family group heard of this, one of their men came to take her to their base. There the entire group proceeded to hover over her, showering her with kind attention and much good food. After two days, well-fed and pampered, Eva regained her strength. To this day she remembers them with gratitude.

As time went on the Germans intensified their attacks. Many of the forest dwellers died; other underground members were arrested in the city. Marylka decided that she and Eva should make a trip to Białystok in case more couriers were arrested. If this happened, Eva could step in and continue the contacts between the forest partisans and the recently established Anti-Fascist Committee in Białystok. Marylka and Eva's journey to the city passed uneventfully. In Białystok, Eva met Ania Rud, a courier passing as a Belorussian Christian. Ania worked in the kitchen of the Ritz Hotel and lived in a modest room. Eva sneaked up to the room, bypassing the landlady. She recalls this meeting.

Ania was generous. She gave me her food, claiming that she was not hungry. This did not sound right. She probably wanted me to have enough to eat. When there was a knock at the door, Ania pushed me into the closet. There I stayed listening to the landlady's chatter. When we were alone, Ania insisted that I use her bed, and she slept on the floor. She let me wash up. She was so kind, risking her life in such a matter-of-fact, friendly way.

"How long did you stay?"

One day and one night . . . Before curfew Marylka and I were supposed to reach the forest and pass the entire town. We left, on purpose, around five. Marylka was carrying a shotgun. She could not take it apart, so she wrapped it in newspapers. Only one part she took off, and this she put into her basket. Because she looked like a common Polish girl, and no one paid much attention to her, a typical country girl . . . she would not allow me to walk with her, but some distance from her. Nor did she let me carry a thing. She also had a lot of medicines, and this partly dismantled shotgun. In the late afternoon, people were leaving the movie house, and we were lost in the mob. She felt that this was the best thing to do. We reached the forest around seven in the evening. I could not go before the curfew into the forest, only after; at that time the Germans were unlikely to enter the forest. At the edge of the forest, Marylka went back.

Eva also describes another trip:

I had to go to Białystok to bring information and medication. Because we were so close to the front, it was almost impossible for the Soviets to deliver goods by dropping things from airplanes . . . Our forest never became a partisan sphere. Most of the Soviet partisans were farther away. When the couriers from Białystok could not reach the forest, the Russians wanted me to go to them, to get information and to continue our contacts.

This time Eva was on her own. After she attended to her chores, she still had a few hours on her hands. Ania's room was inaccessible; she was at work. So Eva roamed the streets of her native city. Unthinkingly she approached a building that had once belonged to one of her uncles. Her intense absorption in her surroundings was invaded by a scream: "Catch the Jew! Catch the Jew!" The call came from a woman standing across the street. Suddenly, Eva realized that she was the Jew who had to be caught. Then, with surprise, she saw that instead of coming toward her the woman remained standing there, screaming. Eva recognized the woman as her uncle's janitor. This gave her a jolt. Eva dashed off, passing narrow and twisting streets, courtyards, and alleys. Rushing on, she could not tell whether she was being chased. Followed by the real or imagined scream—"Catch the Jew! Catch the Jew!"—all she cared about was escape.

After countless abrupt turns and twists, Eva ran into a deserted court-yard. In the corner stood an outhouse. Eva locked herself in. For a long, long time she could hear only the pounding of her own heart. Gradually the silence beyond the outhouse spoke of safety. After Eva had ventured out into the courtyard and the street, she was careful not to glance at the occasional passersby. Eva reached Ania's building and gave the agreed-upon tap on the window. Ania invited her in. Inside, in silence, Eva welcomed Ania's hug.

I met with Ania and Eva independently, at different times. Ania told me that as a Communist who lived illegally in Białystok, she belonged to the Anti-Fascist Committee, as did Marylka, Lisa Czapnik, and others. All along, Ania was committed to ghetto-forest cooperation. Whereas Eva would move from the forest into Białystok, Ania would travel from the city to the forest. Eva's partisan role involved a number of courier duties. Ania's participation in the urban Communist underground also included a few courier tasks. Ania, who was a few years older than the teenaged Eva, explains some of her duties: "In the ghetto we would collect jewelry from our relatives and sell it to buy weapons. So we had a few guns by then. We would pay the peasants for the guns they had collected when the Polish and Red Armies were on the run."[26]

After Ania settled in the Aryan sector of Białystok, one of her underground duties was to make contacts with Jewish partisans and, later, helping the newly arrived Soviet partisan organizers. Ania explains, "We had very close contacts with Jewish partisans. Marylka was the first to leave the ghetto and one of the first to go to the forest."

To my "What did you bring to the forest when you went?" she replies,

Sometimes we would go to the village to buy guns. We would dismember them, and we would each take different parts and bring them to the forest . . . We usually dressed like peasants, and we would carry things with us. Sometimes we also brought food. We would put the guns underneath in the baskets and camouflage them with bread and other goods, in case we were stopped . . . When we were going to the forest and were stopped at the post of the Germans, we would joke around and this is how we went through. Once I went with Lisa [Czapnik] and we had some guns in pipes. The pipes were closed, because the guns were inside. The Germans wanted to know what we were doing with these pipes. We told them that the oven didn't work in our place, and we were carrying these pipes for the oven. The Germans were near a bridge that led into the forest. It served as a kind of gate that brought us outside Białystok. There were actually a few gates like this around the city. When you wanted to leave the city, you had to go through one of those gates; the Germans were always there.

During these forest visits Ania refrained from asking questions. When I inquired about specific underground operations, through her answers she emphasized the need for secrecy.

We only knew what we did . . . When we came to the forest, we didn't ask about what they did and where they were. We came to meet the people. That's all. There were small groups, and they would move from place to place. When we visited them, we didn't see any family camps, only young people, young Jews and young Russians . . . Sometimes we stayed a day or two . . . I only went to the forest a few times, not too often.

Unlike Eva, Ania did not engage in actual military operations. She never used a gun, a fact she mentioned casually. In contrast, Marylka volunteered for military missions. And Eva, as a partisan, was automatically included in anti-German missions. The roles of these three women thus varied, although there were occasional overlaps.

Military operations expanded in about 1944, when the organizers arrived from Soviet headquarters. These were parachutists, experts in partisan warfare. The first thing they did was break up the Jewish partisan groups and redistribute their members into several Soviet-controlled detachments. Eva and her two comrades Syrota and Szyjka were separated.

Eva was not happy with these changes.

I had no special privileges in this Soviet otriad. I had to do everything. They didn't treat me in any special way. When they were guarding, I had to guard. I had to be like everybody else . . . But there was one guy who felt sorry for me. When I was exhausted on a mission, he would carry my gun.

Asked about non-Jewish women in this Soviet partisan unit, she mentions Gienia, a Russian, whom she called "a loose woman."

This Gienia was horrible; I did not talk to her. Then she went to another unit . . . [Another woman], Vera, came because the Germans had killed her Communist father. She came in order to take revenge. She was a very decent person. She was also afraid the Germans might kill her, as the daughter of a Communist. She could not stay in the village and ran away to the forest. She was a very attractive, fine woman. Actually, she was Belorussian, not Russian.

Eva emphasizes, "Everybody had to go on military missions. It was all the same. Vera had to go, I had to go; there was no such thing as not going." Many partisans perished during these last stages of the war.

Another partisan whom we first met working in the ghetto and on the Aryan side, Mina Dorn, came late to this part of the forest, in 1944. She describes her military missions.

Once we had to derail a train. We were four men and two women . . . We had to tie the explosives onto the tracks. Women had to do the tying because they had small hands. The Russian woman and I did the tying up of explosives. When we finished, we ran right back; the men stayed on because they had to shoot at the train so it would pass fast. Otherwise, the train might have missed the explosives. This train flew into the air. Later on we destroyed an electrical power station. The men did the job . . . There were many wounded. The women took care of the wounded. We put them on special carts and moved them into the forest. Some of us worked as nurses, even though we had no special training as nurses.[27]

"When you look back, what differences were there between men and women?"

"I saw no differences. Women walked around with their guns just like men. We had to run away, and the Germans were after us, and we ran away just like the men . . . Men always tried to show their macho, that they were superior to us, that we women were inferior to them."

"Was this specifically in the forest?"

"This was both in the ghetto and in the forest, but I didn't even pay attention. The bullets reached all of us, men, women, and children . . . I never paid attention to male-female differences. For example, one night I was guarding the camp where we were sleeping. I did the same thing as the others, walking around and watching. There were men and women there."

The Białystok and Vilna underground movements were similar in many ways. Each ghetto underground had contacts with the local Communists. In both the underground leaders vacillated over how, where, and when to confront the Germans. Up to the end, the Vilna underground's main goal was to start an uprising during the liquidation of the ghetto. Niusia Długi, a member of the FPO (United Partisan Organization) headquarters, explains:

> The Communists on the outside, with whom we cooperated, had an
> influence on what happened inside the ghetto . . . The Jewish under-
> ground wanted to save the people. We thought that during the uprising,
> if we fought, people would have a chance to run away. It was a naive
> dream because people didn't even want us to stand up for them. They
> were not supporting us.[28]

The liquidation of the Vilna ghetto began on September 23, 1943. It was precipitated by several deportations, accompanied by uneven clashes between the Jewish underground and the Germans. In the course of these events, valuable fighters perished, others were deported. The Jewish underground was weakened, morally and militarily. At the same time, disagreements between the Judenrat and the underground groups continued to grow, until finally the ghetto population gave a vote of "no confidence" to the underground. More deportations and the execution of Jacob Gens, the head of the Judenrat, followed. Finally the FPO decided that the only thing left to do was leave the ghetto.

On September 27, after overcoming seemingly insurmountable barriers, a few dozen FPO members arrived in the Rudnicki Forest. Among them were Abba Kovner, the head of the Vilna underground, and Hienia Dobrowski. As an "old-guard Communist," backed up by the Soviets, Hienia became the commander of the Jewish partisan unit in the forest. The Rudnicki Forest, like the woods around Białystok, lacked a well-organized Soviet presence. For a long time most of the partisans had been Jewish. They had found the harsh conditions very difficult. Just as in the Białystok woods, here too women participated in a variety of tasks.

Niusia, one of these women partisans, describes her work and that of other women.

> We went from village to village collecting information from different peasants. This was my main job. We wanted to know where the Germans were and what they were planning. The peasants would tell me . . . Certain peasants we trusted . . . I also went on one of those military expeditions . . . They gave me the honor of pulling the string so the dynamite would explode. That was a very nice feeling. Mostly they went to blow up military trains. Some women would also go on expeditions, for food and so on, but not many. Basically women were not fighters . . . No, many of the women didn't even know how to use guns. Most women were busy with domestic work, in the kitchen, cleaning up, nursing, service jobs. They washed, and cleaned, things like that.[29]

Women engaged in a variety of jobs. In fact, in the summer of 1942 two women from the Vilna ghetto, Vitka Kempner and Izia Mackiewicz, participated in an important sabotage operation to mine a railway track near Wilejka. The mission succeeded. The engine and several wagons filled with munitions were derailed and damaged. The Germans were unaware that Jewish women were responsible for this operation. From 1943 to 1944, the Jewish partisans in the Rudnicki Forest organized thirty-nine anti-German military missions. A document describing these operations mentions the commanders by name. It shows that all missions were headed by men. But for three of these expeditions the names of other participants are listed; three were women. Just as in the woods around Białystok so here women couriers served as important links between the forest and the city of Vilna. Among these women were Vitka Kempner, Zelda Treger, and Sonia Madejsker.[30]

Forest Partisans

In the forests around Białystok and Vilna the participation of women in what were traditionally regarded as masculine roles was due to the harsh conditions rather than to beliefs about sexual equality. In fact, although male partisans seemed to take female contributions for granted, practically none of these women became officers. When the organization of the partisan groups improved and the conditions became less threatening, women's contributions were seen as less essential. Once a partisan presence was well established, women were barred from the more valued military duties. And so, under improved forest conditions women were more likely to be relegated to traditional feminine spheres.

In East European forests the fate of the Jews, both male and female, depended on social, political, and military developments in the region that affected non-Jewish partisan groups, particularly the dominant Soviets. These developments influenced the lives of the Jews differently, and their reactions to the changes depended on their sex, age, class, and other factors.

The German defeat at Stalingrad in 1943 marked a turning point in the Russian-German war. This victory spurred Stalin to make more concerted efforts to increase the efficiency of the Soviet partisan movement. More men from the USSR parachuted into Belorussian forests. Others came in planes that landed at secretly constructed airports close to the woods.

Colonel Sinichkin was a part of this growing initiative. In mid-1943, he parachuted with a group of twenty men into Western Belorussia. Capable and well-trained, he quickly reorganized the large Russian otriad called Iskra. Once he had it working efficiently, he turned to another partisan group and then another, uniting them into a more effective fighting force. He was soon elevated to the rank of general and became commander of a partisan brigade.

Sinichkin ordered the regional otriad commanders to come together for a forest assembly. At this gathering, partisan officers were told that every disturbance they could cause the enemy would be helpful to the front; they must cut rails, burn bridges, cut telephone and telegraph lines, and reduce the enemy's access to food. One of the local commanders recalls how impressed he was by the difference between this and previous assemblies. He noticed a definite order to the proceedings. Each leader gave a report about his detachment while a secretary kept minutes. These were new bureaucratic ways for conducting meetings. Then General Pantileimon Platon, who was in charge of all Russian partisans in the Baranowicze region, arrived. He further stressed how much importance Moscow was placing on an integrated partisan movement. After General Platon's arrival the assembly became larger and more impressive. Many of the otriad commanders had a chance to talk with the general.[31]

Winning the war, although a top priority, was only one of Stalin's objectives. Beyond the defeat of Germany, the USSR had political agendas, some of which involved Poland. Once Stalin felt more secure about the outcome of the war, he began to press his allies, the United States and England, for recognition of the Polish-Russian borders as specified in the Ribbentrop-Molotov Agreement. This called for the return to the USSR of the Polish lands occupied by the Soviets in the fall of 1939. Stalin's aspirations, however, went beyond that. He also wanted a Moscow-sponsored government for all of postwar Poland.[32]

Determined to conquer the region both militarily and politically, Stalin set out to bureaucratize and politicize the Russian partisan movement. Belorussia, with its extensive forests and thousands of forest dwellers, became a crucial part of this plan. As the Soviets consolidated their control over the partisans, they established two separate centers of power, one military, the other political.[33]

Gradually such efforts helped transform the Belorussian forests into an important center of the entire Soviet partisan movement. The Soviet organizers gained more control not only over their own men but also over other groups throughout the region. Occasionally they even managed incursions into adjacent towns and villages. Toward the end of 1943 it was not unusual for local authorities to avoid certain partisan enclaves. The spread of influence was uneven, however, and subject to change.[34]

Although the Soviets succeeded in establishing a firmer grip over their partisans, they never gained full control. To retain their power, they had to compromise, bowing to certain local demands. They tolerated a variety of subgroups with distinct, at times even hostile, aims. And though the Russians were numerically and politically dominant, most of their partisan units remained an ethnic mixture of Russians, Belorussians, Ukrainians, Jews, Poles, and Lithuanians. Each of these groups was politically and socially heterogeneous.

Parallel to this outside influence and in part independent of it was the emergence of new values and sociocultural arrangements throughout the East European forests. In the harsh surroundings of these woods, life was reduced to its basics. Physical strength, an ability to adjust to outdoor life, perseverance, fearlessness, and courage were the qualities that mattered the most. The high value placed on these attributes meant strong support for guerrilla warfare and other military undertakings. An individual's prestige depended on the extent to which he exhibited these qualities. Fighting the Germans showed patriotism. Hero worship was common. But neither hero worship nor the high value placed on warfare necessarily translated into actual combat. Verbal support was often unrelated to a willingness to fight. Few forest dwellers resembled the idealized image of the fearless, heroic fighter.

The military conduct of the Soviet partisans did not necessarily coincide with official claims. Many anti-German moves were planned but never executed. One observer saw "very few heroes":

> Russian partisans did not want to fight. Most were former prisoners of
> war who worked in surrounding villages. When the Germans ordered
> them to transfer to towns, they were afraid, and they ran away to the for-
> est. If the Germans had not collected them from the towns, there would
> not have been a partisan movement. They went to the forest because
> they feared the Germans.[35]

Nevertheless, the more bureaucratized Soviet partisan movement affected the lives of all forest dwellers in eastern Europe. The harsh physical conditions and the pervasive ideology exalting physical strength, fearlessness, and courage acted as an invitation to young men, both Gentiles and Jews, with working-class backgrounds. Most reports concur that the majority of partisans came from the uneducated poor. Eva Kracowski speaks for many when she notes, "The commandant of our group was a former professional thief who spent many years in prison before he was enlisted into the army . . . Many other partisans with high positions were low-life characters, uncouth and rough. They cursed a lot and behaved badly."[36]

The prewar social background of the forest dwellers had an impact on the way they adjusted to partisan life. Eva notes,

In the winter we would wash with snow, rubbing in the snow. But the educated men in our partisan group were too cold, so they didn't wash at all. There was a Doctor Osder; he was much dirtier than I was, even though he was a young man. They told me that I did not behave like the intellectual that I was . . . True, I tried very hard to be one of the majority. I was not particularly brave or anything special, but I tried to fit in. I am talking about the Jewish group now. Because most of partisans washed with snow, I did too. I did exactly what they did. In our group some were former members of different political movements. Most of the young people came from the working classes, not the upper classes . . . They had it much easier; they could more easily adjust to the conditions of the forest.

Occasionally, the disadvantage of having an upper-class background led to unexpected consequences. Abraham Viner came from an educated family in the small town of Nalibock, in the Nalibocki Forest. He thinks that most of the young Jewish men of this town had planned to escape into the forest. Many had underground connections and had never become ghetto inmates. But Abraham himself was moved into a nearby work camp, Dworzec. Viner talked about his experiences:

People were supposed to come to save us. There was a lot of talk about this, but nothing happened. In December 1942, our Polish Catholic supervisor warned us that there was going to be a liquidation of the camp. He advised us to run away on our way to work. There were a few hundred people at the camp. When the guards realized that we were escaping, they started shooting. We scattered in different directions, both men and women. Probably more than a hundred succeeded in escaping. We subdivided into small groups, so as not to be noticed by the peasants. Actually, we were not organized at all. It so happened that I remained with a group of four other people.[37]

As a part of this group, Abraham spent some time hiding and searching for a more permanent solution. Ideally, he hoped to join a partisan unit. During his wanderings he met Israel Kesler, a native of his hometown and a professional thief, who had spent many years in prison. After the Nazi takeover, Kesler had escaped during an early deportation. He had gathered together a group of Jews, acquired arms from his Belorussian friends, and roamed the countryside collecting food and hiding with peasants.

When Abraham met Kesler he asked to be accepted into his unit, but Kesler refused, saying, "'You cannot stay with us. You are not made of the proper material. You would not be able to kill, to fight, you are not fit to be a partisan.' I left; I had no choice. I and the others were not accepted. We were of the same social background. We had no arms, nothing."

Better suited for life in the forest, Kesler looked down on Jews whom he felt did not fit in. In fact, most young working-class men seemed to resent and envy those who had been their social superiors before the war. Many members of the prewar elite who came to the forest faced discriminatory tactics. One upper-class woman tells of an exchange she had with a working-class Jewish partisan:

"Did you study in high school?"
"I did."
"Did you study at the university?"
"I did."
"So what does it give you? Can you make a thicker soup out of it?"
"No."[38]

An anti-intellectual climate was also apparent in the use of coarse language. For the few who came from upper- and middle-class backgrounds this created problems. When Cila Sawicki met an old friend in the forest who, already well adjusted, greeted her with a string of vulgar words, she was shocked. "My ears stood up, and I said to my husband, 'What will happen?' He said, 'We will get used to it.' I never got used to it. I could never use this kind of language."[39] Cila was in the minority.

We have seen that at the initial stages of the German occupation the Jewish male elite were targeted for destruction. Many were murdered; some succeeded in escaping. Only a minority of the elite moved to the forests. Most of the young men in the forests came from working-class backgrounds. They had little trouble adjusting to the rough ways of the woods, although as Jews they experienced other problems.

Connected to the coarse behavior in the forest was an overall acceptance of high alcohol use. One of the few Jewish intellectuals there notes, "People would drink before an expedition and after an expedition. In the winter people drank to feel warmer and in the summer not to feel the heat. Everyone drank, even women . . . Some partisans paid with their lives for this weakness. Sometimes they were attacked as they slept after a drinking spree." Others think that alcohol made life more bearable. Some explain that drinking dulled the pain by bringing forgetfulness or diminishing awareness of the surrounding dangers and horrors.[40] The Soviet partisans, in particular, associated heavy drinking with masculinity. Among Jewish partisans, alcohol consumption accentuated the distinction between the prewar elite and working-class.

The partisans' heavy drinking affected most forest dwellers, either directly or indirectly. Eva Kracowski recalls,

> I had a small ring, a gold ring, a souvenir from home. Soviet partisans took it away from me, supposedly to buy arms, but they spent the money on drinks in the village. They would buy vodka and other things. The Russians were constantly drinking.[41]

Such experiences were common throughout the different regions. In Western Belorussia, Mina Vołkowiski approached Bobkov, the Russian commander of her otriad, for help in locating her husband. Even before she could explain the purpose of her visit, Bobkov had confiscated her wristwatch, presumably to buy alcohol. Mina must have expected this because when she mentioned the loss of her watch to me her tone was casual; she continued to talk about the help he had offered. And another partisan woman recalls that in 1944, when the Soviet partisan movement was at the peak of its organizational strength, Pupko, the commander of her otriad, insisted on collecting

> the gold anyone might have had. Pupko said that he needed it for arms, but he was buying vodka with it. Even if you had a gold tooth, he wanted you to take it out. He was almost always drunk. They drank a lot. He always asked me where I kept my gold. I hid my wedding band and told him that I had nothing.[42]

The respected Jewish partisan Michael Pertzof shared with me an experience of his that reflected the connection between heavy drinking and abusive conduct. In 1944 he had been transferred to the regiment headed by a General Sikorski. One night Pertzof's sleep was interrupted by an order to appear before the general.

> They wanted me to translate. I went to the headquarters . . . As usual, Sikorski was drunk. So I am supposed to ask questions of a German soldier they captured and translate. To start with, Sikorski takes out his revolver and says, "You must translate every word, or else . . . You are not to give me a sentence, but you must translate word by word, into Russian. If not, I'll hit you. You don't translate a word, you get hit." Then Sikorski began to beat the German soldier, who immediately began crying. After this the German seemed half-dead: he did not move, made no sound.
>
> This is when Sikorski turns to me and says, "You are supposed to shoot." What would you have done in my place? If you don't do what he wants you to, you know that something terrible will happen. He is completely drunk. He continues, "You know what he did to your brothers . . ." And I shot him, even though he must have been dead

already. I had to shoot him. It was terrible. Here I was, shooting a dead man. After that, I couldn't eat, I couldn't sleep.[43]

Years later, when Pertzof wrote his memoirs, he did not mention the incident of the German soldier. When I ask about this omission, his responses are emotional, filled with pain: "If I had written about it, would anyone believe me? To be forced to shoot someone who was already dead?" Obviously, he was still haunted by what had happened.

Inevitably, the fate of all the forest dwellers was affected by the unequal distribution of power and a closely related exposure to prejudice and discrimination, which was most prevalent for the Jews. The less forest inhabitants resembled the idealized image of the partisan, the more precarious was their position. Owing to special prejudices, entire categories of people were devalued. Nor was this exclusion necessarily bound by reality. A catch-all term for anyone who was not wanted was "useless people." *Useless people* had a variety of meanings, but broadly it referred to forest dwellers who did not fit the idealized image of the partisan.

There was a resemblance between the Nazi definition of useless people (discussed in chapter 2) and the meaning attached to the term in the forest. Primarily, in the forest "useless people" were those who were perceived as incapable of waging war. Beyond this general view, those who were classified as useless had other attributes as well. And some were placed in the category because of specific prejudices. But it is not easy to sort out the causes and motivations behind the classification. Basically, anyone who was abandoned or dismissed from an otriad was considered "useless." Such a person might be old, very young, a woman, or someone who for one reason or another was considered inadequate or burdensome. Or the person could be a Jew. People might be placed in the category of "useless" at any time for a number of reasons, but the discrimination was often tied to crises that occurred within the forest.

In the Rudnicki Forest food shortages and serious military threats were common. Yet despite the harsh circumstances, Jewish fugitives continued

to pour into the forest. As their numbers increased, rumors of an impending raid to hunt them down sprang up. When these rumors persisted,
Hienia Dobrowski, the female commander of a Jewish otriad, found a solution. Niusia Długi explains how Hienia handled the crisis.

> Out of the enlarged Jewish group Hienia, our commander, selected a
> hundred partisans and ordered them to move out and establish a new
> base, far from the present one. My brother and I were a part of this
> group. Chaim Lazar was appointed as commander . . . The majority
> were women. The men had limited fighting skills. With few guns we left,
> dejected, knowing well that Polish partisans were in the vicinity, ready to
> kill us. All we could do was run away from them and from any other
> dangers.
>
> My brother became ill. He had jaundice. He was yellow, even sort of
> green; he couldn't eat anything. When we reached a swamp he could not
> get himself out of it. The rest of the people ran away. Shlomo Brand
> turned back to help me get my brother out of the swamp. But because
> my brother couldn't walk, Brand left us there. This brother begged me
> to go with the others because otherwise both of us would die. I refused.
> It was fortunate that Jews from a small town were hiding nearby, just a
> few families . . . They took us to a peasant, who put us up in a barn; it
> was winter. After two days, the farmer asked us to leave because the Ger-
> mans were on the way. This happened at night. But where could we go?
>
> I had a gold ruble, a coin that my mother had given me when I went
> to the forest. I explained to the peasant, "My brother cannot walk. Give
> me a wagon to take us somewhere. I can't leave him." I gave the peasant
> the coin. He put us on the sled and drove us into the forest. After a while
> he left us. We waited in the forest until morning. Then we walked from
> peasant to peasant, pretending to be husband and wife and pretending
> to be Christian. Different peasants helped us along the way. Slowly, we
> found our way back to the base . . . There was no way we could have
> made it on our own . . . Only some returned. No one told us how many
> had died. Initially, we were selected to join this group because we were
> superfluous ["useless"].[44]

Much earlier, in the summer of 1942, Mina Vołkowiski had also been shunted into a "useless" group. It happened during a German attack on the Andrejewski Forest. At that stage Mina and her physician husband were members of the Chapajev group, named after its Soviet commander. Mina recalls how they came to be abandoned.

It was a prolonged offensive that lasted until December. First [the commanders] divided us into small groups. The order was to break through the German encirclement. We had no arms. My husband was in one group and I in another. I was in a group with one Jewish woman, Krysia, a beauty. She was Commander Chapajev's mistress. Among us were Chapajev, several fighting men, and a few others. One day we woke up, and Chapajev and the fighters were gone. They left us there, me, his mistress, a woman who was a cook and her young son, and two men, both of whom were very poor fighters. They simply abandoned us. We had to hide. The others began to grumble against us because we were Jewish. Then they too disappeared . . . I and Chapajev's mistress were alone.

Both of us could easily pass for Christian. Krysia had a gun. After a day or so we realized that we were moving around in circles because we came to the place we started from. Searching, we heard a rough, "Hold! Don't move!" We were surrounded by three partisans, strangers . . . They recognized Krysia. We begged them to let us join them. But they could not take us without checking with their commander. Then they asked me what my nationality was. Without thinking, I said Polish. As they left, they promised to come soon to help. Krysia was restless, mistrustful. When we heard heavy steps, she jumped up. Before I had time to say anything, she grabbed her gun and was gone. The heavy steps belonged to the three partisans we had met before. They had come to take us; now they seemed suspicious about Krysia's disappearance . . . Later I heard that Krysia had been shot by Soviet partisans. She was intelligent, smart, beautiful . . .

I moved around with this small partisan group. One day we were told to go to the headquarters. There I heard terrible things about Jews. They blamed Jews for the German attack; they said that the Jews who

were caught gave away partisan secrets. They blamed the Jews for everything. It was shameful the way they spoke about us.

My group had occasional contacts with other detachments. In one of
them a Polish woman, a Communist, recognized me. She told them that
I was a Jew. I didn't know about it . . . Once I was washing and a partisan called me a dirty Jew. I did not react. Winter was approaching, and
we had to subdivide into separate ziemlankas. The woman who told
them who I was felt bad . . . She brought me the news that no one
wanted to accept me because I was Jewish. This is how I learned about
my problem. She advised me to go to the headquarters and ask them to
help me look for my husband. I did.

Mina was fortunate that the commander of Soviet Belorussia, Bobkov, although known for his cruelty and virulent anti-Semitism, protected her and
her husband.[45]

By 1943 the Soviet partisan movement had adopted a more liberal
recruitment policy. All able-bodied men, regardless of their political past,
were invited to join. The purpose was to deprive the Germans of manpower.
From the Jewish perspective it offered a mixed blessing. True, young Jewish men could now more easily gain entrance into Soviet partisan detachments; on the other hand, because the invitation brought in Nazi supporters,
it stimulated anti-Jewish prejudice. In addition, whenever German assaults
led to hardship, the partisans would blame the Jews for any problems created by the raids. From 1943 on anti-Semitism among Russian partisans can
be traced to two immediate sources: the acceptance of men with a pro-Nazi
past, and the stepped-up military engagements.[46] Caught between anti-
Semitic partisan practices and the official Soviet policy for recruiting more
people into the movement, Jews placed their reliance in the official policy.
The anti-Semitic flare-ups continued.[47]

Appearing under different guises, anti-Semitism occasionally seemed to
operate at cross purposes. As a teenager Lidia Brown-Abramson had escaped during the liquidation of the Głębokie ghetto. A Belorussian peasant
brought her to a partisan detachment. Lidia describes the group.

They were former prisoners of war, all Ukrainians. The Germans had given them a chance and incorporated them into their police force . . . But these Ukrainians moved to the partisans with all the guns and all that they got from the Germans. There was one [other] woman in their group, the wife of the commander, a Russian woman. They received me well. I peeled potatoes and helped the commander's wife with other chores.

They made fun of the Jews. They knew more about the Jews than I did. They were cheerful, sang songs. I decided to stop being a Jew. First because they were killing us, and second because they made fun of us . . . Wherever they went they took me with them, and I stayed with them a year and a half . . .

Then six young men came to us, Jewish men. They had been working outside of the ghetto . . . When they heard about the liquidation of their ghetto, they came to us . . . But these partisans killed all the Jews. They would go on an expedition, and each time another of the Jewish boys would not return. It was obvious that they were murdering them. None of them made it.[48]

In Lidia's group the anti-Semitism was selective; it did not apply to her. She had no explanation for this omission, except that the partisans liked her. They probably had gotten used to her and stopped seeing her as a Jew. Lidia's otriad, Radinoff, operated in and around the Bryzina Forest.

When Mina Dorn came to the Białystok forests in 1944, she had an eye-opening experience. As she casually chatted with a Russian woman, she was told, "You Jews always have it good."

I asked her, "Where do you get this idea from?"

She answered, "In our town, the pharmacist was a Jew. When everybody went to the army, he did not. They left him alone. All the Jews know how to get out of things, how not to do things."

I got very upset. I had my little revolver, a gift from my friend Schade, . . . she had one too. We jumped at each other with our weapons. The Jewish commissar, Sanka, passed. He started screaming at us. Then he scolded us separately. To me he explained that we were 17

Jews among 150 partisans and asked, "Do you think that they love us? What do you think, when we go to sleep do you want them to cut off our heads? There is anti-Semitism, and do not start with them." I told him how she carried on and that I could not bear it any more. He said, "Be blind and deaf. We cannot afford to be so sensitive. With one word you can kill the rest of the Jews, all seventeen."[49]

This commander's assessment was echoed by others. One respected Jewish partisan explains,

If you were an outstanding partisan and a Jew, they envied you. They might kill you out of envy. We had a doctor who was a prominent, a superior man. They were envious of him because he performed miraculous operations . . . There was a non-Jewish Russian doctor who was extremely jealous of him, and he would report all kinds of things against him. He wanted to eliminate him . . .

But if you were a poor fighter, let's say not a very good partisan, and a Jew, then they would point out, "See, he is a coward; he has these Jewish qualities." Every partisan, as you know, had a name, a special name, Ivan, Vasily, whatever. But with the Jew, "the Jew" stood in front of the name . . . There was one Jewish partisan who could not take it any more and lost his mind. So he went to the headquarters and threw in a grenade. He went crazy. Of course they killed him for it. But they didn't call him by his name; they talked about him as "the Jew."

Following this incident I was returning from a dangerous mission. I didn't know what had happened, but everybody was shouting, when discussing the case, "Look what a Jew can do!" Of course this kind of attitude depended very much on who the commander was.[50]

Zorach Arluk, a Lida ghetto runaway, joined the Soviet otriad Iskra. Although personally welcome, he was aware of anti-Jewish discrimination. Zorach remembers his partisan experiences:

There was a certain spirit. I began to go on expeditions, to derail trains and to burn all kinds of targets. I participated in twelve expeditions and was respected as a fighter. I felt that it was safer to be with six people than with the entire otriad. If the Germans attacked it would be against the entire unit, not just six. At first we were mobile, constantly on the move, slept in peasant huts. Only in 1944 did we live in the forest.[51]

"What about anti-Semitism?" I ask.

When things went well, all were heroes. When we had difficulties, the Jews were the scapegoats. "They don't know how to fight; therefore, we had losses," they would say. "The Jews know only how to conduct business, not how to fight." In September 1943, Lida ghetto was liquidated. The Jews were pushed into trains destined for Majdanek. Some tried to save themselves by escaping. Two young men jumped off the train and partisans from Iskra brought them to our camp. During a personal search the partisans found that they had some poison.

My commander was a mathematician. Without any examination, he decided that the two Jews had been sent here to poison the food and that they were Nazi spies. He felt that there was sufficient poison for an entire pot of soup. The two fugitives were put into a cellar. When this happened, I was away on a mission. After I returned, I saw the guard next to the cellar and was told what had happened. I went to the commissar and told him, "If you intend to kill these two Jews, you might as well kill all of us because we're going to notify Moscow about this. Whichever of us Jews survives will do it." He asked me to explain what I thought had happened. I told him that in the ghetto there was a commerce in cyanide. Jews wanted to have poison so they could commit suicide when caught by the Germans. The two had the cyanide only for this purpose. "How can you imagine that the Germans would send two Jews to poison our otriad? And then the two would return to the ghetto? What were all of you thinking about?"

Because of Zorach's intervention the guards were removed. But the two men had to go on a special mission. On one of the roads they were to cut down twenty telegraph poles. The two men turned to Zorach for help, convinced that they would be captured and murdered by the Germans. Zorach explained that the Russians were trying to frighten them: these telegraph poles had been out of order for a long, long time. He supplied the two with saws and told them to do as they were told because the area was off-limits to Germans and therefore safe.

The young men went on the assignment; they could see a Soviet partisan on a horse watching them from afar. When they finished, they returned to the camp and from there left to join the Bielski detachment, an all-Jewish partisan group. The men survived, although Zorach has forgotten their names. He feels that mistreatment of Jews by Soviet partisans was common.

Jews who lived in the forest were sensitive to manifestations of partisan anti-Semitism. Just talking about it seemed to hurt them. When the subject came up I would hear different versions of Mina Vołkowiski's story:

How they mistreated Jews! One can write books about that. They would kill Jews, rob them, and mistreat them in many, many ways. Whenever they had a Jewish boy, he would have to do the worst jobs. The Jews were terribly humiliated . . . At one point, around 1944, the Germans supplied arms to a few villages so that they could defend themselves against the partisans. They called it self-defense. Bobkov, our commandant, gave an order to burn one such village. Among those who left was a Jewish boy from Byten . . . In the morning they came back and reported that the whole village was destroyed, but one of the partisans, the Jew, had not wanted to take part, so they shot him. Bobkov explained to me that he could do nothing against anti-Semitism, that this expressed the anger of the people, because the Jews were denouncing partisans and the people were taking revenge for it . . .

One day, I saw among the trees some people in rags hiding and running. Hiding and running. I did not know who they were. When these Jewish people realized that we were a part of the headquarters, they came out, disheveled, looking terribly dirty, neglected, half alive. Some of them I knew. They had no food. The partisans had left them there without any means. I gave them all the food I had, and I told one of the women with a child to find out where I would be and to come to me; I would help her with food. Gusev, the commissar and an avid anti-Semite, turned to me and asked whether, as a Jew, I wanted to join them. But our commandant said, "No, she's coming with us." We stayed not far from them. One of these women whom I knew would come to me for food. I would beg my people for food for them. She would have loved me to stay with her, but what could I do? Later we left. What happened to them I don't know. If they did not kill them, they might have died of hunger.[52]

Because it appealed to innate prejudices and strong emotions anti-Semitism, not surprisingly, led to unpredictable, often irrational consequences that at times undermined the well-being of the partisan movement. In fact, some Russian partisans refused to accept armed young men simply because they were Jewish. Others grudgingly let a few Jewish young men join their otriads. A select number of Jews in the Belorussian forest had benefited from their cooperation while in the ghetto with early Russian forest partisans. Attached to the Słonim ghetto was a camp called Beutelager. There the Germans employed Jews for sorting, cleaning, and fixing various kinds of weapons. The Jews' access to these arms gave them leverage to make contacts with early Soviet partisans who were in need of weapons.

Zvi Shefet (Shepetinski) explains,

In the Słonim ghetto, the underground started with the Communists, the old Communists and the young ones, as well as the Socialists. We had a lot of weapons and transferred many of them to the forest. We would steal them and bring them first to the ghetto, and from the ghetto we took them to the forest. We had supplied the partisans not only with ammunition and guns but also with medicine, food, clothing, and all kinds of other goods. At that time the partisan movement was not well organized. We helped them establish better-equipped partisan groups with the goods we gave.[53]

But not all Słonim ghetto runaways were accepted into the Soviet partisan detachments. Those who were identified as former suppliers of goods had a chance, as had some young armed Jewish men. In the summer of 1942, after the second Aktion in Słonim, Zvi escaped into the forest with a group of twelve relatives that included his parents and sister. Only some of them were taken into a Soviet partisan unit. Zvi, his parents, sister, and a young aunt were rejected. Then, at a partisan center, the sixteen-year-old Zvi was asked to join a Jewish partisan detachment, otriad 51, while his parents, sister, and aunt were transferred into a family camp.

The command of Zvi's otriad was taken over by a decorated Jewish-Russian officer, Yefim Fiodorovich. An instructor in an officer school, he had been sent there from Moscow. Zvi describes what followed.

Fiodorovich transformed our otriad into an exemplary unit. Then we were ordered to move, supposedly to establish a base for our families. This was the official order . . . On the way we came upon the enemy. We had to fight very hard. They surrounded the forest and they attacked us from above. We were close to the marshes. This was in Polesie, during the dry summer of 1942. Soon we ran out of food. The Germans burnt the forest down. In the battle, many fell, including our Jewish commander.

He was a warm-hearted Jew and an excellent fighter. This was a great loss . . . It seems that Fiodorovich, our commander, was killed not by the Germans but by a commander of a Soviet otriad. Fiodorovich was a high officer, and because of his high rank, Russian commanders had to follow his orders. Therefore one of them did away with him. After Fiodorovich died, we, as Jews, had a lot of trouble.

Some Soviet partisans would chase away Jews, or simply leave them when a raid was in progress. This happened to us. They left us, about forty-two of us . . . By chance, we met another Soviet partisan group, Dziadzia Vassia. They were coming back from an expedition, and they accepted us. This was on the border between the Soviet Union and Poland. Most of the officers in this unit were from Siberia. They treated us very well.

In the Belorussian forests the Germans organized two massive attacks, the first in the summer of 1942, the second in 1943. In the second one, Zvi lost his family.

Faced with threatening and unpredictable conditions, Jews in the forest devised unusual strategies of survival. While some successfully cooperated with non-Jewish partisans, others formed their own units. At times these newly created detachments were really family camps, varying in composition, size, and ability to withstand the overpowering dangers.[54]

In Western Belorussia one of these Jewish groups, known as the Bielski otriad, took on the dual role of rescuers and fighters. The founders of this otriad were the three Bielski brothers, Asael, Tuvia, and Zus. They belonged to the small minority of Jewish peasants. Born in the isolated village of Stankiewicze, they were poor and had received limited schooling. But they were familiar with the countryside and independent; the three brothers refused to submit to Nazi terror, escaped into the countryside in the summer of 1941, and never became ghetto inmates.

At first, for safety, each brother went in a different direction. In exchange for food and shelter, each offered his services to Belorussian peasants. Then in the summer of 1942 came news that their parents, two brothers, and scores of relatives and friends had been murdered. This information strengthened the Bielski brothers' determination to protect themselves in more organized ways. They decided to form a Jewish partisan detachment. From Belorussian friends, they acquired a few weapons. With more than thirty followers they formed a unit, appointing Tuvia Bielski as its commander.

A strong and charismatic leader, Tuvia insisted from the start that all Jews, regardless of age, sex, state of health, or any other condition, be accepted into their otriad. Tuvia's open-door policy met with internal opposition from those who considered it a threat to the existence of the group. But Tuvia argued that large size meant greater safety. He never budged from this position. On the contrary, as the Germans stepped up the annihilation of the Jews, Tuvia became more determined and more inventive, devising new means of rescue.

Not only did the Bielski partisans accept all Jews who reached them on their own, but they sent guides into the ghettos to help Jews escape to join the otriad. Bielski scouts would also locate fugitives who roamed the forest and bring them to their base. Jewish partisans who had suffered from anti-Semitism as members of Soviet detachments knew that they could find shelter in the Bielski otriad. In addition, the Bielski partisans punished local collaborators who denounced runaway Jews. In reprisal, the Bielski partisans would kill the collaborators and burn their farms. They would then leave a notice announcing that the Bielski partisans had avenged the death of the person denounced and that all informers would experience the same fate. After a while local peasants stopped their anti-Jewish measures, making the forests safer for fugitives.

Nonetheless, the environment remained hostile. Tuvia Bielski lessened some of the danger by cooperating with Soviet partisans. This cooperation extended to food collection and joint anti-German military ventures, as well as other forms of economic aid.

From 1942 until 1943, the Bielski group led a nomadic existence. Toward the end of 1943, their number having grown to about four hundred individuals, they established a more permanent home in the huge, swampy, partly inaccessible Nalibocki Forest. At this phase their base came to resemble a shtetl, a small town, with many "factories" and workshops.

The establishment of these production units transformed a portion of the Bielski detachment into suppliers of goods and services to the Soviet partisan movement. This change helped neutralize some of the anti-Semitic complaints that the Jews ate too much without contributing anything of value. In addition, the exchanges that were made possible by the workshops and factories improved the economic situation in the Bielski unit, diminishing the burden on the young men who had been sent on the dangerous expeditions to find food.[55]

While the Bielski detachment accepted all Jewish fugitives, the internal organization of the unit was stratified according to criteria that mattered most to the group's existence. The top elite were the Bielski brothers, their wives, some relatives, and close friends. Included in this upper stratum were the people who worked at the headquarters. Next in importance were young men with guns. Below these were craftsmen and artisans, who enjoyed a more privileged position in the second year of the otriad, beginning in the fall of 1943, when the otriad built workshops and factories. Within these various production units, the skilled workers acquired a higher social standing than the unskilled workers or those whose skills were of no use to the camp.

At the bottom of the social ladder were those who engaged in manual unskilled labor, such as kitchen duty, chopping wood, or taking care of the cows and horses. In fact, the bulk of the otriad's members, who had no special skills and no guns, were at the bottom of the social ladder. These people were called *malbushim,* after the Hebrew word for clothes.[56]

Most of the people who had been members of the prewar elite found themselves relegated to the least desirable jobs, with the obvious exception of physicians and nurses. As one member of that elite explains,

The intelligentsia were down, we were depressed, we were not worth much; they made fun of us because we were malbushim. We were not fit for this kind of life. We had no experience with horses, nothing. The rest, the majority of the people, were uneducated, close to the soil . . . I had little in common with them. I really did not know them. I wanted to be close to them, but they did not want us. I worked all the time so that they would not make fun of me.[57]

Another, who was a teenager at the time, describes what happened to her father, who had held a high position in the brewery in Lida.

In the otriad, he became a malbush . . . He was intelligent, educated, but not resourceful at all. He was dirty, neglected, not seen as a human being somehow. No one would have recognized him at all. There were many disappointed people like him.[58]

Another malbush agrees:

My husband came without a gun. He would not have been a great fighter anyway. He had a high school education and he finished the technical school in Vilna . . . In general, the intelligentsia were not prepared to fight. How heroes are made is a question one often hears. We had one man, Baran, a common man, limited in many ways, very limited. To this day we don't know whether he was a hero or an idiot. He only wanted to fight and go on the most dangerous expeditions. He was a great fighter, not afraid of anything.[59]

The malbushim were more apathetic, less interested in what was happening than other partisans. They found it more difficult to elaborate on various aspects of the otriad. For example, when I asked three intelligent women, all former malbushim, to tell me about the workshops, none of them could say much. Each was almost unaware of their camp's activities.[60]

The Amarants, the husband, Shmuel, a former professor of history and the wife, Tamara, his former student, were notable exceptions to this apathy. In our interview, Tamara Rabinowicz, as she is now, recaptured parts of a conversation she had with Tuvia Bielski when she entered the camp. She remembers telling Tuvia at this first meeting, "We have seen so much destruction, we must take revenge."

Tuvia looked at me for a moment and laughed. "Do you know how many Jewish families have perished? And if something were to happen to either of you, then we would lose another family. No. I do not allow families to go on missions." Then he added, "I will give you work, plenty of it, but only those who have no family will fight the Germans." . . . This is what he did . . . Only about 20 percent or so of us were fighters. They were all young men without families . . .

The Bielski brothers wanted my husband to write a history of the otriad. Asael Bielski gave us a place in his ziemlanka for writing. They told my husband that whoever came to the forest, he should write down where he came from, who of his family were killed, and who stayed alive, so we would know what happened. Both brothers had an unusual sense of history.

There were people in the otriad who had arms and who objected to feeding and working for the rest, who could not help themselves. The Bielskis opposed this kind of attitude. The children, the women, and the rest who could not go on expeditions and fight had to be protected. This is how they felt. I heard it with my own ears. I swear to you that this is how it was. I spoke to my husband about Tuvia, in particular. "Look, here is a man with a minimum amount of education, and what deep involvement and historical sense he has." . . . Tuvia knew the peasants, he knew how to curse just like the peasants, he spoke like them. But the warm Jewish heart that he had, this was a great plus, a great treasure;

to save more than 1,200 Jews, this is no small matter! Without Tuvia Bielski in the forest, we would have been killed. We were without money, without arms; we would have been lost.[61]

When I ask her whether she was referred to as a malbush, Tamara answers simply,

Yes, I was a malbush and my husband too. All the intellectuals were malbushim. The lowest-ranking members of the otriad. I had no special skill, at least not the skills that were necessary there. The different craftsmen worked in their respective workshops. I could not do that. So I received all kinds of job assignments—gladly. Three weeks I was in the villages to collect potatoes. Three months I was guarding an airport. Whatever they asked me to do, I did. I kept guard very often . . . as for class, it is interesting that eventually, out of more than 1,200 Jews [in the otriad], only about 30 had higher education. That is, high school or university. The rest were petty merchants of cattle, all kinds of craftsmen, and they had all kinds of other occupations such as poor people had.

The nurse Riva Kantorowicz-Reich, who also came from an upper-class home, roamed the countryside for a few months before she joined the Bielski otriad:

We heard that Bielski was looking for Jews. He had such a beautiful heart—he took everybody. [She cries.] Tuvia was simply collecting Jews. One day he sent people for us. Whenever he heard that a Jew was somewhere in need of protection, he would send his partisans to get them. He himself did not have too many weapons. He did more than he could, much more . . . After I came to Bielski I started working right away. It was my duty to see to it that it was clean in the camp. It was very difficult to keep the place clean. People were filled with lice; conditions were horrible . . .

[Tuvia] was marvelous! He was delighted with every Jew. Whoever came, he would hug and kiss and say, "Thank God I have another Jew." At that time many people were coming to us, and as soon as I told him that I was a nurse, he wanted me to take care of the camp's hygiene.

I didn't know what to do, how to save these people. I saw people scratching and scratching; the lice would not leave them alone; it was horrible to watch. I advised them to pee, to use their urine and wipe themselves with it. I knew that urine had some chemicals that kill lice. In fact, we have seen the lice die. Lice cannot stand urine.

The people had all kinds of *furouncles* [open sores]. I took some fat and the inside of the bullets and mixed it together. It turned into a yellow mass. When smeared on the wound, this paste helped them tremendously with their skin condition.[62]

Abraham Viner and a female friend were both picked up by Bielski's scouts. The two belonged to the intelligentsia, and their initial entry into the otriad stayed with Abraham for the rest of his life.

Tuvia and Asael greeted us warmly. I wore torn clothes and had no shoes. I had rags around my feet. The girl, too, was in rags. We both looked very bad. There was no romantic involvement between us. When the people around us saw us, we heard them say, "Another malbush, and another malbush!" But Tuvia turned to us and said, "In our place, you will live." This stayed with me, and it made a very big impression on me, forever. I came there at the end of February [1943].[63]

"When meeting Tuvia, what did you think?" I ask.

I thought that I had met the Messiah. How can one think any other way? I did all kinds of work, the same as everyone else. I guarded the place, I worked in the kitchen, I had no weapons, nothing . . . Later, Tuvia put me into his headquarters, and I worked there as a clerk. Actually, at that time we rarely went on anti-German expeditions. Once I went with a group to cut down telegraphs. Sometimes we would move from place to place. As soon as more people came, we incorporated them and moved to another base.

The woman who came with Abraham left for a nearby partisan group, the Zorin otriad. Smaller than the Bielski detachment, this otriad was headed by Shlomo Zorin, a former Soviet POW who had escaped captivity in Minsk. The majority in the Zorin group were Russian Jews. This otriad also had an open-door policy, accepting all Jews, regardless of ability or condition. The two otriads cooperated with each other, yet each was also a special island, one of the only havens open to all Jews.[64]

Male-Female Relationships in the Forest

With minor exceptions dictated by dire need, East European forest partisans were inhospitable to those whom they saw as unfit to wage war. "Advanced age," being Jewish, coming from an upper-class background, being a woman: any or all of these could disqualify an individual from membership in a partisan detachment. How did these various characteristics relate to the fate and coping skills of women in general, and Jewish women in particular?

In the forests most men considered women unfit for combat and therefore burdensome. By contrast, the Soviet government praised the women's contributions to guerrilla warfare. Stalin specifically claimed that women partisans symbolized the supreme dedication and patriotic struggle of the country. But although it was widely publicized and carried political backing, the participation of women in the Russian partisan movement was in reality limited. The estimated proportion of women in the Soviet partisan movement ranges from 2 to 5 percent. In contrast to the pro-female government propaganda, the leadership in the forest maintained that the small number of women were all the movement could effectively absorb.[65]

With the few exceptions I mentioned earlier, women who joined Soviet partisan detachments were relegated to unimportant duties. Eagerness to participate or special fitness for a hazardous job seldom had any effect. By and large women were assigned to service jobs involving the kitchen, cooking, and keeping the base clean.[66]

Some historians argue that women were accepted into Russian detachments largely as sex partners. Particularly in the later stages of the war, officers of partisan units from brigade commanders down to battalion commanders would select sexual partners from among the women enlisted in their units. The women became the virtual property of the officers. By implication this gave them officer status, with the privileges that went with the position of their partners but without combat assignments.[67]

Most high-ranking Russian partisans had mistresses. In recognition of this arrangement, the women were given the title "transit wife." Most non-Jewish women were in the forest only because they had a special relationship with a particular man. Only a fraction had come because of a desire to oppose the Nazis, and an even smaller proportion because their lives were in danger. These women as a whole constituted a small minority of forest dwellers, usually an unwelcome minority at that. Sometimes women were unjustly suspected of spying. One partisan, a physician, tells the story of two Russian sisters, idealists, whom the Soviet partisans accused of treason on concocted charges. Both were burned to death in a public execution. None of the witnesses, including the physician, dared to object.[68]

Unlike most of their Christian counterparts, Jewish women came to the forest to escape death. Before entering a forest Jewish fugitives knew that for a woman alone it would be harder than for a man and that the possibility of rape or murder was real. Jewish women realized that powerful men could give them some protection. Indeed, acceptance into a Russian detachment was often contingent on a woman's readiness to become a partisan's mistress. It was common for young girls to sleep with Russian commanders, political heads, or whoever else was in power. And if a partisan, any partisan, helped a woman, he expected to be paid with sexual favors.[69]

I noted earlier that when partisan groups were weak, harassed by the enemy, and eager to fight, they were more likely to include women in their military missions. Some of my findings suggest that participation in anti-German assaults helped shield women from sexual pressures. But when the partisans became more numerous and better organized, women were more likely to be assigned to domestic roles and more likely to be seen as sex objects. And even though most male partisans were eager to have sexual relations with women, they would accuse them of promiscuity; the women they desired as sex partners they viewed with contempt. In conversations between men, for example, the word *whore* was often substituted for the word *woman.* Characteristically, one Russian commissar insisted that "all women were whores unless proven otherwise." The emphasis in his statement was on "proven otherwise."[70]

Most of these negative perceptions were reflected in the actual treatment of women. And the attitudes did not apply only to particular women— Jews, say, instead of Russians, or promiscuous women rather than chaste. When it came to expressions of anti-female prejudice, the male partisans were fairly egalitarian. Partisan reports concur with Eva Kracowski's assessment:

> There was a very bad attitude on the part of the Russians toward all
> women, even the Russian women they were living with. They talked to
> them and dealt with them with contempt, like prostitutes, often accusing
> them as follows: "You came here only to sleep around." . . . They
> screamed at every woman . . . If I hadn't had my friends, the Jews who
> were protecting me and watching over me [Syrota and Szyjka], I don't
> know what might have happened. It was important for a woman to have
> a man as protector. But I had no boyfriend in the forest . . . You may
> think that I am lying, but I am not. You have to understand that I was in
> a group that was exposed to horrible conditions. We hardly ever stayed
> in a proper ziemlanka. There were constant raids.[71]

Eva was living in the forests around the Białystok area, where the life of all partisans was particularly harsh.

Zvi Shefet explained that to the Russians in the forest a woman was "a service giver . . . She had to satisfy a man's sexual needs. If a woman in the forest had no male protector, she had grave problems."[72]

I asked Jewish male partisans how different they thought their lives would have been if they had been women in the Soviet otriads. Michael Pertzof replied,

> I would have had to do what all the women did because conditions were
> so different for women and men. I would have had to work in the
> kitchen and do the things that women did. It was impossible to do
> otherwise. I would have had to connect with somebody to protect me.
> I see in every woman a heroine because they had to do very hard things.

It was much more difficult for a woman. First of all, they were a very small minority in the forest, and as you know, the majority is always right . . . The woman who could somehow manage for herself without a man was a true heroine.

Many other Jewish partisans confirm this, emphasizing the horrible plight of the Jewish women in the forests.[73]

One respondent who agreed in principle that women faced particular hardships had a slightly different perception of why their situation was the way it was. A keen observer, Ephraim (Franek) Blaichman was born in the small town of Kamionka, near the city of Lublin. In 1942, aged nineteen and anticipating trouble, he left home and for a while roamed the surrounding forests and countryside with a small group of Jewish men. After his group had managed to obtain a few arms from local peasants, the Polish Communist Party (PPR) agreed to cooperate with them. Blaichman concurs with most others that fewer women escaped into the forests. Initially his own group of men had two women under their protection: a young unmarried woman and a mother with a child. Because the partisans were armed, they were able to place the two women and the child in the homes of local peasants.

Ephraim muses about the women's life in the forest.

Usually the civilians, the women and older people, were not real fighters. We did not deny the women the chance to fight, but they were not good at it. We did not take them on missions. There were very few women anyway. They did housework. For about a year it was quite safe there; we were almost free, because the Germans were afraid to do too much . . . Actually I was not very often with women, but I always protected them. I was never afraid to give my opinion. I saw some common men who were starting with women, and I made it clear that I did not approve of that, and I felt that one should not let a woman go from hand to hand. If she had one boyfriend, all right, but if a woman went from hand to hand I felt that the whole group would be demoralized.[74]

Asked about specific differences in the situations of men and women, Blaichman at first denied there were any, but his comments showed that he had in fact been aware of them.

I did not see any differences. We were all needy. It was not a normal life. Everyone was trying to stay alive. Yet more men than women ran away and came to the forest. Maybe women felt less in danger and therefore they were less likely to run into the forest? . . . I really don't understand why, but they seemed to have felt safer than men . . . Still, some women did escape into the forest. Later on, I would tell the few women who joined us, . . . "As commanders, as leaders, we took you in, but none of us singly has the right to demand that you do what we want. Singly, none of us is responsible for accepting you. We men accepted you as a group." . . . Later on, they all thanked me for this. It's hard for me to talk about this. [*He becomes very emotional and stops briefly.*] Of course it was difficult for women. It was very difficult for women to live in the forest. You see, it may be hard for you to grasp what life was like . . . There was no running water, no bathrooms, no conditions for life. How people lived through it is hard to imagine . . . Of the two women we protected, one survived. One was killed. Somebody denounced her. At the beginning we didn't know how to hide. In the snow, one could see [footprints], and one of them was killed because of it. The other escaped. The older woman with the child made it.

Most men seem to agree that more men escaped into the woods than women.[75] Jewish women echoed these conclusions as well. But they explain the reason for the difference in numbers in a variety of ways. Some women agree with Eva Kracowski that

it was more difficult for women because around the Białystok Forest conditions were inhuman. Besides, when you think about who went to the partisans . . . I by chance found myself there, by sheer chance . . . There were very few women among the partisans. Maybe there were more in those family groups, but in general there were very few women . . . The Russian partisans looked on women just as sex objects. Yet maybe one should not generalize like this. After all, sometimes women went on missions . . . Basically, the men felt that the women were needed for the officers, for the commanders, and that the women were whores. This is how the men saw them.

Over time, as anti-Semitism increased, Jewish women faced more serious threats and were more frequently refused entry into Soviet otriads. Hostility to Jewish women increased after the German army began suffering
more defeats, and a large number of Nazi collaborators began switching
sides and joining the Russian partisan groups.[76] Jewish women now faced a
double disadvantage, as Jews and as women. Although exact numbers are
not known, it is estimated that a large number of Jewish women perished in
the forests. Of those who survived, some found refuge in Russian units and
some in Jewish detachments. Only a fraction ended up in the scattered family groups. More women were taken in by the large Bielski and Zorin otriads.

As a physician's wife, Mina Vołkowiski had certain advantages. Doctors
were in short supply among the partisans.[77] But even her husband was not
always able to shield her from danger. Beautiful, energetic, and optimistic,
Mina tries to see the positive side of womanhood. Occasionally, when she
revisits the past, she will hesitate, remembering the more hurtful experiences. To her observation that partisans had no respect for women, she adds
as an afterthought, "The relations between men and women were not so
bad. After all, we gave them food. We cooked it. At one point the partisans
wanted to separate us women from men. They wanted to establish an independent women's unit. We had to collect food, wood, and so on. This was
very difficult for me. A Belorussian woman was appointed as our commander. We were in one ziemlanka at the time."

"Were there other Jewish women besides you?"

"Yes, one, Musia; they finished her off."

"How? What happened?"

"Oh, well! This Belorussian commander was awful. She would assign
the hardest jobs to me and Musia. We didn't know how to handle horses,
but we were forced to. When we went on a food expedition to the village, all
the others would go inside the house, and we had to guard the place and the
horses. Musia was shot. I was saved by a miracle."

"What happened?"

"She was asked to clean, and she refused. So they denounced her at the
headquarters. Gusev, the anti-Semitic commissar, came to investigate and

called it [her refusal] sabotage. There was an order that the two of us had to be killed. One of the guys went for a walk with Musia and shot her. Another partisan had an order to kill me. One evening he sat next to me but his hand was shaking. He could not do it. Then our friend Dr. Berkowicz [Berk] heard about it. He came to take me to his place, to assist him with patients. Later on, when Gusev came to visit us, he was shocked to see me still alive. At that time, this story was old. So I stayed there."[78]

Having a connection with an appropriate man could help a woman negotiate the move from the ghetto to a safer place, shielding her from harm and even death. Unprotected women were targets, both from men encountered in the countryside and from partisans who expected sexual favors. Some Jewish women were raped. One woman, who was fourteen when she ran away from the ghetto, describes her experience:

I was walking alone in the forest. A man with a rifle stopped me . . . I thought it was a partisan, but I was not sure. I was frightened. He pretended to be arresting me. He was forty or so, maybe a Belorussian. He told me to follow him and he took me to a tent. Then he forced himself on me . . . He did not ask . . . He just did it. He raped me.

Inside me something broke. I was sick. This feeling stayed and stayed, for years. I could not look at men . . . I had some kind of an inner conflict. I was excited about sex, but I was scared, turned inward. I did not like the physical part of sex. I did not put sex in an important place. I am glad I don't need it . . . I imagine that many women had similar experiences . . . shocking, this rape . . . horrible.[79]

This teenager's experience was not unique. Lidia Brown-Abramson, who was also a teenager at the time, tells her story:

We were running away during a raid, and I returned to the ziemlanka to take something I had forgotten. Right there, one of our partisans grabbed me. After he pushed me flat on my back, he asked "Do you know what ——— means? And ———?" All very vulgar words. I said no. So he replied, "Come, I will show you what it is." It hurt me. I screamed. He got up saying, "You are not yet a woman!" I don't know what he did. I only know that it hurt me. He got angry and left. I ran after them.

When I caught up with my group he was angry, very angry, and said something like, "You are back with us?" He was the only one who was not nice to me. The commander and his wife were kind. He even promised to take me to Moscow after the war.

"What did this experience do to you?" I ask.

What did it do? To this day I see things through my rape. When I see a dog trying to jump on top of another dog, I feel sorry for the female dog. In my home, it is the same thing. All the time I see it before me; it never leaves me. I never enjoy sex, never. I had to agree to it. I have a family, a fine family, but the sexual act I see as exploitation.

I work. There are holidays. Many of the girls get free time off. Once a girl came as a substitute, simple, common . . . She spoke without any embarrassment, "What kind of a husband do I have? I have to wake him up to make me feel good." As I listened to her, I thought about how healthy this woman must be in her soul, how content she must be. She dresses provocatively and says, "This is sexy; a woman has to be sexy." She's primitive, but her soul is healthy. This I envy. I never had it. I never experienced pleasure from sex, never. I waited for my husband not to want it, not to be able to perform.

I asked him, "What will happen when the time comes that you won't be able to have sex?"

"This would be just like when one cuts the wings off a bird."

He is Israeli born, from a village, good-looking, manly. He's charming. I was his first woman. Maybe this was my luck. He doesn't know anything else.[80]

Lidia is not sure that at the time she knew what had happened to her. She said nothing about it to the commandant's wife, who treated her well. Yet she continues to be haunted by that violent act that took place so many years ago. Eager to explain herself, she continues, "I see sex as a thing that I am forced to do, as a thing that I don't want to do. In my mind, I think that one cannot enjoy something that one is forced to do. The act itself looks to me as if the man is doing something to the woman and not the woman to him. He is coercing her, and I see it as something bad."

"Have you tried to get help?"

"No. It is so deep inside me that I cannot. My brain tells me I should, but I cannot. I am not primitive. Even when I am in bed, and it is pleasant and all is well, the moment it comes to sex, something happens, something, which is not good. I am always in control during the sexual act. I never relax, I never let myself go. I also don't know how to love. Particularly when it comes to sex, I don't feel well."

"How do you explain the fact that you think that you were not aware of what this partisan was doing, and yet it still left such an impression on you?"

"When it happened, I did not understand. Then the pain made me feel bad . . . It must be something from home, that this part of the body one should not touch, that one should be left alone. I don't understand."

As the war was coming to an end, Lidia's otriad was attacked by the retreating German army. During the shooting she hid in the marshes. When she finally emerged from her hiding place, she saw dead bodies scattered all over the ground. These bodies of people she had known and liked represented yet another major loss. This was 1944, and the Germans had left. But Lidia was truly alone.

No one knows how common forest rapes were, nor the scars they left upon the victims. But though secrecy surrounds the subject of rape, information about other sexual experiences is more accessible. Jewish women in the forest were forced into sexual relationships by a number of circumstances. Often their protection, their very survival, depended on their willingness and ability to form a sexual liaison. The women's attitudes toward such involvements, based on their own experiences or on their observations of others, varied. Many Jewish women felt that by and large the sexual relationships of the forest were coercive. Yet frequently they distinguished between having a sexual relationship with a Jewish partisan and having one with a non-Jewish partisan. Within the two Jewish otriads in Western Belorussia, the Bielski and the Zorin detachments, women were more likely to see sexual involvement as voluntary. Their perception that they enjoyed greater personal autonomy can be traced to the policies that governed these Jewish otriads.

In the Bielski partisan group, for example, all women were accepted, no matter how they had come to the forest or who they were. Although Lili Krawitz, a nurse, is often critical of the commander, Tuvia Bielski, she describes how he admitted, without any hesitation, her girlfriend, who arrived with a sick elderly mother. Lili emphasizes that the older woman became a burden for the otriad; this was not an isolated instance. But Tuvia maintained his policy of admitting every Jew, man, woman, and child, a procedure that accounts for the high proportion — 30 – 40 percent — of women in the Bielski otriad.[81]

Inside the Bielski camp a few basic rules applied equally to men and women. Each individual was entitled to a certain minimum allotment of food. The commander allowed no deviations from this rule. Further, all adults were required to do guard duty, although a handful were excused because of physical handicaps, age, or excessive nervousness. Tuvia Bielski wanted to see his followers occupied, and he created new opportunities for work in the Nalibocki Forest in 1943, when he settled his partisans there and had them establish more permanent workshops and factories. In addition to the personal satisfaction of the work, workers occasionally received extra food. This, for example, was true for those doing nursing jobs. A nurse was entitled to extra food. Most women took advantage of whatever job opportunities there were.[82]

But although they had some choice about the type of work they would do, women were barred from military missions and food collections, just as in most other otriads. It was rare for a woman to assume even a semi-leadership role. Similarly, just as in most partisan units, so in the Bielski otriad women were viewed by men as sex objects. If a woman were single, young men might try in various ways to seduce her. One of these women describes how men would make their way to her bunk at night. She had a hard time fighting them off. An older woman advised her to keep a branch next to her and to hit whoever approached. She did so, and the next morning noticed a number of bruised faces. The men soon stopped bothering her.[83]

As a rule, such unsolicited nightly advances did not lead to a steady relationship. But as in other otriads, even in the Bielski detachment it was believed that a woman needed someone to take care of her, a "proper" man.[84]

A newly acquired lover was called a *tavo*. It is a Hebrew word, a masculine address, that within the context of the Bielski detachment could be translated "come here." Because men with guns went on food expeditions, a woman who had a steady tavo with a gun would get more, better food than an unattached woman. The social value given to a youth with a gun was also conferred on his girlfriend. In the forest there were no wedding ceremonies; if the relationship continued for a while a couple were treated as husband and wife.

Because a woman without a man had little social clout, most young girls looked for an appropriate tavo. While many women formed a stable relationship with one particular man, some would have casual sex with different men. Others would decide to remain unattached. But a woman with no special skills and no special protectors was placed in the category of malbush.

Sulia Rubin had belonged to the elite in her native town of Nowogrodek. But when she came to the Bielski otriad in 1942, she was ranked as a malbush. At that time each ziemlanka was allotted provisions, and the members cooked their own meals. As a newcomer, Sulia was assigned to low-level duties. She was delegated to cook, but she didn't know how. Nor did she know how to start a fire; to keep whatever little flame she had gotten going she would have to blow and blow. Her face, hands, and neck were usually covered with soot and ashes.

An old man who shared her ziemlanka took pity on her. Although himself weak, he tried to assist her. But as he helped her he would constantly mumble, "What will become of you? How will you manage? How?" Sulia had no answers. Instead of concentrating on her work, she would dream of owning a fur coat; she had come to the forest wearing only a sweater. The otriad tried to supply its members with a minimum amount of clothing, but this was not always possible, and the clothes did not include fur coats.

Overwhelmed by all the changes in her life, Sulia became depressed. Her parents and sister were still in the ghetto. She became convinced that if they were with her, her troubles would disappear. She knew that if she found an appropriate boyfriend, he could bring her family to the forest. Just the idea lifted some of her depression. She began actively searching for a partner.

Among her new friends was an older man who had recently lost his wife and children. He had started drinking heavily and showed no interest in life or women. This man agreed with Sulia that her problems could be solved if she had a tavo. He thought that his younger brother, Boris Rubierzewicki, a brave partisan, a scout, and a regular food collector, would be a good choice.

Soon Sulia was introduced to a simple, uneducated youth who had guts and a gun. Boris had never imagined that he could have had such a refined girl for a wife. Sulia, too, had never met this kind of boy. Though repelled by his common ways, she was impressed by his courage. She admits that it was not a question of love or attraction. She expected two things from the young man: to improve her economic lot and to rescue her family from the ghetto. Boris was interested. As proof of his intentions, he presented her with a fur coat, confiscated during a mission. Although her acceptance of the fur indicated a deal, Sulia continued to keep him at a distance. Before taking the final step she made Boris promise that as long as they were in the forest he would not leave her. She was trying to avoid future humiliation. Boris readily agreed to her demands.

Through guides, Sulia notified her parents about her decision to take a lover. Her mother was opposed to the union. Sulia had known that her mother was a snob; in fact she herself thought that Boris was not good enough for her. Her mother's letter, brought from the ghetto by a scout, protested, "A woman who sells her body to exist, I can understand. But you sold your soul, because you will never leave him."[85] Sulia did not listen to her mother's message. By April 1943, she had a steady tavo.

Sulia's first six months, when she was alone, had been "like six years of Siberian torture; but in that time I learned how to cook well. They taught me how to shoot, I knew how to clean a gun." Sulia notes that after she took up with Boris,

Right away I was dressed. Right away, I got a pair of boots. I had a fur. To have a man who did not look at anybody else and who protected you was something marvelous! Soon we got a permit to build a ziemlanka. I told my two best friends, Raja and Lola, "I have my tavo, the two of you can wait till the end of the war. You will stay with me. Whatever I have I will share with you. Don't rush into any relationship."

Almost fifty years later, still married to the same man, Sulia explains, "It was enough that I did what I had to do. At least I wanted my two best friends to have the freedom to choose someone they loved." Sulia's mother never met the son-in-law she so vigorously objected to. The family were murdered before Boris could arrange for their escape.

How did Sulia feel about Boris, the man?

"I was not attracted to him. I was not attracted to anybody. I was grateful that I was not repulsed by him. Who could be attracted to anybody? Maybe it was abnormal. The commanders I would not go with at all, no matter what. For me, it was just a necessity for survival. Simply put, it was as if I was a woman of the cave; a mate chose me, and I stayed with him."

"Were the women in the forest not interested in sex?"

"I knew that I had a passion inside me, but I could not respond to anybody. Maybe other women did not like it. For me, I could do with it or without it. Sex never ruled my life."

"Do you see yourself as a frigid woman?"

"No! Circumstances were like that. I was disappointed in men; sex for them was a cure for everything. They were like animals. No sooner did the Germans take away their wives [than] they would look for another one. It was animallike. It repulsed me. I have quite a number of friends who were married more than once, not because they loved the man."

When I ask what the main reason was for women to become involved with men in the forest, she answers,

Survival. Why do beauties in the United States marry older rich men? Many women survived alone. Some did it [took tavos] because they liked the guy. The boys had the guns, not the women. A woman was a convenience for a man. The women were cooking, baking; I did not want to do that. When we were moving from place to place, unless you had a man to whom you were attached, you were alone . . . It was very lonely. To me, it was normal that the boy made a pass at you. In the Bielski otriad nobody raped you. I don't believe in sexual harassment . . . Boris had to wait for me. I didn't right away sleep with him. If I [had] agreed [to do so] right away, maybe there would have been time to take out my parents [from the ghetto]. The way it happened, it was too late.[86]

Some women felt that in the woods sex was based on more than just an exchange of services and goods. One explains, "Even though we women did not go out for combat and on food missions, we had to deal with military actions. The Germans would attack us. A woman who had a man with a gun felt more secure."[87]

Lili Krawitz came from an upper-class family. In the ghetto she became attached to a man from the lower classes. She is convinced that without him she would never have left the ghetto or, if she had done so, that she would never have survived. In the Bielski otriad her husband became a fighter, which gave his wife some advantages. She thinks that women who married as she did were completely dependent on their men. Trying to understand these socially unequal marriages, she points out that no one forced a woman to become attached to a particular man. Of her own relationship, she says, "I was hungry for love, like so many other women, and these men gave us love."

For my husband, it was a great thing that he got a supposedly "superior" woman. He was grateful to me for it. He was proud of the fact that I wanted him and behaved very well toward me. I am not even sure whether he loved me or not. For me, his goodness was compensation for everything else.

I don't think that a woman would have sold herself for food, more likely for security. During a raid a man would look after her. It was important. One always lived in fear of what might happen next. How does one live with this fear all alone? A young girl needed someone. I do not agree that women were selling themselves, but it was not love either.

To be sure, it was the men rather than the women who would select the partner. But if a woman did not like the man, no one forced her. She was free to reject a man.[88]

Some relationships were short-lived. In the Bielski otriad, as in most other detachments, the powerful men had the easiest access to women. Tuvia and Zus Bielski took full advantage of these opportunities. In their defense some say that although the two brothers had many affairs, each tried to stay away from married women and women with steady boyfriends.[89]

Chaja Bielski, who was married to Asael, comes to her brother-in-law Tuvia's defense by pointing out that he was a man with whom any woman could easily fall in love. She admits that he was sexually active but insists, "The women were really after him. He was gorgeous and supposedly good in bed." Others echo her statement and emphasize that "he did not force anyone. He never pushed himself on anyone. All the women in the otriad were in love with him. He was extremely attractive, and he was the commander. One always had a way out. Some women even bragged that they slept with him." One male partisan insists that Tuvia respected women, that he gave them a chance to be self-sufficient, adding, "If any of these women became his mistress, it was because they were chasing him."[90]

In an early forest raid Tuvia had lost his second wife, Sonia. The comments about Tuvia's infidelities refer to the period when he was married to his third wife, Lilka, an attractive young woman. When Lilka talks about her forest marriage, she dwells on the positive. She feels that Tuvia taught her a lot about life, about love. Wistfully, she recalls, "When there was danger he always looked after me. He could rely on me, too. I never interfered. I did not nag him. I did not force him to take me or to stay with me." She too defends Tuvia's infidelities, saying, "His private life was his business. If he went on a mission and slept with someone, I did not see, I did not know. Who cared? . . . Even in front of me women would approach him."[91]

Commenting about this third marriage, Chaja notes,

Probably for Tuvia it wasn't a question of love. Lilka was young and beautiful. It was sex. His wife Sonia was killed during a raid. He began to drink too much after that. He wanted to forget. He stayed away for about two weeks. Before that the whole family had lived together, in one tent. This included Lilka and her father. Tuvia returned to the same tent. Lilka and her father were there. She fell in love with him from the moment she met him, before they arrived in the forest.[92]

Lilka's love for her husband was atypical. Most forest unions began when a woman offered sex in exchange for goods, protection, or security. Stories about sexual escapades among the partisans have circulated widely, with few facts to substantiate or refute them. Some accounts deplored what they saw as pervasive promiscuity, while others denied that it took place. Nonetheless, within the Bielski otriad, as elsewhere in the forest, coarse sexual language was part of everyday speech. Men jokingly equated having sexual intercourse with being alive. When he asked a woman to have sex with him, a partisan would say, "Let me check if I am alive."[93]

Yet in the Bielski otriad no one coerced women into a relationship. No woman was ever raped. On the contrary, compared to the Soviet detachments, women in the Bielski unit had a number of options. They had the freedom to refuse a man. No woman was dismissed because she rejected a man. No woman was ever dismissed at all.[94]

Some women opted for celibacy. As one explains,

There were many vulgar men. I did not go for such men. I saw how the partisans behaved sexually. I slept in the same ziemlanka . . . and I felt nauseated by them. I preferred to remain a malbush.

The nurse Riva Kantorowicz-Reich, who was young and attractive, also refused to become involved with men. She preferred to concentrate on her work. She readily admitted that a woman with a lover had more protection, but this was not for her. She felt that as a nurse she was already in a more favorable situation than most other single women. Specifically, she says,

I did not have a difficult time because I was working. I felt good because I was helping people. I knew who needed what and was able to do things for them. I was surrounded by respect, approval. Tuvia protected me, and I did not care about anyone else.

Some women insist that in the Bielski otriad women who refused to become involved with a man were in some ways more respected than those who attached themselves to one.[95]

In contrast to the Bielski otriad, entry into a Soviet partisan unit was often contingent upon a woman's willingness and ability to become an officer's mistress. Not all women were ready to trade sex for protection. More significant, only a fraction of the women were able to negotiate such transactions. Most women lacked the two basic requirements: youth and good looks. A woman with special skills had a better chance of acceptance: a physician, a nurse, even a good cook was likely to be accepted into a Soviet detachment, and she would not have to become someone's mistress. Occasionally a Jewish woman would join a Soviet otriad because she had a connection to a powerful partisan that was unrelated to sex. A man might be allowed to keep his daughter or sister if he were important enough to the otriad. These women also had the privilege of refusing the sexual advances of partisan officers without being dismissed.[96]

Making the women's situation even more precarious, in 1943 rumors began circulating that the Germans had infected Jewish women with venereal diseases and sent them into the forest to spread the illness. The non-Jewish partisans took these and other anti-Semitic rumors seriously. In response some partisan detachments ordered their officers to discard their Jewish mistresses and send them to the Bielski otriad. Some complied, others left the otriad along with their Jewish wives. The few women who had managed to become part of a Soviet otriad as mistresses continued to need a protector, preferably a powerful one.[97]

But women's difficulties did not stop with attachments to "appropriate" men. Having a man in itself created new, painful problems. The forest was an inhospitable place for rearing children. Many loved children, but all knew how hard it would be to see them grow up in these surroundings. None of the partisans wanted babies. Inevitably, however, some sexual liaisons led to pregnancies. In the Bielski otriad, as elsewhere, women had to carry most of the burdens of unwanted pregnancies. Abortions were common and performed under trying circumstances, with inadequate instruments and no medication. Dr. Hirsh, the camp physician who also acted as gynecologist for the Bielski otriad, was kept busy performing abortions not only on women from his detachment but also on those from the surrounding Soviet otriads.[98]

The doctor, thin and smiling, could always be found working, his instrument case in hand. Soon his surgical reputation had spread far and wide. In payment for his services the doctor would receive such valued provisions as fat, pork, flour, and other food. In addition to the food, which Dr. Hirsh got from partisans who went on food missions, the doctor demanded gold coins from those who could afford them. It was rumored that both his instrument bag and a special bag he wore tied around his neck were filled with gold coins. Nonetheless, women from the Bielski otriad who could not afford his fees were accommodated free of charge. And although most people agreed that no children were to be born in the forest, in the Bielski otriad nothing happened to the few exceptions. Two or three babies were born.[99]

Many of the young women who were sexually active had one or more abortions. One woman died during the procedure. After the war some of these women had difficulty becoming pregnant. To this day former women partisans find it hard to talk about these experiences. Some who had several abortions are bitter, blaming the men for not practicing birth control. Still haunted decades later, most of these women seem frank about their feelings. Many agree with the woman who complained, "After all, I paid with my body; did I need pregnancies too? It depended on him, not on me."[100]

A few of the women who reached the forest were already pregnant. If the pregnancy was advanced, the woman would be allowed to give birth, then the newborn baby would usually be taken away and killed. As in other forests, in Rudnicki no woman was supposed to keep her baby. The commander, Hienia Dobrowski, was very strict about this rule. Hienia had left her husband and son in the Vilna ghetto to come to the forest with her lover. When she became pregnant, however, she ignored the rule. She gave birth to a baby girl and kept her. The baby, Hienia, and her lover all survived.[101]

Like Dr. Hirsh in the Bielski otriad, other forest physicians, including

Dr. Vołkowiski, were kept busy performing abortions. Among Dr. Vołkowiski's patients was the mistress of Bobkov, the commander of the otriad. Once the doctor's wife, Mina, paid a visit to another base, where she met a woman with a newborn baby at her breast. Mina stopped to chat with the beautiful mother, Irka, and learned that she was the mistress of Paweł Progniagin, the chief of staff of the regiment headed by General Sikorski. When the baby was born, the couple had been ordered to discontinue their relationship. They were to give up the baby, and Irka expected to be moved to another otriad. Progniagin's efforts to intervene had had no effect. As Mina later heard, the baby was taken away; no one ever knew what happened to her. Irka was sent to a small otriad. There, dejected, she remained until the arrival of the Red Army. This was not an unusual case.[102] In the forest, pregnancy, whether terminated or completed, was always filled with regrets and painful choices.

For an attractive woman to become a center of attention was potentially threatening for her and those close to her. For example, Mina and her physician husband were separated several times by circumstances. She was fortunate that during most of these periods she was able to stay at the headquarters, protected by Commander Bobkov. Many partisans were eager to sleep with her and would anxiously watch one another to see if anyone else had succeeded. Although Mina was shielded, she would feel more and more uncomfortable. On one occasion, aware of her predicament, Kasian, a partisan friend, helped locate her husband. Once the doctor was back, the men kept their distance. But even her husband's presence did not protect her from another unexpected danger.

One day in 1944 General Sikorski, the abusive drunk described earlier who was the head of the regiment in the Polesie region, paid a visit to the Bobkov brigade. Mina describes his visit:

I had not met General Sikorski before. He arrived with his entire headquarters. We had all assembled to greet him . . . Such an ugly man, like an ape. Fat and horrible looking. He noticed me. During the meal he talked to me. He seemed to like me and told me that he would help my husband advance. Soon, he said, the war would end, and before that happened he wanted me to move to his place. When I said no, he continued to press, adding that he would extend a formal invitation. Of course, knowing how the partisans liked to promise and brag, I shrugged it off.

Later, Bobkov told us that the members of our headquarters, including me and my husband, had been invited to Sikorski's place for dinner. The dinner was festive. Lavish. General Sikorski gave presents to all the women. Then he called Dr. Blumowitch, the head doctor, and announced that he was removing him from the post and was giving it to Dr. Volkowiski. This scared me. My husband did not want this kind of a job. He was a modest man. Blumowitch was very talented, a good organizer. The commander became furious [when my husband refused]. He kept insisting. My husband argued that he was not suited for this kind of work. The general insisted, "You will have the position, and Blumowitch will do everything." All my husband said was no. The general called Paweł Progniagin, the chief of staff, and urged him to persuade my husband. My husband refused. Angry, possibly drunk, the general ordered Progniagin to kneel and proceeded to hit him with a whip. There was chaos, confusion, and shooting. They were all drunk.

We ran away; half dead, we reached our base. We returned as heroes. Bobkov escaped with us. Later Bobkov went to see Sikorski to find out why he had insisted. After all, he said, there were beautiful girls there, much better looking than I. Sikorski felt that I had seduced him with my eyes. This ended the story.[103]

Mina was fortunate that Bobkov had stood up for them. But as Bobkov never tired of telling his men, as a commander he was replaceable, but a doctor was much harder to get.

The partisan Eva Kracowski faced similar dangers. In 1944, after the arrival of a few Soviet parachutists in the Białystok forests, the Jewish male partisans in her otriad decided that the way to shield her from the sexual advances of the Soviets was to announce that she was engaged to Szyjka, one of the two Jewish men with whom she had escaped from the ghetto. This story was partly true; Szyjka did indeed hope to marry Eva after the war. For her part, Eva liked him as a friend but had never promised to become his wife. After the war they remained friends but never married.

Eva emphasizes that when she was a partisan she had no sexual drive whatsoever. She feels that this might have been due to the horrendous conditions in the forest. For a year Eva stopped menstruating and felt as if something had died inside her. Everything except the will to survive had lost its value.[104]

Another partisan, in the Belorussian forests, felt less harassed. As a little girl, Rachel Kasińska, now Bilerman, had come from Denmark to Minsk because Rachel's father, a Lubavitcher Hasid, felt that there were not enough Jews in Copenhagen. To remain Jewish, he believed, the family had to live in Belorussia. When the Germans began occupying Minsk, Rachel was married and the mother of two boys. By August 1941, she had lost her husband. Rachel and one of her sisters, also a war widow, pooled their resources. Each had two children, and each found employment outside the ghetto that gave them a chance to earn money by smuggling goods. One day the sisters returned home to find their four children gone. The Germans had taken them away during an Aktion.

Distraught, the two mothers now decided that there was nothing to keep them in the ghetto. The sisters planned an escape and invited their coworkers on the outside to join them. After bribing a guard, Rachel and her sister slipped away with a group of eleven women. They roamed the countryside for several hours, then finally approached a Belorussian woman to ask whether it was safe to enter the forest. The woman warned them against it, adding that partisans were present. This was the answer they had hoped for, and they hurried into the woods.

There they met Jewish men who directed them to a partisan center that might help place them in an otriad. At this center Rachel met a Jewish partisan fighter and scout from Nalibock. Eventually the two became lovers. This man, Szymonowicz, took her to the Shashkin brigade, which numbered about a thousand male partisans and only two women, one Jewish and one Russian. Rachel became the third woman, but her sister was refused entry; Szymonowicz took her to the Bielski otriad. The women were delegated to do domestic duties.

Like many others, Rachel had great respect for fighting. As she talks, she reverts continually to her own desire to wage war while making excuses for why she was excluded from military missions. First she blames her poor health. Then she explains that her job preparing food was as important as fighting the Germans. Finally, she explains that her pregnancy kept her away from military missions. All these occasions she saw as missed opportunities to fight.

Rachel is open about the fact that she wanted to end her pregnancy, saying,

> I wanted to have an abortion, but my husband, Szymonowicz, would not let me. Even when I was five months pregnant, I still was eager to stop it. When I heard that in a nearby place someone performed abortions, I climbed into a wagon, ready to go. But my husband ran after me. He screamed and screamed that he would not stop running after me. I had to give in. When we were liberated I had a daughter. There were many abortions. But if my husband would not let me, I could do nothing about it. I worked in the kitchen. I milked cows, made butter and cheese. I was friendly only with the Russian woman who was the mistress of the commander. I had no contact with the other woman. This friend became pregnant and wanted to end the pregnancy. She did all kinds of things. In the end she contracted an infection and died.[105]

The Soviet partisans did not always reject women. Survivors also report cases of special acceptance, protection, and friendship. Rina Raviv and her brother had been separated from their parents by the war. The brother and sister remained in their native town of Baranowicze and were soon forced into a ghetto. Rina, who looked up to her beloved older brother, was disappointed when he got married, to a refugee a few years his senior. The three escaped together into the surrounding forests, where they joined a family group. There Rina's sister-in-law began an affair with the commander of their group, a Jew from Pinsk. In June 1944, Rina's brother failed to come back from a mission. Rumor had it that their commander had had his rival murdered.

At about that time a small group of Soviet parachutists landed in the area to help step up the anti-German operations. For a while they stayed in the nearby village, where they hired a cook and a housekeeper. Rina describes how this affected her.

When my brother died, I was going through a terrible crisis. I gave up on life. I didn't know how to live. I also resented my Jewishness. When I heard that there was a new group of Soviet partisans I thought that maybe I ought to become part of their unit. I went to the village and asked to see General Vitusi. This is what they called the commander. He agreed to talk to me privately. I told him how unhappy I was. I told him about my situation, that my parents were away, my brother was killed, and I didn't want to be a Jew any more. I poured it all out. He said, "All right, if you want to stay with us, I'll keep an eye on you. You will be in the same tent with me. After the war I'll take you to Russia. I have a daughter your age."

I stayed with them for six months. He kept his promise. I would help with the cooking, I would clean the table, I kept busy. I knew German very well, and I would translate some of the news from German into Russian for them . . . All the time the men would leave for different missions; exactly what they did, I don't really know. [106]

"They didn't take you with them?" I ask.

No. There were young men around him who tried to start up with me. They also made all kinds of jokes; some of the jokes were anti-Semitic. They knew that I was Jewish. But he told them not to touch me, not so much as a finger. He also told them not to talk in my presence about Jews, not to make jokes. He was very protective of me. After six months, when they were about to leave, they wanted me to go with them to Bialystok. From there they were going to fly to Russia. He told me that in Russia I could study in Moscow, he would see to it.

When I ask whether he had made a pass at her, she denies it emphatically.

Oh, no, completely no. It's very interesting, but no . . . He had a woman
in the village. He had somebody. He would go to the village and then
come back . . . At the end I told him that I didn't want to go to Russia.
I wanted to go and look for my parents; maybe they had survived. He
said, "If you want to do that, I won't stand in your way." But he was
insulted. He was also worried about me, for he kept saying, "How will
you go? How will you find anything? Where will you go?" I told him
that I wanted to go to Minsk and there I would start looking. Before leaving, he tried again, saying, "I wanted so much to take you to Moscow,
and now you will disappear? You could have been my daughter's friend.
The two of you could have studied together, and you are such a beautiful girl." . . . I was so skinny. I was so miserable looking. I was full of lice.
I was very undernourished, with no breasts.

Vitusi left Rina in the care of a peasant, who was to bring her to a safe place.
From there, he felt, she could start her search more effectively.

Like some other Jewish women in the forest, Rina did not think about
sex at all. She muses, "Maybe I was too young. I think that we were really
preoccupied with survival. People were constantly facing death and only
thought about ways of staying alive. Each day we thanked God for being
alive." Rina never found her parents. Much later, she had a family of her
own. In Rina's case, it was the Soviet rather than the Jewish partisans who
protected her. Her experiences point to the complexities of forest life.

For the male partisans, the desire to survive was usually tied up with the
wish to wage war. Women could also share these ideals, but rarely — and
only grudgingly — were they included in missions that called for combat.
This was true even of a group like the Bielski otriad, which offered more
freedom and privileges to women than most Soviet otriads. The Bielski policy excluded women from military missions. Everyone in the Bielski otriad
was well aware of this condition, and most accepted, even justified it. Asked
what happened to a young woman who reached the Bielski camp alone, one
male partisan summarizes her position:

No one raped her, no one forced her to do anything. She usually tried to
find an appropriate man who would fulfill her needs. Very few women

had guns without the men. The few who had them did so because of their men. Guns were given to men, because they went for military actions and for food expeditions.[107]

When some women complained about these restrictions, they were told that every army needed a large supporting group and that women belonged in that group. In the rare instances when a woman reached the Bielski otriad with a weapon it would be confiscated. Guns belonged to men, not women — this was the law of the forest. Raja Kaplinski, though an independent woman, justifies this custom and insists that Tuvia Bielski needed the guns for the men who went on food missions.[108]

Single, unattached women tended to be dressed in rags, with shoes that threatened to fall apart — or no shoes at all. A woman without shoes had to wait for her turn with the shoemaker, but if she had nothing to bribe him with, her turn might come late, very late.[109] Except for their free entry, the lives of women in the Bielski otriad followed the well-established forest patterns: they were excluded from leadership and combat roles. Moreover, a woman's social standing was determined by the position of the man to whom she was attached. If she remained single, her rank was low unless she had special skills — usually medical.

Most women seem to have made peace with their subordinate roles. Again and again, regardless of the situation they were in, most told me that they agreed that men had to be armed, not women. Nor did they challenge the fact that leadership roles belonged to men. When women did participate in military ventures these expeditions sometimes took unusual turns.

An unexpected incident occurred when Mina Vołkowiski, in a group of Bobkov's partisans, traveled to the huge forest of Bialowiecka Puszcza. Mina describes the event:

> On the way, we had an order to destroy a Ukrainian police station. By that time, the winter of 1943, I knew how to shoot. We surrounded the place at night. Our fighters went inside and brought out the Ukrainian commander. They moved him from hand to hand. It was pitch dark. Eventually, they placed him in front of me. A huge man is in front of me. All I can see is this large person with a leather coat on. I hold him from

behind by his belt. I feel how he trembles, but I am also afraid. I don't know whether I'm supposed to shoot him, but I think, "Will I be able to do it?" Out comes a fighter and asks me, "What are you doing here?" I explained that I am supposed to guard him. This partisan turns to the prisoner: "You stupid, how come you didn't turn around and free yourself from her? You allow such a little woman to keep an eye on you?"

Then he began to scold me: Why don't I keep the gun directly aimed at the prisoner? Others join in screaming at me, then they took the prisoner away. I had enough. Impulsively, furious, I rush inside. There I see a portrait of Hitler. Out of frustration I shot at it, until it was totally demolished. Later, they all laughed at me, how I killed Hitler. From then on, I learned how to keep an eye on prisoners.[110]

Hersh Smolar, the Communist journalist, shared the command of the Komsomolski brigade with two Russians toward the end of his partisan career. Here, as in all brigades, the control was divided between the commandant, who was in charge of military matters; the commissar, who attended to the actual running of the place; and the political head in charge of propaganda and communications—Smolar. The three commanders rotated the night duties. Smolar describes an incident that occurred when he was on duty. That night a guard came to report that he had found a woman crouched under a tree who insisted on seeing the commander.

Afraid of spies, the unit was careful not to accept newcomers, so Smolar asked to see her. When she appeared before him, one look told him that she was Jewish: her sad eyes were an instant giveaway. She told him that she had run away from her ghetto after seeing a German split her child's head in two. Now all she wanted was to inflict pain on the Germans. She was ready to do anything. She had to avenge the death of her baby. She finished by saying that she wanted to be included in all anti-German missions.

Smolar explained that only the commandant in charge of military matters had the power to assign her to this kind of job. In addition, the commander had to interrogate her before the unit could accept her at all. The next day, when Smolar mentioned the woman, the commandant was annoyed. Because of recent rumors that Jewish women were being sent to the forest to poison Soviet partisans, he did not want to bring any into the camp. As far as he was concerned, all women were unwelcome in his brigade. But Smolar interceded on the woman's behalf. He insisted that she was not dangerous and that she should be allowed at least to stay. Finally, as a favor to Smolar, the commandant agreed, saying, "Okay, send her for kitchen work."

The woman, who was about thirty years old and not particularly attractive, was dissatisfied with this assignment. From that moment on, she stopped speaking. She followed orders, worked well, did whatever she was told. The partisans were pleased with her cooking and the other tasks she performed, but she never uttered a word. She would not even respond to Smolar's "Good morning." Compliments on her cooking met with total silence. Her face remained expressionless, as if chiseled in stone. When she would encounter Smolar, her face would occasionally show a glimmer of anger. Then she would turn her head away and look down. The partisans nicknamed her "The Mute One." This lasted for several months, and the Mute One became a fixture in the brigade.

One day five SS men were brought to the headquarters. The partisans knew that they could not keep prisoners; they did not have the means to. Standing orders were to shoot all German prisoners except officers, who were interrogated and then transferred to the partisan head of the region, General Platon. From there a few, particularly the high-ranking officers, were transported by plane to Moscow. Among the SS men caught that day were four officers of low rank and one high-ranking one. All were to be interrogated, but the man of high rank was to be watched especially closely. Since Smolar knew German well, he was in charge of the interrogation. A table was placed outside, which Smolar sat behind, surrounded by partisan officers on both sides. In front of the table stood the five SS men, the one with the highest rank in the middle. Their hands were bound behind them.

Then from afar, Smolar spotted the Mute One coming toward them. He recalls,

I thought to myself, "What does she want? Maybe some food she prepared was ready, or some such thing?" But I had to concentrate on the job . . . Then, in a split second, I saw the woman jump with a knife in hand. She pushed the knife into the back of the highest-ranking officer. He fell instantly and never moved. First came shock, then the horrible realization that our most important catch was gone. The rest of them were just extra baggage. Still, all of them had to reach General Platon.[111]

Arresting the woman did not solve their problem. Nor did it settle her fate. Smolar intervened on her behalf, arguing with the commandant that the woman's death would not accomplish a thing. Impulsively, seething with anger, the Russian issued an order, "From now on, the Mute One is to be included in the worst, most dangerous military operations . . . Let her discover what it really means to fight!" The decision had a miraculous effect on the Mute One. Immediately she began to act and look like a soldier. Her transformation was followed by top performances in one military mission after another. Her reputation as an exceptionally brave fighter grew. She survived the war and accumulated a number of military distinctions.

Occasionally, a fighter from a Soviet detachment could arrange for a daughter or sister to join his otriad. Sometimes these women were given the freedom to choose their own jobs. When I asked people about the possibilities of women becoming partisan fighters, the name Żenia kept popping up. Those who mentioned her minimized the gender distinctions, pointing to her as proof that women were also brave partisans. What they seemed not to recognize was that in and of itself this insistence underscored Żenia's uniqueness.

Curious, I managed to locate the legendary Żenia and met with her for a lengthy interview. Up to and during the war, Żenia Minkow and her family had lived in a small Polish town, Chocieńczyn, three kilometers from the Soviet border. There were eleven Jewish families in the town. When the Germans occupied the area, Żenia's family was a traditional Jewish family, with four children: Żenia, fifteen, an older sister, and two younger siblings both under ten years old. The Jews of Chocieńczyn lived in a ghetto that gave them a certain freedom of movement. The surrounding forests seemed to offer special options for resistance. This was particularly true for the community's young people. Żenia describes the evening they met in a large group to plan their escape into the forest; shortly after the start of the discussion,

> We all cried; we did not want to be parted from our parents, from the very old, and from the very young. So we stayed on. Actually, our parents also spoke about escaping into the forest . . . Our Belorussian neighbors continued to come to us to use our smithy, despite the so-called ghetto. We too were able to go to the villages to buy provisions. We had friendly relations with these Christians, and many of them urged us to escape.[112]

In the Minkow family, the father left first. He became a valued fighter in a Soviet otriad, but because he had two small children, he could not bring the entire family to join him. Eventually, the two youngest children and his wife moved into a special camp that was established for the fighters' families. The family camp supplied the fighters with various services. Commander Sanoff, a warm and caring Christian, headed this group. At the same time, Żenia's father was able to place his two older daughters in his own otriad.

Musing about gender differences, Żenia notes that their fighting unit had at most only five women.

> The commander had a mistress, and two of the partisans brought their wives with them, but none of these women went on military missions. These women cooked and busied themselves with all kinds of domestic chores. I never knew women who had high positions in a fighting unit. I never knew of a female commander or high officer. In the usual otriads, not in family camps, a woman had to have a man to protect her.

Comparing the lives of men and women, Żenia thinks that in the forest men had an easier time. But when she makes this statement, she seems to be limiting her observations to young women and young men. She elaborates further, noting that

> Jews who were not a part of the partisan unit and who lived as an independent family group had it very hard, all of them. The women among such unattached Jews had to attend to the children; they went to the villages and begged for food. Men were afraid to go. Women had it always

harder than men. Today, too, when the woman works, she has two
jobs . . . Maybe now in the younger generation men help a little. But in
those days, a woman had nothing to say. The man had to make all the
decisions. He told her how to build, how to do things. We did not know,
none of us did that.

I asked her whether she and her sister could have joined the otriad on
their own. Her answer comes promptly.

Of course not. Without my father, no. Because he was a respected
fighter, they took us in. A Russian commander, the political head of the
detachment, fell in love with my sister, and she became his mistress . . .
My sister was a beauty, and it could not have just been any partisan who
would fall in love with her; only a high officer would have had a chance.
After the war, they married.

Unlike her sister, Żenia had no boyfriend. She found none of the Jewish men attractive and refused to have anything to do with non-Jewish men.
Żenia preferred to fight, and she became a part of a demolition group. She
explains.

My group consisted of six people, one German, one French, three Russians, and I. We would demolish trains and bridges; we dealt with explosives . . . It was hard work. We would go kilometer after kilometer on
missions. I worked with five healthy Christian men, but they treated me
very well. They never, never abused me in any way. It is possible that my
own behavior contributed to this. I established my position with them
from the very start. I made it clear that I would not tolerate any hands,
any touching. "You can talk but no touching." I was angry with my sister
that she was involved with a non-Jew . . .

When we were on the road, we would enter a village, and they would
feed us. The others ate garlic and onion, but I didn't like them so I lost
my teeth early. I was small in size; I could hardly reach to the cooking
pot—it was too high for me. So I hardly ever got what was at the bottom
of the pot. Later, they took pity on me and gave me special food, but my
teeth were already ruined, they crumbled . . . When we were at the base,
we had to fix our things, wash, do things connected with our own needs.

This took a long time. We would rest for a week or so, and then go on a new mission. Just the walking took a week or two. Then we would rest in the villages.

Once I fell into a river. This happened in March. They dried my clothes in the next village. We wore white coats for camouflage, in winter. There was a time when I had a wound on my body. But usually we had no infections; we were not sick. We stayed on the Russian side of Belorussia. The Christians were very friendly; they were good to us. There were no Jewish groups there.

I ask whether she was afraid.

No, not at all. I would roam alone in the forests. To remain single, every woman had to have a strong character. As a rule, a woman needed the protection of a man. But in this respect I was strong. I was little, cheerful, people liked me. I could sing beautifully. I would always joke around. I had good spirits. The partisans liked me and respected me. They had an endearing name for me, "The Tiny One."

On the way back from an assignment they would tell stories about their sexual escapades in the villages. I pretended to be asleep; I was embarrassed. Some of them would say, "Shhh, the little one is asleep." It was terrible the way they talked about women. I heard stories that made me think that I would never want to marry. I thought that all men were liars who never kept a promise. It was horrible how they behaved and how they talked about these women . . . This made me distrustful of men. And so I told myself that I would only marry a man I loved. Otherwise, I would not marry. I met a very refined fellow, not obnoxious like they were. If he had not approached me the proper way, I would never have married.

Although unusual, Żenia's story underscores what many others have said about women's life in the forest. Żenia was an exception, and she knew it. But her story and her keen observations tell us something about the history of other women. Żenia's unusual circumstances and personality led to unusual opportunities. By comparing Żenia's story with those of other women, we can recognize the experiences that were common to all women.

Little is known about the Jews of wartime Stanisławów, their lives, resistance, and deaths. In this brief and blurred history a chemical engineer named Anda Luft played an unusual role. If we examine this young woman's actions and those of the people around her we shall find some recurrent motifs.

The liquidation of the Stanisławów ghetto began on February 23, 1943. A few Jews with special qualifications were spared; the Germans intended to exploit them for a variety of purposes. Clearing up the deserted ghetto and sorting out the victims' possessions was probably their top priority, although a few factories also continued to operate with Jewish laborers. Seven physicians were kept alive for an unspecified purpose. The Jews all knew that time was running out. They dealt with their circumstances in various ways. Six of the seven physicians collectively committed suicide. Other Jews went into previously prepared hiding places. Still others escaped into the surrounding forests. Among these escapees were Jewish laborers who had been employed outside the ghetto.

The very air breathed by the Jews seemed to warn that the Germans were preparing a final cleanup operation. Among those who escaped were Jewish employees of the Morgoshes leather factory. This group was led by Anda Luft; Dr. Kremizer, a dentist; and a young physician, Dr. Zimmer. During the escape the three commanders, guns in hand, had fired on the pursuing Germans. Defending their people as they ran, these leaders kept the road safe for seventy Jewish laborers. The entire group reached the forests close to the Bystrzyca River in the Carpathian Mountains, where they formed a partisan unit. They had brought along a small reserve of light arms and ammunition. Soon they met with a group of wounded Soviet officers and soldiers hidden in the mountains. Deciding that it would be better to pool their resources, the Jews took in the Soviet partisans. Through the Jewish physicians, the Russians regained their health. They next came upon a Soviet otriad, Kolpak, in a nearby forest. They learned that one of these Russian partisans was a Józef Lenobel, a Jewish ghetto escapee who had entered the Kolpak otriad by pretending to be a Ukrainian named Franko Bilinski.

All along the Germans and their collaborators were vigorously pursuing the partisans. The Kolpak otriad incurred heavy losses as the Germans succeeded in killing most of the members. Lenobel eluded the enemy and joined the Jewish otriad. This detachment was well organized, and it was still run jointly by Anda Luft, Dr. Kremizer, and Dr. Zimmer.

Anda was tall and full of energy. A talented chemical engineer, she had been valued by the German directors of the leather factory, who promised her protection from the SS. But she had distrusted their assurances and preferred to escape with her co-workers. Those who knew Anda praised her intelligence and physical stamina. Although in an advanced stage of pregnancy at the time, she continued to be energetic; her fellow partisans called her "a blessing in the sea of enemies."

The Jewish otriad reacted to the many pressures by splitting into smaller units, each of which had one weapon. These splinter groups turned into virtual watchdogs. Whenever a single German or a small number of them was spotted by any of these Jews, they would attack, killing the Germans and confiscating their weapons. In this manner, the Jews amassed more guns and ammunition. When they saw a larger group of enemy soldiers, the units would disperse as quickly as possible. Later on, they would reassemble at a previously agreed-upon site.

Food collection was undertaken by several men who were able to pass as Christians. Speaking flawless Ukrainian, these armed men had no trouble gathering provisions from the surrounding villages. At the temporary bases, a few women who belonged to the group were in charge of the cooking and other domestic duties. In my sources concerning the unit, these women are not mentioned by name, and I assume that Anda was not one of them.

In the summer of 1943, a large group consisting of members of the Order Police (*Ordnung Politzei*) headed by the Gestapo, entered the forest to clear the area of Jewish partisans. The Jews, prepared, spread out as they had agreed earlier. The commandant of the Order Police, Captain Tausch, alone ventured deeper into the forest. He was caught by the Jewish partisans, who jumped down on him from the tree branches, an original way to launch an enemy assault.

Tausch was bound and marched to the partisan base, where he was brought before the commanders. After a brief trial, he was sentenced to death by hanging. The proud German fell to his knees, crying and pleading for mercy for himself, for his wife, and for his small children, who were awaiting his return. He was reminded of the way he had brutally chased his Jewish victims toward the cemetery, where they would be executed. The partisan judges informed him that considering the nature of his crimes their verdict was unusually mild. Captain Tausch was hanged on a huge branch of a pine tree.

Anticipating renewed attacks, the entire otriad moved quickly to another area. For a few months they managed to elude the enemy. Whenever possible, they would fight, inflicting loss of life and property. On July 11, 1943, Anda gave birth to a baby girl. Two physicians in the unit, Dr. Gerta Lieblein and Dr. Zimmer, assisted in the delivery. Immediately after the birth of the infant a partisan came running with the news he had heard on their radio: on this day the Americans had captured the Italian island of Pantelleria, a position the Germans had fiercely defended. To commemorate both victories of that day, the partisans gave the name Pantelleria to the newborn baby and to their detachment.

But the celebration was short-lived. Their lives were becoming more and more threatened. The initial cooperation that had existed between the Jewish partisans and the Kolpak otriad ceased. A small remnant of the Soviet group moved away. The Jewish otriad had to rely on its own resources as it confronted Germans, hostile villagers, and Ukrainian partisans of the Bandera group. The Bandera partisans (named after their nationalist hero) were well armed, familiar with the area, and blessed with the full support of the local population.

In November 1943, the German police and army also began a series of forest raids. During one of these unexpected assaults several Jews fell, with axes in hand; among them were the Menis brothers, Regina Streit, and a Mrs. Demberg. The rest broke away. This attack was followed by another, initiated by the Bandera partisans in collaboration with local villagers. In the fierce, uneven battle that followed, only a few of the partisans survived. Most died fighting to the end.

Among these fighters was the commander Anda Luft. With Pantelleria, her infant daughter, strapped to her back, Anda continued to fire at the enemy up to the last moment. In the end, riddled with bullets, mother and child fell. Pantelleria the baby and Pantelleria the Jewish otriad each had a short life.[113] This group's history underscores the consistent findings of this book: no matter how resilient and courageous the Jewish women and men were, most were overcome by the ruthless German power.

8

Conclusion

Throughout this book, I have shown the role played by my research method in leading me down paths both familiar and unexpected. As in my earlier works, my current research has concentrated on the voices of the oppressed, voices that come from a variety of sources: wartime diaries, postwar memoirs, a range of other archival materials, and, most important, *direct interviews with Holocaust survivors*. Singly and collectively, these sources offer vivid firsthand accounts of the victims' personal experiences, as well as equally vivid observations about the fate of families, friends, and communities. These rich Holocaust materials have both weaknesses and strengths. Puzzles remain.

I framed my interviews around a set of core questions, which guide but do not control the course of the interview. Sometimes, when listening to survivors' accounts, my respondent would wander down an unusual path, which, in turn, would open up unconsidered new avenues for exploration. During one of those strange detours, something I heard struck a wrong note. It happened in Tel Aviv, in 1995, as I was listening to a Hungarian woman who had been deported to Auschwitz in 1944.

When she mentioned casually that she had been sent to Auschwitz with her parents, I asked, "Could you tell me, how did your father behave during the train ride?"

"Oh, he was very upset."

"In what way was he upset? What did he do?" I wanted to know.

"He was very nervous."

"Yes, but could you describe to me how he acted, what told you that he was nervous?"

"He couldn't help us, and was very, very tense."

At this point, I switched to questions about her mother and how she had behaved. These queries received similarly vague answers. This went on and on. Probing seemed to be of no use. Faced with an impasse, I decided to change direction, leave these questions, and return to them later. This is when I heard her say, "I was not with my father and mother when they were deported. I did not come to Auschwitz with them."

Trying not to act surprised, I asked her whom she had traveled with. This time she said that she had been deported with her older sister and the sister's two small children. They lived in a different community, and the sister's husband, a Hungarian Jew, had been drafted into the "auxiliary service," a part of the Hungarian army. (Of the 130,000 Jewish men who were drafted into this service an estimated 30,000 to 40,000 had perished.)[1] This survivor explained that her parents had sent her to help her sister take care of the children. During the deportation of the community, she was transferred to Auschwitz with them.

I suppressed my natural inclination to comment on her initial distortion and inquired instead, "Can you describe in detail what happened as the train was taking you to Auschwitz and right after it arrived there?"

The woman responded by offering a moving account about what happened before and after their arrival. She described the unexpected, painful separation forced on her by the crowd from her sister and the two little ones. She went on to speak with precision about her life in Birkenau and subsequent transfers to other camps. I was rarely forced to probe. A keen observer, this survivor was eager to share her story and most willingly answered my questions. When we seemed to be approaching the end of the interview I ventured to ask why at the beginning she had spoken about reaching Auschwitz with her parents, rather than with her sister and the children. She explained that she had been interviewed in the past and the interviewers were not interested in details: "These things did not matter to them. So I wanted to simplify the exchange just to keep it to what an interviewer would want." This woman's evidence is a valuable example of the advantages of listening and probing, as well as of the danger of interviewing survivors several times; they may suffer from respondents' fatigue.

In the summer of 1995 I continued my research, locating survivors in several European cities. In Basel, my Swiss friends Martina and Vincent Frank introduced me to several Holocaust survivors. I was particularly excited about meeting Richard Glazar, a Czech economist, who now lived in Switzerland. He had participated in the August 2, 1943, Jewish uprising in the death camp Treblinka and was one of the handful of survivors who managed to escape during the uprising. Martina and Vincent invited the Glazars over with the understanding that before dinner, in a separate part of the house, I would interview the former camp inmate. The man impressed me as intellectual and distant. He began by saying that he had been interviewed by a writer for a book about Franz Stangl, the commandant of Treblinka, and had found it a thoroughly disappointing experience because the author distorted his information. In fact, Glazar was still angry when he told me about it. He made it clear that he was not looking forward to our interview. I listened silently while Glazar pointed out that my questioning him was superfluous because his memoir, *Trap with a Green Fence,* was about to be published in the United States. (It appeared later that year.) Glazar ended by saying that since he agreed to meet me he would grant me a short interview. He hoped that I would not distort his story. This was not a very promising start, but experience has taught me how hard it is to predict the outcome of these meetings.

The interview was conducted in German. I began by asking Glazar about the start of the war. He outlined his past and then turned to the concentration camp experiences that must have had the greatest impact upon his life. This is when I began to probe. But each time I asked a question, he would counter by telling me that I would find the answer in his book. Not convinced, I would repeat the question in a slightly different form. Glazar would insist once again that the book said it all. After about three or four similar exchanges, I prefaced my questions by explaining that even though he might have dealt with the issue in his book I would appreciate hearing about it again. I assured him that I liked to listen to accounts of the same events several times. He did not argue and tried reluctantly to accommodate me. His answers were curt.

Gradually, however, his caveat that this or that issue was mentioned in his book became less frequent. Somewhere in the middle of the interview, Glazar volunteered that he regretted that he had not thought about the issues we were tackling before delivering the book to his American publisher. In the end this interview was filled with thoughtful, insightful comments about life under extreme conditions and the importance of cooperation under such circumstances.

At the time unfamiliar with his book, I felt somewhat uneasy, that I might have made him repeat things he was reluctant to repeat. However, as he relaxed and even complimented me on some specific questions I became conscious of how valuable his remarks (cited in chapter 5) were. His comments contain important historical information, as well as reflections on the need for cooperation in extreme situations, especially those that at best promise only temporary survival. He emphasized again and again that one could not exist in Treblinka without some kind of bonding with others. Woven into his remarks were striking observations about slavery, autonomy, and opposition under conditions of ruthless domination.

My subsequent reading of Glazar's memoir reconfirmed how right I had been to probe patiently, yet stubbornly. Although Glazar's memoir is a historically valuable and important document, it does not deal with the broader insights and implications that grew out of our two-hour interview.

Findings from my direct interviews, archival materials, and published accounts underscore that the closer I came to the victims' own experiences the more varied and insightful did the evidence become. Nevertheless, I am also aware that these valuable data may be problematic. Thus at the outset of this study I dealt with the issue of time and memory. Now I would like to reiterate that even though the memories evoked in these survivors might be contaminated by the lapse of time, my questions about specific issues made the respondents and me partners in the search for dormant memories. And yet what comes out through these direct interviews is in some ways "new." These memories were often buried for decades. It took them time to surface. Throughout my research I was aware that long-buried memories might never resurface without special questioning. As I continued to listen to how the survivors recounted their resurfaced Holocaust experiences, I was gratified to note that although these "new" memories were recounted independently, collectively they revealed certain shared patterns in the respondents' experiences that offer important theoretical insights.

What are these theoretical insights? What are their implications?

The upheavals of World War II rendered most traditions irrelevant and substituted for these traditions seemingly irrational and unpredictable coercive demands. Under such conditions people inevitably become preoccupied with self-preservation. But the focus on self-preservation sometimes leads to efforts at cooperation. There is strength in cooperation and mutual help. Indeed, in extreme conditions, self-preservation depends on cooperation and reciprocal giving even more than under "normal" circumstances.

To the victims who struggle for survival, cooperation may initially appear at best as a distraction, at worst as an impediment to efforts to stay alive. And yet what might start as an attempt to create a glimmer of hope may turn into valid efforts at cooperation. These coping strategies define survival as much as they transcend it. Social scientists assume that the more destructive an environment is, the more survival depends on such mutual help and cooperation. But even though these efforts can be mutually beneficial, under threatening circumstances, people may avoid them. The final outcome, of course, is unpredictable; sometimes negative experiences can induce those who attempted cooperation to give up on life. This seeming inconsistency suggests that in extremely threatening environments only a minority are able to effectively engage in mutual help and cooperation. This, in turn, mirrors reality: in threatened circumstances only a few have a chance to survive.

344

It appears that the more integrated people are into a traditional culture, the harder it is for them to adapt to the coercive political systems that can follow unprecedented upheavals. In addition, the more an individual has benefited from his or her social position the harder that person finds it to adjust to humiliation and oppression. Thus there is often a strong correlation between filling a privileged class position and being socially integrated. However, it is also true that social integration is not dependent upon high rank. For example, older individuals may be rigid conformists even when they are economically deprived. Nevertheless, under severe social disruptions and ruthless domination, high social integration and a privileged class position tend to decrease an individual's ability to cope or survive.

As I have shown throughout this book Jewish strategies of survival and cooperation were primarily influenced by German anti-Jewish measures, applied at different times, with varying degrees of ruthlessness. Nevertheless, these coping devices were also affected by the special characteristics of the prospective victims — their sex, prewar social class, wartime social labels, and a range of other attributes.

And so from most survivor reports I could discern that during the Holocaust, adult women and men, to a greater extent than the very old and very young, traveled on different roads toward the single destination planned for them by the Germans. Men were seen as humiliated, broken by their inability to provide for their families. The horrendous circumstances they had to face left them depressed and apathetic. Mothers or female relatives were generally viewed with admiration for their selfless aid to their families and others. When husbands and fathers were unable to fulfill their roles, adult women and their teenaged children of both sexes rose to the challenge, aiding their families, friends, and communities.

Less tangible, but nevertheless impressive, was the emotional tone that permeated the survivors' reflections on the different experiences of men and women. Their stories were filled with expressions of compassion and sadness. Conspicuously absent from these comments were expressions of hatred or hostility. Even the rare, unflattering images of fathers who were suspected of stealing food from their families came with expressions of surprise and hurt, even excuses — the father had been forced to the action because he was bigger and needed more nourishment, for example. Indeed, most stories were filled with personal regrets and self-recrimination for not doing more for others. The interviewees regretted their inability to avert the horrendous conditions. In reality, however, the evidence suggests that there was a great deal of cooperation, self-sacrifice, and mutual care in their actions.

The Nazi occupation of eastern Europe began with ruthless assaults on Jewish men. Some of the intended victims escaped; others were murdered. The majority of the men who survived these initial assaults were subjected to humiliating mistreatment and prevented from discharging their familial roles as providers and protectors. At the outset and in the ghettos, by barring Jewish men from the fulfillment of their traditional family obligations, the Germans had attacked their core masculine identification. That is, the Germans made it impossible for Jewish men to fulfill the role of protector and placed almost impossible challenges in the fulfillment of that of breadwinner. When Jewish men found themselves unable to do what traditional society expected of them, they frequently became demoralized and depressed. Inevitably, these experiences created a void in the lives of Jewish families and communities.

Women, who traditionally had assumed nurturing, supportive roles, tried to fill the gap by performing some of these traditional male roles. The womens' descriptions of their expanding duties were frequently interwoven with careful justification; most women who stepped into the role of family provider saw in these efforts a natural duty imposed by outside forces. Few blamed the men.

In the past, the traditionally subordinate position of women demanded that they accommodate themselves to the expectations of their more powerful male partners. Habits arose of overall adaptability, which contributed to smoother family relations and a reduction of conflicts.

Before the war Jewish women had typically seen their men as self-assured, capable, in charge. The changes they observed dealt yet another blow to these women's familiar world. Faced with their men's inability to earn a living, many women rose to the occasion. Barred from the role of protector by circumstances, women concentrated on the roles of provider, caregiver, and nurturer. They broadened their duties, showing resourcefulness under circumstances that seemed to offer no options. In a sense, their traditional roles were enhanced, encompassing duties that had not previously been seen to belong to them. Despite the horrendous circumstances and deprivations, some women felt gratified by their ability to make an extra effort on behalf of their families and communities.

In addition, at the initial stage of the occupation and after they had been transported to the ghettos, some women responded to the German oppression by aiding those who were not related to them, thereby expanding their help to the needy and the community. Later, they continued their efforts to help others, both on the Aryan side and in resistance groups. Only in the forest, where the highly patriarchal partisan groups placed a high value on physical strength and military skills, were women hampered in their efforts to assume new roles. The culture of the forest defined women as burdensome or mere sex objects. Here their presence was at best tolerated, in contrast to the attitude shown toward able-bodied men. Of the small minority of Jewish women who entered the forest, most assumed domestic duties or became mistresses of partisan officers — often both. Occasionally, however, when partisans were in dire need of fighters, women were given a chance to participate in military ventures, at which some of them excelled.

Conditions in the forest were harsh for everyone. Nevertheless, the social and psychological baggage that these fugitives brought with them made a difference in their coping skills and efforts to adjust. Even though the forest and the partisan environments were hostile to women, here too their traditional flexibility and readiness to cooperate helped them.

Class distinctions enhanced gender differences. Through their work men generally had been more socially integrated before the war and enjoyed a correspondingly more extensive degree of power than women. Findings consistently show that prewar class distinctions among Jewish males led to differences in their ability to cope with German assaults. Men who had been socially privileged before the war had farther to fall. These upper-class men seem to have had a harder time coping with the constant daily humiliations than lower-class men.

Findings from the forest environment, in particular, add further confirmation to the relation between social integration, the exercise of power, and the ability to cope with unprecedented social calamities. Working-class men, who had probably had to deal with unemployment and poorly paid work in their prewar lives, were better prepared to face wartime deprivations. They tended to be less demoralized by the Nazi catastrophe than men of the upper classes, for whom the wartime experiences were more likely to undermine their dignity. In addition, working-class men were more familiar with jobs that demanded physical exertion. They could more readily take on physically hard labor, which the Germans forced upon all Jewish men.

Women were less affected by their prewar class affiliations than men. Emanuel Ringelblum observed that from the start of the occupation, Jewish women behaved in ways that ignored many of their prewar class distinctions. Women even dressed in similar ways for their work helping to feed their families. One exception I noted had to do with life in the forest, which was often easier for unattached upper-class women. Many Jewish forest fighters, most of whom came from working class backgrounds, were eager to have young women who came from more privileged social backgrounds as their mistresses or wives.[2]

Perhaps the limited effect that a woman's prewar class had on her wartime coping skills resulted from the fact that her class affiliation was only tenuously connected to her core identity as a woman, whereas a man's class was intricately bound up in his masculine identification. Undoubtedly, women suffered when they were deprived of class privileges. But they were not as devastated as men because they were not likely to experience these losses as attacks upon their femininity. A woman's class affiliation has always tended to come from the men to whom she is attached — fathers and husbands. Especially in prewar times, class affiliation for the majority of women was disconnected from feminine identification, although single and modern young women, particularly in urban settings, were exceptions to this traditional pattern.[3]

However, for the majority of adult women, the core of their identification probably lay in their real or anticipated familial roles of wife and mother. It was in these roles that they were particularly vulnerable to German assaults. Almost from the start of the occupation the Germans saw Jewish children as superfluous. In addition, the Nazi decrees against Jewish motherhood functioned as an assault against women's feminine identity and their very lives. Inevitably, women were more affected by rules about motherhood than men.

In most wartime settings the Germans attacked Jewish women through their children, born and unborn. They knew that these children would become adults, and the Nazis saw Jewish adults as a threat to the Third Reich. Prompted by racial fear, the Germans thus targeted Jewish children. They prohibited Jewish pregnancies. Children within the ghettos were deported or starved. Similarly, women who arrived at the camps visibly pregnant or accompanied by small children were immediately gassed. Women nonetheless clung to their role as mother. Even after they had entered a camp, and it was no longer possible to protect their children, mothers refused to abandon them to save themselves. Mothers stayed with their children until the end, easing their journey to death.

The pain Jewish mothers experienced watching their children starve shows up again and again in diaries and memoirs by teenagers who declared themselves grateful that they were not parents. These teenagers were also saddened by their fathers' lack of options and loss of spirit. In general their expressions of compassion were mixed with admiring remarks about their mothers' resourcefulness and devotion to the family and to other needy people. The experience of these teenagers, female and male, in some ways resembled that of their mothers. Their youth left them relatively unconstrained by their past. Because they were not adults they had not yet been fully integrated into the established society. Not yet set in their ways, the young, in fact, seemed more aware of the situation during the war than adults did. They were more open to what was happening around them. Some young men and women formed partnerships for mutual survival. They also helped their mothers in the effort to keep their families alive.

Jewish youths who before the war had belonged to political movements had special advantages. As members of organized groups they were familiar with cooperation and seem to have acquired habits and skills that during the war facilitated their participation in such cooperative ventures as relief for the needy. In many East European ghettos underground movements originated in the remnants of these prewar youth organizations.

At the beginning of the war the Germans had classified some Jews as "useless." Over the years this label disappeared and reappeared under different circumstances. Its meaning was in flux, not very clear, contingent on the attitudes of those who wielded power. To Jews it seemed to be a temporary assessment, directed at those who were of no economic value—the old, children, the sick. It was a long time before Jews realized that, ultimately, the Germans considered them all useless—and all "useless" people were destined to die sooner than the rest. Indeed, most Jews defined as "useless" perished, just as those in power had intended. But not all. I spoke to a few who knew that they had been specifically categorized as "useless" and had survived. While they all wanted to live, they note that most others who felt as they did succumbed. These survivors credited their survival to luck. Nevertheless, in addition to luck or fate, they also mention others who helped them overcome the hardships. This suggests that in addition to the elusive entity we call luck, the survival of the "useless" depended on help from people who wanted them to live. There is little that can be said about what characterized the category of "useless"—the definition would change depending on how those in power perceived the threat. That only a few avoided death underscores both the importance of chance and the value of cooperation under conditions of coercive domination.

Of the various Holocaust settings the Nazi concentration camp came closest to a system of total domination. Yet even there some Jewish prisoners refused to cave in. Precisely because the reality of the concentration camp was so horrendous, many inmates created for themselves make-believe worlds — a blend of dreams, fantasies, friendships and resistance — as an antidote. Either through groups or individually inmates tried to re-create the families they had lost by creating bonds with partners whom they designated Lager mothers, sisters, brothers, and fathers. These new "family" groups functioned as substitutes for what was no more, often creating a link that joined the prisoners' lost past to the hope for a future. Some of these groups shared any extra food that came their way; others recited poetry, sang, read, and engaged in a range of other artistic undertakings. Still others focused on organizing resistance. Usually most of these informal groups engaged in a number of these various activities.

Prisoners seemed to experience their escapes into fantasies and dreams as especially gratifying. Often tied to mothers they loved, these fantasies helped the prisoners detach from the surrounding horrors. Reflecting the power of imagination, these illusions offered comfort and guidance in the labyrinth of terror. Thoughts about mothers usually focused on all that was good. Most of the mothers were gone, but the memories and dreams about them continued. Undoubtedly, the longing contributed to the idealized nature of these images. But in addition, it may be that the more idealized the image of the mother was, the more effective were the dreams and fantasies about her. Such escapes into fantasy may have improved the prisoners' hold on life.

The concentration camp environment erased most prewar social distinctions and offered little that was conducive to self-preservation, mutual help, and cooperation. Nevertheless, most inmates who belonged to bonding groups and made use of fantasies and dreams agree that the desire to escape from the camp environment, a longing for some autonomy, and the need for help and protection led to a proliferation of bonding groups. Moreover, no matter how brief, how illusory these groups were, membership in them forged links between the past and the future.

Our world has had a long history of social eruption followed by ruthless political domination. How potent a coercive society has been usually depends, in part, on the history of the oppressed before the upheaval, for this affects how they cope with oppression. It seems that the more fully integrated and privileged the oppressed had been, the more likely were they to succumb to the new coercive order.

It is important to reiterate a consistent finding: the more devastating the social upheaval, the greater the need for cooperative, mutually supportive, collective efforts. Commenting upon contemporary society, the philosopher Daniel Callahan notes, "In hard times, options are fewer, choices are nastier . . . Hard times necessitate a sense of community and the common good . . . Hard times demand restraint in the blaming of others for misfortune . . . But an ethic of autonomy stresses responsibility only for one's free, chosen, consenting relationships."[4]

In a recent reexamination of John Stuart Mill, the philosopher Susan Anderson discusses Mill's ideas about the value of cooperation. According to Mill, mutual association "is riveted more and more as mankind are further removed from the state of savage independence."[5] In addition, frequent upheavals followed by periods of suppression of various groups reflect the high value placed on the exercise of power, competition, and subjugation, all of which relate to patriarchal principles.

But no matter how ruthless the oppression is, the characteristics of the oppressed, their coping strategies, may not affect the outcome but do influence, at least in part, the quality of life. This consistent finding indirectly supports Georg Simmel's theory that even in a master-slave relationship the master has to consider what the slave does: no matter how asymmetrical the relationship, the powerful must take the powerless into account. On the other hand, the more symmetrical interactions are, the more cooperative they are. This also means that cooperative relationships are more likely to rely on principles of equality than are relationships based on competition.[6]

From this it may also follow that the powerful partners in relationships have to take into account both the structures and the dynamics that emanate from their subordinate partners. I define "structures" as the characteristics of the oppressed and "dynamics" as their coping skills. Who they are versus what they do.

More specifically, the more accustomed prospective victims are to performing nurturing and cooperative roles, the more able they are to adapt to changing circumstances. These conclusions touch on other formulations. In 1938, in response to Hitler's rise to power, Virginia Woolf reaffirmed her opposition to patriarchal principles. She emphasized that the high value patriarchy places on domination, competition, social differentiation, and jealousy creates a predisposition to war. Woolf felt that gender differences stem from differential power, a condition that might be remedied by social change. Examining women's skills in nurturing and cooperation and their tendency to provide one another with mutual support, she concluded that if societies were to reassess these traditional womanly roles as more valuable, they might be redirected into pacifist paths. Tzvetan Todorov echoes Woolf's sentiments when he asserts that "values I have called feminine have been seriously undervalued throughout Western history, it is vital that they now acquire the importance they deserve."[7]

I see some affinity between these views on patriarchy and war and the implications of my research. Both suggest that a social order that values cooperation over competition, equality over domination, mutual support over conflict, can reduce the violence and social eruption that in turn lead to systems of excessive domination, human devastation, war, and genocide.

Some empirical validation for this theory can be found in the history of the Bielski otriad, a group of Jewish partisans that took on the dual role of rescuers and fighters in the Belorussian forests. Bowing in part to the need to wage war in the forest, the Bielski partisans, under the rule of their charismatic leader, Tuvia Bielski, nonetheless focused their energies on cooperation, rescue of the oppressed, and survival. Unlike other otriads, the group admitted all Jewish refugees, regardless of age, sex, or circumstance. Gradually this group also took on the task of finding and rescuing fugitives who had few other options. And so the Bielski otriad became a unit defined by openness, cooperation, and emphasis on survival. These partisans participated in military expeditions because they had to, because this was the accepted way, rather than because they wanted to. Although they could not avoid combat, the Bielski partisans nevertheless stressed mutual help and protection. In the end their policy proved successful.

Estimates of the death rate for Jewish partisans who joined Soviet fighting detachments go as high as 80 percent, while those of the death rate for other Soviet partisan units hover around 33 to 52 percent. As a rule, Jewish family camps had much higher death rates. Many family camps were left unprotected by partisans and their entire membership perished.[8]

In contrast to these figures, the estimated losses for the Bielski otriad do not exceed 5 percent. When in the summer of 1944 the Red Army reconquered these forests, the Bielski unit had grown to more than 1,200 individuals. Most of them were older people, women, and children—precisely the people who were not welcome in most forest shelters. The history of this Jewish group attests to the importance of cooperation and mutual assistance.[9]

As unexpected as it was gratifying, the story of the Bielski otriad played a double role in my current research. Initially, it alerted me to gender differences in the forest. And now, at the conclusion of my research on gender and the Holocaust, it offers further confirmation of the view that in times of upheaval, in the ruin of traditional society, cooperation and mutual protection rather than combativeness and competition promote greater odds of survival.

The German occupation created violent, destructive, and unpredictable worlds, worlds in which most conventional, traditional, and cultural values lost their effectiveness. For the Jews in particular, life was reduced to the most fundamental aspects of human existence, its bare essentials. When traditions and conventions are stripped away, we are confronted with an uncluttered view of the human condition. The study of the Holocaust provides a unique opportunity to gain a better understanding of life in extremis. By delving into the world of radical domination and devastation, this book offers valuable lessons about how women and men coped during a time of extreme social upheaval. These lessons not only underscore important differences between women and men; they also emphasize the universal need among people in extreme situations for cooperation and mutual care.

Notes

Chapter 1: Voices from the Past

1 After the war Gruber wrote a memoir, *I Choose Life,* about his wartime experiences.

2 Hilberg, *Perpetrators Victims Bystanders,* 126. For a discussion of variations in the temporary treatment of men and women see 126–130.

3 See my *Defiance,* chap. 12, pp. 154–169.

4 Studies of family life during the 1930s Depression show a consistent association between male unemployment and family conflict. A few classic studies are Bakke, *Unemployed Worker;* Cavan and Ranck, *Family and the Depression*; and Komarovsky, *Unemployed Man and His Family.*

5 See Karen Anderson, "World War II," in *Women's Studies Encyclopedia,* ed. Helen Tierney (Westport, Conn.: Greenwood, 1989), 3:489–490, and Trey, "Women in the War Economy."

6 Jacqueline Cochran and Maryann Bucknum Brinley, *Jackie Cochran: An Autobiography* (New York: Bantam, 1987), pp. 165–176; a program about Cochran aired on Public Television on the evening news program of May 24, 1999.

7 See Noggle, *Dance with Death.*

8 For discussions of methodological problems in the study of the Holocaust, see two of my articles that despite similar titles deal with different methodological issues: "Diaries and Oral History: Reflections on Methodological Issues in

Holocaust Research," in Shapiro, *Holocaust Chronicles,* 267–276, and "Methodological Considerations: Diaries and Oral History."

9 For a few discussions of this issue see Bower and Gilligan, "Remembering Information Related to Oneself"; Conway, *Written By Herself;* Herman, *Trauma and Recovery;* Hoffman, "Reliability and Validity in Oral History"; and Lummis, "Structure and Validity in Oral Evidence."

10 Using testimonies of survivors Christopher R. Browning was also confronted by similar methodological problems; as he notes, "The testimonies, not surprisingly, frequently contradict one another concerning chronology, dates, persons and events," (*Nazi Policy, Jewish Workers, German Killers*), 91. Despite these difficulties, Browning, as I do, relies on such testimonies.

11 Hilberg, in *Perpetrators Victims Bystanders* (126–138), compares men and women in a variety of ways but refrains from quantitative comparisons of the number of deaths. In a private letter to me, written on July 2, 1995, Hilberg said, "To answer your question about the death rates of men and women: such figures as we have or can calculate from data at hand are only partial, although more and more of these statistics turn up every year." Independently Israel Gutman told me (March 2000) that exact figures about death rates of Jewish women & men are unavailable.

I am convinced that we can gain insights into the destruction of European Jewry and issues of gender even though exact death tolls of Jewish women and men are unavailable. In contrast, Joan Ringelheim emphasizes the centrality of quantitative comparisons of the murders of Jewish women and men. In "The Holocaust: Taking Women into Account," Joan Ringelheim writes: "My work on deportations and death figures connected with the mobile killing operations, ghettos and camps has led me to conclude that more Jewish women were killed than Jewish men. Jewish women's chances for survival were not equivalent to those of Jewish men" (22). Basically the same conclusions reappear in two of her more recent publications: "Women and the Holocaust: A Reconsideration of Research," in Rittner and Roth, *Different Voices,* 373–405, and "The Split Between Gender and the Holocaust," in Ofer and Weitzman, *Women in the Holocaust,* 340–350. Ringelheim's tables and discussions offer no overall figures of the populations on which the percentages of murdered women and men were based.

12 For a fascinating discussion of misuses of statistical measures see Jaffe and Spirer, *Misused Statistics.*

13 This definition relies on Max Weber's formulation of power: see Weber, *Essays in Sociology,* 180, and *Theory of Social and Economic Organization,* 152.

14 See Cantor, *Jewish Women, Jewish Men;* Johnson, *Gender Knot,* 5; Bruce Kokopeli and George Lakey, "More Power than We Want: Masculine Sexuality and Violence," in Anderson and Collins, *Race, Class and Gender;* and Charlene Sprentak, "Naming the Cultural Forces That Push Us Toward War," in Russell, *Exposing Nuclear Phallacies,* 53–62. A few examples of cross-cultural publications about the universality of patriarchy are Malinowski, *Sex and Repression in Savage Society,* and *Sexual Life of Savages;* Mead, *Male and Female;* Murdock, *Social Structure;* and Sanday, *Female Power and Male Dominance.* Two studies that focus on the centrality of patriarchy in Jewish traditions are Fromm, *Love, Sexuality, and Matriarchy,* 46–75, and Aschkenasy, *Eve's Journey,* especially the chapters entitled "Woman and Oppression" and "Female Strategy," 109–249.

15 For theoretical discussions on the effects that differential power has upon the interactions of different role partners, see Merton, *Social Theory and Social Structure,* 370–379, and Wolff, *Sociology of Georg Simmel,* 181–300.

16 Quoted in Bluel, *Sex and Society in Nazi Germany,* 56; see also Stephenson, *Women in Nazi Society,* 8–9, 13.

17 Bluel, *Sex and Society in Germany,* 62, 54. At the first general membership meeting of the Nazi party in January 1921, Hitler is already quoted as saying, "Woman can never be admitted into the leadership of the party or into the Executive Committee." In fact, in the Third Reich women were declared ineligible for jury service because Hitler felt that "they cannot think logically or reason objectively since they are ruled only by emotion" (Waite, *Psychopathic God,* 58–59). At his table talks, which took place at Berghof, in Berchtesgarden, Hitler is quoted as saying, "However intelligent she was a woman could not separate matters of feeling from matters of intellect in politics" (Picker and Hoffman, *Hitler Close Up,* 112).

18 Koonz, *Mothers in the Fatherland,* 160, 166–167, 183, 217, 255.

19 Marion A. Kaplan suggests that the Nazis set out to destroy the patriarchy within the Jewish German family in *Between Dignity and Despair,* 59.

20 See Des Pres, *The Survivor,* 53–72; and Fackenheim, "Spectrum of Resistance During the Holocaust."

21 Ringelblum, *Kronika Getta,* 585. See also Dobroszycki, *Chronicle of the Łódź Ghetto;* Kermisz, *To Live with Honor and Die with Honor;* and Ringelblum, *Notes from the Warsaw Ghetto.*

22 Hilberg, *Destruction of the European Jews,* 684–704.

23 Katz and Ringelheim, *Proceedings of the Conference on Women Surviving.*

24 Collections include Ofer and Weitzman, *Women in the Holocaust,* and Rittner and Roth, *Different Voices.* Books focusing on German women include Koonz,

Mothers in the Fatherland; Owings, *Frauen;* and Stoltzfus, *Resistance of the Heart.* A few examples of publications with *women* or *sisters* in the title are Distel, *Frauen im Holocaust;* Fuchs, *Women and the Holocaust;* Gurewitsch, *Mothers, Sisters, Resisters;* Kremer, *Women's Holocaust Writing;* Ofer and Weitzman, *Women in the Holocaust;* and Ritvo and Plotkin, *Sisters in Sorrow.*

25 The journalist Gabriel Schoenfeld, in an article entitled "Auschwitz and the Professors" (*Commentary,* June 1998), initiated a heated debate on academia and the study of gender and the Holocaust. His article led to a series of letters that appeared in the *Wall Street Journal.* I was the author of one of them. Schoenfeld continued on the same path with "How Much Holocaust Is Too Much?" I took part in a discussion at the closing session of the workshop "Women in the Holocaust" at the Hebrew University, Jerusalem, June 1995. Among those who seemed to be voicing certain concerns about the study of gender and the Holocaust were such notable scholars as Israel Gutman and Yehuda Bauer.

26 For a clear statement about the centrality of Jewishness see Gisela Bock, "Racism and Sexism in Nazi Germany: Motherhood, Compulsory Sterilization, and the State," and Marion Kaplan, "Jewish Women in Nazi Germany: Daily Life, Daily Struggles, 1933-1939," in Rittner and Roth, *Different Voices,* 162-186, and 188-212. A fascinating, but as yet unpublished, paper by Anna E. Rosmus underscores the special significance of an individual's Jewishness rather than gender, "The Pre-Nazi Town That Chose a Jewish Sex Symbol: Gender, Anti-Semitism, and Politics in Passau, 1919-1929."

27 The following are just a few examples of gender studies from the field of anthropology: Linton, "Age and Sex Categories"; Malinowski, *Sex and Repression in Savage Society,* and *Sexual Life of Savages;* Mead, *Male and Female;* Murdock, *Social Structure;* and Sanday, *Female Power and Male Dominance.*

28 A few such examples are: Shmuel Geler, Yad Vashem, 1556/112; Margot Dränger, Yad Vashem, 03/1686; Hana Stołowicki, Yad Vashem, 3439/193 (the spelling of the name Dränger varies; in future references I shall use the spelling of the particular source).

Chapter 2: In the Beginning

1 Vladka Meed, personal interview, New York, 1994. It was not unusual for Polish anti-Semites to identify Jews who joined breadlines. Jews who were singled out not only lost their chance to receive bread but were also physically abused in public. Among those who have mentioned this common practice is the eminent historian Emanuel Ringelblum; for his comments see *Polish-Jewish Relations During the Second World War,* 37-38.

2 Noakes and Pridham, *Nazism, 1919–1945*, Vol. 3: *Foreign Policy, War and Racial Extermination*, 1050–1053 (quote on 1052). Early assaults against Jewish men less frequently included women and children and the destruction of Jewish property; these are vividly described by Martin Gilbert in *The Holocaust*, 84–108. For a more complete description of the early murder of Jews, see Hilberg, *Destruction of the European Jews*, 177–256.

3 See *Warsaw Diary of Adam Czerniakow*, 85–91.

4 These issues are raised in my study *When Light Pierced the Darkness*, 40–41.

5 Ringelblum, *Polish-Jewish Relations*, 42.

6 Kaplan [Kapłan], *Scroll of Agony*, 53, 134. Similar descriptions appear in Ringelblum, *Polish-Jewish Relations*, 38–53.

7 See Améry, *At the Mind's Limits*, 21–40; Des Pres, *The Survivor*, 53–71; Fackenheim, "Spectrum of Resistance During the Holocaust." For one of many photographs of Jews being humiliated, see the jacket of Christopher Browning's *Ordinary Men*, which depicts self-satisfied uniformed German soldiers looking straight into the camera while a disheveled orthodox Jew half-kneels in front of them with raised hands, looking at the camera with a bewildered gaze. To the side and in the back of this picture Jews stand with hands raised above their heads. Inside the book following p. 40 are the full version of this photograph and another picture depicting an identical scene: self-satisfied Germans and humiliated Jews. Examples of similar images are also included in *Chronicle of the Łódź Ghetto*. For a picture of a bemused member of the notorious 101 Police Battalion watching while his comrade amuses himself by cutting off the beard of an orthodox Jew see Goldhagen, *Hitler's Willing Executioners*, 245.

8 See Filip Friedman, "Zagłada Żydow Polskich w Latach 1930–1945," 168; Israel Gutman described the work gangs to me in various personal communications.

9 See Hilberg, *Destruction of the European Jews*, 162–168; Kaplan, *Scroll of Agony*, 55.

10 For a discussion of the gradual expropriation of Jewish laborers and the loss of their earning capacity, see Hilberg, *Destruction of the European Jews*, 90–105, and Yahil, *Holocaust*, 159–171. For moving descriptions of the consequences of this policy see Ringelblum, *Notes from the Warsaw Ghetto*, 194–207.

11 For discussions about the conflict between those who wanted to use Jews for work and those who wanted to murder them see: Browning, *Nazi Policy*, 58–89, and Hilberg, *Destruction of the European Jews*, 332–345.

12 Vladka Meed, personal interview.

13 Eva Galer, personal interview, New Orleans, 1992. (Parenthetically, I noticed that

a seemingly disproportionate number of the women I interviewed were named Eva. Probably at the time it was a popular name among East European Jews.)

14 Eva Galer spoke to me about how the jobs of teenage boys and girls with Polish peasants alleviated family hunger. Ephraim Blaichman described how at the beginning of the German occupation, he began wheeling and dealing with local peasants; his "illegal" activities helped support his large family. (Ephraim Blaichman, personal interview, New York, 1995.) In another case of a teenager taking the initiative, Lisl Cade told me how her father, a prominent Jewish lawyer in Vienna, lost his spirits after the annexation of Austria in 1938. When the twelve-year-old Lisl insisted that she could not endure staying in the country, the father told her that she could go ahead and make the arrangements for emigration. She took the challenge and applied for a visa to England. Later that year she and her parents moved to England. (Lisl Cade, personal interview, New York, 1987.)

15 Tonia Rotkopf-Blair, personal interview, New York, 1994. Many children are haunted by memories of their humiliated fathers. Henia Shenberg vividly remembers the beatings her father received at the beginning of the war. She mentions it in her personal interview (Paris, 1995). Sandra Brand describes how she was forced to watch her Hasid father dance to the drums of a German soldier. This scene included her father's fall, beatings, and the presence of an enthusiastic crowd of onlookers, Germans, and Gentile neighbors. Without success Sandra tried to stop the spectacle by asking the German to beat her instead of the father. See Brand, *Between Two Worlds*, 94-95. There is also additional and consistent evidence showing how fathers' degradations and loss of spirit humiliated teenage boys. Such examples are scattered throughout this book. For a discussion of the spontaneity of the outrages, see Kaplan, *Scroll of Agony*, 44-53.

16 Tonia Rotkopf-Blair, personal interview. Similarly, when at the start of the German occupation Israel Shaham's father lost his important post in the Zionist Organization in Poland, he could do little for his family. Shaham's mother stepped in and arranged all the complicated formalities, which led to their emigration to Palestine in February 1940. (Israel Shaham, personal interview, Jerusalem, 1995.)

17 For a historical overview of initial Jewish destruction in the freshly conquered Eastern territories, see: Hilberg, *Destruction of the European Jews*, 191-219. Martin Gilbert, in *The Holocaust*, 154-212, concentrates on Eastern Europe in 1941; he includes descriptions of Jewish reactions to these initial assaults. For another, brief mention of this issue see my *When Light Pierced the Darkness*, 5-6.

18 Jürgen Förster, "Wehrmacht and the War of Extermination against the Soviet Union," in Rothkirchen, *Yad Vashem Studies*, 7-34 (quote on p. 15). Arno Mayer

is convinced that the Judeocide of the twentieth century was closely interwoven with the Nazi-led crusade against Bolshevism from 1941 to 1945. See his *Why Did the Heavens Not Darken?* 224; for an interesting discussion and a different position see Browning, *Path to Genocide,* 59-121.

19 See Herbert, *Nationalsozialistische Vernichtungspolitik,* 48-54; Karl Jäger, commander of Einsatzkommando 3, on the extermination of Lithuanian Jews, 1941, in Arad, Gutman, and Margaliot, *Documents on the Holocaust,* 398-400. Jürgen Matthäus contributed an insightful, extensive historical analysis about the regional patterns of murder, following the outbreak of the 1941 German-Soviet war in the eastern region. His paper will appear in Yad Vashem's multivolume *History of the Holocaust,* as a chapter in volume 2, edited by Christopher R. Browning, which is devoted to the origins of the Final Solution (forthcoming from University of Nebraska Press).

20 After the German retreat, in 1944, a war-crimes commission from Moscow came to investigate. When they dug up the bodies, Riva identified her husband by his pajamas, finally putting an end to her lingering hopes. (Riva Kantorowicz-Reich, personal interview, Tel Aviv, 1989.)

21 Eva Kracowski, personal interview, Tel Aviv, 1995. In his account of the horrors that came with the German conquest of the city of Białystok, the historian Szymon Datner mentions the prominent Dr. Kracowski, who perished along with eight hundred to a thousand prominent Jewish men in the great synagogue fire, which continued to burn for days; this June 27, 1941, event is known as the Black Friday massacre (Datner, *Walka i Zagłada Białystockiego Getta,* 12-13). Datner describes both the actual horrors and rumors about plans for Jewish destruction on pages 14-15 and 25-27.

22 Zvi Shefet (Shepetinski), personal interview, Tel Aviv, 1995.

23 Despite this assumption, occasional humiliating measures were directed against Jewish women. For example, a report dated February 1940 describes well-dressed Jewish women who were seized on the streets of Warsaw. They were forced to wash floors but received no rags to wash with, so they used their underwear. After they had finished, they had to put the underwear back on. Such incidents notwithstanding, abuses of women were much less common than those against men. See Ringelblum, *Kronika Getta Warszawskiego,* 89.

24 Sandra Brand, personal interview, New York, 1995.

25 This is my free translation from the Polish; see Ringelblum, *Kronika Getta Warszawskiego,* 67. This diary was part of the Oneg Shabath archive created by Ringelblum.

26 Hilberg, *Destruction of the European Jews,* 458-473.

27 Berta Benau-Hutzler, personal interview, Ramat Gan, 1995.

28 In Germany, too, the Jews thought that the men were in greater danger than the women, and therefore more men than women emigrated. See Kaplan, *Between Dignity and Despair*, 132–144.

29 Berta Benau-Hutzler, personal interview. Since 1997 I have had frequent conversations with a Slovakian Jew, Helen Spitzer-Tichauer, known as Zippi, about her experiences in Auschwitz. During one of these conversations I learned that she and Berta Benau had gone to the same high school in Bratislava and that they had been good friends since kindergarten. Indeed, some of the first-hand information I learned from Berta and Helen served as independent sources of data validation. This is true for the predeportation date as well as the time they spent in Auschwitz, 1942–1945.

Chapter 3: Life in the Ghetto

1 Probably the underground archive workers had access to the ghetto prison and obtained Mrs. F.'s story from her. However, there is a slight discrepancy concerning the sum of money involved. Emanuel Ringelblum, in *Notes from the Warsaw Ghetto*, 237, reports that one of the women, the mother of three children, was killed for lack of 100 zlotys. She had offered the policeman 50 and he had demanded 150. In the Polish version, *Kronika Getta Warszawskiego*, 338, Ringelblum states that the woman offered the policeman 50 zlotys but he wanted 100. See also Yad Vashem, JM/217/4, pp. 3–4, 12–14. Mrs. F. was a part of Cecylia Ślepak's study, a part of the Ringelblum underground archive, Oneg Shabat. On the imposition of the death penalty laws, see Dawidowicz, *Holocaust Reader*, 67, and Tec, *When Light Pierced the Darkness*, 27–39.

2 On the attitude of Jews toward the proposed ghettos, see Perechodnik, *Am I a Murderer?* 8, and Adler, *In the Warsaw Ghetto*, 5–9.

3 For the building of the Warsaw ghetto, see Hilberg, Staron, and Kermisz, *Warsaw Diary of Adam Czerniakow*. The diary is filled with many anxious entries about the establishment of the ghetto (in particular, 200–220). See also Nehemiah Titelman "Setting Up a Closed Ghetto," in Kermisz, *To Live with Honor*, 143–145, and Ringelblum, *Notes from the Warsaw Ghetto*, 82–90. I am also indebted to a 2001 personal communication with Israel Gutman.

4 See Hilberg, *Destruction of the European Jews*, 166–168, 174.

5 See Yehuda Bauer, "The Judenräte — Some Conclusions," and Raul Hilberg, "Conscious or Unconscious 'Tool,'" in *Patterns of Jewish Leadership*, 393–405, 31–44; Trunk, *Judenrat*, 40–45.

6 In his recent book *The Politics of Memory: The Journey of a Holocaust Historian*,

Raul Hilberg discusses the controversy which grew up between him and Hannah Arendt, much of which had to do with the role of the Judenräte during the Holocaust. See also his *Perpetrators Victims Bystanders,* 105–117. Irena Lusky describes her job as a clerk in the Vilna ghetto Judenrat in a personal interview (Tel Aviv, 1995); see also Irena Lusky, *Traverse de la Nuit,* 50–55. On the Wieliczka Judenrat, see Trunk, *Judenrat,* 20.

7   Chaim A. Kaplan was particularly critical of the Judenräte; see *Scroll of Agony,* 337–339. See also Philip Friedman, "Social Conflicts in the Ghetto," in Ada J. Friedman, *Roads to Extinction,* 145–150; Gutman, *Jews of Warsaw,* 78; Ringelblum, *Notes from the Warsaw Ghetto,* 140; and Smolar, *Minsk Ghetto,* 53.

8   Philip Friedman, "Social Conflicts in the Ghetto," 150.

9   Ibid., 144–145. See also Adelson, and Lapides, *Łódź Ghetto,* 175; Dobroszycki, *Chronicle of the Łódź Ghetto,* 93; and Kogon, *Theory and Practice of Hell,* 188–192.

10 See Emanuel Ringelblum, "The History of Social Aid in Warsaw During the War," in Kermisz, *To Live with Honor,* 338–344.

11 Ibid., 340; Sara Kadosh, "Joint Distribution Committee," in Laqueur, *Holocaust Encyclopedia,* 363–370.

12 "Jewish Welfare Society," and Emanuel Ringelblum, "The House Committee," in Kermisz, *To Live with Honor,* 345–352.

13 Bauer, *History of the Holocaust,* 169–191; Mark Dworzecki, "The Day-to-Day Stand of the Jews," Gutman and Rothkirchen, *Catastrophe of European Jewry,* 386–99; Gutman, *Resistance,* 71–98.

14 Yad Vashem, JM/217/4, 3–4.

15 Yad Vashem, JM/215/3. My translation from the Polish. Ślepak was deported from the Warsaw ghetto in the summer of 1942, so this statement had to have been made before that time.

16 Ringelblum, *Kronika Getta,* 394. My translation from the Polish.

17 Ibid., 462–463. Mrs. Mokrska's first name does not appear.

18 Roma Nutkiewicz-Benatar, personal interview, Kvar Shmariahu, Israel, 1995. In a moving article based on her wartime recollections, Irena Sendlerowa, a heroic rescuer of Jews, describes in detail how the ghetto youths participated in the welfare operations of the Warsaw ghetto house committees. See: "O Działalności Kół Młodzieży Przy Komitetach Domowych w Getcie Warszawskim," *Biuletyn Żydowskiego Instytutu Historycznego* 2/118 (1981): 91–118.

19 Gutman, *Jews of Warsaw,* 120–132.

20 Israel Gutman, "The Genesis of the Resistance in the Warsaw Ghetto," in Marrus, *Nazi Holocaust,* vol. 17: *Resistance to the Holocaust,* 180–184.

21 The excessive overcrowding of Nazi ghettos suggests that the majority of ghetto inhabitants were refugees. Even the poorest city inhabitants rarely had to live under such cramped conditions, sometimes with as many as fifteen people to a room. On life in the ghetto, see Ofer, "Cohesion and Rupture." Among the few who did not experience the horrendous conditions were the Catholic converts in the Warsaw ghetto and the German Jews from Hamburg in the Minsk ghetto. Each had special privileges, respectively discussed by Ringelblum, *Notes from the Warsaw Ghetto,* 138, 146–147, 214, and Smolar, *Minsk Ghetto,* 102–103. For a vivid diary written by a German Jew who was evacuated to the Riga ghetto see Kogon, *Theory and Practice of Hell,* 188–192. While all sources agree that food shortages were pervasive in ghettos, there are some variations about the amount of calories allotted to inmates and the degree of hunger suffered. According to Gutman, only about 3 percent of the Warsaw ghetto population belonged to the upper class and suffered no food shortages (*Jews of Warsaw,* 76). For additional descriptions of the plight of starving inmates in the Warsaw ghetto see Ringelblum, *Notes from the Warsaw Ghetto,* 189, 205–206, 251, 281; Roland, *Courage Under Siege,* 103–104, 98; and Sierakowiak, *Diary* (the book is permeated with comments about starvation).

22 Karla Szajewicz-Frist, personal interview, Tel Aviv, 1995.

23 Chava Grinberg-Brown, personal interview, Israel, 1992. Chava lives on a farm (a Moshav), Bnei Atarot, close to Tel Aviv.

24 Ibid.; some women concurred with these views; they remarked on how fortunate they were not to have had children so that they were not forced to watch them starve; see Janina Bauman, *Winter in the Morning,* 85. See also: Edelman, *Ala z Elementarza,* 80–81, who says that in the ghetto being a mother was the worst thing.

25 Alexandra Sołowejczyk-Guter, personal interview, Bat-Yam, Israel, 1995.

26 Itke Brown, now known as Lidia Abramson, personal interview, Tel Aviv, 1995. I shall refer to her either as Lidia Brown-Abramson or as Lidia Abramson. Several teenage girls told me how gratified they were by being able to help their families. Among them was Miriam Akavia (personal interview, Tel Aviv, 1995), who told me that for a while she took care of the household in the Kraków ghetto while her parents worked; Pesia Bernstein (personal interview, Israel, 1995), who took care of her younger siblings and the household from the time her mother died, in 1937.

27 Alexandra Sołowejczyk-Guter, personal interview. Zahava Ziskowicz-Adam (personal interview, Tel Aviv, 1995) told me how proud she was when her mother made her a blue coat. When she wore it for the first time in the Vilna ghetto she

thought that "it was the most beautiful thing in the world; I was so happy. Then I wanted a ring, and my parents indulged me and made a ring for me."

28 Vladka Meed, personal interview, New York, 1994.

29 Eva Galer, personal interview, New Orleans, 1992.

30 Ita Shapiro, personal interview, Hertzlia, Israel, 1995. Ita is married to a professor and usually goes by her married name of Einder. She wanted me to refer to her as Shapiro in remembrance of her family. Another one of these exceptions was Zahava Ziskowicz-Adam (personal interview), who lived in the Vilna ghetto. Zahava describes her father as extremely resourceful and intelligent; he was "very strong, full of knowledge . . . He even invented an explosive and was a part of the ghetto underground . . . Since he had three children and a wife, he could not leave the ghetto with the others as a partisan." His participation in the Vilna underground, and his ability to help the resistors with munitions probably gave him a feeling of self-respect that kept him from depression.

My father was also an exception; he never lost his spirit. During the war he was fortunate in that the German who took over his factory treated him as a human being, giving him a chance to protect his family as well as others. This consideration may have allowed my father to keep his sense of usefulness, perhaps even have a feeling of autonomy. I describe him in my memoirs, *Dry Tears*.

31 Naomi Zeif, personal interview, Tel Aviv, Israel, 1995. Among those who claimed that no one in Białystok starved to death are Mina Kizelstein-Dorn (personal interview, Tel Aviv, 1995) and Shamay Kizelstein (personal interview, Yehud, Israel, 1995). My discussion is also based on Shamay Kizelstein's unpublished memoir, "Paths of Fate," and personal interviews with Eva Kracowski and Ania Rud (both Tel Aviv, 1995).

32 Mina Kizelstein-Dorn, personal interview.

33 Shamay Kizelstein, personal interview.

34 Some of the extensive archival materials appear in Adelson and Lapides, *Łódź Ghetto,* and Lucjan Dobroszycki, *Chronicle of the Łódź Ghetto.* Another important document is Dawid Sierakowiak's diary, which is filled with profound observations about history, philosophy, politics, and much more. As in most documents from ghettos, towering over all other topics are comments about food and hunger. The diary is more than 270 pages long, and each page has five or more entries. Almost every entry mentions food or hunger. Woven into these observations are comments about Sierakowiak's father and mother: how they related to each other and how they dealt with issues of food (*Diary of Dawid Sierakowiak*). See also the Łódź diary by Jakub Poznański, *Pamiętnik z Getta Łódzkiego.*

35 Sierakowiak, *Diary,* entry of April 19, 1942 (p. 156); pp. 178-243.

36 Ibid., entry of September 4, 1942 (p. 216); entry of September 5, 1942 (p. 220). Dawid survived his mother by only a year (see p. 268).

37 Zyskind, *Stolen Years,* 92-93. Another example comes from Alexandra Sołowejczyk-Guter (personal interview): in the Warsaw ghetto, a friend confided in her that her husband had changed from a most agreeable, fine man to a person who would secretly steal her food. The friend was too embarrassed to confront her husband. She told Alexandra that she was waiting for the war to end, after which she would divorce him. The couple survived, but the woman did not divorce her husband, and after the war she never mentioned her husband's wartime transgressions again; Mrs. Guter also refrained from bringing up the subject.

38 Zyskind, *Stolen Years,* 43.

39 Ibid., 156. It is interesting that not only did Sara supply her father with food, but she also arranged a place for him in the hospital. Zyskind did not limit her assistance to her father. She describes how during lunchtime at her workshop the workers would collect food for those who were more needy than they. Each of the laborers contributed one spoonful of soup from his or her midday meal to another person.

40 Sierakowiak, *Diary,* 93.

41 Ibid., 244.

42 Rosenfeld, cited in Adelson and Lapides, *Łódź Ghetto,* 262-263. Rosenfeld was deported in August 1944 to Auschwitz, where he perished (501).

43 Dobroszycki, *Chronicle of the Łódź Ghetto,* 289.

44 Sierakowiak, *Diary,* 174. On hunger and its effect on the intellect, see Eitinger, "Auschwitz — A Psychological Perspective," in Gutman and Berenbaum, *Anatomy of the Auschwitz Death Camp,* 469-482, and *Choroba Głodowa.*

45 Sierakowiak, *Diary,* 183; Dobroszycki, *Chronicle of the Łódź Ghetto,* 226.

46 Vladka Meed, personal interview; Meed, "Jewish Resistance in the Warsaw Ghetto," 12.

47 Rudashevski, *Diary of the Vilna Ghetto,* 128-129. I am grateful to Jane Lillibridge for stimulating some of these ideas about cultural activities.

48 Dobka Freund-Waldhorn, personal interviews, Kvar Shmariahu, Israel, 1995, 1996.

49 See my "Historical Perspective: Tracing the History of the Hidden Child Experience," in Marks, *Hidden Children,* 273-291.

50 Adelson and Lapides, *Łódź Ghetto,* 352.

51 Quoted in ibid., 328, 330-331.

52 Ibid., 320-359. Particularly touching in this description is the heart-wrenching

lament of an unnamed father who has lost his little daughter and blames himself (348–349). See also Dobroszycki, *Chronicle of the Łódź Ghetto*, 248–255.

53 On the deportations of 1942 see Browning, *Ordinary Men*, xv; Friedman, "The Extermination of the Polish Jews During the German Occupation, 1939–1945," in Ada Friedman, *Roads to Extinction*, 211–243; Gilbert, *Holocaust*, 252–351; and Yahil, *Holocaust*, 404–456.

54 On Korczak's orphanage and deportation see Korczak, *Ghetto Diary*, and Lifton, *King of Children*. Among the staff members who went with Korczak was Stefania Wiliczyńska, the manager of the Children's Home. Probably secretly in love with Korczak, she had worked with him since 1911. There are slightly different versions of the procession to the waiting cattle cars. See Dawidowicz, *War Against the Jews*, 307, and Aaron Zeitlin, "The Last Walk of Janusz Korczak," in Korczak, *Ghetto Diary*, 7–63.

55 The story is told in Szwajger, *I Remember Nothing More*, 54–58, and Edelman, *Ala z Elementarza*, 73–75. See also Krall, *Shielding the Flame*, 9, who quotes Edelman as saying that a doctor offered cyanide to the children. He further asserts that the doctor had given her own cyanide to these children. This disagrees with Szwajger's account. Charles G. Roland, in *Courage Under Siege* (184–185), also refers to the fact that cyanide was given to the children. He seems to rely on the Krall reference mentioned above. However, later (180) Roland mentions Adina Szwajger, claiming that she gave morphine to a room full of children. In this instance he correctly refers to Szwajger's book.

Chapter 4: Leaving the Ghetto

1 Itke Brown, now known as Lidia Abramson, personal interview, Tel Aviv, 1995. I shall refer to her either as Lidia Brown-Abramson or as Lidia Abramson.

2 Dina Abramowicz, "The World of My Parents: Reminiscences," *YIVO Annual* 23 (1997): 153. On the breakup of the Vilna ghetto, see also Arad, *Ghetto in Flames*, 429–432.

3 Dobka Freund-Waldhorn, personal interviews, Kvar Shmarjahu, Israel, 1995, 1996.

4 The first armed encounter between the Germans and the Warsaw ghetto resistance lasted only a few days, but it was a prelude to the future uprising. For discussion of these events, see Gutman, *Resistance*, 177–187, and Zuckerman, *Surplus of Memory*, 263–347.

5 Roma Nutkiewicz-Benatar, personal interview, Kvar Shmarjahu, Israel, 1995.

6 A jump from a moving train in no way ensured survival. As Eva Galer's account

shows (personal interview, New Orleans, 1992), often these jumps ended in death.

7 Shamay Kizelstein, personal interview, Yihud, Israel, 1995; I also consulted his unpublished memoir, "Paths of Fate" (1985).

8 Zvi Shefet (Shepetinski), personal interview, Tel Aviv, 1995.

9 Jewish partisan detachments were sometimes attacked by Russian and Polish partisans. See Gutman and Krakowski, *Unequal Victims,* 208, 222; Krakowski, *War of the Doomed,* 37, 41–42, 54; and my *In the Lion's Den,* 182, 185.

10 Luba Garfunk, personal interview, Haifa, 1990. The fate of the Garfunks is also described in my *Defiance,* 129, 141.

11 Eva Galer, personal interview.

12 For a fascinating account of survival as a Polish laborer in Germany, see Ida Fink's memoir *The Journey.* Although it is a novel, it describes Fink's personal wartime experiences.

13 Eva Kracowski, personal interview, Tel Aviv, 1995. For general discussions about what took place in the Białystok ghetto underground see Grossman, *Underground Army.* Chaika Grossman was an underground courier for the Białystok ghetto resistance. Her book is both a wartime memoir and a historical account of the Jewish underground. See also Mark, *Ruch Oporu w Getcie Białostockim.*

14 The Communists took a while to organize after the outbreak of the German-Russian war in 1941. Because the Communists were weak, they were willing to take in less-committed people to augment their numbers. Indeed, they were less selective than other political parties. As an upper class apolitical woman, Kracowski fell into the category of "not well qualified" individuals who were accepted only by the Communist organization because they were not as choosy.

15 See my *When Light Pierced the Darkness,* 70.

16 See Philip Friedman, "The Destruction of the Jews of Lvov," in Ada J. Friedman, ed., *Roads to Extinction,* 244, 321. Sandra Brand describes these events as well in *Roma,* 184–189.

17 Sandra Brand, personal interviews, New York, 1994, 1995.

18 In her books Brand refers to Julius by the name Fischer. She did not give his real name because in 1978 when she wrote her book *I Dared to Live,* she thought that perhaps his German Gentile children might not like to learn that their father was Jewish. When I interviewed her in 1995, she felt more relaxed about such issues.

19 Alexandra Sołowejczyk-Guter, personal interview, Bat-Yam, Israel, 1995.

20 When I was researching my book *When Light Pierced the Darkness,* I found that most wealthy Jews had become poor by the time they managed to move to the

Aryan side. Many of them had either lost their fortunes early or had been forced to leave suddenly, without taking anything of value with them (27–39).

21 Mina Vołkowiski, personal interviews, Tel Aviv, 1994, 1995. It was not unusual for upper-class Jews to be rebuffed by underground organizations on the grounds that they would not fit into the life in the forests or into the life of the underground. We saw this in the case of Eva Kracowski. In *Defiance*, I describe a former teacher, Abraham Viner, who was rejected by a Jewish partisan group because he was an intellectual (98). I heard a similar story from Irena Lusky (personal interview, Tel Aviv, 1995). Lusky told me that because of her upper-class background she was denied entrance into Aba Kovner's resistance group.

22 Chava Grinberg-Brown, personal interview, Israel, 1992. Chava lives on a farm (a Moshav), Bnei Atarot, close to Tel Aviv.

23 Ania Rud, personal interview, Tel Aviv, 1995.

24 Lusia Grosman-Sternberg, personal interview, Tel Aviv, 1995.

25 Miriam Akavia, personal interview, Tel Aviv, 1995. See also Akavia's *An End to Childhood*.

26 Ruth Hudes-Tartako, personal interview, Tel Aviv, 1995.

27 For additional examples of children who escaped only to return to their families, see Edelman, *Ala z Elementarza*, 80–81, and Friedländer, *When Memory Comes*.

28 For the story of the Nowogródek breakout see my *Defiance*, 188–192. I discuss other large-scale escapes in *In the Lion's Den*, 135–148.

29 Amiora Ackerman, personal interview, Tel Aviv, 1995. Mrs. Ackerman still lives in Belgium, but I interviewed her when she was on a visit to Israel.

30 Shulamit Einhorn-Roitman, personal interview, Tel Aviv, 1995.

31 For a history of the OSE see Dwork, *Children with a Star*, 55–65; for a more extensive account of its history and activities see Sabine Zeitoun, *L'Oeuvre de Secours aux Enfants (O.S.E.) sous l'occupation en France* (Paris: Editions L'Harmattan, 1990), and Samuel, *Sauves les enfants*.

32 Rose and Edith Margolis, personal interview, Elmhurst, Illinois, 1993. The Margolis sisters are so attached to each other that they insisted on being interviewed together. Rather than lose the chance to hear their story, I agreed. This was an exception.

33 Claire Prowizur-Szyper, personal interview, Tel Aviv, 1995. I also relied on a memoir written by Prowizur-Szyper, *Conte à Rebours*.

Chapter 5: The Concentration Camps

1 Rita Weiss-Jamboger, personal interview, Tel Aviv, 1995.

2 Judith Rubinstein, Yad Vashem, 03/4483.

3 When referring to the camps I shall use the synonymous terms *camp, concentration camp,* and *Lager* interchangeably. Only when relevant will I distinguish between them.

4 Sofsky, *Order of Terror,* 15.

5 Michael Berenbaum, Preface, and Shmuel Krakowski, "The Satellite Camps," both in Gutman and Berenbaum, *Anatomy of the Auschwitz Death Camp,* vii, 50.

6 Sofsky, *Order of Terror,* 5.

7 See Yehuda Bauer, "Discussion," in Gutman and Saf, *Nazi Concentration Camps,* 39.

8 Goldhagen, *Hitler's Willing Executioners,* 171; Sofsky, *Order of Terror,* cites a total of 10,006 Nazi camps (292). For a classic study of the concentration camp system see Kogon, *Theory and Practice of Hell.* For descriptions of a variety of camps and discussion of the proportion of inmates who perished in them see: Czesław Madajczyk, "Concentration Camps as a Tool of Oppression in Nazi-Occupied Europe," in Gutman and Saf, *Nazi Concentration Camps,* 47–68, and Franciszek Piper, "The Number of Victims," in Gutman and Berenbaum, *Anatomy of the Auschwitz Death Camp,* 61–76.

9 On "total institutions" see Goffman, *Asylums.* Drawing on Goffman's theoretical formulations and concentrating on empirical evidence from the Warsaw ghetto, Ilana Geva wrote an impressive M.A. thesis, "The Warsaw Ghetto as a Total Institution" (Bar Ilan University, Israel, 1988). The description of the concentration camps offered by Wolfgang Sofsky in *The Order of Terror* (14) closely resembles Goffman's definition of a total institution.

10 Otto Kraus and Erich Kulka, in *Death Factory,* estimate that 80 percent of the Jews who were sent to Auschwitz were gassed on arrival. According to another estimate, 90 percent or more of the Jews arriving at Auschwitz were herded directly into the gas chambers without being entered on the register: see Walter Laqueur, Foreword, to Czech, *Auschwitz Chronicle,* xvi. In the death camps specifically created for the murder of Jews the percentage of those who perished on arrival was higher. For figures on admissions and deaths in selected camps from 1933 to 1945 that reflect the annihilation pressures in these camps see Sofsky, *Order of Terror,* 39, 43. The process of killing through work is described in Felicja Karay, "Skarżysko-Kamienna," in Gutman, *Encyclopedia of the Holocaust,* 4:1360–1362; see also Karay, *Death Comes in Yellow.* For a thorough discussion of how the annihilation of the Jews took precedence over economic considerations in the Third Reich see Hilberg, *Destruction of the European Jews,* 332–345.

11 Levi, *Drowned and the Saved,* 120. For examples of German brutality see Améry, *At the Mind's Limits,* 21–40; Browning, *Ordinary Men;* Goldhagen, *Hitler's Will-*

ing Executioners; Des Pres, *The Survivor;* and Shmuel Krakowski, "Satellite
Camps," 54. Emil Fackenheim, in "Spectrum of Resistance During the Holocaust," views the Nazi policy of Jewish dehumanization as an end in itself rather
than subordinate to the goal of Jewish destruction.

12 The following is only a sample of the many sources that describe the different
treatment of Jewish and non-Jewish prisoners: Borowski, *This Way for the Gas,
Ladies and Gentlemen;* Israel Gutman, "Social Stratification In the Concentration Camps," in Gutman and Saf, *Nazi Concentration Camps,* 144–176; Hermann
Langbein, *Die Stärkern,* 122; Sofsky, *Order of Terror,* 128; Cohen, *Human Behavior in the Concentration Camp,* 120; and Frankl, *Man's Search for Meaning,*
3–4. Two excellent articles on the treatment of Gypsies are Raul Hilberg,
"Gypsies," in Laqueur, *Holocaust Encyclopedia,* 271–277, and Yehuda Bauer,
"Gypsies," in Gutman and Berenbaum, *Anatomy of Auschwitz,* 441–455.

13 Zahava Ziskowicz-Adam, personal interview, Tel Aviv, 1995.

14 Helen Spitzer-Tichauer (known as Zippi), personal interview, New York, 1997.
Since that interview Zippi has generously continually provided me with answers
whenever I contacted her. Zippi is a walking encyclopedia about Birkenau and
Auschwitz, where she was imprisoned for almost three years.

15 Among the men I asked about headshavings were Aronek Kierszkowski (now
known as Arnold Kerr; personal interview, Westport, Connecticut, 1996),
Shamay Kizelstein (personal interview, Yehud, Israel, 1995), and Menachem
Rubyn (personal interview, Ramat Gan, 1995). The literature contains many
examples of women who were traumatized by the headshaving ceremony. A particularly devastating reaction is offered by Ruth Nebel: "The Story of Ruth," in
Bridenthal, Grossmann, and Kaplan, *When Biology Became Destiny,* 343.

16 Ester Margolis-Joffee, Yad Vashem, 03/1645. For a discussion of the living quar-
ters, see Robert-Jan van Pelt, "A Site in Search of a Mission," in Gutman and
Berenbaum, *Anatomy of the Auschwitz Death Camp,* 93–156, and, for more detail,
Dwork and van Pelt, *Auschwitz,* 307–353, and Des Pres, *The Survivor,* 53–71.

17 Koonz, *Mothers in the Fatherland,* 407. There were occasional but short-lived
exceptions to the division of families, such as Auschwitz's Jewish family camp
and Gypsy camp. These facilities were designed for specific purposes and did
not last. See Yehuda Bauer, "Gypsies," and Nili Keren, "The Family Camp,"
in Gutman and Berenbaum, *Anatomy of the Auschwitz Death Camp,* 441–455,
and 428–440.

18 Helen Spitzer-Tichauer (Zippi), personal interview.

19 Tonia Rotkopf-Blair, personal interview, New York, 1996.

20 Eva Braun, Yad Vashem, 03/6526.

21 Frankl, *Man's Search for Meaning;* Donat, *Holocaust Kingdom.*

22 For accounts of illegal correspondence see Borowski, *This Way for the Gas, Ladies and Gentlemen,* 134, and Hart, *I Am Alive,* 75. It was the custom for prisoners to smuggle such letters for one another free of charge.

23 Naomi Zeif, personal interview, Tel Aviv, 1995.

24 Tola Szwarc-Chudin, personal interview, Tel Aviv, 1995. Such experiences were quite common. Another prisoner describes an almost identical encounter; from a distance she saw her brother walking with a group of male prisoners, but when she called out his name, and he turned around, his guard immediately began hitting him (Birenbaum, *Hope Is the Last to Die,* 87).

25 Zahava Ziskowicz-Adam, personal interview.

26 Berta Benau-Hutzler, personal interview, Ramat Gan, 1995. Helen Spitzer-Tichauer (Zippi) also talked to me about the Dutch women in Birkenau and how quickly they perished in the Lager (personal communication, 2001).

27 De Jong, *Netherlands and Nazi Germany,* 23.

28 Helen Spitzer-Tichauer (Zippi), personal interview.

29 Shoshana Kahn, personal interview, New York, 1993.

30 Bracha Winger-Ghilai, personal interview, Chulon, Israel, 1995.

31 Hadassa Moldinger, personal interview, Jerusalem, 1995. Although she worked for Yad Vashem for years, Hadassa had refused to be interviewed for any purpose. This was her first interview. In deference to her wishes I did not tape the interview, but I did take extensive notes. (She was only the second of the hundreds of respondents I interviewed who refused to be recorded.) At her request I sent her a transcribed copy of the interview in English.

32 Gerda Nothmann-Luner, personal interview, Elmhurst, Illinois, 1993.

33 Dobka Freund-Waldhorn, personal interviews, Kvar Shmarjahu, Israel, 1995, 1996.

34 Naomi Zeif, personal interview.

35 Karla Szajewicz-Frist, personal interview, Tel Aviv, 1995.

36 Miriam Rubyn, personal interview, Ramat Gan, 1995.

37 On Skarżysko Kamienna see Ida Buszmicz, Yad Vashem, 03/2798; Felicja Karay, personal interview, Bat-Yam, Israel, 1995; and Róża Bauminger, *Przy Pikrynie i Trotylu,* 36. The camp was dismantled in 1944.

38 See Karay, "Skarżysko-Kamienna," and *Death Comes in Yellow.*

39 There are a few similarities between this camp and the work camp Strachowice, described by Christopher R. Browning in *Nazi Policy, Jewish Workers, German Killers.* In both camps the men and women tended to mingle more freely. Browning notes that the reason may have in part been Jewish participation in the internal administration of these camps (89–115).

40 Felicja Karay, personal interview. Hannah Levy-Hass, in *Inside Belsen,* assumes that it is a fact that a man's body responds differently to hunger and cold than a woman's: "It is a fact, and many doctors say the same today, that a woman can adapt herself better to suffering than a man. (Not to physical effort, because a man is physically stronger.) A man's body suffers much more when subjected to hunger, fatigue, or cold" (107–108). Commenting on the overall mortality rates of men and women in concentration camps, Germaine Tillion, writes in *Ravensbrück,* "The mortality rate among men in the camps was higher than that of women, an inequality due at least in part to the different aptitudes of the sexes. Women have a greater ingenuity in many things touching directly on the simple preservation of life" (39).

41 Ida Buszmicz, Yad Vashem, 03/2798.

42 Felicja Karay, personal interview. Ruth Bondy claims that in Theresienstadt, "the number and percentage of men punished far exceeded those of women (the ratio was about four men punished to one woman punished)" ("Women in Theresienstadt and the Family Camp in Birkenau," in Ofer and Weitzman, *Women in the Holocaust,* 317).

43 Henia Shenberg, personal interview, Paris, 1995.

44 Bela Chazan-Yaari, personal interview, Tel Aviv, 1995.

45 Ella Lingens-Reiner, *Prisoners of Fear,* 38, feels that men had a harder time in the camps.

46 Aronek Kierszkowski (Arnold Kerr), personal interview.

47 Shamay Kizelstein, personal interview.

48 Rita Weiss-Jamboger, personal interview.

49 See Des Pres, *The Survivor,* 89; and Cohen, *Human Behavior in the Concentration Camps,* 148–152.

50 Jan Sehn, "Food," in *Chief Commission for the Investigation of Nazi Crimes in Poland,* 55; Levi, *Survival in Auschwitz,* 67.

51 Helen Spitzer-Tichauer (Zippi), personal interview.

52 Levi, *Drowned and the Saved,* 114.

53 Ada Wiener-Goldberg, Yad Vashem, 03/3224. Such experiences were frequent. Dvora Salzberg tells a similar story. In her case, a bowl of soup was offered to six women without a spoon. This, too, led to horrible scenes with jealous outbursts and name calling (Yad Vashem, 03/2341).

54 When Elie Wiesel's father thought that he was about to be gassed, he insisted that Elie take his eating utensils. In a real sense, these utensils were the son's only inheritance. (The father's fear turned out to be a false alarm, and he lived a while longer.) The occasion is movingly described in Wiesel, *Night,* 85–86. Similarly,

Primo Levi received utensils from his friend Shmulik, when he knew that he had been condemned to death (Anissimov, *Primo Levi*, 139).

55 Bracha Winger-Ghilai, personal interview.

56 Hadassa Moldinger, personal interview; Arieh Eitani, personal interview, Herzlia Pituach, Israel, 1995.

57 Ita Shapiro, personal interview, Herzlia, Israel, 1995. Among those who praised the taste of raw potatoes are Karla Szajewicz-Frist, Bracha Winger-Ghilai, and Tola Szwarc-Chudin.

58 Ina Weiss, Yad Vashem, 03/1341.

59 Tola Szwarc-Chudin, personal interview.

60 Renée Hofland, Yad Vashem, 033/1294.

61 Shoshana Kahn, personal interview.

62 It is generally agreed that for most camp inmates the sexual drive disappeared. See Kautsky, *Teufel and Verdamte*, 229–230; Laska, *Women in the Resistance and in the Holocaust*, 181; Maurel, *An Ordinary Camp*, 94; Tedeschi, *There Is a Place on Earth*, 115; and Weinstock, *Beyond the Last Path*, 235–236. Camp survivors concur that they lost interest in sex. Tadeusz Borowski thinks that when prisoners had enough food and rest they were ready to have sex (*This Way for the Gas, Ladies and Gentleman*, 108).

63 Leon Eitinger, "Auschwitz—A Psychological Perspective," in Gutman and Berenbaum, *Anatomy of the Auschwitz Death Camp*, 473; Jean Améry, *At the Mind's Limits*, 9. The term *Musulmann* is used for camp prisoners who were on the verge of death from starvation. The spelling seems to vary, depending on the source; see Danuta Czech, "The Auschwitz Prisoner Administration," in Gutman and Berenbaum, *Anatomy of the Auschwitz Death Camp*, 369–371. Eugen Kogon calls them "Moslem" (*Theory and Practice of Hell*, 319); Levi says "Mussulman" (*Drowned and the Saved*, 81); Richard L. Rubenstein and John K. Roth use "Musselmänner" (*Approaches to Auschwitz*, 186). I shall use "Musulmann" for both the singular and plural. On the effects of starvation see also Pwełczyńska, *Wartości A Przemoc*, 93.

64 Rachel Aronowicz, Yad Vashem, 03/3306. My translation from the Polish.

65 Ibid.; Sofsky, *Order of Terror*, 25.

66 Levi, *Drowned and the Saved*, 84. Mistreatment of the Musulmann has been reported in a number of sources. For a few examples see Sofsky, *Order of Terror*, 204; Birenbaum, *Hope Is the Last to Die*, 110; and Levi, *Survival in Auschwitz*, 80–81.

67 On women's work see Eva Braun, Yad Vashem, 03/6526; and Irena Strzelecka, "Women," in Gutman and Berenbaum, *Anatomy of the Auschwitz Death Camp*, 407. Shamay Kizelstein (personal interview) described conditions at Buna.

68 Roma Nutkiewicz-Benatar, personal interview, Kvar Shmarjahu, Israel, 1995.
69 Arieh Eitani, personal interview.
70 Ibid. Elie Wiesel movingly describes the execution in Auschwitz of a Pipel who was loved by all who knew him in *Night*, 74–76.
71 Arieh Eitani, personal interview. Tzvetan Todorov, in *Facing the Extreme*, argues that inmates' defiance, even suicide, enrages guards because it challenges their power. They and not the prisoners should be making the decisions about when the prisoners are going to die (63).
72 Tonia Rotkopf-Blair, personal interview.
73 Menachem Rubyn, personal interview.
74 Ruth Hudes-Tatarko, personal interview, Tel Aviv, 1995.
75 Lucy Mandelshtam, Yad Vashem, 03/5591.
76 Tola Szwarc-Chudin, personal interview.
77 Bracha Winger-Ghilai, personal interview.
78 Dvora Rosenbaum-Fogel, personal interview, Tel Aviv, 1995.
79 Tonia Rotkopf-Blair, personal interview.
80 Dobka Freund-Waldhorn, personal interviews.
81 Edith Lasman, personal interview, Tel Aviv, 1995.
82 Felicja Karay, personal interview.
83 Naomi Zeif, personal interview; Tola Szwarc-Chudin, personal interview.
84 Levi, *Survival in Auschwitz*, 35–36.
85 Ibid., 36.
86 Menachem Rubyn, personal interview.
87 For a description of the death marches see Goldhagen, *Hitler's Willing Executioners*, 327–371.
88 Discussions about medical treatment in concentration camps abound. A few examples are Lifton, *Nazi Doctors;* Micheels, *Doctor 117641;* and Irena Strzelecka, "Hospitals," in Gutman and Berenbaum, *Anatomy of the Auschwitz Death Camp*, 379–392.
89 Weinstock, *Beyond the Last Path*, 43. On the treatment of mothers with small children and their responses see Cohen, *Human Behavior in the Concentration Camp*, 117–120; Kraus and Kulka, *Death Factory*, 114; Kubica, "Children," in Gutman and Berenbaum, eds. *Anatomy of the Auschwitz Death Camp*, 422; Borowski, *This Way for the Gas, Ladies and Gentlemen*, 43; and Bondy, "Women in Theresienstadt and the Family Camp in Birkenau," 324–325.
90 A German Jew, Charlotte had escaped to the south of France during the war. She was arrested and moved to the transit camp Drancy, then deported to Auschwitz. Although she was murdered at the age of twenty-six, Charlotte left more than

NOTES TO PAGES 162–167

seven hundred paintings as her visual autobiography. See Felstiner, *To Paint Her Life,* 204. On the fate of pregnant women in general, see Irena Strzelecka, "Women," in Gutman and Berenbaum, *Anatomy of the Auschwitz Death Camp,* 405.

91 See Perl, *I Was a Doctor in Auschwitz,* 80–86; and Tillion, *Ravensbrück,* 77.

92 Elias, *Triumph of Hope,* 146–157.

93 Ruth Hudes-Tatarko described to me in a personal interview (Ramat Gan, 1995) how she saw an SS man in her barracks roughly remove a newborn infant. Sara Nomberg-Przytyk, in *Auschwitz,* tells the story of Esther, a pregnant woman in Birkenau who refused to discontinue her pregnancy. No matter how strongly others would try to explain the situation, she clung to the idea that everyone, including Dr. Mengele, would be enchanted with her baby. Esther's infant was beautiful. But when her baby boy was only two days old, there was a selection in the hospital block. Every patient had to parade nude in front of Dr. Mengele and the SS man assisting him. When Esther's turn came, the inevitable happened: "She left naked, in her arms she held the baby. She held it up high as though she wanted to show them what a beautiful and healthy son she had" (71).

94 Dvora Rosenbaum-Fogel, personal interview. Celina Strachen, Yad Vashem, 03/2955, also tells about a postwar delivery by a former concentration camp inmate. In *Ravensbrück,* Germaine Tillion reports that between October 1944 and March 1945 an estimated 850 infants were killed in Ravensbrück hospital to save their mothers (78).

95 Lucy Mandelshtam, Yad Vashem, 033C/1135.

96 Ania Rubinger, Yad Vashem, 03/6393.

97 Karla's story is told in Nomberg-Przytyk, *Auschwitz,* 85–88.

98 Miriam Rubyn, personal interview; see also Jackson, *Elli,* 85, 87, and Hart, *I Am Alive,* 81.

99 Among the teenagers I discussed in chapter 3 who tried to take on the role of the family's breadwinner and partial protector, readers will recall Zvi Shefet (Shepetinski), Eva Galer, Shamay Kizelstein, and Vladka Meed. Several of the survivors I interviewed described siblings who knowingly chose to remain with their parents. Among them were the sister of Sulia Rubin (personal interview, Saddle River, N.J., 1989), Luba Rudnicki (personal interview, Tel Aviv, 1989), and Ania Rud (personal interview, Tel Aviv, 1995). Alina Edelman-Margolis, in *Ala z Elementrza,* describes a young woman who went to the concentration camp with her mother even though she had a place prepared for her in the Aryan side and the necessary papers (68–69).

100 Dobka Freud-Waldhorn, personal interviews.

101 Dr. Aptowicz looked after his son from age nine, after his wife was shot by Ukrainians on July 26, 1941, to age twelve. When the two finally arrived at Buchenwald, in Germany, their survival depended on organized help. The Buchenwald underground had set aside an area in two blocks in which to protect Jewish children. One of the blocks housed boys aged sixteen to eighteen, while the second one contained boys from twelve to sixteen, although two were aged eight and nine. These two worked in the kitchen, a place that offered extra food. In charge of the second block was Emil Carlebach, a Jew, a Communist, and a prisoner since 1939. Carlebach had devoted himself to the rescue of children, and he took over the care of Dr. Aptowicz's son. The Buchenwald arrangement showed how desperately some inmates fought to save Jewish children. See Dr. Ryszard Aptowich [Aptowicz], Yad Vashem, 03/2712 and Weinstock, *Beyond the Last Path*, 127, 191–193. For a variety of relationships between fathers and sons, some showing mutual help and devotion, see Olga Lengyel, "Scientific Experiments," in Rittner and Roth, *Different Voices*, 315; and Tedeschi, *There Is a Place on Earth*, 98.

102 Quoted in Jackson, *Elli*, 86.

103 See ibid., 94–95; Heinemann, *Gender and Destiny*, 18–21; and Sara R. Horowitz, "Women in Holocaust Literature: Engendering Trauma Memory," in Ofer and Weitzman, *Women in the Holocaust*, 370.

104 Roma Nutkiewicz-Benatar, personal interview; Miriam Akavia, personal interview, Tel Aviv, 1995. See also Bondy, "Women in Theresienstadt and the Family Camp in Birkenau," 315; Olga Lengyel, "Scientific Experiments," in Rittner and Roth, *Different Voices*, 315; and Tedeschi, *There Is a Place on Earth*, 98.

105 Arieh Eitani, personal interview.

106 Edith Lasman, personal interview; Frankl, *Man's Search for Meaning*, 5–6. During my interviews similar sentiments were spontaneously and consistently expressed by Dvora Fogel, Bracha Winger-Ghilai, Shamay Kizelstein, Ita Shapiro, Helen Spitzer-Tichauer (Zippi), Rita Weiss-Jamboger, among others.

107 Levi, *Drowned and the Saved*, 132.

108 Ibid., 142 (see also p. 143); Améry, *At the Mind's Limits*, 18. A prisoner from Buchenwald voiced a slightly different opinion, arguing that the upper-class intellectual prisoners had a particularly hard time because they were individualists and therefore less likely to benefit from cooperation and mutual help. See Weinstock, *Beyond the Last Path*, 125–126.

109 See Levi, *Drowned and the Saved*, 134.

110 See, for example, Buber-Neumann, *Milena*, 163, and Lewinska, *Twenty Months at Auschwitz*, 111.

111 Ada Wiener-Goldberg, Yad Vashem, 03/3224.
112 Menachem Rubyn, personal interview.
113 Miriam Rubyn, personal interview.
114 Bracha Winger-Ghilai, personal interview.
115 Gerda Nothmann-Luner, personal interview.
116 See, for example, my "On Forgiveness," in "The Symposium" of Wiesenthal, *Sunflower*, 241–247. The entire symposium contains essays on forgiveness. An earlier set of essays on the same topic is also included Wiesenthal's *Sunflower*.
117 Felicja Karay, personal interview. See also Des Pres, *The Survivor*, 121, 136. For an insightful treatment of the intricate relation between collectivity and individuality, see Slater, *Pursuit of Loneliness*. For arguments about the connection between cooperation and survival see Leon Eitinger, "Auschwitz—A Psychological Perspective," in Gutman and Berenbaum, *Anatomy of the Auschwitz Death Camp*, 475, and Todorov, *Facing the Extreme*, which argues that in concentration camps "survival was impossible without the help of others" (35).
118 Tillion, *Ravensbrück*, xxii. See also Kogon, *Theory and Practice of Hell*, 255–273; Kraus and Kulka, *Death Factory*, 1–3; Langbein, *Against All Hope*, 393–394; and Weinstock, *Beyond the Last Path*, 154.
119 See Des Pres, *The Survivor*, 89; and Cohen, *Human Behavior in the Concentration Camps*, 148–152.
120 See Sofsky, *Order of Terror*, 158.
121 See, among others, Booth, "Sex and Social Participation"; Chodorow, "Family Structure and Feminine Personality," in Rosaldo and Lamphere, *Woman, Culture and Society*, 43–66; Roy G. D'Andrade, "Sex Differences and Cultural Institution," and Walter Mischel, "A Social Learning View of Sex Differences in Behavior," in Maccoby, *Development of Sex Differences*, 174–204 and 51–81; Gilligan, *In a Different Voice*, 8–17, 170; Heinemann, *Gender and Destiny*, 6–7; Miller, *Toward a New Psychology of Women*, 83–89; and Tannen, *You Just Don't Understand*, 24–25, 71.
122 See Baumel, "Social Interaction Among Jewish Women in Crisis During the Holocaust"; and Benisch, *To Vanquish the Dragon*. Benisch was a member of this group.
123 Sybil Milton, "Women and the Holocaust: The Case of German and German-Jewish Women," in Bridenthal, Grossmann, and Kaplan, *When Biology Became Destiny*, 311–312.
124 Karay, *Death Comes in Yellow*, 247.
125 Koonz, *Mothers in the Fatherland*, 408. The following are but a few books by Jewish male prisoners that discuss their participation in such groups: Arditti,

Will to Live; Donat, *Holocaust Kingdom;* Glazar, *Trap with a Green Fence;* Levi, *Survival in Auschwitz;* Pisar, *Of Blood and Hope;* Weinstock, *Beyond the Last Path;* and Wells, *Janowska Road.* Memoirs by women include Benisch, *To Vanquish the Dragon;* Berger, *Tell Me Another Morning;* Gluck, *My Story;* Pawlowicz and Klose, *I Will Survive;* Tedeschi, *There Is a Place On Earth;* and Zyskind, *Stolen Years.* I have not come across a single Lager autobiography that does not mention bonding of some kind as a part of the prisoners' experiences.

126 Publications about cooperative groups only occasionally recognize the need to compare men and women. Thus, Lillian Kremer, in *Women's Holocaust Writing,* emphasizes women's greater capacity for bonding and friendship than men's, but she relies only on women's memoirs. And in an interesting paper by Ami Neiberger, "An Uncommon Bond of Friendship, Family and Survival in Auschwitz," in Rohrlich, *Resisting the Holocaust* (133–149), the author concentrates only on bonding by women. In contrast, see Heinemann, *Gender and Destiny,* which calls for comparisons of male and female bonding groups (3–4). Alexander Donat, in *Holocaust Kingdom,* 237, and Eugen Kogon, in *Theory and Practice of Hell,* 27, both suggest that men helped one another but they shied away from verbal expressions of compassion. It is not known how pervasive this taciturnity was and whether it was true of only men. Many women talk about close and warm camp friendships, many of which continued after the war.

127 Roma Nutkiewicz-Benatar, personal interview.
128 Gerda Nothmann-Luner, personal interview.
129 Tola Szwarc-Chudin, personal interview.
130 Ita Shapiro, personal interview.
131 Dobka Freund-Waldhorn, personal interviews.
132 Irena Lusky, personal interview, Tel Aviv, 1995. The Vilna women who at various times were employed by the AEG during the war collectively published a book privately called *Women's War: The Story of a Forced Labor Camp* (in Hebrew).
133 Irena Lusky, personal interview. See also Lusky's book *La Traverse de la nuit,* which contains descriptions of many interesting war experiences. This book was also published in Hebrew by Kibbutz Beit Lohamei Hagetaot in 1981.
134 Shoshana Kahn, personal interview. At that time Vilna was part of Poland.
135 Bracha Winger-Ghilai, personal interview.
136 Ruth Hudes-Tatarko, personal interview, Tel Aviv, 1995.
137 Menachem Rubyn, personal interview.
138 See Donat, *Death Camp Treblinka,* a collection of memoirs by former prisoners of Treblinka, and Sereny, *Into That Darkness.*

139 Richard Glazar, personal interview, Basel, 1995. See also Glazar's *Trap with a Green Fence*. The quotes in the text come from the interview.

140 See Gutman and Krakowski, *Unequal Victims*, 106.

141 Aronek Kierszkowski (Arnold Kerr), personal interview.

142 Shamay Kizelstein, personal interview.

143 This account is based on a brief, unpublished memoir given to me by the author, Shamay Kizelstein, "Paths of Fate, Auschwitz-Birkenau No. B-1968." The literature is filled with examples of how groups helped keep their members alive.

144 Shamay Kizelstein, personal interview.

145 Ibid.

146 Kogon, *Theory and Practice of Hell*, 314.

147 On various artistic activities see Fenelon, *Playing for Time;* Green, *Artists of Terezin;* Karas, *Music in Terezin;* Troller, *Theresienstadt;* Świebocka, *Auschwitz;* and Langer, *Art from the Ashes*. In *Trap with a Green Fence*, Richard Glazar discusses how "entertainments" were used for humiliation in Treblinka (117–125); for another description of an SS-sponsored public boxing competition see Steinberg, *Speak You Also*, 21–27.

148 See, among others, Lucy Mandelshtam, Yad Vashem, 033C/1135. Ruth Elias, another prisoner, concurs with Lucy's assessment. For Ruth, watching and listening to various artistic presentations had the effect of spiritual nourishment, shielding her from her surroundings (Elias, *Triumph of Hope*, 84).

149 Zahava Ziskowicz-Adam, personal interview; Aronek Kierszkowski (Arnold Kerr), personal interview.

150 Celina Stranchen, Yad Vashem, 03/2955.

151 Bracha Winger-Ghilai, personal interview.

152 Ita Shapiro, personal interview. Singing as a common pastime is reported by many others.

153 Miriam Rubyn, personal interview.

154 Tonia Rotkopf-Blair, personal interview; Levi, *Survival in Auschwitz*, 52.

155 Irena Lusky, personal interview.

156 Felicja Karay, personal interview.

157 Karay, *Death Comes in Yellow*, 247.

158 Roma Nutkiewicz-Benatar, personal interview.

159 Zahava Ziskowicz-Adam, personal interview.

160 Tola Szwarc-Chudin, personal interview.

161 Dobka Freund-Waldhorn, personal interviews.

162 Ruth Hudes-Tatarko, personal interview, Ramat Gan, Israel, 1995.

163 See especially Langer, *Holocaust Testimonies*, 4.

NOTES TO PAGES 206–213

Chapter 6: Hiding and Passing in the Forbidden Christian World

1 Ruth Flakowicz, Yad Vashem, 033/15.

2 See Davidowicz, *Holocaust Reader*, 67; Bartoszewski, "Egzekucje Publiczne w Warszawie"; Ringelblum, *Notes from the Warsaw Ghetto*, 236; and Berenstein et al., *Eksterminacja Żydów Na Ziemiach Polskich w Okresie Okupacji Hitlerowskiej*, 121–122.

3 Bartoszewski, "Egzekucje Publiczne w Warszawie"; Friedman, *Their Brothers' Keepers;* Iranek-Osmecki, *He Who Saves One Life;* Datner, *Las Sprawiedliwych;* Berenstein et al., *Eksterminacja Żydów Na Ziemiach Polskich w Okresie Okupacji Hitlerowskiej;* Klukowski, *Dziennik z Lat Okupacji;* Ziemiński, "Kartki Dziennika Nauczyciela w Łukowie"; and Hirszfeld, *Historia Jednego Życia*, 407.

4 Tec, *When Light Pierced the Darkness*, 45.

5 The following are a few of the many sources that describe what life was like for the Poles under the Nazi occupation: Bartoszewski, *1859 Dni Warszawy*, and *Straceni Na Ulicach Miasta;* Landau, *Kronika Lat Wojny i Okupacji* (Landau tried to survive by passing but was caught); Korboński, *Polish Underground State;* and Wroński and Zwolakowa, *Polacy i Żydzi*.

6 In Germany fewer women, Jewish or non-Jews, were arrested and persecuted than men. See Johnson, *Nazi Terror*, 359–361; Kaplan, *Between Dignity and Despair*, 80. Claudia Koonz, in *Mothers in the Fatherland*, presents evidence that before 1938 no Jewish woman was arrested in Germany (335). Court records indicate that of those accused and found guilty of crimes during the Third Reich, 20 percent were women (334). Koonz also emphasizes that women had much more freedom to move around than men (327).

7 Tec, *When Light Pierced the Darkness*, 23.

8 Tola Szwarc-Chudin, personal interview, Tel Aviv, 1995.

9 Karla Szajewicz-Frist, personal interview, Tel Aviv, 1995.

10 Dvora Rosenbaum-Fogel, personal interview, Tel Aviv, 1995.

11 For a thorough account of Jewish experiences on the Aryan side in Holland, see Presser, *Destruction of the Dutch Jews*, 381–405, and Valkhoff, *Leven in Een Niet-Bestaan*, 136–39. I am grateful to Marion Pritchard for directing me to this Dutch source and for translating it for me.

12 Tec, *When Light Pierced the Darkness*, 184.

13 Tola Szwarc-Chudin, personal interview.

14 Alexandra Sołowejczyk-Guter, personal interview, Bat-Yam, Israel, 1995.

15 Ania Rud, personal interview, Tel Aviv, 1995.

16 Alexandra Sołowejczyk-Guter, personal interview.

17 Fanya Gottesfeld-Heller, personal interview, New York, 1995; see also Heller, *Strange and Unexpected Love*.

18 Alexandra Sołowejczyk-Guter, personal interview; Dr. A. Liebesman-Mikulski, Yad Vashem, 033/1093.
19 Anita Adler, personal interview, Basel, 1995.
20 Ania Rud, personal interview.
21 Moses Lederman (personal interview, New York, 1979) told me that when he boarded a train for Warsaw he stumbled over the body of a young Jew. No one could have taken this young man for a Jew. Lederman later learned that the man had tried to leave for Warsaw but had the misfortune of being recognized by a Polish high school friend, who immediately denounced him. Asking no questions, a German shot him on the spot. For additional cases see my *When Light Pierced the Darkness,* chap. 2, and *Defiance,* where I tell the story of Dr. Zyskind, a young surgeon who had an almost perfect Aryan appearance. Near his destination (a forest bunker), he was recognized by a Belorussian policeman with whom he attended public school. The policeman denounced him, and Dr. Zyskind was executed after considerable torture, under which he revealed no secrets (58).
22 Alexandra Sołowejczyk-Guter, personal interview.
23 See my *When Light Pierced the Darkness,* 33–34.
24 See Kubar, *Double Identity,* 46–48.
25 See Rachel Adler, "The Jew Who Wasn't There," in Heschel, *On Being a Jewish Woman,* 14, and Heller, *On the Edge of Destruction,* 158, 227.
26 See Zborowski and Herzog, *Life Is with People,* 132; Tec, "Sex Distinctions and Passing as Christians"; Cantor, *Jewish Women, Jewish Men;* and Gershon Bacon, "The Missing 52 Percent: Research on Jewish Women in Interwar Poland and Its Implications for Holocaust Studies," and Paula E. Hyman, "Gender and the Jewish Family in Modern Europe," in Ofer and Weitzman, *Women in the Holocaust,* 56 and 33.
27 Alexandra Sołowejczyk-Guter, personal interview. Indeed, when Henryk Grynberg's mother stayed with her Polish friend in Warsaw, the friend refused to take him in because she was afraid that as a boy he was much more likely to bring on disaster (Grynberg, *Childhood of Shadows,* 79).
28 Sandra Brand, personal interview, New York, 1994; see also Brand, *I Dared to Live,* 61–66.
29 Vladka Meed, personal interview, New York, 1994. Jeanette Nestel was painfully aware of the problems created by Jewish "sad eyes" (Yad Vashem 03/6550).
30 See my memoir, *Dry Tears,* especially p. 68.
31 Ringelblum, *Polish-Jewish Relations During the Second World War,* 103–104.
32 Ania Rud, personal interview.
33 Anita Adler, personal interview.

34 See my *In the Lion's Den*. Oswald Rufeisen survived the war by hiding, passing as a Gentile, and by becoming a partisan in the forest.

35 For discussions of this issue see Goldstein, *Stars Bear Witness*, 201, 211, 216, 222; Gross, "Aryan Papers in Poland"; and Gross, "Unlucky Clara."

36 Alexandra Sołowejczyk-Guter, personal interview. Contrary to Alexandra's experience, Bernard Goldstein claims that even during the Polish uprising in Warsaw the Polish underground discriminated against Jews (*Stars Bear Witness*, 244).

37 Tec, *When Light Pierced the Darkness*, 213n15.

38 Eva Safczycka, personal interview, Tel Aviv, 1995. Eva's married name is Strich, but she preferred to be referred to by her maiden name.

39 Leah Silverstein, personal interview, Washington, D.C., 1997; Leah Silverstein, U.S. Holocaust Memorial Museum Archive, Transcript of Interview RG-50. 030*363. For other accounts see Kubar, *Double Identity*, 9–14; Kuchler-Silberman, *One Hundred Children;* and Szyfman, *Moja Tułaczka Wojenna*

40 Eva Galer mentions teenagers who helped feed their families by working on surrounding farms (personal interview, New Orleans, 1992); for other examples of teenage boys who worked on farms, see also my *Defiance*, 24–40; Kuper, *Child of the Holocaust*, 68–97; Grynberg, *Childhood of Shadows*, 45–48; and Oliner, *Restless Memories*.

41 Chava Grinberg-Brown, personal interview, Bnei Atarot, Israel, 1992.

42 Oswald Rufeisen, whose mother raised geese, remembers with pain her perpetually injured fingers. For a detailed description of the thankless task of raising geese, see my *In the Lion's Den*, 11–12.

43 Tema Rotman-Weinstock, Yad Vashem, 033/635.

44 It is not unusual for interviewees to request anonymity about their sexual experiences. It is, however, unusual for them to claim that a rape had no impact upon their lives.

45 For a description of my personal involvement in the black market as a buyer and seller see *Dry Tears*, 148–153, and 165–184. On local black market activities involving mainly young Jewish boys, see Ziemian, *Cigarette Sellers*.

46 Rina Eitani, personal interview, Hertzlia Pituach, Israel, 1995. As I explain later, it was dangerous for Jewish men to go to Germany disguised as Poles. Rina's brother was one of the rare men who succeeded.

47 Accounts disagree about whether women or men were more likely to extend help to Jews. See Henry, *Victims and Neighbors*, 104; Koonz, *Mothers in the Fatherland*, 335; and Tec, "Sex Distinctions." It may be that whether women or men were more likely to offer help varied with the kind of help needed.

48 Zwia Rechtman-Schwarz, personal interview, Tel Aviv, 1995. Ida Fink spent part of the war as a Polish laborer in Germany. She knew about two Jewish men who worked in Germany disguised as Poles (personal communication, 1998).

49 Eva Galer, personal interview, New Orleans, 1992.

50 Miriam Gold-Kowadło, Yad Vashem, 03/1181.

51 Zwia Rechtman-Schwarz, personal interview.

52 Lusia Grosman-Sternberg, personal interview, Tel Aviv, 1995.

53 See Ida Fink's *The Journey*, a novel based on the author's experiences, for the story of one such escape. I also received a personal communication from Ida Fink, in 1998.

54 Bronka Klibanski, "In the Ghetto and in the Resistance," unpublished paper delivered at the International Workshop on Women in the Holocaust at Hebrew University of Jerusalem, June 1995; see also Bronka Klibanski, Yad Vashem, 033/1351. Another courier, Bela Chazan (Yaari), was arrested as a Polish resister and survived the rest of the war in Auschwitz (personal interview, Tel Aviv, 1995).

55 Ringelblum, *Kronika Getta Warszawskiego*, 377–378. This is my free translation from the Polish; an English translation by Jacob Sloan is available in *Notes from the Warsaw Ghetto*, 273–274.

56 Leah Silverstein, U.S. Holocaust Memorial Museum, RG-50.030*363. See also Liza Chapnik, "Grodno Ghetto," unpublished paper delivered at the International Workshop on Women in the Holocaust at Hebrew University of Jerusalem, June 1995; Vladka Meed, personal interview; and Meed, *On Both Sides of the Wall*.

57 Vladka Meed, personal interview.

58 Ibid.

59 Bronka Klibanski, Yad Vashem, 033/1351.

60 Leah Silverstein, U.S. Holocaust Memorial Museum Archive.

61 Leah Silverstein, personal interview.

62 Leah Silverstein gave me a Polish copy of this essay; it was also translated into Hebrew in its entirety, published in *Yalkut Moreshet* 50 (1991). This is my free translation from the Polish.

63 Leah Silverstein, personal interview. On how hard it is to piece together historical events, see Zuckerman, *Surplus of Memory*, 348–376, and Rufeisen, *Pożegnanie z Milą*.

64 Mina Kizelstein-Dorn, personal interview, Tel Aviv, 1995. In *The Underground Army*, Chaika Grossman discusses Arthur Schade and the help he gave to the Jewish underground (185–186).

65 Schade was listed in the Yad Vashem Department for the Righteous Among the Nations in the January 1, 1998, report.

66 Fanya Gottesfeld-Heller, personal interview; and Heller, *Strange and Unexpected Love.*

67 Sandra Brand, personal interview; Brand, *I Dared to Live.* Peschel was listed in the Yad Vashem Department for the Righteous Among the Nations in the January 1, 1998, report.

68 Particularly in southern France, the distinctions between retaining a Jewish identity and taking on a Christian identity were sometimes blurred. Similarly, as late as 1942 some Jews in France felt that having a child protected a Jewish mother from deportation. Indeed, this is why the mother of Claire Sokołofsky became pregnant (Claire Sokołofsky, personal interview, Paris, 1995). For an interesting collection of children's memories of war, see David, *A Child's War.* For an overview of the fate of Jewish children see Dwork, *Children with a Star.* A rare autobiography of a young Jewish boy who survived from the age of four to seven in the concentration camp Bergen-Belsen, first published in Dutch (I read it in Polish) is Oberski, *Lata Dzieciństwa.* See also my "A Historical Perspective: Tracing the History of the Hidden-Child Experience," in Marks, *Hidden Children,* 273–291, and "Between Two Worlds."

69 Zwia Rechtman-Schwarz, personal interview.

70 Margot Dränger, Yad Vashem, 03/1686.

71 Fela Sztern, personal interviews, Winnipeg, 1979, 1994; Tec, *When Light Pierced the Darkness,* 43–44, 49.

72 Edzia Wilder, Yad Vashem, 033/645.

73 Sandra Brand, personal communication, 1998.

74 Cyla Menkes-Fast, Yad Vashem, 033/634. This is my translation from the Polish.

Chapter 7: Resistance

1 Eva Kracowski, personal interview, Tel Aviv, 1995.

2 See Reuben Ainsztein, "The Białystok Ghetto Revolt," in Suhl, *They Fought Back,* 136–143; Lisa Chapnik, "The Grodno Ghetto and Its Underground: A Personal Narrative," in Ofer and Weitzman, *Women in the Holocaust;* Grossman, *Underground Army,* 270–305; Bronka Klibanski, Yad Vashem 033/1351; and Mark, *Ruch Oporu w Getcie Białostockim,* 235–250.

3 See Roger S. Gottlieb, "The Concept of Resistance." For a discussion of different forms of Jewish resistance see Bauer, *Jewish Emergence from Powerlessness,* 27–40 and my "Jewish Resistance."

4 See, for example, de Jong, "Anti-Nazi Resistance in the Netherlands," in *European Resistance Movements*, 137–149; and Michel, *Shadow War*, 13.

5 Michel, *Shadow War*, 185. See also Vakar, *Belorussia*, 191, which strongly supports this assessment. It is widely known that the process of Jewish destruction involved several stages: identification, expropriation and removal from gainful employment, isolation, murder. These stages were all accompanied by measures of degradation, selective terror, and murder.

6 On the flat terrain of Holland, see De Jong, *The Netherlands and Nazi Germany*, 31.

7 Jan Karski, personal communication, December 1999. On Allied indifference see Philip Friedman, "Jewish Resistance to Nazism," in Ada Friedman, *Roads to Extinction*, 387–408. Henri Michel, in *Jewish Resistance During the Holocaust*, 372, and in particular in *Shadow War*, 355, emphasizes that the Allies were not interested in the European resistance movements in general. He also shows how handicapped the Jews were compared to other groups (*Shadow War*, 179–180; and *Jewish Resistance During the Holocaust*, 365–375). On the relative powerlessness of the resistance movements, see Michel, *Shadow War*, 356, and De Jong, *The Netherlands and Nazi Germany*, 29: "Resistance appears to be a subject full of romance."

8 Michel, *Shadow War*, 355, 358.

9 See Karski, *Story of a Secret State*, 280–281, and Wood and Jankowski, *Karski*, 99.

10 On the development of the resistance movements see my *Defiance*, 94–107, and Philip Friedman, "The Extermination of the Polish Jews During the German Occupation, 1939–1945," in Ada Friedman, *Roads to Extinction*, 211–243.

11 Karski, *Story of a Secret State*, 281.

12 On how German and Jewish women in Germany were less likely to be arrested and persecuted than men see Kaplan, *Between Dignity and Despair*, 80. Claudia Koonz, in *Mothers in the Fatherland*, shows that in Germany before 1938 no Jewish woman was arrested (335). Court records show that in general of those accused and found guilty during the Third Reich, 20 percent were women (334). Koonz also emphasizes that women had much more freedom to move around than men (327). In an interview (Westport, Connecticut, 1994) Marion Pritchard emphasized that in urban centers, the rescuing of Jews was performed mainly by women who worked as couriers. This was because women were less conspicuous and less likely to be arrested than men.

13 Thea Epstein, personal interview, Tel Aviv, 1995.

14 Claire Sokołowski, personal interview, Paris, 1995.

15 See Tec and Weiss, "Historical Injustice."

16 See Draenger, *Justyna's Narrative*, and Lubetkin, *In the Days of Destruction and Revolt*. Dov Levin notes that there were many more women fighters among Jewish partisan fighters in the forests around Vilna than among non-Jewish partisans (*Fighting Back*, 219).

17 Shulamit Einhorn-Roitman, personal interview, Herzlia, Israel, 1995.

18 Fela Isboutsky-Szmidt, personal interview, Tel Aviv, 1995.

19 Although some of these Soviet soldiers may have been deserters, others were left behind because of special circumstances. The Russians were retreating fast and chaotically, and remnants of the army might have inadvertently been left behind. Yitzhak Arad describes the Red Army's limited means of transportation in *Ghetto in Flames*, 30. See also Smolar, *Minsk Ghetto*, 4-8, 17. Smolar talked to me about how the retreating army seemed to abandon some of the Jews who wanted to leave with it (personal interviews, Tel Aviv, 1989, 1990).

20 It is estimated that in the first six months of the war the Germans took more than 3.5 million Soviet soldiers prisoner. In *Keine Kameraden Die Wehrmacht*, Christian Streit claims that by March 1942, 2 million of these prisoners had been murdered. Streit also notes that about 57 percent of the 5.7 million Soviet POWs perished. See also Earl Ziemke, "Composition and Morale of the Partisan Movement," in Armstrong, *Soviet Partisans in World War II*, which notes that Nazi policies toward Russian POWs consisted of economic exploitation and murder. And economic exploitation was simply an intermediary step to death. Economic exploitation in turn was closely related to political and economic conditions (143). These ideas are supported by Reuben Ainsztein (*Jewish Resistance*, 243), and Martin Gilbert (*Second World War*, 373).

21 Seventy-seven percent of Polish Jewry lived in urban centers. See Lestchinsky, "Economic Aspects of Jewish Community Organization in Independent Poland," and "Industrial and Social Structure of the Jewish Population of Interbellum Poland"; see also Polonsky, *Politics in Independent Poland*, 42. On the hardships suffered by Jewish refugees in the forest, see Ainsztein, *Jewish Resistance*, 307-338; Bauer, *History of the Holocaust*, 271; Bar-Oni, *The Vapor*; Cholawski, *Soldiers from the Ghetto*, 147; Krakowski, *War of the Doomed*, 28; and Levin, *Fighting Back*, 206-207.

22 Ainsztein, *Jewish Resistance*, 279; Vakar, *Belorussia*, 192.

23 During my interviews, several couriers separately praised Marylka Różycka highly for her selfless contributions to the underground. More praise appears in Grossman, *Underground Army*, 270-305, and Bronka Klibanski, Yad Vashem 033/1351.

24 See Grossman, *Underground Army,* 306–317; Ania Rud, personal interview, Tel Aviv, 1995; Mark, *Ruch Oporu w Getcie,* 94; Meed, *On Both Sides of the Wall,* 75–102; Szwajger, *I Remember Nothing More;* and Tec, *When Light Pierced the Darkness,* 40–84. One of the few male Jewish couriers was Simcha Rotem, the author of *Memoirs of a Warsaw Ghetto Fighter.*

25 Eva Kracowski, personal interview.

26 Ania Rud, personal interview, Tel Aviv, 1995.

27 Mina Kizelstein-Dorn, personal interview, Tel Aviv, 1995.

28 Niusia Długi, personal interview, New York, 1997.

29 Ibid.

30 On the train sabotage see Arad, *Ghetto in Flames,* 261; and Document No. 1251, Archives of the Jewish Historical Institute, Warsaw (p. 120), published in Ajzensztajn, *Ruch Podziemny w Gettach i w Obozach.* The partisans are listed in D.1.4650, Moreshet Archives: "Operations Diary of a Jewish Partisan Unit in Rudnicki Forest, 1943–1944," reproduced in Arad, Gutman, and Margaliot, *Documents of the Holocaust,* 463–471. On female couriers in Vilna see Arad, *Ghetto in Flames,* 435. Arad notes that Sonia Madejsker was actively engaged as a courier between Vilna and the surrounding forests. Shortly before the German retreat she was arrested. She attempted suicide and was taken to a hospital, where she died without revealing the names of any of the partisans (*Ghetto in Flames,* 456). Anna Siewner spoke about Madejsker to me with much admiration. Anna was grateful to her for helping her escape from the Vilna ghetto to the Rudnicki Forest (personal interview, Tel Aviv, 1995).

31 *Yehudei Yaar* and Tuvia Bielski, personal interview, Brooklyn, N.Y., 1987; Lazar Malbin, personal interviews, Tel Aviv, 1987, 1988; and *Sefer Hapartisanim Hajehudim,* vol. 1, p. 446. Hersh Smolar sees the arrival of Platon, whose real name was Vasilli Tschernishov, as an important step in the reorganization of the partisan movement (personal interviews, Tel Aviv, 1989, 1990).

32 See Davies, *God's Playground,* vol. 2, pp. 466–472, and Karski, *Great Powers and Poland,* 403–411.

33 See John A. Armstrong and Kurt De Witt, "Organizational Control of the Partisan Movement," in Armstrong, *Soviet Partisans in World War II,* 73–139; Bor-Komorowski, *Secret Army,* 119–120; and Michel, *Shadow War,* 219.

34 See my *In the Lion's Den,* 181.

35 Mina Vołkowiski, personal interviews, Tel Aviv, 1994, 1995. See also Michel, *Shadow War,* 185; Vakar, *Belorussia,* 191. Both these historians agree that the basic motivation for coming to the forest was survival rather than patriotism or the desire to fight the enemy. Even after the Russian-German war turned in favor

of the Soviet Union, it was some time before the Soviet partisans became an effective force. Some believe that up to the end, partisan combat was less extensive than officially claimed: Pinchas Boldo, personal interview, Haifa, 1990. Oswald Rufeisen, a member of the Ponomarenko otriad, believes that the partisan battles and heroism have been highly exaggerated. See my *In the Lion's Den*, 201-202.

36 Eva Kracowski, personal interview.

37 Abraham Viner, personal interview, Haifa, 1989.

38 Tamara Rabinowicz, personal interview, Haifa, 1990. These distinctions were noted by most Bielski partisans. A few examples are Shmuel Geler, Yad Vashem, 1556/112; Raja Kaplinski, personal interviews, Tel Aviv, 1987-1989; and Riva Kantorowicz-Reich, personal interview, Tel Aviv, 1989. Zvi H. Isler, Yad Vashem, 1706/113, in particular, as a physician and thus of the upper classes was very sensitive to these distinctions and tried to participate in activities associated with the working class.

39 Cila Sawicki, personal interview, Tel Aviv, 1989.

40 Shmuel Geler, Yad Vashem, 1556/112. Among those who expressed the view that drinking dulled the pain of forest life are Lilka Bielski, personal interview, Brooklyn, N.Y., 1988; Eva Kracowski, personal interview; Sulia Rubin, personal interview, Saddle River, N.J., 1988.

41 Eva Kracowski, personal interview.

42 Mina Vołkowiski, personal interviews; Mina Kizelstein-Dorn, personal interview.

43 Michael Pertzof, personal interview, Tel Aviv, 1995.

44 Niusia Długi, personal interview.

45 Mina Vołkowiski, personal interviews.

46 In 1943 special teams of well-trained officers were sent from Moscow into the Belorussian forests. These new arrivals introduced strict codes of conduct, prohibiting drinking, card playing, and stealing from civilians. In part these new measures improved the attitudes toward Jews. They also resulted in more protection for the Jews. However, these positive changes left intact many forms of anti-Semitism. And they did not succeed in establishing strict military discipline. See Ainsztein, *Jewish Resistance in Occupied Eastern Europe*, 333-335; Alpert, *Destruction of Słonim Jewry*, 317-323; and Tenenbaum, *Underground*, 393.

47 Determined to increase the number of partisans and to deprive the Germans of manpower, the Soviets devised various unorthodox ways to achieve this goal. See Michel, *Shadow War*, pp. 184-185, and Vakar, *Belorussia*, 193-194. For a discussion of the effects of this open-door policy on the forest Jews, see Arad, *Partisan*, 138; Bauer, *Jewish Emergence from Powerlessness*, 32; Cholawski, *Soldiers*

from the Ghetto, 147; Levin, *Fighting Back,* 183-185; Raja Kaplinski, personal interviews, Tel Aviv, 1987-1989; and Hersh Smolar, personal interviews.

48 Itke Brown, now known as Lidia Abramson, personal interview, Tel Aviv, 1995. I shall refer to her either as Lidia Brown-Abramson or as Lidia Abramson.

49 Mina Kizelstein-Dorn, personal interview.

50 Michael Pertzof, personal interview.

51 Zorach Arluk, personal interview, Tel Aviv, 1988. Although he was recognized as a brave fighter in the Iskra detachment, Zorach was only allowed to keep his wife with him. He had to place his wife's parents in the Bielski otriad, where they survived the war.

52 Mina Vołkowiski, personal interviews. The lack of concern and heartlessness of Commanders Bobkov and Gusev about the fate of Jewish fugitives is emphasized by Leon Berk, in many pages of *Destined to Live.* For a few examples see 141-143. Shmuel Ostrowski, in his "Diary of War and the Holocaust" (unpublished diary in Yiddish), Yad Vashem, 7970, refers to Bobkov as an anti-Semite who was "cruel toward the Jews, killing them at any pretext" (89).

53 Zvi Shefet (Shepetinski), personal interview, Tel Aviv, 1995. Judith Graf, who like Shefet comes from Słonim, also describes the activities of Beutelager pretty much the way Shefet did (Yad Vashem, 2978/220).

54 For examples of the instability and precarious position of these camps, see Arad, "Jewish Family Camps in the Forests: An Original Means of Rescue," in Gutman and Zuroff, *Rescue Attempts During the Holocaust,* 333-353. Lea Garber Kowenska, a member of a small family group in the Lipiczańska Forest, movingly describes the great suffering and mutual caring that touched the lives of that group ("Dos vos hot sich fargidenkt oyf aibik"). In an unpublished Yiddish memoir made available to me by her daughter, Kowenska further describes her life in the forest. In her group of fifteen people there were seven children. Some were orphans whom she and others had picked up on the way to the forest. See also Merin and Porter, "Three Jewish Family Camps in the Forests of Vołyń," and Tenenbaum, *Underground,* 404.

55 This discussion of the Bielski partisan detachment is drawn from my book *Defiance.* Initially, Tuvia Bielski and his group named themselves the Zukov otriad. Later, when the partisans in this area became better organized, they renamed themselves the Kalinin otriad. But in fact, they were never referred to by either of these names but called always the Bielski otriad.

56 See Amarant, *Nevo Shel Adam.* This hierarchy was described by practically everyone I spoke to. A few examples are Tamara Rabinowicz, Pinchas Boldo, and Baruch Kopold, all personal interviews, Haifa, 1990, and Chaja Bielski, personal interviews, Haifa, 1987-1990.

57 Cila Sawicki, personal interview.
58 Hana Stołowicki, Yad Vashem, 3439/191.
59 Luba Garfunk, personal interview, Tel Aviv, 1989. Baran was a legendary figure: fearless, brave, not very intelligent. Pesia Bairach talked about him in the same way Luba did (personal interview, Tel Aviv, 1990). See also *Sefer Hapartisanim Hajehudim,* 402.
60 Riva Kaganowicz-Bernstein, personal interview, New York, 1988; Cila Sawicki, personal interview; Rosalia Gierszonowski-Wodakow, personal interview, New York, 1989.
61 Tamara Rabinowicz, personal interview. Dr. Amarant did write a history of the Bielski group, but it was confiscated by the Russians when he and his wife were traveling through Romania to Israel. In Israel Dr. Amarant wrote another history from memory.
62 Riva Kantorowicz-Reich, personal interview, Tel Aviv, 1988.
63 Abraham Viner, personal interview.
64 The Zorin group, headed by Sholem Zorin, a construction worker and former Red Army sergeant, consisted mainly of Jewish fugitives from Minsk. Soviet partisans helped establish it and named it unit 106. But like the Bielski otriad, the Zorin otriad was always called by the name of its leader. The history of this unit is described in Hersh Smolar's *Minsk Ghetto,* 106–108.
65 Jack N. Porter notes that the literature about the partisan movement does not admit that women were treated in a sexist fashion. See his "Jewish Women in the Resistance," in Kowalski, *Anthology of Armed Resistance to the Nazis,* vol. 1, p. 292. See also Earl Ziemke, "Composition and Morale of the Partisan Movement," in Armstrong, *Soviet Partisans in World War II,* 147.
66 See my *In The Lion's Den,* 195.
67 See Ziemke, "Composition and Morale of the Partisan Movement," 147–148.
68 Hersh Smolar (personal interviews) told me about the term "transit wife." On the women who were executed, see Berk, *Destined to Live,* 173–177.
69 This point was made by Chaja Bielski (personal interviews, Haifa, 1987–1990), Raja Kaplinski (personal interviews), and Lili Krawitz (personal interview, Tel Aviv, 1989). On Jewish women in the forest see *Sefer Hapartisanim Hajehudim,* vol. 1, p. 442, and Solomian-Loc, *Woman Facing the Gallows,* the personal account of a Jewish partisan and the discrimination she had to face as a woman in a Soviet otriad.
70 The officer is quoted in Berk, *Destined to Live,* 173. Hersh Smolar mentioned the usage of *whore* for *woman* (personal interviews). It is interesting that some women used these expressions as well: see my *Defiance,* 136.

71 Eva Kracowski, personal interview.

72 Zvi Shefet (Shepetinski), personal interview.

73 Michael Pertzof, personal interview. Among the respondents who agreed are Baruch Kopold (personal interview, Haifa, 1989), Abraham Viner (personal interview), and Moshe Bairach (personal interviews, Tel Aviv, 1987–1989).

74 Ephraim Blaichman, personal interview, New York, 1996. The name Franek was given to him in the forest.

75 Among male Jewish partisans who agree with this observation are Moshe Bairach, Baruch Kopold, Hersh Smolar, Abraham Viner.

76 Particularly for the last year of the war an estimated 10 to 20 percent of the Soviet partisan movement consisted of former German collaborators. See Ziemke, "Composition and Morale of the Partisan Movement," 147. Several Jewish partisans reported increased anti-Semitism in the Soviet otriads in the last years of the war. Among them are Zorach Arluk (personal interview), Jashke Mazowi (personal interview, Tel Aviv, 1989), Mordechai Ginsburg (Yad Vashem, 3682/270), and Itzyk Mendelson (Yad Vashem, 3355/186).

77 Despite the shortages of doctors, some of the Jewish doctors still experienced discrimination in the partisan units. Dr. Berk, for example, was refused entry into a Polish detachment and encountered overt anti-Semitism in the Soviet otriad he joined (Berk, *Destined to Live,* 97, 122). Dr. Michael Temchin, in *The Witch Doctor,* emphasized the advantages that doctors had.

78 Mina Vołkowiski, personal interviews. In *Destined to Live* Dr. Berk describes how he brought Mina to his own otriad.

79 A partisan in the Bielski otriad, this woman asked me not to mention her name in connection with the rape. I interviewed her for about three hours, and only near the end did she mention it.

80 Itke Brown (Lidia Brown-Abramson), personal interview.

81 Lili Krawitz, personal interview, Tel Aviv, 1989. The presence of many old people attests to this policy. No clear-cut figures are available for the number of women. The estimate of 30–40 percent was offered by several partisans (Moshe Bairach, personal interviews, Tel Aviv, 1987–1989; Raja Kaplinski, personal interviews, Tel Aviv, 1987–1989; Lazar Malbin, personal interview, Tel Aviv, 1989).

82 Riva Kantorowicz-Reich emphasizes how important the extra food was (personal interview).

83 Sulia Rubin, personal interviews, Saddle River, N.J., 1988, 1995. I reinterviewed her specifically for this book.

84 This view was expressed by practically everyone. A few examples are Chaja Bielski, personal interviews; Eljezer Engelstern, Yad Vashem, 3249/233; and Shmuel Geler, Yad Vashem, 1556/112.

85 Sulia Rubin, personal interview. In a sense, her mother was right: Sulia remained married to the man for close to fifty years.

86 Sulia Rubin, personal interview, 1995. (This was a second and much later interview.)

87 Pesia Bairach, personal interview, Tel Aviv, 1990.

88 Lili Krawitz, personal interview. Lili described many such marriages that had lasted a lifetime. She was still groping for explanations and answers.

89 Ibid. Lili was particularly adamant when she talked about their sexual escapades. But toward the end of the interview, she acknowledged that nowadays men sleep with their secretaries and other women who are dependent on them.

90 Chaja Bielski, personal interviews; Pesia Bairach, personal interview; Abraham Viner, personal interview.

91 Lilka Bielski, personal interview. Sonia Bielski, the second wife of Tuvia Bielski, was killed during a German raid in January 1943 near Chrapiniewo. Tuvia was particularly affected by the death of his second wife. Some refer to him as "a broken man"; others say that he was in a deep depression because he loved her very much (Tec, *Defiance*, 92, 260).

92 Chaja Bielski, personal interview.

93 Luba Garfunk, personal interview, Tel Aviv, 1989.

94 When Arkie Lubczanski disobeyed an order and was banned from the otriad, his "wife" was not included in this order. In fact, she voluntarily left with him but then returned because no Russian otriad would take her. She was accepted into the Bielski group.

95 Riva Kaganowicz-Bernstein, personal interview; Riva Kantorowicz-Reich. Lili Krawitz and Sulia Rubin were among those who thought unattached women had more respect in the otriad (personal interviews).

96 Chaja Bielski spoke about the necessity for most women to become mistresses (personal interview). But as I noted earlier, doctors, in particular, were in short supply, as were nurses, and they were usually welcomed into Soviet detachments. Zorach Arluk was able to keep his wife with him in the Iskra otriad, but he had to send his wife's parents to the Bielski otriad (personal interview).

97 Moshe Bairach and Hersh Smolar told me about these rumors in personal interviews. Fanny Solomian-Loc was one of the women who refused to become attached to a Russian partisan and suffered because of it. She describes her experiences in *Woman Facing the Gallows*.

98 Amarant, *Nevo Shel Adam*.

99 See ibid. Shmuel Geler writes that two or three children were born in the forest (Yad Vashem 1556/112).

100 A number of women expressed similar sentiments. Not to betray their trust, I do not include their names.

101 Niusia Długi, personal interview; Anna Siewner, personal interview, Tel Aviv, 1996.

102 Mina Vołkowiski, personal interviews. This was by no means an isolated occurrence. For other cases see Berk, *Destined to Live*, 162–164; Schulman, *A Partisan's Memoir*, 145; and Solomian-Loc, *Woman Facing the Gallows*, 125.

103 Mina Vołkowiski, personal interviews.

104 Eva Kracowski, personal interview.

105 Rachel Bilerman, personal interview, Tel Aviv, 1995. Rachel belongs to the small minority of those I interviewed who disliked Tuvia Bielski. In fact, spontaneously, several times she would make some statement minimizing his accomplishments. This might be due in part to the fact that Zymonowicz, her husband, was a close friend of Israel Kesler, who plotted against Tuvia and was eventually executed by the Bielski otriad. In addition, her respect for armed opposition might have diminished Tuvia's special accomplishments in her eyes; he was more concerned with the rescue of Jews. Rachel and her sister both survived the war.

106 Rina Raviv, personal interview, Tel Aviv, 1995.

107 Baruch Kopold, personal interview, Haifa, 1990.

108 Raja Kaplinski, personal interviews. Pesia Bairach described how she was told that she belonged in the support group (personal interview). Dov Levin, in *Fighting Back*, describes how Soviet partisans took away arms from both men and women partisans, and he quotes one woman as vehemently objecting to being disarmed: "We haven't come here to hide but to fight. We bought our weapons at a high price and we should not be robbed of them. We proved ourselves before we came to the forest" (183–185). Hersh Smolar also mentioned that some women would not let themselves be disarmed. But he admits that this was rare (personal interviews).

109 Moshe Bairach, personal interviews; Shmuel Geler, Yad Vashem 1556/112.

110 Mina Vołkowiski, personal interviews.

111 Hersh Smolar, personal interview.

112 Żenia Minkow, personal interview, Chedera, Israel, 1995.

113 Dr. A. Liebesman-Mikulski survived the war by living illegally on the Aryan side around his native area of Stanislawow. He describes his family's wartime experiences in a Yad Vashem document, 033/1093. After the war Dr. Liebesman-Mikulski collected information from the few remaining, scattered Jews who were a part of the Pantelleria otriad. These partisans were Jozef Lenobel, who at the

time lived as a farmer in Israel near Natania; Dr. Kremizer, a dentist, who was living in South America; Max Hellman, living in West Germany; and Nachman Feuer, living in the United States. Dr. Liebesman-Mikulski also incorporated the results of his investigation into a portion of the Yad Vashem document also listed as 033/1093. My history of the Pantelleria group is based on these documents.

Chapter 8: Conclusion

1 See Hilberg, *Destruction of the European Jews*, 517-518. For a concise summary of the relation between Hungary and the Third Reich, see pp. 508-554.

2 Ringelblum, *Kronika Getta Warszawskiego*, 67. For a detailed discussion of this pattern of working-class partisans taking upper-class mistresses and its implications, see my *Defiance*, 154-169.

3 On how women fit into the stratification system, see Acker, "Women and Social Stratification"; French, *War Against Women;* Gillespie, "Who Has the Power?"; and Gilligan, "Woman's Place in Man's Life Cycle."

4 Daniel Callahan, "Minimalist Ethics: On the Pacification of Morality," Beckwith, *Do the Right Thing*, 53-54.

5 Anderson, *On Mill*, 58.

6 Simmel, *Sociology of Georg Simmel,* 181-189.

7 Woolf, *Three Guineas*, 21, 78-80; Todorov, *Facing the Extreme*, 295. Coming from a very different direction, ideas presented by the scientist Robert Jastrow suggest a broad theoretical similarity to Todorov's and Woolf's views. In *Until the Sun Dies,* Jastrow asks why "the Age of Reptiles [has] given way to the Age of Mammals" (101-105). He concludes that the answer lies in qualities the mammals developed over time which the reptiles lacked: mutual care and cooperation, superior intelligence, and special flexibility and adaptability.

8 One historian, Shmuel Krakowski, estimates that 80 percent of Jews who were in armed Jewish partisan groups perished (*War of the Doomed,* 303). For death rates in other units see Dov Levin, "Baltic Jewry's Armed Resistance to the Nazis," in Kowalski, *Anthology of Armed Resistance to the Nazis,* vol. 3, pp. 42-48. On the family camps see Arad, *Partisan from the Valley of Death to Mount Zion,* 115-134; for additional descriptions of the plight of family camps in different areas, see Merin and Porter, "Three Jewish Family-Camps in the Forests of Volyn, Ukraine, During the Holocaust."

9 These issues are more extensively explored in my *Defiance*, 204-209.

Bibliography

Abramsky, Chimen, Maciej Jachimczyk, and Antony Polonsky, eds. *The Jews in Poland*. New York: Blackwell, 1986.

Acker, Joan. "Women and Social Stratification: A Case of Intellectual Sexism." *American Journal of Sociology* 78 (January 1973): 936–945.

Adelson, Alan, and Robert Lapides, eds. *Łódź Ghetto: Inside a Community Under Siege*. New York: Viking, 1989.

Adler, H. G. *Theresienstadt, 1941–1945*. Tübingen: Mohr, 1960.

Adler, Jacques. *The Jews of Paris and the Final Solution: Communal Response and Internal Conflicts, 1940–1944*. New York: Oxford University Press, 1987.

Adler, Stanisław. *In the Warsaw Ghetto, 1940–1943: An Account of a Witness*. Jerusalem: Yad Vashem, 1982.

Ainsztein, Reuben. "The Bandera-Oberlander Case." *Midstream* 6, no. 2 (Spring 1960): 17–25.

———. *Jewish Resistance in Nazi-Occupied Eastern Europe*. New York: Barnes and Noble, 1974.

———. "The Jews of Poland Need Not Have Died." *Midstream* 4, no. 4 (Autumn 1958): 2–4, 101–103.

———. *The Warsaw Ghetto Revolt*. New York: Holocaust Library, 1979.

Ajzensztajn, Betti, ed. *RUCH PODZIEMNY W GETTACH I W OBOZACH* [The underground in ghettos and camps]. Warszawa: Centralna Żydowska Komisja Historyczna w Polsce, 1946.

Akavia, Miriam. *An End to Childhood*. Ilford, Essex: Vallentine Mitchell, 1995.

Alpert, Nachum. *The Destruction of Słonim Jewry: The Story of the Jews of Słonim During the Holocaust*. New York: Holocaust Library, 1989.

Amarant, Shmuel. *Nevo Shel Adam* [The oasis of man]. Tel Aviv: Published privately with the help of Misrad Hahinuch V Tarbut, 1973.

Améry, Jean. *At the Mind's Limits: Contemplations by a Survivor on Auschwitz and Its Realities*. Trans. Sidney Rosenfeld and Stella P. Rosenfeld. Bloomington: Indiana University Press, 1980.

Anderson, M. L., and P. H. Collins, eds. *Race, Class and Gender: An Anthology*. Belmont, Calif.: Wadsworth, 1992.

Anderson, Susan Leigh. *On Mill*. Belmont, Calif.: Wadsworth, 2000.

Anissimov, Myriam. *Primo Levi*. Woodstock, N.Y.: Overlook, 1999.

Apenszlak, Jacob. *The Black Book of Polish Jewry*. New York: American Federation of Polish Jews, 1943.

Arad, Yizhak. *Bełżec, Sobibór, Treblinka: The Operation Reinhard Camps*. Bloomington: Indiana University Press, 1987.

———. *Ghetto in Flames: The Struggle and Destruction of the Jews in Vilna in the Holocaust*. New York: Holocaust Library, 1982.

———. *The Partisan: From the Valley of Death to Mount Zion*. New York: Holocaust Library, 1979.

Arad, Yitzhak, Israel Gutman, and Abraham Margalit, eds. *Documents on the Holocaust: Selected Sources on the Destruction of the Jewry of Germany and Austria, Poland and the Soviet Union*. Jerusalem: Yad Vashem, 1981.

Arad, Yitzhak, Shmuel Krakowski, and Shmuel Spector, eds. *The Einsatzgruppen Reports: Selections from the Dispatches of the Nazi Death Squads' Campaign Against the Jews, July 1941 – January 1943*. New York: Holocaust Library, 1989.

Arditti, Leon. *The Will to Live*. New York: Shengold, 1996.

Arendt, Hannah, *Eichmann in Jerusalem: Reflections on the Banality of Evil*. New York: Viking, 1963.

Arieti, Silvano. *The Parnas*. New York: Basic Books, 1979.

Armstrong, John A., ed., *Soviet Partisans in World War II*. Madison: University of Wisconsin Press, 1964.

Aschkenasy, Nehama. *Eve's Journey*. Philadelphia: University of Pennsylvania Press, 1986.

Ash, Timothy Garton. *The Uses of Adversity*. New York: Random House, 1989.

Aubrac, Lucie. *Outwitting the Gestapo*. Lincoln: University of Nebraska Press, 1993.

Bakke, E. Wight. *The Unemployed Worker: A Study of the Task of Making a Living Without a Job*. New Haven: Yale University Press, 1940.

Baolhwar, Neera Kapur. "Altruism Versus Self-Interest: Sometimes a False Dichotomy." *Social Philosophy and Policy* 10, no. 1 (1993): 90–117.

Barkai, Meyer, ed. *The Fighting Ghettos*. New York: Lippincott, 1962.

Bar-Oni, Bryna. *The Vapor*. Chicago: Visual Impact, 1976.

Bart, Pauline B., and Eileen Geil Moran, eds. *Violence Against Women: The Bloody Footprints*. Newbury Park, Calif.: Sage, 1993.

Bartoszewski, Władysław. "EGZEKUCJE PUBLICZNE W WARSZAWIE W LATACH, 1943–1945" [Public executions in Warsaw, 1943–1945]. *BIULETYN GŁÓWNEJ KOMISJI BADANIA ZBRODNI NIEMIECKICH W POLSCE* 6 (1946): 211–224.

———. *1859 DNI WARSZAWY* [Warsaw's 1859 days]. Kraków: Wydawnictwo Znak, 1974.

———. *STRACENI NA ULICACH MIASTA* [Lost on the streets of the city]. Warszawa: Książka I Wiedza, 1970.

Bartov, Omer. *Hitler's Army: Soldiers, Nazis, and War in the Third Reich*. New York: Oxford University Press, 1991.

Bauer, Yehuda. *A History of the Holocaust*. New York: Franklin Watts, 1982.

———. *The Holocaust in Historical Perspective*. Seattle: University of Washington Press, 1978.

———. *The Jewish Emergence from Powerlessness*. Toronto: University of Toronto Press, 1979.

———. *Jews for Sale?* New Haven: Yale University Press, 1994.

———. *Rethinking the Holocaust*. New Haven: Yale University Press, 2001.

Bauman, Janina. *Winter in the Morning: A Young Girl's Life in the Warsaw Ghetto and Beyond, 1939–1945*. New York: Free Press, 1986.

Bauman, Zygmunt. *Modernity and the Holocaust*. Ithaca: Cornell University Press, 1989.

Baumel, Judith Tydor. *Double Jeopardy: Gender and the Holocaust*. London: Vallentine Mitchell, 1998.

———. "Social Interaction Among Jewish Women in Crisis During the Holocaust: A Case Study." *Gender and History* 17, no. 1 (April 1995): 64–84.

Bauminger, Arieh L. *The Fighters of the Cracow Ghetto*. Jerusalem: Keter, 1986.

Bauminger, Roża. *PRZY PIKRYNIE I TROTYLU: OBÓZ PRACY PRZYMUSOWEJ W SKARŻYSKU KAMIENNEJ* [The forced-labor camp Skarżysko-Kamienna]. Kraków: Centralny Komitet Żydow Polskich, 1946.

Baxter, Janeen, and Emily W. Kane. "Dependence and Independence: A Cross-National Analysis of Gender Inequalities and Gender Attitudes." *Gender and Society* 9, no. 2 (April 1995): 193–215.

Beauvoir, Simone de. *The Second Sex*. New York: Vintage, 1989.

Beckwith, Francis, ed. *Do the Right Thing: A Philosophical Dialogue on the Moral Issues of Our Time.* Boston: Jones and Bartlett, 1996.

Benisch, Pearl. *To Vanquish the Dragon.* Jerusalem: Feldheim, 1991.

Berenstein, Tatiana, et al., eds. *EXTERMINACJA ŻYDÓW NA ZIEMIACH POLSKICH W OKRESIE OKUPACJI HITLEROWSKIEJ* [Jewish extermination on Polish soil during the Hitlerite occupation]. Warszawa: Żydowski Instytut Historyczny, 1957).

Berg, Mary. *Warsaw Ghetto.* New York: Fischer, 1945.

Berger, Zdena. *Tell Me Another Morning: A Novel.* New York: Harper, 1961.

Berk, Leon. *Destined to Live.* Melbourne: Paragon, 1992.

Berkowitz, Sarah Bick. *Where Are My Brothers? From the Ghetto to the Gas Chamber.* New York: Helios, 1965.

Bierman, John. *Righteous Gentile: The Story of Raoul Wallenberg, Missing Hero of the Holocaust.* New York: Viking, 1981.

Birenbaum, Halina. *Hope Is the Last to Die.* Armonk, N.Y.: Sharpe, 1996.

Bluel, Hans Peter. *Sex and Society in Nazi Germany.* New York: Lippincott, 1973.

Bolles, Edmund B. *Remembering and Forgetting: An Inquiry into the Nature of Memory.* New York: Walker, 1988.

Booth, Alan. "Sex and Social Participation." *American Sociological Review* 37 (April 1972): 183–193.

Bor-Komorowski, Tadeusz. *The Secret Army.* London: Gollancz, 1951.

Borowski, Tadeusz. *This Way for the Gas, Ladies and Gentlemen.* New York: Penguin, 1976.

Bower, G. H., and S. G. Gilligan. "Remembering Information Related to Oneself." *Journal of Research and Personality* 13 (1979): 420–432.

Bożykowski, Tuvia. *Between Falling Walls.* Ghetto Fighters' House, Israel: Ghetto Fighters' House, 1972.

Brand, Sandra. *Between Two Worlds.* New York: Shengold, 1982.

———. *I Dared to Live.* New York: Shengold, 1978.

———. *Roma.* New York: Shengold, 1992.

Brenner, Rachel Feldhay. *Four Women Confronting the Holocaust.* University Park: Pennsylvania State University Press, 1997.

Bridenthal, Renate, Anita Grossman, and Marion Kaplan, eds. *When Biology Became Destiny.* New York: Monthly Review Press, 1984.

Bridenthal, Renate, and Claudia Koonz, eds. *Becoming Visible: Women in European History.* Boston: Houghton Mifflin, 1977.

Browning, Christopher R. *Nazi Policy, Jewish Workers, German Killers.* New York: Cambridge University Press, 2000.

——. *Ordinary Men*. New York: Harper, 1992.

——. *The Path to Genocide*. New York: Cambridge University Press, 1995.

Brownmiller, Susan. *Against Our Will: Men, Women and Rape*. New York: Simon and Schuster, 1975.

Buber-Neuman, Margarete. *Milena*. New York: Schocken, 1989.

Buchler, Yehoshua. "First in the Vale of Afflictions: Slovakian Jewish Women in Auschwitz, 1942." *Holocaust and Genocide Studies* 10, no. 3 (Winter 1996): 299–325.

Cantor, Aviva. *Jewish Women, Jewish Men: The Legacy of Patriarchy in Jewish Life*. San Francisco: HarperSanFrancisco, 1995.

Cargas, Harry James, ed. *When God and Man Failed: Non-Jewish Views of the Holocaust*. New York: Macmillan, 1981.

Cavan, Ruth Shone, and Katherine Howland Ranck. *The Family and the Depression*. Chicago: University of Chicago Press, 1938.

Chevrillon, Claire. *Code Name Christiane Clouet*. College Station: Texas A&M University Press, 1995.

Cholawski, Shalom. *Soldiers from the Ghetto*. New York: Herzl, 1980.

CHOROBA GŁODOWA [Starvation illness]. Warsaw: American Joint Distribution Committee, 1946.

Cochran, Jacqueline, and Maryann Bucknum Brinley. *Jackie Cochran: An Autobiography*. New York: Bantam, 1987.

Cohen, Elie A. *Human Behavior in the Concentration Camp*. London: Johnathan Cape, 1954.

Conway, Jill Ker, ed. *Written by Herself: Autobiographies of American Women, An Anthology*. New York: Vintage, 1992.

Czech, Danuta. *Auschwitz Chronicle, 1939–1945*. New York: Henry Holt, 1989.

Dallin, Anthony. *German Rule in Russia, 1941–1945: A Study of Occupation Policies*. New York: Octagon, 1980.

Datner, Szymon. *LAS SPRAWIEDLIWYCH* [The forest of the righteous]. Warszawa: Książka I Wiedza, 1968.

——. *WALKA I ZAGŁADA BIAŁOSTOCKIEGO GETTA* [The struggle and destruction of the Białystok ghetto]. Łódź: Czytelnik, 1946.

David, Janina. *A Square of Sky/A Touch of Earth: A Wartime Childhood in Poland*. New York: Penguin, 1981.

David, Kati. *A Child's War: World War II Through the Eyes of Children*. New York: Four Walls, Eight Windows, 1989.

Davies, Norman. *God's Playground: A History of Poland*. 2 vols. New York: Columbia University Press, 1982.

Dawidowicz, Lucy. *The War Against the Jews, 1933–1945*. New York: Holt, Rinehart and Winston, 1975.

Dawidowicz, Lucy, ed. *A Holocaust Reader*. New York: Behrman House, 1976.

De Jong, Louis. *The Netherlands and Nazi Germany*. Cambridge: Harvard University Press, 1990.

Delbo, Charlotte. *None of Us Will Return*. New York: Grove, 1968.

Des Pres, Terrence. *The Survivor: An Anatomy of Life in the Death Camps*. New York: Oxford University Press, 1976.

Distel, Barbara, ed. *Frauen im Holocaust*. Gerlingen, Germany: Bleicher Verlag, 2001.

Dobroszycki, Lucjan, ed. *The Chronicle of the Łódź Ghetto: 1941–1944*. New Haven: Yale University Press, 1984.

Dobroszycki, Lucjan, and Jeffrey S. Gurock, eds. *The Holocaust in the Soviet Union: Studies and Sources on the Destruction of the Jews in the Nazi-Occupied Territories of the USSR, 1941–1945*. Armonk, N.Y.: Sharpe, 1993.

DOCUMENTY ZBRODNI I MĘCZEŃSTWA [Documents of crimes and torture]. Kraków: Żydowska Komisja Historyczna w Krakowie, 1945.

Donat, Alexander, *The Holocaust Kingdom: A Memoir*. New York: Holt, Rinehart and Winston, 1965.

Donat, Alexander, ed. *The Death Camp Treblinka: A Documentary*. New York: Holocaust Library, 1979.

Draenger, Gusta Davidson. *Justyna's Narrative*. Ed. Eli Pfefferkorn and David H. Hirsch. Trans. Roslyn Hirsch and David H. Hirsch. Amherst: University of Massachusetts Press, 1996.

———. *PAMIĘTNIK JUSTYNY* [Justyna's Diary]. Kraków: Wojewódzka Żydowska Komisja Historyczna, 1946.

Dribben, Judith Strick. *A Girl Called Judith Strick*. New York: Cowles, 1970.

Druks, Herbert. *The Failure to Rescue*. New York: Speller, 1977.

———. *Jewish Resistance During the Holocaust*. New York: Irvington, 1983.

Dunin-Wąsowicz, Krzysztof. *Resistance in the Nazi Concentration Camps, 1933–1945*. Warsaw: Polish Scientific Publishers, 1982.

Durkheim, Emile. *The Rules of Sociological Method*. Glencoe, Ill.: Free Press, 1950.

Dwork, Debórah. *Children with a Star*. New Haven: Yale University Press, 1991.

Dwork, Debórah, and Robert Jan van Pelt. *Auschwitz: 1270 to the Present*. New York: Norton, 1996.

Eckardt, Alice L., ed. *Burning Memory: Times of Testing and Recokoning*. New York: Pergamon, 1993.

Eckman, Lester, and Chaim Lazar. *The Jewish Resistance: The History of the Jewish*

Partisans in Lithuania and White Russia During the Nazi Occupation, 1940–1945. New York: Shengold, 1977.

Edelman, Alina Margolis. *ALA Z ELEMENTARZA* [Ala's childhood]. London: ANEKS, 1994.

Ehrenburg, Ilya, and Vasily Grossman, eds. *The Black Book: The Ruthless Murder of Jews by German-Fascist Invaders Throughout the Temporarily Occupied Regions of the Soviet Union and in the Death Camps of Poland During the War of 1941–1945.* New York: Schocken, 1981.

Eibeshitz, Jehoshua, and Anna Eilenberg-Eibeshitz, eds. *Women in the Holocaust: A Collection of Testimonies.* Vol. 1. New York: Remember, 1991.

Eisenberg, Azriel, ed. *Witness to the Holocaust.* New York: Pilgrim, 1981.

Elias, Ruth. *Triumph of Hope.* New York: Wiley, 1998.

Elkins, Michael. *Forged in Fury.* New York: Ballantine, 1971.

Engel, David. *In The Shadow of Auschwitz: The Polish Government in Exile and The Jews, 1939–1942.* Chapel Hill: University of North Carolina Press, 1987.

Engelking, Barbara. *NA ŁĄCE POPIOŁÓW: OCALENI Z HOLOCAUSTU* [On the field of ashes: Saved from the Holocaust]. Warsaw: Wydawnictwo Cyklady, 1993.

Engelking, Barbara, and Jacek Leociak. *GETTO WARSZAWSKIE* [Warsaw ghetto]. Warszawa: Wydawnictwo, IFISPAN, 2001.

Epstein, Cynthia Fuchs. *Deceptive Distinctions: Sex, Gender, and the Social Order.* New Haven: Yale University Press, 1988.

Erlichman-Bank, Sujka. *LISTY Z PIEKŁA* [Letters from Hell]. Białystok: Krajowa Agencja Wydawnicza, 1992.

European Resistance Movements, 1939–1945. International Conference on the History of the Resistance Movements. New York: Pergamon, 1960.

Fackenheim, Emil L. *From Bergen-Belsen to Jerusalem: Contemporary Implications of the Holocaust.* Jerusalem: Hebrew University of Jerusalem, 1975.

———. "The Spectrum of Resistance During the Holocaust: An Essay in Description and Definition." *Modern Judaism* 2 (1982): 113–130.

Fein, Helen. *Accounting for Genocide: Victims — and Survivors — of the Holocaust.* New York: Free Press, 1979.

Felstiner, Mary Lowenthal. *To Paint Her Life: Charlotte Salomon in the Nazi Era.* New York: HarperCollins, 1994.

Fenelon, Fania. *Playing for Time.* New York: Berkeley, 1983.

Ferderber-Salz, Berta. *And the Sun Kept Shining.* New York: Holocaust Library, 1980.

Ferencz, Benjamin B. *Less Than Slaves: Jewish Forced Labor and the Quest for Compensation.* Cambridge: Harvard University Press, 1979.

Figes, Eva. *Patriarchal Attitudes*. New York: Stein and Day, 1970.

Fink, Ida. *The Journey*. New York: Farrar, Straus and Giroux, 1992.

———. *A Scrap of Time and Other Stories*. New York: Schocken, 1987.

Flinker, Moshe. *Young Moshe's Diary: The Spiritual Torment of a Jewish Boy in Nazi Europe*. Jerusalem: Yad Vashem, 1965.

Fogelman, Eva. *Conscience and Courage*. New York: Doubleday Anchor, 1994.

Frank, Anne. *The Diary of a Young Girl: The Definitive Edition*. New York: Doubleday, 1995.

Frankl, Viktor. *Man's Search for Meaning*. New York: Simon and Schuster, 1962.

Fraser, Kennedy. *Ornament and Silence*. New York: Knopf, 1996.

French, Marilyn. *The War Against Women*. New York: Ballantine, 1992.

Friedl, Ernestine. *Women and Men: An Anthropologist's View*. New York: Holt, Rinehart and Winston, 1975.

Friedländer, Saul. *When Memory Comes*. New York: Farrar, Straus and Giroux, 1979.

Friedman, Filip. "ZAGŁADA ŻYDÓW POLSKICH W LATACH 1930–1945." *BIULETYN GŁÓNEJ KOMISJI BADANIA ZBRODNI NIEMIECKICH W POLSCE* 6 (1946): 165–208.

Friedman, Philip. *Roads To Extinction: Essays on the Holocaust*. Ed. Ada J. Friedman. Philadelphia: Jewish Publication Society of America, 1980.

———. *Their Brothers' Keepers*. New York: Crown, 1957.

Fromm, Erich. *Love, Sexuality, and Matriarchy: About Gender*. New York: Fromm International, 1997.

Fussell, Paul. *Wartime: Understanding and Behavior in the Second World War*. New York: Oxford University Press, 1989.

Geva, Ilana. "The Warsaw Ghetto as a Total Institution." M.A. thesis, Bar Ilan University, 1988.

Gies, Miep. *Anne Frank Remembered: The Story of the Woman Who Helped to Hide the Frank Family*. New York: Simon and Schuster, 1987.

Gilbert, Martin. *Atlas of the Holocaust*. New York: Macmillan, 1982.

———. *The Holocaust: A History of the Jews of Europe During the Second World War*. New York: Holt, Rinehart and Winston, 1985.

———. *The Second World War: A Complete History*. New York: Henry Holt, 1989.

Gillespie, Diar L. "Who Has the Power? The Marital Struggle." *Journal of Marriage and the Family* 33 (August 1971): 445–458.

Gilligan, Carol. *In a Different Voice*. Cambridge: Harvard University Press, 1993.

———. "Woman's Place in Man's Life Cycle." *Harvard Educational Review* 49, no. 4 (November 1979): 31–46.

Glazar, Richard. *Trap with a Green Fence: Survival in Treblinka*. Evanston, Ill.: Northwestern University Press, 1995.

Goffman, Erving. *Asylums: Essays on the Social Situation of Mental Patients and Other Inmates*. New York: Doubleday, 1961.

Goldhagen, Daniel J. *Hitler's Willing Executioners*. New York: Knopf, 1996.

Goldstein, Bernard. *The Stars Bear Witness*. New York, Viking, 1949.

Gollwitzer, Helmut, Käthe Kuhn, and Reinhard Schneider. *Dying We Live: The Final Messages and Records of the Resistance*. New York: Pantheon, 1956.

Gottlieb, Roger S. "The Concept of Resistance: Jewish Resistance During the Holocaust." *Social Theory and Social Practice* 9, no. 1 (Spring 1983): 31–49.

Green, Gerald. *The Artists of Terezin*. New York: Schocken, 1978.

Gross, Nathan. "Aryan Papers in Poland." *Extermination and Resistance, Historical Sources and Material* 1 (1958): 79–86.

———. "Unlucky Clara." *Yad Vashem Bulletin* 15 (1964): 55–60.

Grossman, Chaika. *The Underground Army: Fighters of the Białystok Ghetto*. New York: Holocaust Library, 1987.

Gruber, Samuel. *I Choose Life*. New York: Shengold, 1978.

Grynberg, Henryk. *Childhood of Shadows*. London: Vallentine, Mitchell, 1969.

Gurdas, Luba Krugman. *The Death Train*. New York: National Council on Art in Jewish Life, 1978.

Gurewitsch, Brana, ed. *Mothers, Sisters, Resisters*. Tuscaloosa: University of Alabama Press, 1998.

Gutman, Israel. *Fighters Among the Ruins: The Story of Jewish Heroism During World War II*. Washington, D.C.: B'nai B'rith Books, 1988.

———. *The Jews of Warsaw, 1939–1945: Ghetto, Underground, Revolt*. Bloomington: Indiana University Press, 1982.

———. *Resistance: The Warsaw Ghetto Uprising*. Boston: Houghton Mifflin, 1994.

Gutman, Israel, ed. *Encyclopedia of the Holocaust*. 4 vols. New York: Macmillan, 1990.

Gutman, Yisrael, and Michael Berenbaum, eds. *Anatomy of the Auschwitz Death Camp*. Bloomington: Indiana University Press, 1994.

Gutman, Yisrael, and Cynthia J. Haft, eds. *Patterns of Jewish Leadership in Nazi Europe, 1933–1945: Proceedings of the Third Yad Vashem International Historical Conference, Jerusalem, April 4–7, 1977*. Jerusalem: Yad Vashem, 1979.

Gutman, Yisrael, and Shmuel Krakowski. *Unequal Victims: Poles and Jews During World War II*. New York: Holocaust Library, 1986.

Gutman, Yisrael, and Livia Rothkirchen, eds. *The Catastrophe of European Jewry*. Jerusalem: Yad Vashem, 1976.

Gutman, Yisrael, and Avital Saf, eds. *The Nazi Concentration Camps: Structure and Aims, the Image of the Prisoner, The Jews in the Camps; Proceedings of the Fourth Yad Vashem International Historical Conference, Jerusalem, January 1980.* Jerusalem: Yad Vashem, 1984.

Gutman, Yisrael, and Efraim Zuroff, eds. *Rescue Attempts During the Holocaust: Proceedings of the Second Yad Vashem International Historical Conference, Jerusalem, April 8-11, 1974.* Jerusalem: Yad Vashem, 1977.

Hallie, Philip P. *Lest Innocent Blood Be Shed: The Story of the Village of Le Chambon and How Goodness Happened There.* New York: Harper and Row, 1979.

Halter, Marek. *La Mémoire inquiete, il y a cinquante ans: Le Ghetto de Varsovie.* Paris: Editions Robert Laffont, 1993.

Hart, Kitty. *I Am Alive.* London: Abelard Schuman, 1961.

Heilbrun, Carolyn G. *Writing a Woman's Life.* New York: Norton, 1988.

Heinemann, Marlene E. *Gender and Destiny: Women Writers and the Holocaust.* Westport, Conn.: Greenwood, 1986.

Heller, Celia S. *On the Edge of Destruction.* Detroit: Wayne State University Press, 1994.

Heller, Fanya Gottesfeld. *Strange and Unexpected Love: A Teenage Girl's Holocaust Memoirs.* Hoboken, N.J.: KTAV, 1993.

Henry, Frances. *Victims and Neighbors: A Small Town in North Germany Remembered.* South Hadley, Mass.: Bergin and Gravey, 1984.

Herbert, Ulrich. *Nationalsozialistische Vernichtungspolitik, 1939-1945.* Frankfurt: Fischer Verlag, 1998.

Herman, Judith Lewis. *Trauma and Recovery.* New York: Basic, 1992.

Herzog, Elizabeth. *Life Is with People.* New York: International Universities Press, 1952.

Heschel, Susannah, ed. *On Being a Jewish Woman: A Reader.* New York: Schocken, 1983.

Heyes, Peter, ed. *Lessons and Legacies, The Meaning of the Holocaust in a Changing World.* Evanston, Ill.: Northwestern University Press, 1991.

Heyman, Eva. *The Diary of Eva Heyman.* Jerusalem: Yad Vashem, 1974.

Hilberg, Raul. *The Destruction of the European Jews.* New York: New Viewpoints, 1973.

———. *Perpetrators Victims Bystanders: The Jewish Catastrophe, 1933-1945.* New York: Harper-Collins, 1992.

———. *The Politics of Memory: The Journey of a Holocaust Historian.* Chicago: Ivan R. Dee, 1996.

Hilberg, Raul, Stanisław Staron, and Josef Kermisz, eds. *The Warsaw Diary of Adam Czerniakow: Prelude to Doom.* New York: Stein and Day, 1982.

Hillesum, Etty. *An Interrupted Life*. New York: Pantheon, 1983.

Hirszfeld, Ludwik. *HISTORIA JEDNEGO ŻYCIA* [A life history]. Warsaw: Pax, 1957.

Hoffman, Alice G. "Reliability and Validity in Oral History." *Today's Speech* 22 (Winter 1974): 23–27.

Iranek-Osmecki, Kazimierz. *He Who Saves One Life*. New York: Crown, 1971.

Jackson, Livia E. Bitton. *Elli: Coming of Age in the Holocaust*. New York: Times Books, 1980.

Jaffe, A. J., and Herbert F. Spirer. *Misused Statistics: Straight Talk or Twisted Numbers*. New York: Dekker, 1987.

Jaggar, Alison J., and Paula S. Rothenberg, eds. *Feminist Frameworks: Alternative Theoretical Accounts of the Relations Between Women and Men*. New York: McGraw-Hill, 1993.

Jastrow, Robert. *Until the Sun Dies*. New York: Norton, 1977.

Johnson, Allan G. *The Gender Knot*. Philadelphia: Temple University Press, 1997.

Johnson, Eric A. *Nazi Terror: The Gestapo, Jews and Ordinary Germans*. New York: Basic, 1999.

Kaplan, Alice. *The Collaborator*. Chicago: University of Chicago Press, 2000.

Kaplan, Chaim A. *Scroll of Agony: The Warsaw Diary of Chaim A. Kaplan*. Trans. and ed. Abraham I. Katsh. New York: Collier, 1973.

Kaplan, Marion A. *Between Dignity and Despair*. New York: Oxford University Press, 1998.

———. *The Jewish Feminist Movement in Germany*. Westport, Conn.: Greenwood, 1979.

Karas, Joža. *Music in Terezin, 1941–1945*. New York: Beaufort, 1985.

Karay, Felicja. *Death Comes in Yellow: Skarżysko-Kamienna Slave Labor Camp*. Amsterdam: Harwood, 1996.

Karski, Jan. *The Great Powers and Poland, 1919–1945: From Versailles to Yalta*. New York: University Press of America, 1985.

———. *Story of a Secret State*. Boston: Houghton Mifflin, 1944.

Katz, Esther, and Joan Miriam Ringelheim, eds. *Proceedings of the Conference on Women Surviving the Holocaust*. New York: Institute for Research in History, 1983.

Kautsky, Benedict. *Teufel und Verdamte*. Vienna: Verlag Der Wiener Volksbuchhandlung, 1948.

Kazik. *See* Rotem, Simha.

Kermish, Joseph, ed. *To Live with Honor and Die with Honor: Selected Documents from the Warsaw Ghetto Underground Archives "O.S."* Jerusalem: Yad Vashem, 1986.

Kiedrzyńska, Wanda. *Ravensbrück*. Warszawa: Książka i Wiedza, 1965.

Kiełar, Wiesław. *Anus Mundi*. New York: Times Books, 1972.

Kizelstein, Shamay. "Paths of Fate: Auschwitz-Birkenau No. B-1968." Yad Vashem.

Klein, Gerda Weissman. *All But My Life*. New York: Farrar, Straus and Giroux, 1992.

Klibanski, Bronka. "In the Ghetto and in the Resistance." Paper delivered at the International Workshop on Women in the Holocaust at Hebrew University of Jerusalem, June 1995.

Klukowski, Zygmunt. *DZIENNIK Z LAT OKUPACJI ZAMOJSZCZYZNY. 1939 – 1944* [Zamość: Diary during the occupation, 1939 – 1944]. Lublin: Lubelska Spółdzielnia Wydawnicza, 1958.

Kogon, Eugen. *The Theory and Practice of Hell*. New York: Berkeley, 1980.

Kohn, Moshe M., ed. *Jewish Resistance During the Holocaust: Proceedings of the Conference on Manifestations of Jewish Resistance, 1968*. Jerusalem: Yad Vashem, 1971.

Kohn, Nahum, and Howard Roiter. *A Voice from the Forest*. New York: Holocaust Library, 1980.

Komarovsky, Mira. *The Unemployed Man and His Family*. New York: Dryden, 1940.

Koonz, Claudia. *Mothers in the Fatherland: Women, the Family and Nazi Politics*. New York: St. Martin's, 1987.

Korboński, Stefan. *The Polish Underground State: A Guide to the Underground*. Boulder, Colo.: East European Quarterly, 1978.

Korczak, Janusz. *Ghetto Diary*. New York: Holocaust Library, 1978.

Kossoudji, Sherrie A., and Laura J. Dresser. "Working Class Rosies: Women Industrial Workers During World War II." *Journal of Economic History* 52, no. 2 (June 1992): 431–446.

Kowalski, Isaac, ed. *Anthology of Armed Resistance to the Nazis, 1939 – 1945. 3* vols. New York: Jewish Combatants Publishing House, 1986.

Koweńska, Lea Garber. "Dos vos hot sich fargidenkt oyf aibik" [What is remembered forever]. *Żurnol fun Sovietisher Heimland* [Journal of the Soviet Homeland] 4 (1971): 92–102.

Krakowski, Shmuel. *The War of the Doomed: Jewish Resistance in Poland, 1942 – 1944*. New York: Holmes and Meier, 1985.

Krall, Hanna. *Shielding the Flame*. New York: Henry Holt, 1986.

Kraus, Otto, and Erich Kulka. *The Death Factory: Documents on Auschwitz*. New York: Pergamon, 1966.

Kremer, S. Lillian. *Women's Holocaust Writing: Memory and Imagination*. Lincoln: University of Nebraska Press, 1999.

Kubar, Zofia S. *Double Identity: A Memoir*. New York: Hill and Wang, 1989.

Küchler-Silberman, Lena. *One Hundred Children*. New York: Doubleday, 1961.

Kuper, Jack. *Child of the Holocaust.* New York: Doubleday, 1968.

Laguardia, Gemma Glück. *My Story.* New York: David McKay, 1961.

Landau, Ludwik. *KRONIKA LAT WOJNY I OKUPACJI* [The chronicle of the war and occupation]. 3 vols. Warszawa: Państwowe Wydawnictwo Naukowe, 1962.

Langbein, Hermann. *Against All Hope: Resistance in Nazi Concentration Camps, 1938–1945.* New York: Paragon House, 1994.

———. *Die Stäkeren: Ein Bericht aus Auschwitz und Anderen Konzentrantionslagern.* Köln: Bund Verlag, 1982.

Langer, Lawrence L. *Holocaust Testimonies: The Ruins of Memory.* New Haven: Yale University Press, 1991.

———. *Preempting the Holocaust.* New Haven: Yale University Press, 1998.

Langer, Lawrence L., ed. *Art from the Ashes: A Holocaust Anthology.* New York: Oxford University Press, 1995.

Laqueur, Walter, ed. *The Holocaust Encyclopedia.* New Haven: Yale University Press, 2001.

Laska, Vera. *Women in the Resistance and in the Holocaust: The Voices of the Eyewitnesses.* Westport, Conn.: Greenwood, 1983.

Latour, Amy. *The Jewish Resistance in France, 1940–1944.* New York: Holocaust Library, 1981.

Lengerman, Patricia M., and Ruth A. Wallace. *Gender in America.* Englewood Cliffs, N.J.: Prentice-Hall, 1985.

Lengyel, Olga. *Five Chimneys: The Story of Auschwitz.* New York: Howard Fertig, 1983.

Lestchinsky, Jacob. "Economic Aspects of Jewish Community Organization in Independent Poland." *Jewish Social Studies* 9, nos. 1–4 (1947): 319–338.

———. "The Industrial and Social Structure of the Jewish Population of Interbellum Poland." *YIVO Annual Social Science* 2 (1956–1957): 243–269.

Levi, Primo. *The Drowned and the Saved.* New York: Summit, 1986.

———. *Survival in Auschwitz.* Trans. Stuart Wolf. New York: Collier, 1965.

Levin, Dov. *Fighting Back: Lithuanian Jewry's Armed Resistance to the Nazis, 1941–1945.* New York: Holmes and Meier, 1985.

Levy-Hass, Hannah. *Inside Belsen.* Totowa, N.J.: Barnes and Noble, 1982.

Lewińska, Pelagia. *Twenty Months at Auschwitz.* New York: Lyle Stuart, 1968.

Lifton, Betty Jean. *The King of Children.* New York: Schocken, 1988.

Lifton, Robert Jay. *The Nazi Doctors.* New York: Basic, 1986.

Lingens-Reiner, Ella. *Prisoners of Fear.* London: Victor Gollancz, 1948.

Linton, Ralph. "Age and Sex Categories." *American Sociological Review* 7 (1942): 589–603.

Lomax, Judy. *Women of the Air*. New York: Dodd, Mead, 1987.

Loy, Rosetta. *First Words*. New York: Henry Holt, 1998.

Lubetkin, Civia. *In the Days of Destruction and Revolt*. Ghetto Fighters' House, Israel: Ghetto Fighters' House, 1981.

Lummis, T. "Structure and Validity in Oral Evidence." *International Journal of Oral History* 2, no. 2 (1981): 109–119.

Lusky, Irena. *La Traverse de la nuit*. Geneva: Livre Metropolis, 1988.

Maccoby, E., ed. *The Development of Sex Differences*. Stanford: Stanford University Press, 1966.

Malinowski, Bronisław. *Sex and Repression in Savage Society*. Chicago: University of Chicago Press, 1927.

———. *The Sexual Life of Savages*. Boston: Beacon, 1987.

Mark, B., *RUCH OPORU W GETCIE BIAŁOSTOCKIM* [The underground movement in the Białystok ghetto]. Warszawa: Żydowski Instytut Historyczny, 1952.

Marks, Jane. *The Hidden Children: The Secret Survivors of the Holocaust*. New York: Ballantine, 1993.

Marrus, Michael, ed. *The Nazi Holocaust*. vol. 17: *Resistance to the Holocaust*. Westport, Conn.: Meckler, 1989.

Marrus, Michael R., and Paxton, Robert O. *Vichy France and the Jews*. New York: Schocken, 1983.

Martin, Elaine, ed. *Gender Patriarchy and Fascism in the Third Reich*. Detroit: Wayne State University Press, 1993.

Maurel, Micheline. *An Ordinary Camp*. New York: Simon and Schuster, 1958.

Mayer, Arno. *Why Did the Heavens Not Darken?* New York: Pantheon, 1989.

Mead, Margaret. *Male and Female*. New York: Dell, 1949.

———. *Sex and Temperament in Three Primitive Societies*. New York: William Morrow, 1935.

Meed, Vladka. "Jewish Resistance in the Warsaw Ghetto." *Dimensions* 7, no. 2.

———. *On Both Sides of the Wall: Memoirs from the Warsaw Ghetto*. Washington, D.C.: Holocaust Library, 1993.

Mendelsohn, Ezra. *The Jews of East-Central Europe Between the World Wars*. Bloomington: Indiana University Press, 1983.

Merin, Yehuda, and Jack Nusan Porter. "Three Jewish Family Camps in the Forests of Vołyń, Ukraine, During the Holocaust." *Jewish Social Science* 156, no. 1 (1984): 83–92.

Merton, Robert K. *Social Theory and Social Structure*. Glencoe, Ill.: Free Press, 1957.

Meyer, Peter. *The Jews in the Soviet Satellites*. Syracuse, N.Y.: Syracuse University Press, 1953.

Micheels, Louis J. *Doctor 117641*. New Haven: Yale University Press, 1989.

Michel, Henri. *The Shadow War: European Resistance, 1939–1945*. New York: Harper and Row, 1972.

Michelson, Frida. *I Survived Rumbuli*. New York: Holocaust Library, 1979.

Miller, Jean Baker. *Toward a New Psychology of Women*. Boston: Beacon, 1976.

Miller, Nancy K. *Subject to Change: Reading Feminist Writing*. New York: Columbia University Press, 1988.

Millett, Kate. *Sexual Politics*. New York: Simon and Schuster, 1990.

Murdock, George Peter. *Social Structure*. New York: Macmillian, 1949.

Neumann, Margarete Buber. *Milena: The Story of a Remarkable Friendship*. New York: Schocken, 1989.

Noakes, J., and G. Pridham, eds. *Nazism, 1919–1945:* Vol. 3, *Foreign Policy, War and Racial Extermination*. Exeter, Eng.: University of Exeter, 1988.

Noggle, Anne. *A Dance with Death: Soviet Airwomen in World War II*. College Station: Texas A&M University Press, 1994.

Nomberg-Przytyk, Sara. *Auschwitz: True Tales from a Grotesque Land*. Chapel Hill: University of North Carolina Press, 1985.

Nyiszli, Miklos. *Auschwitz: A Doctor's Eyewitness Account*. New York: Fawcett, 1960.

Oberski, Jona. *LATA DZIECIŃSTWA* [Childhood]. Warszawa: Książka i Wiedza, 1988.

Ofer, Dalia. "Cohesion and Rupture: The Jewish Family in East European Ghettos During the Holocaust." *Studies in Contemporary Jewry* 14 (1998): 143–165.

Ofer, Dalia, and Lenore J. Weitzman, eds. *Women in the Holocaust*. New Haven: Yale University Press, 1998.

O'Kelly, Charlotte G., and Larry S. Carney. *Women and Men in Society: Cross-Cultural Perspectives on Gender Stratification*. 2nd ed. Belmont, Calif.: Wadsworth, 1986.

Oliner, Samuel P. *Restless Memories: Recollections of the Holocaust Years*. Berkeley: Judah L. Magnes Museum, 1986.

Ostrowski, Shmuel. "Of War and the Holocaust." Unpublished diary (Yiddish). Yad Vashem, 7970.

Owen, Alison. *Frauen: German Women Recall the Third Reich*. New Brunswick, N.J.: Rutgers University Press, 1994.

Pawełczyńska, Anna. *WARTOŚCI A PRZEMOC, ZARYS SOCJOLOGJCZNEJ PROBLEMATYKI OŚWIĘCIMA* [Values and oppression: Outline of sociological problems in Auschwitz]. Warszawa: Państwowe Wydawnictwo Naukowe, 1973.

Pawłowicz, Sala, and Kevin Klose. *I Will Survive*. New York; Norton, 1962.

Perechodnik, Calel. *Am I a Murderer?* Boulder, Colo.: Westview, 1996.

Perl, Gisella. *I Was a Doctor in Auschwitz*. New York: International Universities Press, 1948.

Peukert, Detlev J. K. *Inside Nazi Germany: Conformity, Opposition, and Racism in Everyday Life*. New Haven: Yale University Press, 1987.

Picker, Henry, and Heinrich Hoffman, eds. *Hitler Close Up*. New York: Macmillan 1969.

Pisar, Samuel. *Of Blood and Hope*. Boston: Little, Brown, 1979.

Poliakov, Leon. *The History of Anti-Semitism*. New York: Schocken, 1974.

Polonsky, Antony. *Politics in Independent Poland, 1921–1939*. Oxford: Claredon, 1972.

Porter, Jack Nusan, ed. *Jewish Partisans: A Documentary of Jewish Resistance in the Soviet Union During World War II*. Vol. 1. New York: University Press of America, 1982.

Poznański, Jakub. *PAMIĘTNIK Z GETTA ŁÓDZKIEGO* [Łódź ghetto memoir]. Łódź: Wydawnictwo Łódzkie, 1960.

Prawdzic-Szlacki, Janusz. *NOWOGRÓDCZYZNA W WALCE, 1940–1945* [Nowógrad is fighting]. London: Oficyna Poetow I Malarzy, 1976.

Presser, J. *The Destruction of the Dutch Jews*. Trans. Arnold Pomerans. New York: Dutton, 1969.

Rashke, Richard. *Escape from Sobibor: The Heroic Story of the Jews Who Escaped from a Nazi Death Camp*. Boston: Houghton Mifflin, 1982.

Ringelblum, Emanuel. *KRONIKA GETTA WARSZAWSKIEGO* [Chronicle of the Warsaw ghetto]. Warszawa: Czytelnik, 1983.

——. *Notes from the Warsaw Ghetto: The Journal of Emanuel Ringelblum*. New York: Schocken, 1975.

——. *Polish-Jewish Relations During the Second World War*. Ed. Józef Kermisz and Shmuel Krakowski. Jerusalem: Yad Vashem, 1974.

Ringelheim, Joan. "The Holocaust: Taking Women into Account." *Jewish Quarterly* 39, no. 3 (1992): 19–23.

Rittner, Carol, and Sandra Myers, eds. *The Courage to Care: Rescuers of Jews During the Holocaust*. New York: New York University Press, 1986.

Rittner, Carol, and John K. Roth, eds. *Different Voices: Women and the Holocaust*. New York: Paragon House, 1993.

Ritvo, Roger A., and Diane M. Plotkin. *Sisters in Sorrow*. College Station: Texas A&M University Press, 1998.

Rohrlich, Ruby, ed. *Resisting the Holocaust*. New York: Berg, 1998.

Roland, Charles G. *Courage Under Siege*. New York: Oxford University Press, 1992.

Rosaldo, Michelle Zimbalist, and Louise Lamphere, eds. *Woman, Culture and Society*. Stanford: Stanford University Press, 1974.

Rosenberg, Blanca. *To Tell at Last.* Urbana: University of Illinois Press, 1993.

Rotem, Simha (Kazik). *Memoirs of a Warsaw Ghetto Fighter: The Past Within Me.* New Haven: Yale University Press, 1994.

Rowbotham, Sheila. *Woman's Consciousness, Man's World.* London: Pelican, 1973.

Rubenstein, Richard L., and John K. Roth. *Approaches to Auschwitz: The Holocaust and Its Legacy.* Atlanta: John Knox Press, 1987.

Rudashevski, Yitskhok. *The Diary of the Vilna Ghetto, June 1941–April 1943.* Ghetto Fighters' House, Israel: Ghetto Fighters' House, 1973.

Rufeisen, Hela Schüpper. *POŻEGNANIE MIŁEJ 18: WSPOMNIENIA ŁĄCZ-NICZKI ŻYDOWSKIEJ ORGANIZACJI BOJOWEJ.* Kraków: Wydawnictwo "Beseder" S.C., 1996.

Russell, Diana E. H., ed. *Exposing Nuclear Phallacies.* New York: Pergamon, 1989.

Sakowska, Ruta. *DWA ETAPY* [Two phases]. Warszawa: Wydawnictwo Polskiej Akademii Nauk, 1986.

———. *LUDZIE Z DZIELNICY ZAMKNIETEJ* [People in the closed quarters]. Warszawa: Państwowe Wydawnictwo Naukowe, 1975.

Samuel, Vivette. *Sauves les enfants.* Paris: Liana Levi, 1995.

Sanday, Peggy Reeves. *Female Power and Male Dominance: On the Origin of Sexual Inequality.* New York: Cambridge University Press, 1981.

Sanday, Peggy Reeves, and Ruth Gallagher Goodenough, eds. *Beyond the Second Sex.* Philadelphia: University of Pennsylvania Press, 1990.

Schoenfeld, Gabriel. "How Much Holocaust Is Too Much? When Hitler Stole the Pink Rabbit." *Journal of the Jewish Theological Seminary* 9, no. 1 (Fall 1999): 8, 9, 20.

Schulman, Faye. *A Partisan's Memoir: Woman of the Holocaust.* Toronto: Second Story Press, 1995.

Schwarz, Leo W., ed. *The Root and The Bough.* New York: Rinehart, 1949.

Sefer Hapartizanim Haihudim [The Jewish partisan book]. Merchavia, Israel: Sifriat Hapoalim, 1958.

Seidel, Rochelle G. "Women's Experiences During the Holocaust—New Books in Print." *Yad Vashem Studies* 28 (2000): 363–378.

Sendlerowa, Irena. "O DZIAŁALNOŚCI KÓŁ MŁODZIEŻY PRZY KOMITE-TACH DOMOWYCH W GETCIE WARSZAWSKIM." *BIULETYN ŻYDOWSKIEGO INSTYTUTU HISTORYCZNEGO* 2, no. 118 (1981): 91–118.

Sereny, Gitta. *Into That Darkness: From Mercy Killing to Mass Murder.* New York: McGraw-Hill, 1974.

Shaffer, Kay T. *Sex Roles and Human Behavior.* Cambridge, Mass.: Winthrop, 1981.

Shapiro, Robert Moses, ed. *Holocaust Chronicles: Individualizing the Holocaust*

Through Diaries and Other Contemporaneous Personal Accounts. Hoboken, N.J.: KTAV, 1999.

Shelley, Lore, ed. *The Union Kommando in Auschwitz.* New York: University Press of America, 1996.

Sierakowiak, Dawid. *The Diary of Dawid Sierakowiak: Five Notebooks from the Łódź Ghetto.* New York: Oxford University Press, 1996.

Silberman, Lena Küchler. *One Hundred Children.* New York, Doubleday, 1961.

Silten, R. Gabriele S. *Between Two Worlds: Autobiography of a Child Survivor of the Holocaust.* Santa Barbara, Calif.: Fithian Press, 1995.

Simmel, Georg. *The Sociology of Georg Simmel.* Ed. Kurt H. Wolff. Glencoe, Ill.: Free Press, 1950.

Slater, Philip. *The Pursuit of Loneliness.* Boston: Beacon Press, 1976.

Smolar, Hersh. *The Minsk Ghetto: Soviet Jewish Partisans Against the Nazis.* New York: Holocaust Library, 1989.

Sofsky, Wolfgang. *The Order of Terror: The Concentration Camp.* Princeton: Princeton University Press, 1997.

Solomian-Loc, Fanny. *Woman Facing the Gallows.* Amherst, Mass.: Word Pro, 1981.

Steinberg, Lucien. *Not as a Lamb.* Farnborough, Eng.: Heath, 1970.

Steinberg, Paul. *Speak You Also.* New York: Henry Holt, 1996.

Stephenson, Jill. *Women in Nazi Society.* New York: Barnes and Noble, 1975.

Stoltzfus, Nathan. *Resistance of the Heart: Intermarriage and the Rosenstrasse Protest in Nazi Germany.* New York: Norton, 1996.

Streit, Christian. *Keine Kameraden Die Wehrmacht Und Die Sowietischen Krieggefangenen, 1941–1945.* Stuttgart: Deutsche Verlag Anstalt, 1978.

Strobl, Ingrid. *Das Feld des Vergessens.* Berlin: Edition ID-Archiv, 1994.

Stroop Report, The: A Facsimile Edition and Translation of the Official Nazi Report on the Destruction of the Warsaw Ghetto. New York: Pantheon. 1979.

Suhl, Yuri, ed. *They Fought Back: The Story of the Jewish Resistance in Nazi Europe.* New York: Schocken, 1967.

Świebocka, Teresa, ed. *Auschwitz: A History in Photographs.* Bloomington: Indiana University Press, 1993.

Szmaglewska, Seweryna. *Smoke over Birkenau.* New York: Henry Holt, 1947.

Szmajzner, Stanisław. *Hell in Sobibór: The Tragedy of a Jewish Adolescent.* New York: Edition Bloch, 1968.

Szwajger, Adina Blady. *I Remember Nothing More: The Warsaw Children's Hospital and the Jewish Resistance.* New York: Simon and Schuster, 1990.

Szyfman, Arnold. *Moja Tułaczka Wojenna [My Wartime Wanderings].* Warsaw: Wydawnictwo Obrony Naraodowej, 1946.

Szyper, Claire Prowizur. *Conte à rebours*. Brussels: Louis Musin, 1979.

Tannen, Deborah. *You Just Don't Understand: Women and Men in Conversation*. New York: William Morrow, 1990.

Taylor, Shelley E., et al. "Biobehavioral Responses to Stress in Females: Tend-and-Befriend, Not Fight-or-Flight." *Psychological Review* 107, no. 3 (2000): 411–429.

Tec, Nechama. "Between Two Worlds." *Journal of Literature and Belief* 18, no. 1 (1998): 15–26.

———. *Defiance: The Bielski Partisans*. New York: Oxford University Press, 1993.

———. *Dry Tears: The Story of a Lost Childhood*. New York: Oxford University Press, 1982.

———. *In the Lion's Den: The Life of Oswald Rufeisen*. New York: Oxford University Press, 1990.

———. "Jewish Resistance: Facts, Omissions, and Distortions." Occasional Paper, United States Holocaust Memorial Museum, Research Institute. Washington, D.C.: Research Institute of the United States Holocaust Memorial Museum, 1997.

———. "Methodological Considerations: Diaries and Oral History." *Holocaust and the Arts* 4, no. 1 (2000): 87–94.

———. "Sex Distinctions and Passing as Christians During the Holocaust." *Eastern European Quarterly* 18, no.1 (March 1984): 113–123.

———. *When Light Pierced the Darkness*. New York: Oxford University Press 1986.

Tec, Nechama, and Daniel Weiss. "A Historical Injustice: The Case of Masha Bruskina." *Journal of Holocaust and Genocide Studies* 7, no. 3 (Winter 1997): 366–377.

Tedeschi, Guiliana. *There Is A Place on Earth: A Woman in Birkenau*. New York: Pantheon Books, 1992.

Temchin, Michael. *The Witch Doctor: Memoirs of a Partisan*. New York: Holocaust Library, 1983.

Tenenbaum, Joseph. *Underground: The Story of a People*. New York: Philosophical Society, 1952.

Tillion, Germaine. *Ravensbrück: An Eyewitness Account of a Women's Concentration Camp*. New York: Anchor, 1975.

Todorov, Tzvetan. *Facing the Extreme*. New York: Henry Holt, 1996.

Trey, J. E. "Women in the War Economy—World War II." *Review of Radical Economics* 4 (July 1972): 40–57.

Troller, Norbert. *Theresienstadt: Hitler's Gift to the Jews*. Chapel Hill: University of North Carolina Press, 1991.

Trunk, Isaiah. *Jewish Responses to Nazi Persecution*. New York: Stein and Day, 1979.

———. *Judenrat*. New York: Stein and Day, 1977.

Vakar, Nicholas P. *Belorussia: The Making of a Nation.* Cambridge: Harvard University Press, 1956.

Valkhoff, Ziporah. *Leven in een Niet-Bestaan.* Utrecht: Stiehing ICODO, 1992.

Vrba, Rudolf. *I Cannot Forgive.* New York: Sidgwick and Jackson, 1964.

Waite, Robert G. L. *The Psychopathic God, Adolf Hitler.* New York: New American Library, 1978.

Weber, Max. *Essays in Sociology.* Ed. H. H. Gerth and W. Mills. New York: Oxford University Press, 1953.

———. *The Theory of Social and Economic Organization.* Glencoe, Ill.: Free Press, 1947.

Weinstock, Eugene. *Beyond the Last Path.* New York: Paul and Gaer, 1947.

Weitz, Shirley. *Sex Roles: Biological, Psychological, and Social Foundations.* New York: Oxford University Press, 1977.

Wells, Leon. *The Janowska Road.* New York: Macmillan, 1963.

Wiesel, Elie. *Night.* New York: Avon, 1969.

Wiesenthal, Simon. *The Sunflower.* New York: Schocken, 1997.

Wołozhiński-Rubin, Sulia. *Against the Tide: The Story of an Unknown Partisan.* Jerusalem: Posner and Sons, 1980.

Wood, Thomas, and Stanisław M. Jankowski. *Karski: How One Man Tried to Stop the Holocaust.* New York: Wiley, 1994.

Woolf, Virginia. *Three Guineas.* New York: Harcourt Brace Jovanovich, 1966.

Wrónski, Stanisław, and Maria Zwolakowa. *POLACY I ŻYDZI, 1939–1945* [Poles and Jews, 1939–1945]. Warszawa: Książka I Wiedza, 1971.

Wyman, David S. *The Abandonment of the Jews.* New York: Pantheon, 1984.

Yahil, Leni. *The Holocaust: The Fate of European Jewry.* New York: Oxford University Press, 1990.

Yehudei Yaar [Forest Jews, As Told to Y. Ben Dor by Tuvia and Zus Bielski, Sonia and Lilka Bielski, and Abraham Viner]. Tel Aviv: Am Oved, 1946.

Zassenhaus, Hiltgunt. *Walls.* Boston: Beacon, 1974.

Zawodny, Janusz K. *Death in the Forest: The Story of the Katyn Forest Massacre.* New York: Hippocrene, 1988.

Ziemian, Joseph. *The Cigarette Sellers of Three Crosses Square.* Minneapolis: Lerner, 1975.

Ziemiński, Stanisław. "KARTKI DZIENNIKA NAUCZYCIELA W ŁUKOWIE Z OKRESU OKUPACJI HITLEROWSKIEJ" [Pages from the diary of a teacher from Łuków during the Hitlerite occupation]. *BIULETYN ŻYDOWSKIEGO INSTYTUTU HISTORYCZNEGO* 27 (1958): 105–112.

Zuccotti, Susan. *The Holocaust, the French, and the Jews.* New York: Basic, 1993.
———. *The Italians and the Holocaust.* New York: Basic, 1987.
Zuckerman, Yitzhak. *A Surplus of Memory.* Los Angeles: University of California Press, 1993.
Zyskind, Sara. *Stolen Years.* Minneapolis: Lerner, 1981.
Zywulska, Krystyna. *I Came Back.* New York: Roy, 1951.

Acknowledgments

This book grew out of a prolonged journey that was marked by expected and unexpected detours and revelations. Many of the obstacles and road bumps were smoothed by generous aid from a number of sources. I am grateful for the opportunity to thank those groups and individuals whose care and interest were reflected in their readiness to invest their valuable time in efforts that helped me complete this book.

Assuming the role of developmental editor, Jonathan Brent, editorial director of Yale University Press, read several versions of *Resilience and Courage*. His comments, voiced during our frequent meetings, were always stimulating, always illuminating, and were vital to this project. Jonathan's special attention to my book improved its quality, while transforming the writing process into a valuable learning experience. If this book could talk, it would join me in praising Jonathan's insightful comments, which he so generously shared.

I am grateful to Senior Manuscript Editor Susan Laity for her sensitive and valuable input into this project. Susan's concise thinking and dedication added clarity to my writing. I am fortunate, indeed, that the Press assigned her to edit my book.

Very much appreciated is the patient, efficient help I received from editorial assistant Gretchen Rings. Gretchen's willingness to listen and to take care of things simplified the often-complex process of book making.

I should also like to thank my agent, Pam Bernstein, for her efforts on my behalf and for bringing this book to Yale University Press.

Over the years I have received invaluable support from the University of Connecticut, especially from those who, like me, have been affiliated with the Stamford campus. I am particularly indebted to Jacquelyn Joseph-Silverstein, associate vice chancellor and director of the Stamford campus, for her gracious encouragement and generous help. For their consistently caring support I am grateful to associate directors Sheila Moore and Terry Reilly. I would also like to thank the library staff, particularly Nancy Romanello and Shelley Roseman, whose heroic efforts supplied me with hard-to-find literature, often in foreign languages.

This book has benefited from the generosity of my colleague Patricia Cramer, who read most of its chapters at both early and late stages. At each reading, Pat offered extensive and valuable comments. Joel Blatt, with whom I have been co-teaching for years, frequently served as a springboard for my ideas. I appreciate his patience and willingness to engage in discussions on many issues. I also would also like to thank Julian Reitman for guiding me through my many computer questions. Equally generous with her computer skills was my colleague Maggie Levy. For expert copying and recopying I am grateful to Rosa James.

My 1995 appointment as a Fellow at the International Institute for Holocaust Research at Yad Vashem, Jerusalem, gave me a chance to expand and deepen my research. Israel Gutman, at that time director of the institute, took great interest in my work. I appreciate his constant counsel, which continues to this day. During my stay at the institute I shared an office with Yehuda Bauer; I would like to thank him for his hospitality and care. For years Shmuel Krakowski, beginning with his tenure as head of the archives at Yad Vashem and continuing to the present, has been most supportive in directing me to relevant and important archival holdings. I appreciate his encouragement and input. I would also like to thank Judith Kleiman of Yad

Vashem for helping me find archival materials. My thanks go to Iris Berlazky for sharing survivor tapes and for directing me to individual survivors to interview. I appreciate as well the help of Sara Bender, a colleague at the institute, for arranging interviews for me with survivors who had participated in her research. Many others in Israel helped me find new materials and established contacts for me with new interviewees. For such efforts I would like to thank my daughter, Leora Tec; Renanna Ben-Gurion; Martina and Vincent Frank; the late Anita Gandelsman; Ilana Geva; Barry Kaplan; Miriam Kaplan; and David Leshem. I am particularly grateful to respondents who helped me find additional interviewees: Zvi Shefet (Shepetinski); Ruth Hudes-Tartako, Mina Vołkowiski, and Dobka Freund-Waldhorn.

The U.S. Holocaust Memorial Museum in Washington, D.C., offered me a Senior Research Fellowship at the Miles Lerman Center for the Study of Jewish Resistance in 1997, which further facilitated my research. My participation in the professional seminars sponsored by the institute that were specially designed for the fellows helped me clarify many issues. In addition, the museum's library resources and extensive archival holdings increased the scope of my work. For the various ways they eased my many research tasks, I am indebted to William Connelly, Elisabeth Koenig, Aron Kornblum, Amy Rubin, and Mark Ziomek. I would also like to thank Benton Arnovitz for his careful reading of the preliminary chapters of my book. For the duration of my museum fellowship and beyond, my work has benefited greatly from Jürgen Mattäus's readings and comments. A keen observer and an excellent historian, Jürgen offered consistently insightful observations. Our exchanges continue to enhance the quality of my work. I would also like to thank all those at the Jewish Historical Institute in Warsaw and the Yivo Institute for Jewish Research in New York who facilitated my research.

At different stages of this project I have consulted Raul Hilberg, and I am grateful for his caring, patient consideration of my numerous questions. My thanks also go to Monika Adamczyk-Garbowska, who has shown a special interest in my work; I am particularly grateful for the time she devoted to going over the Polish entries in my bibliography. For helpful comments about early portions of this book I would like to thank my friends Rochl and George Berman, Daniel Weiss, and Toby Appleton. I am also indebted to Jane Lillibridge for listening carefully to my dictation and for her perceptive comments throughout. I wish to thank Susan Alderman for trying to keep my computer files in order and for locating "lost" documents. I also appreciate Sandy Grant's prompt responses to my SOSes about computer troubles and her expert work fixing the problems.

I am fortunate to have had my family's constant, loving support. My husband Leon's patience was particularly welcome during my occasional crises. Invariably, his optimism and support helped me move on and overcome the seemingly insurmountable obstacles. My daughter Leora's approval and readiness to respond to my doubts and questions gave me comfort. My son, Roland, has examined each chapter at various stages of completion. Roland's sense of style and his original, substantive comments smoothed the road toward the completion of this complex and at times frustrating undertaking.

I deeply admire those individuals who for hours allowed me to probe their painful memories. Readers of this book will know how central the contribution of these interviewees has been. My boundless gratitude and appreciation is directed to these respondents: Amiora Ackerman, Anita Adler, Miriam Akavia, Tamar Amarant, Zorach Arluk, Moshe Bairach, Pesia Bairach, Bracha Bartfold-Abrahami, Berta Benau-Hutzler, Pesia Bernstein-Pertzof, Chaja Bielski, Ephraim Blaichman, Pinchas Boldo, Dina Borowac, Sandra Brand, Lidia Brown-Abramson, Bela Chazan-Yaari, Irena Deuel-Lusky, Shulamit Einhorn-Roitman, Arieh Eitani, Rina Eitani, Thea Epstein, Dobka Freund-Waldhorn, Eva Galer, Luba Garfunk, Richard Glazar, Fanya Gottesfeld-Heller, Chava Grinberg-Brown, Lusia Grosman-Sternberg, Ruth Hudes-Tartako, Riva Kantorowicz-Reich, Fela Isboutsky-Szmidt, Shoshana Kahn, Raja Kalmanowicz, Rachel Kasińska-Bilerman, Arnold Kerr (Aronek Kierszkowski), Shamay Kizelstein, Mina Kizelstein-Dorn, Baruch Kopold, Eva Kracowski, Lili Krawitz, Edith Lasman, Niusia Lubocki-Długi, Rose Margolis-Abrams, Edith Margolis-Adelman, Vladka Meed, Miriam Meirowicz-Rubyn, Żenia Minkow, Hadassa Moldinger, Moshe Nikopajewski, Gerda Nothmann-Luner, Roma Nutkiewicz-Benatar, Michael Pertzof, Claire Prowizur-Szyper, Rina Raviv, Zwia Rechtman-Schwarz, Dvora Rosenbaum-Fogel, Tonia Rotkopf-Blair, Sulia Rubin, Menachem Rubyn, Ania Rud, Felicja Schachter-Karay, Hermann Schmelzer, Hela Schüpper-Rufeisen, Israel Shaham, Ita Shapiro, Zvi Shefet (Shepetinski), Henia Shenberg, Anna Siewner, Lea Silverstein, Hersh Smolar, Claire Sokołowski, Alexandra Sołowejczyk-Guter, Helen (Zippi) Spitzer-Tichauer, Lea Susenski, Karla Szajewicz-Frist, Fela Sztern, Tola Szwarc-Chudin, Marion van Binsberger-Pritchard, Abraham Viner, Mina Vołkowiski, Rita Weiss-Jamboger, Bracha Winger-Ghilai, Tamar Yaari, Naomi Zeif, and Zahava Ziskowicz-Adam.

Index

Labor under German occupation: ghetto systems, 39–40; humiliation and attacks connected to, 32, 103; of illegal Jews, 222–241; Judenräte as supplier of, 23, 32, 40; low economic value of Jewish, 23–24; Nazi laws on, 207–208; roundups, 22–23, 33; unemployment, male, 4; unproductive people, murder of, 40; of youth, 26, 27, 32, 46
Lager system, 122
Lasman, Edith, 156–157, 169
Lazar, Chaim, 290
Lederman, Moses, 382n21
Leipzig camp, 200
Lenobel, Józef, 336, 394–395n113
Levi, Primo, 140, 148, 158, 159, 170
Libraries, 43, 44
Lida ghetto, 85
Liebesman-Mikulski, A., 213, 394n113
Lieblein, Gerta, 338
Lipowa work camp, 1–2
Łódź (Poland), 26–29, 47
Łódź ghetto, 28, 39, 62, 63–64, 65, 69–70
Lower class. See Class
Lubaczów ghetto, 55, 87
Lubetkin, Civia, 266
Luft, Anda, 336, 337, 338, 339
Lusky, Irena, 184–185
Lvov (Ukraine), 94–95, 105, 235–236, 254
Lvov ghetto, 102–104, 106

Mackiewicz, Izia, 281
Madejsker, Sonia, 282, 388n30
Majdanek camp, 85, 129, 149–150, 178, 182–183
Malbushim (partisan rank), 301–303, 315
Mandelshtam, Lucy, 164–165
Margolis, Anna, 71, 72, 73
Margolis, Edith and Rose, 113–115
Margolis-Joffee, Ester, 126
Masarek, Rudi, 189
Mass killings: of men, 30–32, 33, 41; in Russian-held territories, 29–30; of

Russian prisoners of war, 270; of women and children, 30, 32, 33
Meed, Ben, 243
Meed, Vladka, 20, 54–55, 66, 218–219, 242, 243–244
Melines transit camp, 116
Memory: accuracy of, 4, 7–8; resurfaced, 1–2, 17–18, 344
Men in concentration camps: cigarette cravings of, 169; class background and, 169–170; coping skills of, 132–138, 169–170, 345; cruel treatment of, 130, 132, 137; cultural activities of, 197, 201; food and nourishment needs of, 137–138, 141; head shaving, 125–126; hygiene of, 157, 158–159; separation of sexes and, 128; in support groups, 176–177, 188–196; in uprisings, 188–191
Men under German occupation: communism associated with male elite, 29–30; depression of, 15, 25, 27, 35, 48, 54, 64, 107, 113, 217; emigration of, 15, 36; enterprising and resourceful, 56–57, 58–62, 74, 111, 365n30; escape of, 15, 22, 109–110, 118; escape of children and, 88, 89, 117; food theft from family members, 62, 63–64, 345–346, 366n37; hidden, 209, 211–213, 223, 243; humiliation and assaults on, 22, 24, 25, 26–27, 32, 104, 360n15; loss of protector/provider role, 24–25, 26, 27–28, 35, 36, 37, 48, 51, 53, 73–74, 96, 115, 345, 346; mass killings of, 30–32, 33, 41; passing on Aryan side, 207, 210–211, 215, 217, 220–221, 223, 225, 232–233; prisoners of war, 1–2; roundups of, 22–23, 33; separations from family, 15, 49–50; special danger to, belief in, 33, 34, 36, 37; targeting of male elites, 30–32, 207–208, 264, 287; in western Europe, 110–18. See also Judenräte; Labor under German occupation; Partisans, Jewish
Mengele, Josef, 155, 163, 164, 376n93
Menis brothers, 338
Menkes-Fast, Cyla, 254–255

Partisans, Russian *(continued)*
331–332; ghetto refugees to, 77, 80, 90,
93, 98–99, 256–260, 271, 297–298; idealized image of, 284–285, 289; inhospitable
to "useless" people, 289–291; rapes by,
311–313; sexual encounters of, 4, 291, 305–
307, 309, 313, 321, 323–325, 334; Soviet initiatives and control over, 282–284; women's
participation with, 278–280, 281, 282, 305,
306, 325–328, 329–335
Partisans, women: abortions of, 321–323, 326;
anti-female prejudice, 307, 310; celibacy of,
320–321, 334; hardships of, 307–309; with
Jewish groups, 273–275, 281, 310, 314–321,
328–329; male protectors of, 306, 307, 308,
311, 318, 327–328; in military operations,
274–275, 278–280, 281, 306, 329–335, 339,
347; participation and acceptance of, 272,
305, 325–328; pregnancy and childbirth,
321–323, 326, 338; rape of, 311–313; sexual
encounters with Jewish partisans, 314–320;
sexual encounters with Russian partisans,
4, 291, 305–307, 309, 313, 321, 323–325,
334; subordinate roles of, 281, 282, 305,
308, 310, 314, 329, 337, 347
Passing on Aryan side: Christian protectors
and, 209, 222, 224, 225–229, 246–247; as
cooperative effort, 95–97, 209; couriers
and underground workers, 102, 241–245,
276–277; danger and unpredictability of,
206–209, 213–214, 241; denouncement
and blackmail in, 206, 207, 214, 215, 220,
226, 241, 242, 382n21; documents for, 95,
102, 103–104, 105, 106, 215–216, 218, 219–
220; fear, anxiety, and depression, 217–218,
246; Gestapo interrogation and, 205–206;
knowledge of native culture and, 216–217,
227–228, 234, 239; labor *(see* Labor on
Aryan side); loneliness of, 242–243, 244;
love relationships, 211–213, 245–249; men's
vulnerability, 210, 221, 223, 232–233, 265;
motherhood and, 250–255; Nazi laws on,
206; physical appearance and, 210–211, 215;

in Polish underground, 221–222; return to
ghetto, 104–106; sadness of Jewish eyes
and, 218–219; self-assurance, 219–221,
235–236; sexual encounters, 224, 229–231,
246–247; in western Europe, 111
Patriarchal ideology: anti-Jewish policies and,
11–12, 264; gender roles and, 9–10; Nazi,
10–11, 357n17; in oppressive societies, 9,
352–353
Peltel, Shlomo, 20, 24
Peltel, Vladka, 24–25
Peretz, I. L., 66
Pertzof, Michael, 288–289, 307–308
Peschel, Rolf, 248, 253
Phillips Company, 173, 180, 181–182
Physicians. *See* Doctors
Picz, Janina, 102
Pietruszka, Wacek, 97
Płaszów camp, 197
Platon, Pantileimon, 283
Poland: anti-Semitism in, 21–22, 358n1; con-
centration camp system in, 123; German
takeover of, 20; labor transfers to Germany,
207, 232–241; persecution and deportation
of Poles, 122, 207; Soviet political agenda
in, 283; underground in, 221, 243, 248;
Warsaw uprising of *1944*, 221–222, 248.
See also Christian protectors; German
occupation; Ghettos; Labor on Aryan
side; Passing on Aryan side
Police. *See* Gestapo; SS (German Security
Police)
Polish Communist Party (PPR), 308
Polish language, Jewish women's knowledge
of, 216
Ponomarenko, Pantileimon, 272
Powerlessness, men's feelings of, 26, 37,
73–74
Pregnancy, prohibition against, 40, 68, 75,
349
Pregnant women: on Aryan side, 249–250; in
concentration camps, 162–164; partisans,
321–323, 326, 338